THE 101 GREATEST PLAYS

Michael Billington has been theatre critic of the *Guardian* since 1971 and of *Country Life* since 1986. He is the author of biographies of Harold Pinter and Peggy Ashcroft, critical studies of Tom Stoppard and Alan Ayckbourn, a celebration of Ken Dodd and a collection of reviews, *One Night Stands*. He has also edited *Directors' Shakespeare: Twelfth Night* and *Stage and Screen Lives* selected from the *Dictionary of National Biography*. He frequently lectures and broadcasts on the arts, teaches drama for the University of Pennsylvania and is a Visiting Professor at King's College London and an Honorary Fellow of St Catherine's College, Oxford.

Michael Billington's *State of the Nation: British Theatre Since 1945*, also published by Faber, won the Theatre Book Prize 2008.

Further praise for *The 101 Greatest Plays*:

'A pleasure to read . . . there is probably nobody currently living who has the knowledge, experience and memory of Michael Billington when it comes to writing a book of this type . . . A book that is simultaneously important and enjoyable. Who could ask for anything more?' Philip Fisher, *British Theatre Guide*

'The elegance and vigour of [Billington's] writing . . . backed by his unparalleled banks of theatrical knowledge and wisdom makes these essays a joy to read.' *Scotsman*

'Extremely readable . . . a great book for theatre lovers and an indispensable book for theatre practitioners and students. I cannot recommend it too strongly.' *Mature Times*

'What is fascinating about Billington's preferences is his high respect for the text . . . He is a focused and generous champion for the written word, who can give dozens of equally convincing readings of the same play, and is always ready to meet the political questions they ask head on. He knows what he's doing.' *Huffington Post*

MICHAEL BILLINGTON

THE
101
GREATEST
PLAYS

FROM ANTIQUITY
TO THE PRESENT

First published 2015
by Guardian Books, Kings Place, 90 York Way, London, N1 9GU
and Faber & Faber Ltd, Bloomsbury House,
74–77 Great Russell Street,
London, WC1B 3DA

This paperback edition published in the UK in 2016
This paperback edition published in the USA in 2016

Typeset by K.DESIGN, Somerset
Printed and bound by CPI Group (UK) Ltd, Croydon CR0 4YY

A CIP record for this book
is available from the British Library

ISBN 978-1-78335-031-5

FSC
www.fsc.org
MIX
Paper from
responsible sources
FSC® C013604

4 6 8 10 9 7 5

TO THE PLAYWRIGHTS,
LIVING AND DEAD

Contents

Introduction

The 101 Greatest Plays? I know: it sounds a bit arrogant. Who, after all, has the encyclopedic knowledge to make such a list? But I promise the book was written in a spirit of intellectual enquiry rather than out of any sense of omniscience: I simply wanted to find out for myself what the qualities were that made for first-rate drama. I initially thought of writing a book entitled *101 Great Plays*. But it was Antonia Fraser – who, I should add, bears no responsibility for my choices or the content – who encouraged me to raise the stakes and make it not just 'Great' but 'The Greatest'. I see her point: that makes the book more of a challenge, a provocation and the prelude to a debate in which everyone is free to join.

What, I will be asked, were my criteria? That's hard to answer. Definitions of greatness change from age to age. Dramatic forms are also the product of time and circumstance: as Alain Robbe-Grillet once pointed out, a five-act verse tragedy about a prince enjoined to kill his usurping uncle would not automatically be considered a masterpiece if it were written today.

But as I drew up my initial list of plays, I had one basic idea in my mind: that the very best plays are rooted in their historical moment and yet have a sustainable afterlife. In writing the book,

I found the list constantly changed as I made exciting discoveries and read more widely. But I never gave up on the idea that a great play is both an expression of its time and open to multiple reinterpretations.

There is, however, no iron-clad formula that makes a great play: if there were, more people would write one. What happened was that, through writing the book, I found myself revealing my own predilections. I realised that I was instinctively drawn to plays which display moral ambivalence, are rooted in close observation, blend the tragic and the comic and exude the life and energy that Baudelaire thought were the preconditions of any work of art. As we get to the modern era, readers will find I have a strong preference for plays with a realistic bias. But even here there are striking exceptions. One of the joys of doing the book was to learn that there are very few inflexible rules when it comes to drama.

I cannot stress too strongly the subjective nature of the enterprise. I have tried to cover a wide historical span from Aeschylus to the present. Geographically, the book is defined by my own experience: if, for instance, I say nothing about Indian or Far Eastern drama, that is because I don't know enough about them to speak with any degree of confidence. The final choices are mine and no one else's, determined by a lifetime of reading and theatregoing. I guess that, during nearly fifty years as a critic, I must have seen some 9,000 plays. I have tried to use that experience in the book and make constant reference to particular productions that reinforce my notion of greatness. This is a book about plays on the stage as well as on the page.

Eyebrows will doubtless be raised about my final selection: the omissions even more than the inclusions. I'd just say two things. I could easily draw up a long list of writers – living as well as dead – whom I profoundly admire but who don't appear in the book. If they are around today, I trust they will forgive me. There are also many plays with a claim to greatness that, for one reason or another, don't appear in the book. Some Shakespeareans will be outraged – indeed already have been – to discover that I have left out *King Lear*. I admit it's a craggily awesome play in which Shakespeare sounds the depths of human suffering. I can only say that, after a lifetime of seeing and reading it, I find it structurally unwieldy: the Gloucester sub-plot too consciously mirrors the main plot, and I find Edgar's refusal to identify himself to his father both inexplicable and needlessly cruel. Beckettians will also be astonished that there is no *Waiting for Godot*. I hope the reasons will become apparent later on: I can only say that, while I fully acknowledge the play's historic significance, I also feel that it has lost its capacity to shock or surprise. One last word about my choices. They were dictated by strong personal preference rather than a desire to prove a point or to be fully representative. In other words, questions of gender and ethnicity arose only after I had made my selection rather than before. I'd be the first to recognise that a woman critic or one from a black or Asian background would arrive at a wholly different list from my own. But then so would just about everyone else.

As for the form of the book, it consists largely of explanatory essays that I hope will be of interest to the general reader and the drama student. But astute readers will notice that, later in the book, I occasionally turn to dialogue between an old male critic and a young female one. You can easily identify the old man: the young woman, I should quickly explain, is a fictional composite. Tom Stoppard once said that 'writing dialogue is the only respectable way of contradicting myself'. And that's precisely why I used the form: to challenge my own assumptions about specific plays and writers. It's also great fun to occasionally swap expository prose for dialectical argument.

In the end, I can only say that the book is intended as a celebration of the art of the dramatist. That may seem obvious, but it is worth stressing when, out of an understandable desire to democratise the theatrical process, the status and authority of the solo writer is constantly being challenged. This book is a response to the current threat to the playwright. I just hope it will provoke readers into coming up with their own definition of greatness and deciding which plays meet its requirements. So let the debate begin.

Michael Billington
London 2015

1

The Persians

AESCHYLUS
(c.525–456 BC)

We gathered in the Brecon Beacons on a sunny August evening in 2010 to see the oldest surviving play in Western drama. No one who was there will ever forget Mike Pearson's National Theatre Wales production, staged in and around a hilltop military village built by the British army to train troops in hand-to-hand fighting. But we weren't simply responding to the resonance of the site or engaging in an act of cultural piety. What we discovered – or at least I did – was that Aeschylus from the start had unearthed a fundamental principle of drama: that it should contain moral and political ambivalence and that its meaning should vary according to circumstance.

Just look at the basic facts. Aeschylus wrote the play in 472 BC. That was a mere eight years after the events it describes: the annihilation of the Persians by the Athenians at the Battle of Salamis. That, in turn, makes it the only extant Greek tragedy to deal with an historical, as opposed to mythical, event. Given that every able-bodied Athenian male citizen (around 30,000) would have been conscripted to fight in the battle, it seems virtually certain that many in the audience would have had vivid memories of Salamis. Yet Aeschylus takes the bold decision to tell the story from the vantage point of the vanquished rather than the victors. Imagine a British movie of the late 1940s dealing with the bombing of Dresden from a German perspective or a Jewish dramatist populating a play about the 1948 Arab–Israeli War with a cast of Palestinians and you begin to grasp the audacity of Aeschylus' concept.

But this raises the fundamental question of what kind of play *The Persians* really is. Philip Vellacott, translator of the Penguin Classics version, says the play's purpose was 'the gratification of the natural pride of the Athenians in their achievement'. Edith Hall sees the play as the starting point of an Orientalism in which the European imagination has dominated Asia 'by conceptualizing its inhabitants as defeated, luxurious, emotional, cruel and always dangerous'. Meanwhile yet another scholar, A. J. Podlecki, argues that the original Athenian audience had almost to forget who they were and 'concentrate on the common humanity which they shared with their former enemy'. So what exactly is *The Persians*? A patriotic battle-cry? Anti-Persian propaganda? A humane tragedy? It can be any or all of those things depending on your point of view, which is one of the reasons why it is a still-vibrant play that, even more than *The Oresteia*, establishes a pattern for Western drama.

At times, it palpably exults in Athenian supremacy. The action takes place in the Persian court, where a chorus of old men and the queen mother, Atossa, await news of the outcome of Xerxes' expedition against the Athenians. The answer soon comes in a speech from a messenger describing how the Persians have been annihilated in the sea-fight at Salamis. He even recalls the triumphalist cry of the Athenians as they go into battle, described thus in the excellent version by Kaite O'Reilly in the aforementioned production: 'Liberation! Sons of Greece, to battle! For the freedom of your homeland, your children and your wives, fight! For your ancestral gods, your forefathers' graves, all or nothing! Now is the time! Strike! All is at stake!'

This celebrated passage had a long afterlife in that it inspired the French revolutionary anthem, 'La Marseillaise' ('Allons enfants de la Patrie /Le jour de gloire est arrivé'). *The Persians* also led to a patriotic British poem celebrating Nelson's victory over Napoleon at the Battle of the Nile. And Aeschylus' play stimulated Shelley to write his drama *Hellas*, which he prefaced with the claim: 'We are all Greeks . . . our laws, our literature, our religion all have their roots in Greece.'

And yet *The Persians*, far from being a piece of militaristic chauvinism, is more remarkable for its empathy than its exultation. The opening choruses are filled with foreboding at the departure of the flower of Persian youth and at the fate of their abandoned women-folk 'longing for their men in their suddenly too-big beds' (O'Reilly). Atossa has a vivid premonitory dream in which she imagines her son's chariot, drawn by an unbridled Greek, crashing to the ground. And the messenger's description of the battle of Salamis is filled with a cosmic sense of loss and waste. 'I saw,' he tragically says, 'an entire generation die.'

Judging by the three modern revivals I've seen, we inevitably invest Aeschylus' play with our own sense of the horror of war. I remember a production by Alexis Minotis at Epidaurus which, although solidly traditional in style, avoided any note of chauvinistic vainglory. Peter Sellars, the avant-garde American director, staged a version in 1993 where the Persians became the victims of George Bush Senior's first Gulf War. And without making specific reference to the 2003 war with Iraq, Mike Pearson's National Theatre Wales production played on our memories of the recent catastrophic loss of human life.

As with all great classics, we view *The Persians* from our own perspective. But compassion for the conquered is not something invented by us: it is inescapably there in Aeschylus. Towards the play's end we see the ghost of Darius, Xerxes' father, arising from his tomb. While he condemns his son's hubris ('a mortal playing god to gods'), he also expresses pity for future Persian generations. And when Xerxes, a worn and ragged fugitive, makes a climactic appearance, his lamentations rend the air with their self-hating agony. 'Despised,' he says of himself, 'not even Death would take me.'

No one could say what the mood would have been like when the play was first seen at the City Dionysia in 472 BC. But it is difficult to imagine even the most gung-ho Athenian war veteran not feeling a tug of sympathy for the humiliated Persians. And how could any sensitive spectator not be made aware of the vanity of imperial conquest?

But *The Persians* is more than a great play. It is a reminder of how, in most art forms, early works contain the seeds of future development. When Cervantes wrote *Don Quixote* he anticipated the magic realism and self-referential nature of the modern novel, and in silent cinema pioneer directors like D. W. Griffith and Abel Gance used free-ranging cameras or split screens with an expressive energy that makes most modern innovations look feeble. I am not claiming that Aeschylus in *The Persians* prefigures the whole of modern drama. But what he does discover is that one nation's victory is another's defeat, that a play's meaning is defined by circumstance and that drama is, first and foremost, the art of contradiction.

2

Oedipus the King

SOPHOCLES

(*c*.495–406 BC)

Bernard Shaw said you should try everything once except folk-dancing and incest. And it is the taboo against familial sex that ensured that Sophocles' masterpiece, written around 420 BC, some fifty years after *The Persians*, was not seen on the professional British stage until 1912.

The Oedipus myth was too powerful to be ignored entirely. John Dryden and Nathaniel Lee came up with a popular, neo-Shakespearean version in 1678 which tactfully suggested Oedipus had subconscious reservations about having sex with his mum ('An unknown hand,' he says, 'still checked my forward joy'). There was also an 1821 music-drama designed to encourage George IV to lead a path of domestic virtue. But when Edwardian actor-managers, led by Beerbohm Tree, applied for permission to stage Sophocles' play, they met with stonewalling resistance from the censorious Lord Chamberlain, who clearly feared it would set a bad example to the impressionable English. As the playwright Henry Arthur Jones wryly commented, 'Now, of course, if any considerable body of Englishmen are arranging to marry their mothers, whether by accident or design, it must be stopped at once. But it is not a frequent occurrence in any class of English society. Throughout the course of my life, I have not met more than six men who were anxious to do it.'

We may scoff at a ludicrous censorship and the prissiness of past ages, but, given that Sophocles' play has only been visible on British stages for just over a hundred years, how much do we really understand it? Our problem, I suspect, is that we view it through Freudian spectacles as a demonstration of the 'Oedipus complex'. Freud's argument, forcefully presented in his *Interpretation of Dreams*, is that if we are moved by Oedipus' destiny (i.e. that of killing his father and marrying his mother), it is because it might easily have been ours. 'It is the fate of all of us perhaps,' wrote Freud, 'to direct our first sexual impulse towards our mother and our first hatred and our first murderous wish against our father. Our dreams convince us that this is so.'

The danger in seeing the play as a Freudian textbook is twofold. It underestimates the sublime intricacy of Sophocles' plot, to which Aristotle paid due tribute. It also undermines the unresolved tension, within the play, between the power of fate and free will. The Freudian reading makes Oedipus a victim of destiny. In much the same way tradition-bound academics, such as F. L. Lucas, saw Greek tragedy 'as man's answer to this universe that crushes him so pitilessly'. Both readings, in short, are wilfully determinist. But the brilliance of Sophocles' play lies precisely in the extent to which it shows the hero exercising choices dependent on character. That is the source of its modernity rather than its embodiment of primal sexual urges.

What, after all, does Sophocles show us in Oedipus? A man who can be seen as hubristic or heroic – possibly both – who makes a series of bad choices. At a pivotal moment Oedipus reveals that he was once told by a drunk in Corinth that he was not, as he supposed, the son of the king, Polybus. So what did he do? He went to Delphi, consulted the oracle and was told that he would kill his father and marry his mother. Armed with these dual pieces of information – that Polybus may not be his 'father' and that he would one day commit parricide and incest – you'd have thought Oedipus would have gone about his daily business with a certain caution. Not a bit of it. He instantly flees Corinth and, on the road to Thebes, impulsively kills an old man. And having been installed as Theban king after solving the riddle of the Sphinx, he marries the widow of his predecessor, Laius, and makes no enquiry about his forerunner's fate. Even what we'd now call the 'back-story' shows Oedipus to be guilty of hideous rashness.

In the immediate present, Sophocles offers a vivid character-study of a flawed human being: no plaything of the gods but an arrogant autocrat who, in his unceasing quest for truth, is also perversely admirable. Oedipus believes that his earlier rescue of Thebes from the clutches of the Sphinx has lent him total inviolability: 'I saved the state with my genius,' he boastfully proclaims in Don Taylor's brisk translation for BBC Television. And with stunning psychological insight, Sophocles shows Oedipus' belief in the invincibility of power leads him to ignore all the warnings he is given. The play amounts to a series of existential choices in which the seer Tiresias, the brother-in-law Creon and the wife-mother Jocasta all urge Oedipus not to go on. Even the old shepherd, who locks the story into place by revealing that he was ordered to take the three-day-old Oedipus from Laius' court and kill him but hadn't the heart to do so, underscores a key point about the play: that the tension between the preordained and personal impulse is never-ending. It is the point definitively made by Bernard Knox in his introduction to the Penguin Classics edition, one of the great pieces of modern criticism. 'Oedipus,' writes Knox, 'is the free agent who, by his own self-willed action, discovers that his own predicted destiny has already been fulfilled.'

Through its perfect structure and endless tension between fate and free will, the play has left its imprint on Western drama: Ibsen, especially, is Sophocles in a Norwegian frock-coat. But how do you stage the play? As a big spectacle or with austere simplicity? As a star-vehicle or a director's showcase? In isolation or, along with *Oedipus at Colonus* and *Antigone*, as part of a Theban trilogy? By now most formats have been tried. Max Reinhardt's ground-breaking 1912 production at Covent Garden was a variant on an earlier version seen in Germany: it began apparently with a vast crowd surging through the auditorium and ended with the blinded Oedipus making his cathartic exit by groping his way through the audience. Clearly, director's theatre at its most thrilling.

In contrast, a 1945 London revival was chiefly remembered for Olivier's bravura performance: 'Olivier's famous "Oh! Oh!" when the full catalogue of his sin is unfolded,' wrote Tynan, 'must still be resounding in some high recess of the New Theatre's dome.' Other productions have stressed the ritualistic aspects of the play: Tyrone Guthrie presented it in giant, primitive masks in Stratford Ontario and Minneapolis in the 1950s and 1960s. Peter Hall, at the Olivier in 1996, opted for a similarly stylised approach, although the masks were on a more human scale, and Alan Howard was able to convey the destructive zeal of Oedipus' quest for self-knowledge.

But, for me, it was Jonathan Kent's 2008 revival, also at the Olivier, that finally unlocked the play's complexity. There was a mixture of hauteur, paranoia and pride in Ralph Fiennes's city-suited Oedipus that led him to declare of his Corinthian youth, in Frank McGuinness's translation, 'I was the one to beat in that city.' Yet there was also something heroic about Fiennes's obsessive self-discovery. At the last, it became impossible to withhold one's pity from this fallen, blood-spattered figure urging his children to 'lead a good life, better than your father's'. I felt I'd finally got close to the heart of Sophocles' play: one that shows, within an immaculate structure, that flawed characters are capable of huge suffering and that a belief in the workings of destiny does not exclude human responsibility. That's what Sophocles teaches us, and these lessons were to leave their visible fingerprint on drama over the next two and a half millennia.

3

Helen

EURIPIDES

(*c.*480–407 BC)

We are slightly in awe of Aeschylus and Sophocles. Euripides, however, seems 'one of us'. His tone is sceptical and ironic, he's irreverent about the gods, preoccupied by sex and appalled by the destructive horror of war. What's not to like?

For all those reasons his plays have been seized on by modern directors and actors. *Medea*, with its aggrieved outsider avenging herself on a faithless husband, has become part of the feminist canon: it has yielded fine productions by Deborah Warner, Jonathan Kent and Carrie Cracknell and fire-breathing performances from Fiona Shaw, Diana Rigg and Helen McCrory. Katie Mitchell has set *Women of Troy* and *Iphigenia at Aulis* in a world of bureaucracy and concrete bunkerdom to heighten Euripides' modernity. And I've seen *The Bacchae* staged everywhere from the National Theatre (by Peter Hall) to a Northampton print-works (by Laurie Sansom) to make its point about the danger of either uninhibitedly indulging or fiercely repressing our darkest passions.

Yet I'd choose *Helen*, first performed in 412 BC, when Euripides was sixty-eight, as his greatest play. My reason is that it invents a wholly new form: tragi-comedy. We always accept the rigid categories of classical drama, yet here Euripides, with the lightest of touches, offers a savage indictment of war's futility. You can point to a raft of later plays, from Shakespeare's *Troilus and Cressida* to Shaw's *Arms and the Man* and Giraudoux's *The Trojan War Will Not Take Place*, which satirically debunk Homeric myth and posturing heroism. What is extraordinary is that Euripides, at a time when dramatic forms were only just taking root, shows their infinite flexibility.

He starts from a wittily outrageous premise (admittedly one that scholars say owes something to work by the great lyric poet Stesichorus and the historian Herodotus): that the Helen who went to Troy was a phantom, a mere cloud-puppet made by Hera to spite Aphrodite. The real Helen, in Euripides' version, has spent seventeen years living in Egypt as a model of marital fidelity. So instantly we are into a comedy of mistaken identity. Paris, who abducted the beautiful Spartan queen, thinks he's had the world's most desirable woman but, as Euripides' heroine tartly observes, 'I am afraid there is no Helen of Troy.'

Having prepared the ground, Euripides develops it with quicksilver finesse. First we get the fun: Helen encamped in a graveyard to avoid the clutches of the predatory Egyptian king. Then the mood darkens as she learns, from a Greek soldier, of the death of her mother and her fraternal twins, Castor and Pollux. But lightness returns with the arrival of her shipwrecked husband, Menelaus, in the guise of a tattered derelict. Neither Helen nor Menelaus, at first, recognise each other: when they do, they can't wait to make up for seventeen lost years. But the big joke is that Helen is quick on the uptake while Menelaus is a slowcoach who can't quite get his head round the idea that he sailed to Troy in pursuit of a shadow.

The whole play is a testament to female resourcefulness. Don Taylor, who did a fine translation for BBC Television, says of Euripides' Helen that 'she reminds us of nothing so much as one of Shaw's life-force girls, an Ann Whitefield or Lady Cecily Waynflete or Major Barbara'. She is certainly just as clever. It is Helen who begs the Egyptian king's sister not to snitch about Menelaus' sudden arrival. It is Helen who feigns mourning on the false grounds that Menelaus is dead. And it is Helen who comes up with the master plan that enables both her and her husband to escape: she promises she'll marry the Egyptian king if only he will give herself and her ragged accomplice (i.e. Menelaus) a ship in which to carry out the funeral obsequies according to Greek custom. Helen not only motors the plot, she is one of the most likeable female protagonists in world drama.

But what makes this a great play is Euripides' ability to reconcile apparent contradictions. On one level, the play is pure comedy about a long-postponed marital reunion. On another, it is a fierce critique of the futility of war.

When Kenneth Tynan saw the play staged at Epidaurus in 1962, he got rather tetchy about the idea it was a tribute to marital love. 'Last Sunday,' he wrote, 'when Helen and Menelaus were reunited after seventeen years' separation, 14,000 people burst into spontaneous applause. Their delight was moral and reflected a simple, wholehearted approval of marital reconciliation. That simplicity, that naïve wholeness of response is something we cannot hope to recapture. I state this as a fact, without nostalgia and without regret.' But who is the 'we' to whom Tynan refers? And Tynan defeats his own argument by showing that Euripides' denouement appeals to some deep-seated desire to see a separated couple rematched. To deny that power is to dismiss much of world drama including Shakespearean comedy from *The Comedy of Errors* to *The Winter's Tale*.

The real genius of *Helen* lies in the fact that it disturbs even as it delights. It is worth recalling that this play first appeared in 412 BC, when the war between Athens and Sparta, which began in 431, had reached an especially disastrous phase: news of the destruction of the fleet in the Sicilian expedition, and the loss of at least 10,000 men, had reached Athens in 413 and, according to Thucydides, induced communal panic. Within six months of that debacle, Euripides writes a play that simultaneously offers a redemptive optimism and questions the whole purpose of war. The idea that Troy was toppled because of a phantom Helen threads its way through the play like a seam of blood. And the point emerged strongly in the Frank McGuinness translation used for a 2009 Shakespeare's Globe revival starring a memorably fetching Penny Downie. In the McGuinness version a servant says to Menelaus:

> We all saw a city ripped asunder,
> Men breathing their last – for the sake of what?
> An illusion, a dream-nothing, nothing,
> We fought the Trojan War over nothing.

Later in the play a lyric ode from the Chorus addresses Helen, supposedly of Troy, with the lines:

> Your birth was the death of that great city,
> Its streets and towers are now opened tombs.
> What was that fight for – illusion and dream?
> Are gods like men – nothing is what it seems?
> Sad nightingale, poor birds of the air,
> Sing the damnation of all warmongers.

The point was not lost on a London audience who, in 2003, had seen a British government, led by Tony Blair, join forces with American troops in an Iraqi war over weapons of mass destruction that proved as illusory as the phantom Helen. It was also a war that, in the name of liberation, cost an estimated 100,000 Iraqi lives.

If Euripides' play speaks to us today, it is because it breaks all boundaries. It lauds female ingenuity, hymns marital reunion and combines the affirmativeness of comedy with a critique of military conflict. You can call the play whatever you like: political romcom, optimistic tragedy, feminist prototype. The label scarcely matters. What makes the play supremely modern is Euripides' glorious ability to transcend categories and embrace opposites.

4

Assembly-Women

ARISTOPHANES
(c.448–380 BC)

I've always had a soft spot for Aristophanes. I suspect it stems
from playing a minor role in a version of *The Birds* staged by John
McGrath in an Oxford college garden in the summer of 1959: my
memory is of a joyous production in which slapstick mingled
with satire and Peter Snow offered a stunning impersonation
of General de Gaulle. I've also sat through a number of rousing
(and sometimes arousing) versions of *Lysistrata*: most people
now forget that it was this story of a female sex-strike that in 1957
provided the newly formed English Stage Company with one of
its greatest box-office hits. And I loved the 1974 Burt Shevelove/
Stephen Sondheim version of *The Frogs*, which became the first
musical ever to be staged in a swimming pool.

So why have I chosen the little-known *Assembly-Women* (the
title given to *Ecclesiazousai* by Stephen Halliwell, from whose
excellent Worlds' Classics translation I quote below)? It comes
late in Aristophanes' career, usually being dated around 392 BC.
It is dismissed by many commentators: even someone who writes
as astutely about Aristophanes as Maurice Bowra says that 'the
old gay bawdry has become calculated and cold-blooded, even
at times depressing'. Coming as it does some twelve years after
Athens' defeat in the Peloponnesian War, it might seem to lack

the political urgency of plays like *Acharnians* (425 BC) and *Peace* (421 BC) in which Aristophanes was writing pacifist tracts. Yet, whatever academics may say, I'd put in a strong plea for *Assembly-Women*: not only for its flamboyant gaiety but for its radical message. In effect, it makes the same point that Caryl Churchill was to articulate nearly two millennia later in *Top Girls*: that you can't have true feminism without socialism.

I admit that the play resembles *Lysistrata*. It starts with the female protagonist Praxagora (whose name suggests she is 'active in the Agora', or public life) entering in male drag and putting to her sluggish female followers her Big Idea: that, given the corrupt state of Athenian affairs, women take over the reins of government. In effect, Praxagora stages a *coup d'état*. She packs the Assembly with sisterly supporters, all sporting beards and male cloaks, who vote overwhelmingly for female power. And where are all the men while this is happening? As Aristophanes makes clear, in ribald scenes involving Praxagora's husband and his neighbours, they're faffing around in frocks since their wives have whipped their clothes as well as their political authority: transvestism in short, becomes a metaphor for political role-reversal.

But Praxagora doesn't stop at taking over government. She also envisages a new world of economic communism:

My plan is that all property from now on must be shared.
We must abolish rich and poor, with one man farming acres
While down the road another lacks enough land for his grave.
Or one man owning many slaves, another owning none.
I now decree that everyone must share the same resources.

As if it were not enough to propose that private property be handed over to the city for equal distribution, Praxagora goes several stages further. She decrees that the nuclear family be replaced by communes, that women be shared both for sex and procreation and that, in order not to privilege the good-looking of either gender, the less well-favored will come head of the queue. As Praxagora succinctly says:

> The law now states explicitly
> It's the ugly ones who get first fuck.

The boldness of the idea is breathtaking. As Halliwell points out, the Utopian notions that Aristophanes outlines were very much in the air in Athens in the later fifth and early fourth centuries. Book 5 of Plato's *Republic* advocates that, in the ideal state, women be part of government and that a form of sexual communism be practised. But Plato confines his ideas to the ruling class. And the audacity of Aristophanes lies in taking the abstract proposals of Athenian intellectuals and giving them vivid life on a public stage. For the first time in Western drama, basic ideas about economic and sexual redistribution are being theatrically debated: the fact that both the Athenian audience and the actors were men gives the political ideas more, rather than less, piquancy.

But how much was Aristophanes endorsing or satirising Attic communism? He leaves it to us to decide. No one could deny that Praxagora is a dynamic visionary who has the eloquence of the true pathfinder. She damns the ineptitude, laziness and corruption of the existing Assembly, many of whose members turn up just to claim their statutory three obols of pay per day: since that was about a third of the daily rate for top jobs, the parallel with our own House of Lords is striking. But Praxagora also envisages a world in which age is privileged over youth, ugliness over beauty and no one should ever feel sexually excluded.

There is, of course, a catch in all this. Praxagora herself remains top-cat: a Mrs Thatcher with revolutionary leanings. You could, in fact, raise the same objection to her Utopian vision that Sebastian airs when Gonzalo in *The Tempest* outlines his idea of an egalitarian commonwealth. 'No sovereignty,' says Gonzalo. 'Yet he would be king of it,' retorts Sebastian. And Aristophanes, as a comic writer, naturally contrasts the idealistic dream with the practical reality. One filthily funny episode shows a visibly erect young man being fought over by a trio of ancient hags while his nubile sweetheart looks on in fury. Claiming that her sexual rivals are old enough to be her lover's mother, the young girl warns:

> If you older women should implement this law
> You'll make the city swarm with Oedipusses.

But the richness of the play lies in its ability to show both sides of the equation: to embody the potential, as well as the pitfalls, of a revolutionary proposal. And although Bowra was not one of the play's most fervent admirers, he pins down the essential quality of Aristophanes' work. 'It conveys,' he says, 'the reality of Athenian life even in a world of fantasy.' *Assembly-Women* may be predicated on an unlikely transfer of political power, but it is filled with a sense of urban verismo. This is a world where muggers haunt the streets at night, where paupers walk around half-naked and where Athenian democracy is in the hands of depraved officials. Aristophanes may, in his vision of a city run by women, have had his head in the clouds as far as fourth-century Athens was concerned, but, in his portrait of the chicanery, corruption and civic grottiness of a society run by men, he had his feet firmly on the ground. Like all first-rate satirists, Aristophanes shows us life as it might be and life as it actually is, and it is that, along with its radical politics, that makes this the most enticing, if one of the least-known, of Attic comedies.

5

The Brothers Menaechmus

PLAUTUS

(c.254–184 BC)

Aristophanes died in 380 BC. The Roman dramatist Plautus was born in 254 BC. In that time comedy underwent a momentous change. The textbooks tell us that Aristophanes, at his peak, represented the Old Comedy: a bawdy, lyrical-satirical choral extravaganza. After that came the New Comedy, symbolised by Menander (342–293 BC). Instead of topsy-turvy fantasy it presented stock characters in stock situations: in the words of classical scholar Erich Segal, 'its locale was the city, its people the bourgeoisie, its plots romantic'. But then a populist entertainer arrives in the shape of Plautus, who, while adapting the plots of the New Comedy, gives them something wholly fresh: manic ingenuity, verbal exuberance, a pervasive sexiness. You wouldn't call him a great satirist in that he seems more interested in pure laughs than lethal lampoons. But his influence is all over modern theatre from the political comedies of Dario Fo to the crowd-pleasing farces of Ray Cooney.

If I seize on *The Brothers Menaechmus* (*Menaechmi*), it is because it is both his funniest play and the one that confirms the length of the Roman's reach. Shakespeare uses Plautus' plot as the basis for *The Comedy of Errors* and then ups the ante by giving us not one but two sets of identical twins. Shakespeare's play generated a 1938 Rodgers and Hart Broadway musical, *The*

Boys of Syracuse. Then in 1962 Burt Shevelove and Larry Gelbart brilliantly combined a number of Plautus plots to create *A Funny Thing Happened on the Way to the Forum*, for which Stephen Sondheim wrote the music and lyrics. When that came to London in 1963 Frankie Howerd played the wily slave Pseudolus (who lent his name to one of Plautus' plays), who supervises the action. Howerd did it with such leering, buttonholing expertise that he went on to play a distinctly similar character, Lurcio, in a BBC Television series, *Up Pompeii*, that ran for two seasons in 1969–70 and spawned a subsequent film. Strange to think that every time Frankie Howerd beckoned the camera towards him in *Up Pompeii* to proclaim 'This is the Prologue' he was doing much the same as the lead actor who came on stage in *The Brothers Menaechmus* around 200 BC to announce, 'Now here's the plot. Please listen with your full attention span.'

What's exhilarating about Plautus is that he gives us all the back-story in eighty lines. We are to imagine twins separated at the age of seven. One has been brought up in Epidamnus and, thanks to his adoptive dad, has money, status and a dowried, though disagreeable, wife. The other twin was reared in Syracuse and, though poor, has come to Epidamnus in search of his long-lost brother. There's no hint of the death-threat that hangs over the boys' father in *The Comedy of Errors*: here he's long gone. What we get is inventive fun and the first stirrings of theatrical self-consciousness. Today we call it 'meta-theatre'. For Plautus it was simply a way of reminding his Roman audience that they were part of the act: that all theatre is an imaginative conspiracy between the watchers and the watched. The clever slave who is the eponymous hero of *Pseudolus* compares himself to a playwright 'transforming baseless lies into a semblance of the truth'. In much the same way the Prologue to *The Brothers Menaechmus* reminds us (in Segal's translation): 'This town is Epidamnus, while the play is on.' Tomorrow, however, it will be somewhere else just as the actors will change 'From pimp to papa or to lover pale and wan, To pauper, parasite, to king or prophet, on and on.' In addition to self-awareness you find in Plautus three key elements that, like it or not, were to become staples of comedy and farce down the centuries: mistaken identity, misogyny and madness.

The first of these is obviously crucial to a play about twins. But Plautus is shrewd enough to ensure that we always know which twin is which by giving them perceptibly different character traits. EM (or the resident Epidamnus Menaechmus) is a cunning, lecherous but browbeaten bourgeois: SM (the visiting Syracuse Menaechmus) is a more easy-going, good-natured adventurer, albeit with an acquisitive streak. One can't stress too much the importance of the audience always being ahead of the game. In *The Venetian Twins* (1747) Goldoni made his identical heroes an urban Romeo and a Bergamo bumpkin. In the same way Feydeau in *A Flea in Her Ear* (1907) was to make his lookalike protagonists a middle-class insurance-man and a gormless hotel porter. Plautus doesn't go that far but he still has the nous to mark out the crucial differences.

His other stroke of genius is to allow the identity mix-ups to revolve around a dress that is constantly changing hands. First EM pinches it from his wife to give to his mistress, Erotium. Then Erotium, mistaking her man, hands it over to the visiting SM to get it distinctively embroidered. Next EM, who's being harassed by his wife, asks Erotium to return the dress only for her to claim he's already got it. In the meantime SM finds himself confronted by EM's outraged wife, who demands the dress back and eventually summons her father, who has the visiting twin classified insane. There's much more, but this gives one some idea how a simple prop motors the plot before the confusion is cleared up and the wrongs, so to speak, are redressed.

Misogyny is a trickier topic. We've seen how Euripides and Aristophanes created witty female protagonists. Plautus reverts to stock types. In this play EM's wife is a straightforward virago and Erotium a beguiling sex-object. It's a pattern you find repeated down the ages – the shrew and the temptress – and, without exonerating it, I'd say that it's a by-product of the kind of comedy in which situation takes precedence over psychology. Even if EM and SM are differentiated, it is only because the logic of the plot and audience comprehension demand it. Rather than condemn Plautus for lack of sexual enlightenment, I would just make two points. One is that Plautus undermines Roman notions of masculinity: EM here not only steals his wife's dress but at one point puts it on, feyly saying to his parasite, 'Tell me that I'm so attractive.' The other point is one made by Segal: that the sexual stereotypes allow the homes occupied by EM and his mistress to represent symbolic opposites. 'We see in the two on-stage houses,' writes Segal, 'a contrast between the atmosphere of everyday and that of holiday or, as Freud would express it, the Reality Principle versus the Pleasure Principle. Needless to say, Pleasure emerges triumphant for that is the theme of all comedy.'

Yet madness is also present in the play. It is there in a literal sense. SM is first deemed insane by his supposed father-in-law, and, once categorised as mad, he decides to act the part. A doctor is called to examine and section him, which he duly does. The only trouble is the doc eventually picks on the wrong twin, EM, who is about to be carted off to the bin by four burly bodyguards when he is rescued by SM's good-hearted servant. But Plautus' play deals with the larger, disorienting madness of a stranger arriving in a foreign city and being familiarly greeted while the long-term resident finds himself a stranger in his own world. Identity is called into question, nothing is quite what it seems and, as Eric Bentley wrote of Feydeau's farces, 'one touch, we feel, and the whole thing might go spinning into space'. Plautus was primarily an entertainer. But *The Brothers Menaechmus* introduces us, with pioneering zest, to a host of ideas that were to become common currency in comedy and farce. There is acknowledgement of theatre's theatricality; the notions of marriage as a trap, adultery as a risk, the servant as wiser than the master; above all, the idea that in life you can't achieve harmony and reconciliation without first experiencing disorder and delusion. I just wish someone would revive this delirious piece, which I've only seen done by students, to show that Plautus is the godfather of modern comedy and farce.

6

The Mysteries

---

adapted by TONY HARRISON

(1937–)

It's a big leap from classical Rome to medieval Britain, but in the mystery plays, written at the end of the fourteenth century, one finds the roots of our native drama. This is where it all starts.

The basic facts are familiar. Collectively the plays cover the Bible story from the Creation to the Day of Judgement. Four complete cycles survive: York, Towneley (from Wakefield), Chester and the Ludus Coventriae (deriving, despite its name, from Norfolk). The cycles are diverse in scope and style and are the work of unknown hands. And the plays themselves were performed, at Corpus Christi, on travelling carts or 'pageants' and were sponsored by the appropriate guilds: the shipwrights undertook Noah, the goldsmiths the Magi, the bakers the Last Supper. We know that the plays were popular for two centuries, were banned under the Reformation and were dismissed as primitive by later generations: Byron thought them 'very profane productions'.

But the strange paradox is that they have been systematically rediscovered in secular post-war Britain. York, Chester, Coventry have all staged local cycles, and, when I first came to London in 1964, I saw a stunning re-creation of the Wakefield plays at Bernard Miles's Mermaid Theatre. But it was Tony Harrison ('a Yorkshire poet who came to read the metre') who achieved a brilliant theatrical synthesis in his version of *The Mysteries*: a trilogy comprising The Nativity, The Passion and Doomsday that began its life, in Bill Bryden's unforgettable production, on the National Theatre terraces on Easter Saturday 1977 and ended up being staged in its entirety at Henry Irving's old theatre, the Lyceum, in 1985.

Why do I give these plays, in Harrison's exemplary version, such prominence? First, because they reveal the hunger for realism that, with occasional digressions, dominates British drama for the next six centuries. You see this most clearly in the masterly scenes of the Crucifixion, which are the work of an anonymous writer who, because of his rugged alliteration and emphasis on the sheer difficulty of the task in hand, has been dubbed 'the York realist'. This appetite for the particular comes out perfectly in Harrison's version. The 'knights' assigned to crucifying Christ are individualised workmen equipped with toolbags, lengths of rope, hammers and nails. But, although they're keen to get the job done and pick up their wages, it's more difficult than they thought. First they make the auger-holes on the cross too far apart so that Christ's hands have to be stretched till they can reach them. Then, having laid Christ out on the cross, they can't lift it because of his weight. Finally, with the aid of a ladder and ropes attached to the cross, they heave it precariously into position. 'Him as made mortice made it too wide,' moans the fourth knight. 'That's why it waves. Young gormless get!' Finally wedges are hammered into the base of the cross to make it secure. The most iconic image in the Christian faith thus becomes a prototypical 'work-play'. You can trace a direct line between this and David Storey's *The Contractor*, which, in 1969, showed another group of wage-driven Yorkshiremen having similar difficulties erecting a wedding marquee.

Realism is one aspect of the British dramatic character. Another is a capacity for the comic: a desire, against all the Aristotelian belief in unity of tone, to parodically puncture seriousness. This mixture of the homely and exalted is at its best in the famous Wakefield *Secunda Pastorum*, the Second Shepherd's play, in which the journey of the Magi to the Bethlehem stable is immediately followed by a rollicking farce about an attempt to pass off a cribbed sheep as a cradled infant. Even here there is a strong vein of realism. The oppressed shepherds are first heard moaning on the moor about being 'over-taxed' and 'down-ground', claiming, 'We have no rights allowed by these gentry-men.' For them the loss of a sheep is a serious business. That explains why they are outraged when they find the wife of the thieving Mak nursing the stolen animal in swaddling clothes as if it were the baby Jesus: 'Saw I never in a cradle A horned lad ere now,' one of the shepherds sagely mutters. You can take this as a mark of the Gothic imagination which, as in the paintings of Bosch and Bruegel, mingles the holy and the grotesque. For me it's also a clue to that juxtaposition of the serious and the comic which – although evident in Euripides – helps to define British drama and finds its richest expression in Shakespeare.

I don't think it's fanciful to argue that Shakespeare learned a lot from the mystery plays. We know that a cycle was played in Coventry, not far from Stratford, as late as 1581, when Shakespeare was seventeen. What he would have seen was drama's power to mix the earthy and the elevated. Abraham says to Isaac, whose life he has been called on to sacrifice, 'Make thee ready, my dear darling For we must do a little thing': the words, in context, are as sublime in their simplicity as Lear's 'Prithee undo this button' before his death. And when Hamlet warns the players against rant and bombast, what does he say but 'It out-Herods Herod': a clear reference to the roaring tyrant of *The Mysteries*, who cries, in Harrison's version, 'I am the king of all mankind, I bide, I beat, I loose, I bind.'

Glynne Wickham in *Shakespeare's Dramatic Heritage* takes the argument even further and suggests that *Macbeth* plays on popular recollections of *The Mysteries*. Hell in both the York and Towneley cycles was fortified like a castle and guarded, on behalf of Beelzebub, by a character called Rybald: it's but a short journey to Shakespeare's drunken porter, who mans Macbeth's gate, hears the same knocks on the door as occur in the Harrowing of Hell and who instinctively cries, 'Who's there, i' the name of Belzebub?' Wickham goes on to point out how much Macbeth has in common with the medieval Herod: both tyrants whose peace of mind is destroyed by prophecies of a rival and who hires assassins to murder all potential opponents, including children. Obviously Shakespeare's Macbeth is a thousand times subtler than Herod, but the folk memory lingers on.

I don't, however, mean to suggest that these medieval plays are crude or simplistic. In fact, they show their audience's ability to embrace multiple levels of reality. Take the scenes in Doomsday, where the resurrected Christ appears to his uncomprehending disciples and imagine that you are a fourteenth-century spectator in York or Wakefield. You would have been watching a recognisable local worthy playing Christ. You would also have been confronted by an embodiment of the most spiritual force in your existence. On yet another level you would have seen a character who confirms his physical existence to the sceptical apostles by eating fish and taking honey. It is a moment beautifully realised in Harrison's version and made even stronger when the doubting Thomas is instructed to put his finger in Christ's wounds and cries, 'My hand is bloody with thy blood.' But whose blood exactly? That of the crucified Christ or that from a pool supplied to the props department by a local butcher?

I am not patronising the credulity of the medieval mind. When I saw the Bryden–Harrison version at the National I was fascinated by my own and the audience's response. How was it that we were all so moved by a Creation myth long derided by Darwinists, by the story of a virgin birth not susceptible to reason and by a Day of Judgement depending on a Manichaean notion of Heaven and Hell? Was it simply that we were away-day Christians nostalgic for a religion we may have been taught in childhood? Were we simply overcome by the skill of the presentation? Or was it proof yet again of the contradictory nature of drama, which can make you surrender emotionally to what you doubt rationally? It may have been any one or all of those things. All I know is that, for those of us present, it was a momentous encounter with the origins of English drama.

7

Edward II

CHRISTOPHER MARLOWE

(1564–93)

I first saw Marlowe's play presented by the Cambridge society that bears his name in a dingly dell in Stratford-on-Avon in the summer of 1960. I was mesmerised by its momentum, its poetry, its dizzying shifts of focus. I have seen it many times since, notably in 1969, when a flamboyantly restless Ian McKellen paired it with a more ceremonial *Richard II* in a stunning Prospect diptych, and in 1990 at Stratford's Swan, when Simon Russell Beale made the leap from being, in his own words, the 'RSC's resident poof' to highly accomplished tragedian. There are, of course, other Marlowe plays I might include in my top 101. But *Tamburlaine* ('the story of Giant the Jack-killer', said C. S. Lewis) becomes a bit wearing, *The Jew of Malta* is too self-consciously ironic, and *Doctor Faustus*, for all its sublime poetry, too broken-backed. If I plump for *Edward II* it is because it looks back to the medieval wheel-of-fortune play and forward to the idea of a tragic hero destroyed by his erotic obsessions. In many ways, Edward II's fate foreshadows that of Oscar Wilde: both men who believe that it is better to be beautiful than to be good, both men ruined by a fixation with widely detested emotional parasites: Piers Gaveston in Edward's case, Bosie in Wilde's.

I wouldn't, however, want to push the comparison too far.

What is startling, when you go back to *Edward II*, is how much it revolves around class as well as sex. What angers the burly English barons who surround the king is less his homosexual infatuation with Gaveston than his love-object's lowly origins. In one extraordinary speech Mortimer Senior lists all the classical heroes who sported with their 'minions': since these include Alexander, Hercules, Achilles, Tully and Socrates, it's an impressive gay club. But Mortimer junior gives the game away in his response:

> Uncle, his wanton humour grieves not me,
> But this I scorn that one so basely born
> Should by his sovereign's favour grow so pert
> And riot it with the treasure of the realm.

That note of class-antagonism resounds throughout the play: at various times Gaveston, who wins not just sexual favours but grand titles from the king, is described as 'base and obscure', a 'base peasant', an 'ignoble vassal' as well as a 'sly, inveigling Frenchman' and a 'dapper Jack'. That last phrase is especially significant. What the lords loathe is that a bumptious opportunist like Gaveston has been given the keys to the kingdom. It is not hard to see in the style-conscious, self-promoting Gaveston a projection of the author himself. Marlowe was, after all, the son of a Canterbury shoemaker, was recruited into the spy trade while still at Cambridge and found himself defended by the Queen's Privy Council, including Lord Burghley, Archbishop Whitgift and Francis Walsingham, when the university sought to defer his degree. Gaveston may be the source of the king's downfall. He also has the cocksure defiance of the social arriviste.

Marlowe's erratic genius, however, lies in his ability to keep shifting the dramatic perspective, and not just in the case of Gaveston. Edward initially seems almost child-like in his helpless obsession with his favourite and in his whimsical dispensation of titles:

> I here create thee Lord High Chamberlain,
> Chief Secretary to the state and me,
> Earl of Cornwall, King and Lord of Man

As Peter Conrad has shrewdly pointed out, 'Power means for Edward the requisitioning of fantasies, the fending off of a reproving adult reality. He deploys it like someone playing Tamburlaine in a nursery-game.' McKellen was particularly good at highlighting the king's infantile tendencies: he dispensed honours with the promiscuous abandon of a charity-event Santa Claus dishing out Christmas presents and, whenever his impulses were checked, chewed testily on a bronze medallion. What Marlowe does for much of the play is allow us to see Edward through the eyes of his mutinous nobles and his discarded queen: our impression is of a reckless emotional and financial spendthrift throwing the realm into confusion.

But Marlowe, writing in the early 1590s, a good four years before Shakespeare's *Richard II*, has the born dramatist's gift for contradiction. His Edward starts out an impulsive child. But there is a pivotal moment when he asks to have one last glimpse of Gaveston, who's been taken prisoner in the king's war with his nobles, before he is executed. Eventually the nobles come round to the king's request only for the double-dealing Warwick to ambush the prisoner and strike off his head. This may be the start of Edward's downfall: it also marks a crucial change in our attitude. It allows Marlowe to achieve a decisive tonal shift whereby Edward gains sympathy in defeat, the high-aspiring Mortimer turns into a Machiavellian villain, and Isabella moves from a wronged queen into a conniving adulteress. Shakespeare learned from, and in many ways improved upon, Marlowe's play in *Richard II*. But even he has nothing as fine as the scene where Edward, imprisoned in a damp and stinking cesspit, is visited by his exotic assassin, Lightborn, whose name has echoes of Lucifer: born in light but expelled to darkness. Lightborn is no ordinary killer but a man whose speciality is aural, or oral, penetration. In Naples he learned not only how to poison flowers but

> To strangle with a lawn thrust through the throat
> Or, whilst one is asleep, to take a quill
> And blow a little powder in his ears,
> Or open his mouth and pour quicksilver down.

For Edward death comes by means of a stamped-on table and the insertion of a poker in the anus. But many actors and directors have seized on the voluptuous kinship that exists between the king and his killer. In Toby Robertson's Prospect production Robert Eddison's Lightborn bathed the king's body with sensual thoroughness before death, and McKellen clung fiercely to his assassin as if craving some kind of erotic consummation. Joe Hill-Gibbins, in his freewheeling 2013 National Theatre version, even had the same actor, Kyle Soller, doubling as Gaveston and Lightborn; lover and killer in one man.

Marlowe's play, covering the period from 1307 to 1330, occasionally sprawls and gives one little sense of the England beyond the confines of the court. But it captures, for the first time in English drama and in exquisitely melancholic language, a sense of the solitude of monarchy:

> But what are kings, when regiment is gone,
> But perfect shadows in a sunshine day?

Marlowe, following classic example, also shows how tragedy derives less from external circumstance than internal flaw: in this case Edward's emotional instability and erotic obsession. But Marlowe's greatest achievement, which was to have a profound influence on Shakespeare and later dramatists, is to determine how we watch a play: to show that one of drama's highest pleasures lies in the subversion of instinctive moral judgements, leaving the viewer in a state of excited confusion.

8

Love's Labour's Lost

WILLIAM SHAKESPEARE

(1564–1616)

The young Shakespeare, as most scholars agree, was heavily indebted to Marlowe. But Shakespeare, in his early plays of the 1590s, achieves effects beyond the reach of his contemporary. The magnificent central play of Shakespeare's *Henry VI* trilogy offers a panoramic picture of a divided England. *The Comedy of Errors* is a model of tight farcical plotting. And *Titus Andronicus*, for all its feast of horrors and its Moorish Marlovian villain in Aaron, plumbs the depths of human suffering.

But it is in *Love's Labour's Lost*, conventionally dated to 1594, a year after Marlowe's death, that Shakespeare displays the first full flowering of his genius. Like the later *Midsummer Night's Dream*, the play has no acknowledged source. But the main point is that this is a comedy that both satirises and delights in verbal display, leading Harold Bloom to remark that it outdoes Milton and James Joyce in its linguistic exuberance. It is also a corrective comedy: one that punctures the follies of youth, and male vanity in particular, without ever lapsing into trite moralising. On top of that zest and high spirits are coloured by a sense of transience, time and death in a way that defines Shakespearean comedy. Rarely performed between the 1590s and the 1840s, it is a play that has come into its own in modern times. Of the dozen or so productions I have seen in the last fifty years, one burns in the memory: that by John Barton for the RSC in 1978 that, with its cascading leaves and gathering dusk, captured perfectly the play's Chekhovian beauty.

You have to start, however, with the play's language and Shakespeare's ability to explore everything in the Elizabethan linguistic locker. But language is never divorced from character, as you see in Berowne. He is a figure, memorably incarnated by actors as diverse as Ian Richardson, Michael Pennington and David Tennant, who delights in paradox and pun, sense and sound and rhetorical flights of fancy. He also uses intricate wordplay to expose the absurdity of the King of Navarre's proposal that he and his companions devote three years to fasting, celibacy and monastic study in order to achieve fame. As Berowne says:

> Light seeking light doth light of light beguile;
> So, ere you find where light in darkness lies,
> Your light grows dark by losing of your eyes.

That first line, with its four variations on the word 'light', was glossed by Harry Levin as meaning 'intellect, seeking wisdom, cheats eyesight out of daylight'. The language is dense, packed, playful. It also pins down the central idea: that to search for immortality through academic seclusion is a denial of life. But it's a mark of Shakespeare's dramatic instinct that he makes the play's sceptical hero a study in self-infatuation. We see Berowne in many different ways: as a comically corrective force, as a scourge of his colleagues' oath-breaking hypocrisy and as a verbal spendthrift who finally forswears 'maggot ostentation'. But it was Barton's production that brilliantly showed how Berowne, for all his verbal prowess, needed to be taught a crucial lesson in humility: during the pageant of the Nine Worthies

Pennington's Berowne cruelly seized a flag borne by the Spanish Don Adriano and careered around the stage with it, only to find it wrenched from his grasp by Jane Lapotaire as his adored and angry Rosaline.

Like Berowne, all the other characters discover that language offers no protection against reality. Don Adriano, who delights in extravagant rhetoric and who hilariously describes how the king loves to dally with his 'excrement' (thankfully, he means his moustache), is finally hitched to an illiterate dairy maid. Holofernes, the pedantic schoolmaster who peppers every sentence with Latin tags, is verbally sabotaged during the pageant when his Judas Maccabeus is treated as if he were Judas Iscariot. Even the modest curate, Sir Nathaniel, is dismayed when shown to be 'a little o'erparted' in essaying the role of Alexander the Great; though it is hard not to warm to a character who earlier describes Holofernes' dinnertime conversation, with finicky precision, as 'learned without opinion, strange without heresy'.

But why is it that audiences still warm so readily to a play packed with Elizabethan word-juggling and obscure classical allusions? I suspect it is because it acknowledges life's complexities and shows the chill hand of death intruding on the comedy. It has become fashionable to update the action and underscore it with the distant rumble of guns like those heard by Virginia Woolf and the Bloomsberries in their Sussex retreat in 1914: a transposition first used by Robin Phillips at Stratford Ontario in 1978 has since been adopted by Ian Judge in 1993, Trevor Nunn in 2003 and Christopher Luscombe in 2014 in various RSC and National revivals. It's a concept that can come off but it's essentially redundant, since Shakespeare does the work for us with the climactic intrusion of the black-clad Marcade in one of the most sensational entrances in world drama:

MARCADE: God save you madam.

PRINCESS: Welcome, Marcade,

   But that thou interruptest our merriment.

MARCADE: I am sorry, madam, for the news I bring

   Is heavy in my tongue. The King your father –

PRINCESS: Dead, for my life!

MARCADE: Even so; my tale is told.

BEROWNE: Worthies away, the scene begins to cloud.

Shakespeare himself directs the scene perfectly, and the play's succeeding 200 lines are among his most astonishing in effecting a transition from exuberant fun to chastening separation. There is none of the romantic pairing conventionally associated with comedy. Instead the King of Navarre and his followers are assigned a series of penitential tasks by the Princess of France and her ladies: that for Berowne, inducing laughter in 'the speechless sick', seems especially severe. Some commentators, including John Kerrigan, spy the possibility of redemption among these arrogant males: others, such as Harold Bloom, are sceptical about any possibility of happy reunions for the lovers. But Shakespeare early in his career lays down an important marker: comedy, he shows, doesn't have to end in romantic closure but can be an open-ended affair, allowing the audience to speculate on the afterlife of the characters. Instead of marital pairing Shakespeare ends with two songs in celebration of spring and winter: a significant reversal of the logical order that, as Kerrigan points out, reflects the play's movement from youthful 'delight' to cold death and divorce. And in the songs themselves Shakespeare offers unforgettably graphic images, as sharp and precise as you'd find in a Ted Hughes poem: we can all easily envisage a winter where 'birds sit brooding in the snow And Marian's nose looks red and raw'. It's a play that never ceases to move or amaze me. It's a young man's play, written by what might be a word-spinning Elizabethan Tom Stoppard testing the resources of language to the limit. At the same time, it's palpably the product of a Warwickshire countryman who realises that sophisticated wordplay and academic fame are subject to the implacable rhythm of the seasons and the stark fact of death.

9

Henry IV Parts One and Two

WILLIAM SHAKESPEARE

(1564–1616)

I'm with Kenneth Tynan on this. He wrote in 1955 that 'the two parts of *Henry IV* are the twin summits of Shakespeare's achievement'. No plays ever written can match their panoramic social vision: their ability to combine court and country, poetry and prose, a private drama of fathers and sons and a public account of the state of the nation. I have loved these plays since I first saw them in Bernard Hepton's production at the old Birmingham Rep in 1960. If I had one day of my life left to spend in a theatre, I think I would choose a first-rate revival of these twin masterpieces.

Where to begin? One way might be by stressing the plays' constant dual perspective. On one level, we are in the England of the early fifteenth century; on another, the scenes in the Eastcheap tavern reek of Elizabethan London. And that duality can be applied to character. You can see Prince Hal as a calculating, cold-blooded politician or as a man undertaking a self-imposed education in kingship. And scarcely any figure in world drama arouses such contradictory emotions as Falstaff. At one extreme, articulated by W. H. Auden, he is a figure of supernatural, Christ-like charity: at another, he is a fleshed-out embodiment of Vice as seen in the medieval morality plays. As Adrian Poole has written in the latest Penguin edition, 'it is hard to speak of Falstaff without being too generous or too censorious': Shakespeare's genius lies in creating a figure of such multi-dimensional complexity that no single adjective can ever pin him down.

Falstaff's positive qualities hardly need to be stressed: his vitality, wit, verbal inventiveness, intellectual resourcefulness, carnivalesque sense of fun. I've seen many fine Falstaffs, including Hugh Griffiths, Brewster Mason, John Woodvine and Desmond Barrit, who have brought out these and other qualities. But the two actors who, for me, have most successfully highlighted Falstaff's predatory instinct and tragic dimension are Robert Stephens and Anthony Sher in, respectively, 1991 and 2014 RSC revivals. Both reminded us that Falstaff is a ruthless operator with a casual disregard for human life. As his ragged military recruits filed across the stage towards certain death at the end of *Part One*, Sher almost off-handedly dismissed them as 'food for powder, food for powder. They'll fill a pit as well as better', a line that produced a look of appalled horror in Alex Hassell's Prince Hal. Both Sher and Stephens rigorously desentimentalised Falstaff, showing how he abuses the generous hospitality and innocent credulity of Justice Shallow: 'If a young dace be a bait for the old pike,' he heartlessly announces, 'I see no reason in the law of nature but I may snap at him.' But both actors also brought out Falstaff's essential solitude: Sher was the archetypal pub-charmer with no home-life, and when Stephens came to the line 'If I had a thousand sons, the first human principle I would teach them should be to forswear thin potations', his voice audibly cracked at the end of the first phrase. It was a moment of recognition for Falstaff: an awareness not only of his own childlessness but of his imminent rejection by his surrogate son.

Shakespeare's greatest comic figure turns out to be one of his most tragic. But there is another tragic figure in these two plays: namely, the king. Traditionally, the role has gone to actors, such as Harry Andrews and Eric Porter, skilled at conveying a marble grandeur. But both Julian Glover in Noble's 1991 production and Jeremy Irons in Richard Eyre's 2012 BBC Television version brought something more to the role. Glover started as an unforgiving Old Testament patriarch who provoked rebellion by his curt dismissal of the Percys and alienated his son by treating him as a recalcitrant hooligan: at one moment Hal, having earned his father's praise for his courage in battle, rushed impetuously towards him, only to be met by Mr Glover's implacable, basilisk stare. But, like Irons in the TV production, Glover also showed every facet of the king's insomniac guilt and the pathos of his longing to achieve absolution by religious pilgrimage.

Individual tragedies are seen against a background of national turmoil. But the two plays also display Shakespeare's matchless gift for conveying the realistic texture of everyday life (something that makes nonsense of the presumed authorship of the plays by Francis Bacon or the Earl of Oxford). It is instructive to learn that 45 per cent of *Part One* and 52 per cent of *Part Two* are written in prose. And for the vigour and sinew of that prose you have only to look at a little-regarded prelude to the Gadshill robbery in *Part One*. The scene takes place in a Rochester inn-yard at dawn and involves a conversation between two carriers:

> SECOND CARRIER: Peas and beans are as dank here as a dog, and that is the next way to give poor jades the bots. This house is turned upside down since Robin Ostler died.
> FIRST CARRIER: Poor fellow never joyed since the price of oats rose, it was the death of him.

This is the authentic sound of two working men having a professional whinge: it tells us that old nags have been given stomach worms ('the bots') by damp fodder. But moreover this brief exchange offers a vivid snapshot of Elizabethan realities. If the price of oats was the death of Robin Ostler, it is a reflection of the terrible harvests England suffered between 1593 and 1596, which tripled prices and led to periods of dearth. In the midst of a play about the Middle Ages Shakespeare provides a glimpse of his own times.

I also can't resist quoting a passage in *Part Two* where Mistress Quickly publicly threatens Falstaff, in front of the Lord Chief Justice, with an action for breach of promise:

Thou didst swear to me upon a parcel-gilt goblet,
sitting in my Dolphin chamber at the round table by a
sea-coal fire, upon Wednesday in Wheeson week, when
the prince broke thy head for liking his father to a singing-
man of Windsor – thou didst swear to me then, as I was
washing thy wound, to marry me, and make me my lady
thy wife.

This is pure Dickens in its circumstantial detail: an anticipation of Mrs Bardell in *The Pickwick Papers* and, even more strikingly, the talkative Mrs Nickleby ('I recollect dining once at Mrs Bevan's, in that broad street round the corner by the coachmaker's, where the tipsy man fell through the cellar-flap of an empty house nearly a week before the quarter-day, and wasn't found until the new tenant went in – and we had roast pig there'). But the speech is even more than that. It captures the comic garrulity and fantastic memory of a wronged woman, who talks as if she's already appearing in court. Its reference to 'a singing-man of Windsor' also shows Shakespeare's use of a dual time-frame: there is a possible allusion to a priest involved in a plot against the historical Henry IV and a topical gibe at Elizabethan court and cathedral musicians frequently accused of drunkenness.

The richness of Shakespeare's prose reaches its apogee in the famous scenes in Justice Shallow's Gloucestershire orchard in *Part Two*. Shakespeare captures to naturalistic perfection the zig-zag mental processes of the old and their ability to leap in a second from the monumental to the mundane. For that one has only to listen to Justice Shallow: 'Death, as the Psalmist saith, is certain to all; all shall die. How a good yoke of bullocks at Stamford fair?' But behind the fugal richness of Shakespeare's prose and his portrait of Shallow's rose-tinted memories of his madcap youth, much else is going on: an evocation of a tiny Cotswold Eden from which Falstaff is necessarily excluded and, as Adrian Poole points out, a reminder of Shakespeare's sociable instincts in the little friendship that unexpectedly wells up between Bardolph and Shallow's servant, Davy.

Of course, there are vital contrasts between the two parts of *Henry IV*: the first bristles with energy and action while the second is filled with sickness, decay and intimations of mortality. But I see them, essentially, as one great play that works on any number of levels: a bildungsroman about the education of a prince, a tragi-comic portrait of Hal's surrogate father counterpointed by the agonised suffering of his real one and a wide-angled vision of a nation that embraces the realm's diversity. The two plays are not only Shakespeare's finest work, they remain one of the enduring peaks of world drama.

10

Hamlet

WILLIAM SHAKESPEARE

(1564–1616)

How does one write about a play of such amazing richness? Perhaps it is best simply to itemise a few of the multiple reasons for its enduring fascination.

(1) No other work in world drama is so obviously defined by its historical and geographical context: it becomes, quite simply, a different play depending on when and where you see it. In Western democracies, *Hamlet* has traditionally been viewed as a character-study of a complex, restlessly inquisitive individual; in oppressive dictatorships, it becomes a form of subversive protest against the encroaching state. Yuri Lyubimov's 1971 production for Moscow's Taganka Theatre was dominated by a swivelling mobile curtain that became, as occasion demanded, a castle wall, a cover for eavesdroppers, a symbol of power crushing any obstacles in its path. Similarly when the veteran actor Ion Caramitru played Hamlet in a Bucharest production that came to the National Theatre in London in 1990, we seemed to be in a decaying, cobwebbed autocracy that was an image of Ceaucescu's Romania. No dictator is foolish enough to ban *Hamlet*; yet throughout the second half of the twentieth century the play was seized on as a form of licensed protest against state oppression.

(2) *Hamlet* also alters according to time as well as place:

something that I've noticed in the fifty or so productions I've seen in Britain since my first at Stratford-on-Avon in 1956 with Alan Badel. Two particular changes strike me. Elsinore, as a court initially on a war-footing and as a place contaminated by espionage, has come into greater prominence as we more often play a full text: the moment you include the crucial scene where Polonius sets Reynaldo to spy on Laertes, you immediately establish the idea of the viral infection of eavesdropping. In recent times, it has also become fashionable to frame the action to suggest that what we are watching may be Hamlet's delusional fantasy. This was the governing idea behind Ian Rickson's 2011 Young Vic production, where Michael Sheen's Hamlet was clearly the inhabitant of a psychiatric institution. David Farr's 2013 RSC production also began with Jonathan Slinger's Hamlet squatting in what looked like a public-school fencing-gym, scribbling a few lines in a notebook and uttering the words 'Who's there?' as if all that followed was the product of his imagination. It is as if, in our self-preoccupied age, we feel we can only cope with the play's prodigality by treating it as the outcome of neurosis or feverish creativity.

(3) More than any play in world drama, *Hamlet* is also defined by its lead performer. 'In point of fact,' wrote Oscar Wilde in 'The Critic as Artist', 'there is no such thing as Shakespeare's Hamlet. If Hamlet has something of the definiteness of a work of art, he also has all the obscurity that belongs to life. There are as many Hamlets as there are melancholies.' Writing in 1891, Wilde took the view that the actor's individuality was a vital part of the interpretation; although that may seem a product of *fin de siècle* romanticism, it is inescapably true. Michael Redgrave, whom I saw play Hamlet in 1958 when he was fifty, brought to the role his own mix of intellectual curiosity, aristocratic demeanour, bottled hysteria and tortured sensibility: all reasons why his Hamlet is still

the one I love best. But there are many subsequent Hamlets I have deeply admired: David Warner (1965) for his baffled insecurity; Albert Finney (1976) for his muscularity and sense of danger; Michael Pennington (1980) for his post-Gielgudian music; Sam West (2001) for his anti-authoritarian rage; David Tennant (2010) for his darting mischief and irony. Of the three female Hamlets I've seen, the great German actress Angela Winkler also invested the role with a tenderness in her treatment of Ophelia that eludes most male interpreters. Hamlet is an obliging role with an infinite spectrum of possibilities. Even in the most politically engaged production, it remains a revelation of temperament: part of the power of Lyubimov's production lay in the fact that Hamlet was played by Vladimir Vyssotsky, a stocky, impassioned folk-singer with a cult-following among the Russian young.

(4) The play's limitless potential extends to most of its lead characters. Claudius can be played as a deep-dyed villain. More often today we see him as a shrewd politician and capable ruler coping with an unpredictably wayward nephew, an idea perfectly embodied by Patrick Stewart, who confronted David Tennant's Hamlet, at the end of the play scene, with a controlled fury rather than the usual panicky hysteria. I've also seen every form of Ghost: a clanking giant (Peter Hall's 1965 production), an emanation from within Hamlet himself (Jonathan Pryce at the Royal Court), a spectre entering on a rearing, battle-maddened charger (Patrice Chereau's 1989 Berlin production), a tormented wraith clearly on parole from Purgatory (Greg Hicks in Michael Boyd's 2004 production). Ophelias equally range from the quietly mutinous (Glenda Jackson) to the distractedly lovelorn (Pippa Nixon). More than any other Shakespeare play, *Hamlet* provides its actors with interpretative latitude.

(5) But part of the play's appeal is that it poses endless conundrums. Some of these are structural and depend on whether

one follows the First Quarto, Second Quarto or the Folio edition. The most famous example is the placement of 'To be or not to be', which in the First Quarto becomes Hamlet's second soliloquy and therefore appears before the arrival of the Players and Hamlet's determination to catch the conscience of the king. Many directors see this as more logical, which is why I think it is wrong. For me, it's a measure of the play's insoluble richness that Hamlet, having come up with a concrete plan of action, then contemplates suicide and meditates on life's meaning.

But the whole text is riddled with contradictions. Why does Hamlet tell us in Act 2 Scene 2 that he has 'foregone all custom of exercises' and in Act 5 Scene 2, before the duel with Laertes, that 'Since he went into France I have been in continual practice'? Why does the Ghost, within the space of a few lines, invoke the Christian idea of purgatory ('for the day confined to fast in fires') and the pagan concept of the afterlife ('the fat weed that roots itself on Lethe wharf')? And why does Horatio, having explicitly heard from Hamlet how he contrived the execution of Rosencrantz and Guildenstern on their arrival in England, later tell that country's ambassador that Hamlet 'never gave commandment for their death'?

There are a thousand such puzzles within the play. And that, I'd suggest, is one reason for its never-ending popularity, along with its narrative pulse, its cognitive power, its political resonance, its novelistic characterisation, its mellifluous verse, all of which contribute to a text 'whose vitality', as Professor Terence Hawkes memorably wrote, 'resides in its plurality'.

11

Twelfth Night

WILLIAM SHAKESPEARE
(1564–1616)

As I've suggested in writing about Euripides' *Helen*, the supposedly rigid division between comedy and tragedy was subverted from the earliest days of Western drama. But Shakespeare takes the process even further in this astonishing, opal-like play, one performed, according to the testimony of a London barrister, John Manningham, at Middle Temple in 1602 and, in the words of scholar Michael Dobson, as 'self-consciously experimental a play as Shakespeare ever wrote'.

It is experimental in that it harks back thematically to the nine comedies Shakespeare had already written (children separated at sea, confusion between twins, a heroine forced to disguise herself as a boy) while prefiguring the late romances. But it is also experimental in its use of music to show a romantic comedy imbued with a sense of mortality and in its effortless interweaving of laughter and sadness.

If you think I exaggerate, you have only to look at the extraordinary ramifications of the plot. By the end of *Twelfth Night*, a precarious happiness has been achieved. Orsino is to be married to a woman, Viola, whom he has adored in the guise of a boy. Meanwhile Olivia, even more ardent in her passion for Cesario/Viola, is hitched to her love-object's newly arrived male twin. This opens up the possibility of some decidedly adventurous Illyrian holiday weekends. Will Orsino still yearn for his wife to dress as a boy? Will Olivia, having been so fervently attracted to the disguised Viola, be able to surrender her entirely? It is a stock joke in modern productions for Olivia's cry of 'Most wonderful!' – on being confronted by the indistinguishable twins – to be taken as a hint of intriguing future sexual permutations.

But what of the other characters? Towards the play's end the tortured Malvolio vows revenge not just on his immediate tormentors but on 'the whole pack of you'. The class-conscious Sir Toby, who earlier dismissed Malvolio with 'Art any more than a steward?', is married to a waiting-gentlewoman, Maria, and cruelly rejects his masochistic meal-ticket, Sir Andrew. And Antonio, prepared to sacrifice his freedom and even his life in his passionate pursuit of Sebastian, finds himself –like that other Antonio in *The Merchant of Venice* – excluded from the world of sexual harmony. It is fitting that the final words are left to yet another of the play's outsiders, Feste. In his sublime, concluding song he compresses the seven ages of man into four stanzas and yet suggests the continuity both of human life, in its kaleidoscopic blend of joy and cruelty, and of theatrical performance itself.

But that raises the question of how one presents the play and captures the shifting moods of Shakespeare's Illyria. It is a work that, like Mozart's *The Magic Flute*, always gives pleasure no matter how it is done. However, of the forty or so productions I've seen, three stand out for their ability to capture the play's tonal shifts and specifically English form of magic realism: those by Peter Hall (1960), John Barton (1969) and Sam Mendes (2002). Some directors have chosen to emphasise the play's exotic otherness. Bill Alexander in his 1987 RSC production took the real Illyria, on the Adriatic coast, as his setting and highlighted the white walls, intense heat and air of pervasive madness. Michael Grandage at Wyndham's in 2008 ushered us into a world that suggested pre-1914 Casablanca. And Gregory Doran in his 2010 Stratford revival gave us a Levantine Illyria full of bustling bazaars and bushy-bearded priests.

There's nothing wrong with any of those choices, and each production had its individual delights: Derek Jacobi's fastidious Malvolio, who looked as if he'd strayed into Morocco from Midhurst, in the Grandage version and Alexandra Gilbreath's feckless, reckless Olivia in Doran's production. Yet I'm always struck by the precision of Shakespeare's social comedy and the text's invincible Englishness. When Sir Andrew says 'I had as lief be a Brownist as a politician' he is referring to a sectarian Cambridge theologian, Robert Browne, whose followers set up their own independent East Anglian church. Malvolio's allusion to 'The lady of the Strachy married the yeoman of the wardrobe' may be equally obscure to modern ears but still anchors the play in a stratified English class system. Even something as simple as Antonio's 'In the south suburbs, at the Elephant, is best to lodge' suggests he knows his way round the London inns. Illyria, as a place, may have romantic, far-away connotations. Yet the play relies on profoundly English social structures and localised references.

That is why I come back to my chosen trinity of great productions. Peter Hall, who first directed the play at Stratford in 1958, revised and revived it for the RSC's opening season in 1960, and I remember it for many things. Lila de Nobili's gauzy design was a symphony in russet that combined oak-panelled Caroline rooms with walled English gardens. But Hall's genius was to show that the play's romance was imbued with high-spirited fun, and its comedy with a grave melancholy. This was achieved partly through casting. Olivia – a role traditionally reserved for mature actresses – was played by Geraldine McEwan as a youthfully skittish poseuse affecting a love for a dead brother. Dorothy Tutin's Cavalier pageboy Viola balanced lyrical passion with mischievous amusement at the unintended consequences of her disguise: her cry of 'Poor lady', on realising the depth of Olivia's passion, brought the house down. But the comedy of the romance was balanced by the brooding paranoia of Richard Johnson's manic-depressive Aguecheek and the light and shadow of Max Adrian's abrasive Feste.

John Barton in 1969 achieved, if possible, an even more perfect Chekhovian balance between laughter and tears. In contrast to Tutin, Judi Dench's Viola had a sturdy, steadfast, even spiritual quality so that 'Disguise, I see thou art a wickedness Wherein the pregnant enemy does much' was imbued with tremulous self-doubt. Donald Sinden's Malvolio (partly inspired by Graham Sutherland's portrait of a jaundiced Somerset Maugham) was also riotously funny in the letter-reading scene, as he shot Robeyesque glances of mock-reproof at the dirty-minded audience, and yet tragic in his downfall. And it was a sign of Barton's eye for social detail that Elizabeth Spriggs's Maria was no pert serving-maid but a fiftyish Scottish spinster who saw that her last chance of ensnaring Sir Toby lay in devising the cruel humiliation of Malvolio.

The Chekhovian parallels were reinforced in Mendes's 2002 Donmar production when he cross-cast *Twelfth Night* with *Uncle Vanya*. Having already played Chekhov's eponymous hero, Simon Russell Beale was perfectly equipped to play Malvolio as a tragically self-deluded figure who, in a letter-reading scene transposed to his bedroom, interrupted his Bible studies to engage in masturbatory erotic fantasies. Helen McCrory moved with equal conviction from Chekhov's Yelena to Shakespeare's Olivia: both disruptive figures steeped in the narcissism of the truly beautiful. Yet there was also something wanly comic about the Pozzo–Lucky relationship of Paul Jesson's Sir Toby and David

Bradley's Sir Andrew, who, in the drinking scene, sat on a sofa happily breaking wind together.

Set in an Edwardian country house backed by a large, empty frame that was variously filled with images of the adored and idealised, Mendes's production reminded us that the perpetual marvel of *Twelfth Night* is that reality and fantasy, mirth and melancholy, comedy and tragedy are ultimately inseparable. In Antonio's resonant words, 'An apple cleft in two is not more twin.'

12

The Malcontent

JOHN MARSTON
(1576–1634)

Here is yet another play that makes a bonfire of the categories. Much academic ink has been spilt on trying to decide what exactly it is. Tragi-comedy? Revenge drama? Savage satire? But the joy of John Marston's invigorating Jacobean play lies in its ability to defy classification. If it survives – as it undoubtedly has in revivals at Nottingham Playhouse (1973) and Stratford's Swan (2002) – it is for a variety of reasons: its Shakespearean echoes, its self-referential theatricality, its feast of language. Words simply seem to spill out of Marston as you might expect of a man who trained as a Middle Temple lawyer and ended as a Hampshire priest.

The Shakespearean echoes are evident in the play's provenance. Scholars deduce that *The Malcontent* was conceived for the indoor Blackfriars Theatre in 1603 and first performed there by the children of the Chapel Royal: exactly the kind of boy actors whom Hamlet inveighs against as 'little eyases' (meaning young, untrained hawks) in a waspishly topical, sublimely irrelevant passage invariably cut from modern productions. But, having been written to be performed by precocious kids in an exclusive, indoor, private theatre, Marston's play proved such a hit that it transferred to the inclusive, outdoor, public Globe, complete with a brand-new Induction by John Webster and large-scale revisions by Marston himself.

All this belongs to the arcana of stage history. What really matters is that the genius of Shakespeare pervades *The Malcontent* like the local imprint in a stick of rock. The plot revolves around a deposed Genoese duke who turns up at the court of his usurper in the guise of a rogue satirist, Malevole, to execute revenge. Allusions to *Hamlet*, in both vocabulary and sentence structure, are constant. 'Art there, old truepenny,' cries Malevole to Mendoza, a Machiavellian courtier who is the play's true villain. And Mendoza at one point delivers an encomium on women ('in body how delicate, in soul how witty, in discourse how pregnant, in life how wary, in favours how judicious, in day how sociable and in night how – O pleasure unutterable') that sounds like a dirty-minded burlesque of Hamlet's 'What a piece of work is a man'. Throw in references to guilt-ridden insomnia (as in *Henry IV Part Two*) and the reliability of enemies over friends (*Twelfth Night*) as well as the whole premise of ducal disguise (*Measure for Measure*) and you have a play that shows how much Jacobean drama was saturated in Shakespeare.

That sounds like a negative virtue. But Marston's play has numerous positive qualities. Its plot is witty, ingenious and surprising. You come expecting a retributive bloodbath. What you see is Malevole ultimately joining forces with his usurper, now disguised as a hermit, to outwit the lecherous, treacherous Mendoza. If *Hamlet* subverts the revenge drama by exposing the fundamental futility of its eye-for-an-eye code, *The Malcontent* becomes the first drama to show how brain-power can overcome bestial brutality. The result is a high-spirited revenge comedy in which no one dies.

In Malevole himself, Marston also creates one of the greatest outsider-heroes in the dramatic canon. It was no accident that when Antony Sher played Malevole in Dominic Cooke's 2002 RSC production, he was first heard playing the trumpet, the instrument favoured by John Osborne's modern malcontent,

Jimmy Porter, in *Look Back in Anger*. And Malevole has many of the qualities to be found in Osborne's anti-hero: a savage tongue, a caustic humour, a deep-seated sense of morality.

Obviously Malevole's rage is directed against the corruption, chicanery, deceit and double-dealing of an Italianate court, one that stands as a metaphor for an England which in 1603 saw power pass from the decrepit, tantrum-filled, increasingly irrational Elizabeth I to the crafty, voluble, blatantly gay James I. But what attracts one to Malevole, the licensed satirist of a double-dealing court, is the sheer gusto of his invective. 'I'll come among you, you goatish-blooded toderers, as gum into taffeta, to fret, to fret,' he cries on his first entrance. But there is precision, as well as vituperation, in Malevole's misanthropy. At one point, the wily Mendoza seeks to enlist Malevole's support in his plots against the usurping Pietro. 'Wilt fall upon my chamber tomorrow morn?' enquires Mendoza. 'As a raven to a dunghill,' responds Malevole: an exact image of a predator feeding off ordure. And there is a sharp wit to Malevole, as the following exchange shows:

MENDOZA: Malevole, thou art an arrant knave.
MALEVOLE: Who, I? I have been a sergeant, man.
MENDOZA: Thou art very poor.
MALEVOLE: As Job, an alchemist or a poet.
MENDOZA: The duke hates thee.
MALEVOLE: As Irishmen do bum-cracks.

This tart quip is a reminder that, according to one of Thomas Nashe's provocative pamphlets, 'The Irishman will draw his dagger and be ready to kill and slay, if one break wind in his company.' Not, happily, a quality apparent in Ireland today.

The key question is to what extent Malevole is simply Marston's mouthpiece or an objectively drawn character. Marston himself was regarded as a bilious figure by his contemporaries: he was rebuked for 'lifting up your leg and pissing against the world' and, in Ben Jonson's *Poetaster*, the Marston-character is given a pill to vomit up his windy words. But the strongest evidence lies within the play itself, where the satiric, foul-mouthed Malevole constantly whips off his disguise to remind us he is a wronged duke and where lacerating put-downs alternate with Senecan *sententiae*. The protagonist's dual character turns *The Malcontent* into a piece of meta-theatre in which Malevole functions as a surrogate dramatist contriving plots, moving the action forwards and even commenting on the state of theatre ('O, do not rant, do not turn player. There's more of them than can live one by another already').

It also strikes me as significant that Marston eventually moved from the playhouse to the pulpit. He writes with the vigour of a born language-lover whose pen is steeped in vitriol and, through Malevole, typically describes an upwardly mobile adulterer as 'You whoreson, hot-reined, he-marmoset'. At the same time, Marston clearly believes that reconciliation and forgiveness should triumph over crude revenge. Although the play climaxes in one of those masques that, ever since Kyd's *The Spanish Tragedy* (1587) had become the cue for an orgy of bloodletting, Malevole regains his dukedom, reunites separated couples and spares the life of the malign Mendoza. This is what makes Marston unusual: he is a satirist with a charitable heart. Imagine Shakespeare's Thersites crossed with Prospero and you get close to the spirit of this jaundiced but not vindictive Jacobean avenger.

13

A Mad World, My Masters

THOMAS MIDDLETON
(1580–1627)

A mad world indeed. Like Marston, Middleton is a part of a frenzied burst of Jacobean theatrical creativity. Alongside Shakespeare's tragic masterpieces there appears a brilliant new brand of urban comedy, one which that astute scholar Michael Cordner says 'satirically mirrored the unprecedented energies of a capital city whose mushrooming growth, dizzying accumulations of wealth, and complex array of sub-cultures made it feel decisively different in nature, as well as scale, from its nearest English competitors'.

Today Middleton is best known for his later, sombre, torchlit tragedies such as *Women Beware Women* (1621) and *The Changeling* (1622). But he was also a master of comedy, of which *A Mad World, My Masters* (1605) is a fine, fizzing example. Yet again, the play was first produced by one of those boys' companies, the children of St Paul's, which makes one gasp both at their delight in double-entendres and the audience's willingness to hear adolescents making jokes about 'cocks' and 'organs'. Beyond that, however, Middleton's play provides a template for English comedy for several reasons: it brims with inventive situations, plays with the idea of reality and illusion and delights in what you could either call 'moral ambiguity' or 'having it both ways'. Given its comic richness, what's surprising is the play's limited stage history. Barrie Keeffe did a total rewrite in 1977, Shakespeare's Globe staged a more faithful version in 1998 and Sean Foley and Phil Porter edited, rewrote and updated the play for an RSC revival in 2013 that proved immensely popular but left me pining to see Middleton's masterpiece in its original form.

For a start, Middleton was very good on plot. He takes a stock theme – youth versus age – and gives it copious twists. In this instance a young adventurer, Follywit, is out to get his hands on his grandfather's fortune. In order to rob the gullible oldster Follywit adopts a series of disguises: as an aristocratic guest, a skittishly attractive woman, a travelling player. But while money is the main theme, sex spins the sub-plot. In this we see a randy Puritan, Penitent Brothel, avidly pursuing the wife of the insanely protective Master Shortrod Harebrain and, having conquered her, suffering agonies of guilt. Knitting the two plots together is a manipulative go-between, Frances Gullman, who starts as a courtesan and ends up as Follywit's supposedly virginal wife.

I am reminded, yet again, that comedy, more than tragedy, provides a portrait of an age. Here is the early Jacobean world in all its capricious diversity. Follywit and his followers are recently discharged soldiers obsessed with illicitly making money. Penitent Brothel embodies not just poker-faced hypocrisy but the age-old conflict between religious and sexual zeal. Gullman, as her name implies, shows the wiliness of women in playing on men's weaknesses. And Follywit's grandfather, Sir Bounteous Progress, is a classic portrait of the nouveau riche social climber. The name, according to Professor Cordner, derives from the houses built by high aspirers to accommodate the monarch in his or her progress round the country. The joke may be topical, but the type is eternal. The conflict between Sir Bounteous's social grovelling and secret vanity is perfectly captured in a speech he delivers to Follywit who comes to him in the guise of a high-born house-guest:

Your honour had e'en a hunting meal and now I am like
to bring your lordship to as mean a lodging: a hard down
bed, i'faith, my lord, poor cambric sheets, and a cloth
o' tissue canopy. The curtains indeed were wrought in
Venice, with the story of the Prodigal Child in silk and
gold; only the swine are left out, my lord, for spoiling the
curtains.

Even I got a laugh when I read that speech out to an audience
at the Shakespeare Summer School in Stratford; yet, typically, it
was cut from the Foley production of the play they had just seen.
I hate to labour the point, but it seems perverse to revive a great
Jacobean comedy and dilute the richly textured language that is
one of its supreme joys.

Middleton was a great social commentator. He was also
astonishingly daring in his portrayal of sex. Nothing in English
comedy prepares one for the scene in which the ridiculous Shortrod
– whose name tells you everything – is induced to eavesdrop on
his wife's clandestine lovemaking with the puritanical Penitent. In
a wonderful display of aural sex, Mistress Harebrain's orgasmic
moans, groans, sobs and shrieks are camouflaged by a feigned
conversation with a supposedly bed-ridden female patient ('Oh,
no, lay your hand here, Mistress Harebrain. Ay, there, oh there,
there lies my pain'). But sex threads its way through every scene
of this vivacious comedy. Sometimes it is of the broad-bottomed
variety, as when the ostentatiously musical Sir Bounteous asks
his house-guest, 'Come, my lord, how does your honour relish
my organ?' At other moments it relies on the English love of
cross-dressing and confusion of gender: assuming female attire,
Follywit boldly asserts, 'We are all male to th'middle, mankind
from the beaver to the bum.' Yet Middleton also explores the guilt
that accompanies extra-curricular sex. Having enthusiastically

made love to Harebrain's wife, the puritanical Penitent is shaken by remorse and visited by her in the seductive shape of a succubus or female spirit. And when the real Mistress Harebrain turns up for another bout of strenuous sex he passionately rejects her:

> What knows the lecher when he clips his whore
> Whether it be the devil his parts adore?

The Jacobean scholar Alexander Leggatt has argued that Middleton's combination of intrigue comedy and moral revulsion produces only instability; he goes on to make the witty point that the fear of damnation that haunts Middleton's later tragic characters, such as the Cardinal in *Women Beware Women*, shows them using Christianity 'as a superior form of fire insurance'. Yet I detect in Penitent Brothel something more fascinating: an ambivalent mix of lust and misogyny that was to find its fullest expression in the nineteenth-century plays of August Strindberg.

But it wouldn't do to get too solemn about *A Mad World, My Masters*. This is a play of sharp social observation, sophisticated filth and uproarious fun that sets a pattern for English comedy and plays hilarious games with theatre itself. At the climax Sir Bounteous hosts a play-within-a-play in which Follywit, in one last attempt to con the old man, appears disguised as an actor and makes off with a priceless watch. Who should then turn up but a genuine constable who has caught Follywit's thieving accomplices. Assumed to be part of the play, the honest copper finds himself bound and gagged. But Middleton's brilliant pay-off comes later. Follywit, appearing before his granddad as his true self, seems to have got away with the scam when the stolen timepiece suddenly rings in his pocket. 'Have I 'scaped the constable,' he asks, 'to be brought in by the watch?' This strikes me as a dazzling conjunction of actuality and artifice with a witty punchline. It also confirms my belief that Middleton was a comic master who harpooned Jacobean folly while erecting a signpost to a future that was to contain *Carry On* movies, radio's *Round the Horne*, Tom Stoppard's *The Real Inspector Hound* and the transvestite madness of Joe Orton's *What the Butler Saw*.

14

Macbeth

WILLIAM SHAKESPEARE

(1564–1616)

A great play or a great dramatic poem? No one has ever disputed Macbeth's verbal mastery. 'Search where you will,' wrote the novelist and poet John Wain, 'the art of literature can show no more dazzling performance.' But many have questioned the play's theatrical effectiveness. After the headlong velocity of the first two acts, it seems to lose momentum. Aside from the principal pair, the other characters lack definition. Until Olivier at Stratford in 1955, no great actor enjoyed an unqualified triumph as Macbeth. Yet I would argue that, for a variety of reasons, in the last sixty years we have come to see that Macbeth is as brilliantly effective on the stage as it is on the page.

Macbeth shows Shakespeare at the peak of his poetic power. For a shrewd analysis of its verbal skills one has only to turn to William Empson's *Seven Types of Ambiguity* or Frank Kermode's book *Shakespeare's Language*. 'It is surely impossible to deny,' writes Kermode,

> that certain words – 'time', 'man', 'done' – and certain
> themes – 'blood', 'darkness' – are the matrices of the
> language of *Macbeth*. In the period of the great tragedies
> these matrices appear to have been fundamental to

Shakespeare's procedures. One might guess they took possession of him as he did his preparatory reading. That they are thereafter used with conscious intention and skill seems equally certain.

This is a crucial point: that, whatever its occasional vagaries in plotting, Shakespeare's later work is marked by a calculated use of intricate verbal and imagistic repetition.

Kermode also persuasively argues that *Macbeth*, far from being the broken-backed play we often assume, is unified by these insistent repetitions. Take, for instance, the notion of manliness. Lady Macbeth famously spurs Macbeth into murdering Duncan by challenging his virility: 'When you durst do it, then you were a man.' Tremulously shaking before Banquo's Ghost, Macbeth claims, 'What man dare, I dare.' And later, when the callow Malcolm urges Macduff to respond to his family's slaughter by disputing it like a man, Macduff replies, 'I shall do so; but I must also feel it as a man.' Amongst myriad other things, the play offers a sustained enquiry into whether manliness is defined by military valour or emotional sensitivity.

If any one idea dominates *Macbeth*, however, it is that of equivocation. It is there from the very opening lines, when the First Witch asks 'When shall we three meet again? In thunder, lightning or in rain?': three things meteorologically associated are presented as false alternatives. It is also there at the very climax, when Macbeth grasps that these juggling fiends 'palter with us in a double sense'. Unusually, the references to equivocation also help us to date the play with some precision. I have noted before that the Porter scene has echoes of the medieval Mystery plays. It also contains one highly topical Jacobean reference. Imagining himself a porter of 'hell-gate', Shakespeare's drunken janitor goes on to say: 'Faith, here's an equivocator that could swear in both the scales against either scale, who committed treason enough for God's sake, yet could not equivocate to heaven.' This seems a clear allusion to Father Henry Garnet, a Jesuit arrested for his part in the Gunpowder Plot of November 1605, who was the author of *A Treatise of Equivocation*, which defended the morality of giving ambiguous answers under oath, something that did not prevent his being found guilty of treason or his severed head ending up on a pike on London Bridge.

But for all its poetic richness Shakespeare's play has had a chequered theatrical history. While Sarah Siddons was hugely acclaimed for a Lady Macbeth she played many times between 1781 and 1817, few actors until Olivier triumphed as Macbeth. Judging by the historical accounts of Kean, Macready and Irving, it appears that they were unable to reconcile the character's soldierly prowess, imaginative apprehension and tyrannical decline. But I was lucky enough, as a fifteen-year-old schoolboy, to see Olivier's performance, and its dark imprint is with me still. My abiding memory is of Olivier's brooding intensity, malevolent irony (especially in the scene with Banquo's murderers) and climactic despair. When, in the last act, Olivier's Macbeth announced 'that which should accompany old age, As honour, love obedience, troops of friends, I must not look to have', his voice soared on 'troops of friends' as if in recognition of his agonising spiritual solitude. Yet there was enough of the fighter left in this Macbeth for Olivier, on the injunction to 'Lay on, Macduff', to paw the ground like a cornered bull preparing to charge the waiting matador.

Since Olivier's heroic performance, the play has enjoyed a number of spectacularly successful revivals in Britain, and there are two pragmatic reasons for this. One is that directors have often followed Macduff's advice to 'cut short all intermission'. Until recent times, Shakespeare's shortest tragedy became a needlessly prolonged spectacle. James Agate recorded of Lewis Casson's 1927 revival that 'the curtain still descends some two and twenty times which gravely disperses the interest instead of concentrating it'. But ever since Trevor Nunn's landmark 1976 RSC production the fashion has been to do the play straight through, which gives it unity and momentum. Nunn's production was also first staged in Stratford's The Other Place, which lent the play a conspiratorial intimacy. All the action took place on black floorboards inside a white circle, which, as Carol Chillington Rutter pointed out, took on multiple meanings: an occult cipher, a child's playground, a space enclosing inner terror. We ourselves, seated in a surrounding circle, became eerily complicit in the play's events: unforgettably Judi Dench's Lady Macbeth, having invoked the spirits to fill her 'from the crown to the toe top-full of direst cruelty', leaped back in horror as if there were indeed dark, underground forces in operation a few feet away from us.

Since then other directors have profited from Nunn's discovery that *Macbeth* works best in intimate spaces. Gregory Doran's 1999 RSC Swan production, with Antony Sher and Harriet Walter, began by plunging the theatre into total darkness. Rupert Goold's startling 2007 production, with Patrick Stewart and Kate Fleetwood, began in Chichester's Minerva Studio, where Anthony Ward's white-walled set resembled a mix of abattoir, kitchen and military hospital. And in the summer of 2013 Kenneth Branagh and Rob Ashford staged the play in a deconsecrated Manchester church, with the audience seated on two sides of a narrow, traverse stage: it helped, of course, that Branagh himself echoed Olivier's idea of Macbeth as a guilt-haunted figure who here stammered on the initial letters of 'murder' and 'assassination' as if chilled by the words' implications.

It would be absurd to claim that Macbeth is a play whose difficulties have been entirely conquered: everything depends on the integrity, imagination and intelligence with which it is approached. But if it now, more often than not, works theatrically, it is for a variety of reasons. Some, as I've outlined, are purely practical, such as the emphasis on interval-less intimacy. Others are more obviously historical, such as our awareness of the insecurity at the heart of terror and tyranny. But, above all, I suspect we have come to understand that Shakespeare's play is essentially about the uncovering of the criminal to himself. It prefigures Dostoyevsky's *Crime and Punishment* in that Macbeth, like Raskolnikov, is a character who gains a certain sympathy from our unlimited access to his mental agonies and who is simultaneously a free agent and a victim of external fate. We always knew Macbeth was a great poem. Now we also realise that it is the greatest of all plays about the tortured mind and spirit of the murderer cursed with a volatile imagination.

15

Coriolanus

WILLIAM SHAKESPEARE
(1564–1616)

I first fell in love with this play when I appeared as one of the plebeians in an Oxford student production in the spring of 1959. The production had a young Royal Court director in Anthony Page, a set by Sean Kenny and a professional Volumnia in Susan Engel. As we plebs gathered, seemingly every afternoon, to be scolded by Patrick Garland's Coriolanus, phrase after phrase lodged in my consciousness: 'debile wretch', 'Titan of the minnows', 'vagabond exile', 'the city of kites and crows'. Shakespeare's language became part of my being.

My next encounter with the play came later that summer, when I saw Olivier's breathtaking Stratford Coriolanus. Everything you could wish for was there: virility, irony, emotional power, physical audacity. Endless moments are etched on my memory. In the scene where Volumnia urges Coriolanus to conduct himself 'mildly' before the plebeians, Olivier silently mouthed the key word before mimetically retching. In the subsequent banishment, Olivier turned on the mob to proclaim 'your enemies, with nodding of their plumes, fan you into despair': on the word 'fan' Olivier's left hand fluttered before the fickle crowd with ostentatious contempt giving the bizarre impression, as the critic Laurence Kitchin noted, 'of one man lynching a crowd'. Then, at the climax, Olivier plunged head downwards from the twelve-foot-high Tarpeian platform, while his body, held at the ankles by two soldiers, dangled ignominiously like that of the slaughtered Mussolini.

Michael Blakemore in *Stage Blood* records sitting alongside Olivier during a dress rehearsal of Anthony Hopkins's National Theatre Coriolanus. When Blakemore remarked on the greatness of the play, Olivier gently corrected him: 'No, not a great play, a great text.' For Blakemore that fine distinction was a sign of Olivier's intuitive intelligence. Heretically, however, I would take issue with Olivier: *Coriolanus* is a great play as well as a great text.

At its heart lies a political, moral and emotional ambivalence: one that famously led a French production in 1934 to be seen as an incitement to revolution whereas in Nazi Germany the play was admired for depicting a truly heroic Führer. Although different factions lay claim to the play, I treasure a remark once made by John Barton: 'Shakespeare wasn't left-wing or right-wing. He was wing-less.'

One's first instinct may be to regard Coriolanus himself as an arrogant patrician, a blood-soaked fighting-machine and a political simpleton. And there is some truth in all of this: he denies the people their corn, is only fully himself in war and fails to understand that consular power depends on popular support. Yet read the text carefully and you find contradictory aspects to the character. As the conqueror of Corioles, he is offered a tenth part of the city's treasure. His response? 'I do refuse it, And stand upon my common part with those That have beheld the doing.' Shortly afterwards he begs Cominius to free a prisoner on the grounds that 'I sometime lay here in Corioles At a poor man's house: he used me kindly.' And in the great scene where Volumnia urges him to moderate his temper and resolicit the support of the people, he veers back and forth before deciding

I will not do't
Lest I surcease to honour mine own truth
And by my body's action teach my mind
A most inherent baseness.

It is, of course, Coriolanus' eventual capitulation to his mother's will that sows the seeds of his destruction.

Even if the people's tribunes, Sicinius Velutus and Junius Brutus, are less complex, they need to be played from their own point of view rather than as villainous manipulators. They have a legitimate grievance against the hero in that he has sanctioned a civic starvation policy. They also have a duty to defend the people from the man who would 'vent their musty superfluity' in battle. And they read Coriolanus' character correctly:

Being once chafed he cannot
Be reined again to temperance: then he speaks
What's in his heart and that is there
Which looks with us to break his neck.

While it's a shrewd character analysis, in that last line you also see the ugly side of the tribunes: they realise that, by playing on Coriolanus' defects, they can drive him to his death.

For me the play's greatness lies partly in its multi-dimensionality: it is about the attraction, and the danger, of intransigent selfhood in a world of realpolitik. As a psychological document, it is also astonishing. The relationship between Coriolanus and his mother, Volumnia, has an emotional intensity that shows just how much Shakespeare pre-empted Freud. To whom does the hero kneel on his triumphant return from Corioles to Rome? Not to his wife, but to his mother, a gesture that is ironically echoed when Volumnia kneels before her son at the play's end, imploring him not to sack Rome. But Shakespeare shows that Coriolanus is the victim, as well as the recipient, of an overpowering maternal love. Volumnia giddily recalls a time 'when youth with comeliness plucked all gaze his way', imagines her son going to war 'like a harvest-man that's tasked to mow' and shows a quasi-sexual delight in his battle-scars. Yet it is also Volumnia who provokes her son's banishment by bidding him placate the people and signs his death warrant by urging him to make peace with Rome. Not even the Oedipal fervor of the Hamlet–Gertrude relationship can match this: a portrait of the military mother as her son's creator, champion and destroyer.

But there is another relationship in the play just as intense and as powerfully sexual: that between Coriolanus and Aufidius. I only became aware of it when I saw Tyrone Guthrie's 1963 production, which opened the Nottingham Playhouse. Ian McKellen played Aufidius to John Neville's Coriolanus and, at the climax, swooped on his rival's prostrate body with the anguish of a bereaved lover. But look at the text and the clues are all there as to the narcissistic obsession the two men entertain for each other and the homoeroticism of warfare. In his earlier guise as Caius Martius, Coriolanus greets his fellow general Cominius with the news that he feels as merry as on his wedding night 'and tapers burned to bedward'. But his ultimate obsession is with his Volscian counterpart. Hearing in Act 3 that the enemy troops are gathering head and that Titus Lartius has seen Aufidius, Coriolanus' instinctive question is 'Spoke he of me?'

The sexuality of the relationship only becomes fully apparent, however, when the banished Coriolanus goes to Antium and confronts his quondam rival. First Aufidius embraces Coriolanus and tells him 'more dances my rapt heart Than when I first my wedded mistress saw Bestride my threshold', a direct echo of Coriolanus' own idealisation of masculinity over marriage. In one of the most violently sexual passages in all Shakespeare, Aufidius then describes his own eroticised obsession with Coriolanus:

> Thou hast beat me out
> Twelve several times, and I have nightly since
> Dreamt of encounters 'twixt thyself and me –
> We have been down together in my sleep,
> Unbuckling helms, fisting each other's throat –
> And wak'd half dead with nothing.

This suggests 'the very wrath of love' and the way these nightly dreams lead to a sense of post-coital exhaustion. Lest we miss the point, it is underscored when one Antium servant tells another: 'Our general makes a mistress of him: sanctifies himself with his hand and turns up the white o' th' eye to his discourse.' Even that 'white o' th' eye' implies a sexual infatuation. And although Aufidius is goaded beyond endurance by Coriolanus' arrogance, he remains the victim of an obsession that leads him to later provide the play's most sophisticated analysis of his rival's flaws.

Politics. Psychology. Sex. What more can one ask? And all this expressed in language that is both muscular and vividly concrete. If you want an example of Shakespeare's ability to create filmic images, you have only to look at Junius Brutus' description of the popular hunger to catch a glimpse of the returning hero:

> Your prattling nurse
> Into a rapture lets her baby cry
> While she chats him. The kitchen malkin pins
> Her richest lockram 'bout her reechy neck
> Clambering the walls to eye him. Stalls, bulks, windows
> Are smothered up, leads filled, and ridges horsed
> With variable complexions, all agreeing
> In earnest to see him.

You don't have to understand every word to get the picture: 'ridges horsed With variable complexions' tells us that even roof-edges are straddled by people of every kind hungry to catch a glimpse of the conquering hero. This is not only a mark of Shakespeare's genius for packing so much into a single image. It also indicates the magnetism of Caius Martius Superstar, who turns out to be an enemy of the people: yet one more mark of the ambivalence of this bottomlessly fascinating work. Great Text. Great Play.

16

The Alchemist

BEN JONSON
(1572–1637)

Coleridge famously thought *The Alchemist*, *Oedipus Rex* and *Tom Jones* to be 'the three most perfect plots ever planned'; many have praised Jonson's genius in intertwining seven different narrative strands. The critic and Ibsen translator William Archer, writing in 1923, was less impressed. While paying tribute to Jonson's 'sheer brain-power', he thought these Jacobeans a pretty sorry lot: 'the unrelieved ugliness and sordidness, the moral squalor of the whole picture belong to an age which is only laboriously struggling towards civilization'.

Happily, Jonson's comic masterpiece about cozenage has been rediscovered by the modern theatre. I've seen half a dozen productions in my lifetime, all but one of which have been minor triumphs. Two were at Birmingham Rep: the first in 1957, with Albert Finney as Face, was masterly even if the second, in 1996, was a design-dominated dud. The RSC has had two superb revivals: one directed by Trevor Nunn in 1977, the other by Sam Mendes in 1991, with Philip Voss unforgettable as a berouged, epicene Sir Epicure Mammon emitting little gasps of ecstasy as he imagined himself walking 'naked between my succubae'. And both Tyrone Guthrie at the Old Vic in 1962 and Nicholas Hytner at the National Theatre in 2006 put Jonson's supreme comedy of conmanship into modern dress with great effect.

Hytner, however, was clearly forced to confront an issue that faces all directors of *The Alchemist*: what do you do about a play where the situation seems totally familiar but the language is occasionally inaccessible? If you read Robert Butler's background book on the production, *The Alchemist Exposed*, it is clear that Hytner set out to do a version set in 1610 but with a foot in the contemporary world. By the time it reached the Olivier stage in September 2006, Hytner's production had become definably modern. Alex Jennings's Subtle – the supposed alchemist who caters to his clients' dreams – became at different times a camp Californian guru, a white-robed religious leader and a canny Scottish number-cruncher. Simon Russell Beale's Face similarly shifted from blazered naval captain to Dutch-accented alchemist's acolyte. And Lesley Manville's Dol Common moved from tarty criminal to *Tatler*-type aristo with a cut-glass accent. Not only did Jonson's play translate easily into modern dress, Hytner's production underscored the point that the criminal trio create a Genetesque house of illusions in which willing victims act out their own peculiar fantasies.

Anne Barton got it dead right when she wrote that 'fundamentally, *The Alchemist* is a play about transformation, as it affects not metals, but human beings'. Subtle, Face and Dol are themselves in the transformation business: like all con-artists, they are essentially actors putting on different personae to suit their separate audiences. But what is extraordinary is the diversity of their visitors: a cross-section of Jacobean London who all cherish private dreams. In *Volpone* the dupes are mercenary predators, which is why, in performance, they can all be clad in bird-masks. But the brilliance of *The Alchemist* lies in the way Jonson, with Dickensian prodigality, gives each visitor a special diction, vision and unfulfilled need.

We instantly recognise Dapper, the lawyer's clerk who 'consorts with the small poets of the time' and dreams of being a king of the gambling tables. Even more modest in his aims is Abel Drugger, who simply wants a blessing on his tobacco business. This is the role in which Garrick triumphed in the eighteenth century and Alec Guinness in a 1947 revival at the New Theatre, prompting a delirious enconium from Tynan. 'I was overjoyed,' he wrote, 'to watch his wistful, happy eyes moving in dumb wonder, from Face to Subtle: a solid little fellow, you felt, and how eager to help! At last, he puts in a tolerable contribution to the conversation. O altitudo! His face creases ruddily into modest delight and he stamps his thin feet in glee.'

With the arrival of Sir Epicure Mammon we are in a different league: Jonson paints an astonishing picture of a Faustian fantasist who sees himself as both social benefactor and dedicated voluptuary who yearns to feed off 'the swelling unctuous paps of a fat pregnant sow'. If Mammon is heroic in his folly, Ananias and Tribulation Wholesome are scathingly satirised Puritans who contort their flexible consciences to justify the coining of money. And, last but not least, come Kastril and his sister, Dame Pliant: the former is a bone-headed rustic who yearns to quarrel like a fashionable Angry Young Man, and the latter a pliable widow whose obsession with marrying a Spanish grandee amounts to a sexual fetish.

I itemise the characters because Jonson observes them with a particularised relish that not even Shakespeare or Middleton can match. His comedy, which looks backwards to Plautus and forwards to Michael Frayn at his most mathematically ingenious, is also classically structured. Every knock at the door represents either a prospect of money or a potential crisis. Every character has to be kept in a separate compartment, unless it is in the interest of Face or Subtle that they should meet. It is also a measure of Jonson's structural adroitness that we, like the characters themselves, forget about individual ruses. At the end of Act 3 the hapless Dapper is gagged with gingerbread and stuck in a stinking privy to get him out of the way. The play has almost reached its climax before cries from the closet remind us of the hidden Dapper, who emerges only to apologise for eating his gag.

With Jonson, however, one inevitably comes back to the language and whether it is an obstacle to our enjoyment or a source of rich pleasure. Peter Conrad has written that 'the language of *The Alchemist* is a prodigal wastage, like the excrement to which it so often refers'. In the theatre both Nunn and Hytner hired dramatists, respectively Peter Barnes and Samuel Adamson, to prune and clarify a dense text. Sam Mendes has recalled how, after the first read-through, his depressed RSC actors felt they were coping with 'a sort of Swahili text'. But Mendes went on to say that, if you keep the set simple and trust the Jonsonian rhythms, the play soon starts to take off.

My own instinct is that we grossly exaggerate the impenetrability of the language. For a start the play is full of technical, alchemical terms ('Take away the recipient, And rectify your menstrue, from the phlegma') that it is not necessary for us to understand: we should be as blinded by science as the gulled clients themselves. Jonson's genius also lies in creating the perfect idiom for each character. At one extreme, Mammon speaks like a Marlovian over-reacher glorying in the decadent sound of each syllable. At the other extreme, Jonson achieves a breathtaking simplicity: remember the neighbour who, on the unexpected return of the house's rightful owner, recalls hearing a noise from within 'as I sat up, a-mending my wife's stockings'. The play is also full of single lines that, by painting a vivid picture, brand themselves on the memory. I had an English teacher who used to chortle uncontrollably at Ananias's 'Thou look'st like Antichrist in that lewd hat'. And in the play's orgy of sweet filth nothing is funnier than Drugger's observation of his neighbouring rich widow: 'And I do, now and then, give her a fucus.'

The Alchemist is Jacobean comedy at its perihelion: a brilliantly immoral, perfectly structured, panoramically vivid play that creates what David Mamet, in a later study of conmanship, was to call a *House of Games* and that shows that duplicity and deception only work with the active connivance of the victim. If Jonson's masterpiece endures, it is partly because we recognise that we are all dreamers hoping someone will one day realise our secret fantasies.

17

The White Devil

JOHN WEBSTER
(*c*.1580–1633)

Webster, a superbly pungent poet, certainly brought out the phrase-maker in both his admirers and detractors. T. S. Eliot wrote of Webster in his 1920 poem 'Whispers of Immortality' that he 'was much possessed by death / And saw the skull beneath the skin'. Rupert Brooke also vividly encapsulated Webster's world as one in which 'Human beings are writhing grubs in an immense night'. For Shaw, however, Webster was the 'Tussaud laureate' and for William Archer he was a dramatist who wrote 'haphazard or melodramatic romances for an eagerly receptive but semi-barbarous public'.

'Haphazard' is a charge we'll come back to. What is startling is how relatively recent is the appreciation of this mordant master. No record exists of any production of *The White Devil*, first performed in 1612, between the late seventeenth century and a revival by Cambridge's Marlowe Society in 1920. In the last 100 years, however, the play has gained popular currency, and a turning point clearly came with Michael Benthall's production at London's Duchess Theatre in 1947. A young Tynan was excited both by the production and by Webster's language: 'a new poetry,' he wrote, 'tangy and bitter, full of warning and irrepressibly sombre, a realistic ragged poetry which none has imitated save

Beddoes and Shelley'. One might add to that list Harold Pinter. The sixteen-year-old Pinter was with a party of Hackney schoolboys taken to see that production at the Duchess. Among them was his friend Henry Woolf, who later said, 'This was life to the power of twenty-three. It had a terrific impact on Harold and the rest of us.' Indeed so. The dying Flamineo in *The White Devil* cries 'O, I am in a mist' just as his counterpart, Bosola, in *The Duchess of Malfi*, talks of human life as 'a mist of error'. And it can hardly be an accident that for the expiring Andy in Pinter's *Moonlight* 'the past is a mist'.

But why is it that *The White Devil* has come into its own in the last 100 years? I suspect it is because we worry less than our predecessors about the alleged haphazardness of its plot. It is certainly a play in which the focus is always shifting. At times we are drawn to the blood-soaked passion of the heroine, Vittoria, and her adulterous lover, Brachiano: a passion that leads to the convenient murder of her husband and his wife. At other times, we are hypnotised by the vengeful intrigues of the Florentine Francisco and his papal chum, Monticelso. And then there is the ubiquitous figure of Flamineo: 'a self-centred existentialist pimp' in a vivid phrase from Margaret Drabble's novel *The Garrick Year*, but also an acid-tongued commentator who happens to be Vittoria's brother. I think observers exaggerate Webster's defective plotting. In the theatre, I've always found the play perfectly clear. In the excellent Cambridge University Press edition, David Gunby sees off the carpers by pointing out that 'the play works cyclically, by exploiting repetition, parallelism and analogy in language, character and incident'.

All true. But what makes the play so gripping, whether on stage or on page, is Webster's jaggedly brilliant language and fluctuating moral perspective. The purest example comes in the great third act scene where Vittoria is put on trial. We know, from previous evidence, that Vittoria is beautiful, hot-blooded and complicit in the murder of both her husband and Brachiano's wife. Yet Webster in the trial scene shows Vittoria to be witty, defiant and cunning. She quickly sees off a pedagogic lawyer who speaks 'hard and indigestible words'. She boldly defies the ecclesiastical Monticelso, who, with lip-smacking rhetoric, brands her a whore (I recall how in Gale Edwards's 1996 RSC production Philip Voss's cardinal surreptitiously peered down the front of Jane Gurnett's dress even as he inveighed against her 'poisoned perfumes'). And when Monticelso confronts her with evidence of her complicity with Brachiano, she cries with devastating logic:

If you be my accuser,
Pray, cease to be my judge: come from the bench.

The brilliance of the scene lies in the fact that Webster draws our sympathy to the isolated Vittoria through her quick-wittedness, exposes the hypocrisy of her judges and, at the same time, never lets us forget that she is an adulterous accomplice to murder.

Some, of course, deduce from Webster's quicksilver ambivalence that he is muddled or morally anarchic. But I would put it another way. Webster seems curiously modern in that he views the world with sceptical intelligence and sees man as quintessentially alone: in this sense, he is closer in spirit to Camus and Beckett than he is to Shakespeare. There is, however, nothing arid or dry about Webster's philosophy. He expresses much of it through the character of Flamineo, who is that familiar Jacobean figure, the intellectual malcontent, and a witty cynic whose brain is aflame with vivid images. In Webster's overpowering final act we also see that Flamineo, a bawd, hired assassin and fratricide, is a figure of some complexity. Having heard his mother's dirge over the body of the brother he has slain, Flamineo suddenly announces:

I have a strange thing in me, to the which
I cannot give a name, without it be
Compassion.

In the extraordinary final scene we discover yet more facets to Flamineo. First he fakes death by persuading Vittoria and her waiting-woman to shoot him and then goes through parodic death-agonies ('There's a plumber laying pipes in my guts, it scalds'). The moment when Flamineo rises from the ground, having fooled both the audience and his killers, is the finest *coup de théâtre* in Jacobean drama. But when moments later Flamineo and his would-be assassins are themselves stabbed, he utters the following resonant lines:

I do not look
Who went before, nor who shall follow me;
No, at myself I will begin and end.
While we look up to Heaven, we confound
Knowledge with knowledge. O, I am in a mist!

As Alexander Leggatt has written: 'There is no better definition of what we might call the Jacobean world picture: man adrift in an incomprehensible universe.' It is a picture of a world without meaning, value or the comforting consolations of religion. This doesn't, of course, lessen the exuberance of Webster's turbulent theatrical imagination, and there are copious qualities in the play I have barely touched on: its simmering sexuality, its celebration of female resourcefulness, its prodigiously inventive death scenes, in which Brachiano's wife dies by kissing a poisoned picture and Vittoria's husband is strangled as he fails to surmount a vaulting-horse. The more I think about it, the more absurd Shaw's put-down of Webster seems: this is no waxwork show but a play in which the imminence of death lends a fierce intensity to life. If we have learned to love Webster, it is because his language glitters like a diamond in the night, because he gives death a concrete reality and because, ultimately, he is an Absurdist *avant la lettre*.

18

Fuenteovejuna

LOPE DE VEGA
(1562–1635)

Brits boast, with some justice, about the great explosion of drama that took place from the 1580s to the closure of the London theatres in 1642. We hear rather less about the comparable, and longer-lasting, Spanish Golden Age. Ardent Hispanophiles even rate it higher than our own creative blaze. 'The drama,' wrote Somerset Maugham, 'at no time and in no country has flourished so luxuriantly as in Spain during the hundred years that ended with Calderon's death in 1681.' That's a big claim. But it's worth noting that Madrid alone had forty theatres in this period, that we know the names of over 2,000 Golden Age actors and it's estimated that some 30,000 plays were produced.

What is even more extraordinary is that 1,800 of those plays were the work of one man: Lope de Vega, whom Cervantes, no slouch himself, called 'a prodigy of nature'. It is difficult to know whether to be more in awe of Lope the writer, 400 of whose plays survive, or of the man. In the course of a long life he had two wives, three long-term mistresses, countless affairs, fathered fourteen children, suffered imprisonment and exile and entered the priesthood. 'An unregenerate womanizer tied irrevocably to the demands of the flesh,' in the words of the scholar Melveena McKendrick, 'he was at the same time a sincerely devout man attracted relentlessly to the orthodox spirituality that Spain had made its heritage.' He was also a compulsive writer: not just of plays but of all literary forms and, even when sailing with the Spanish Armada to England in 1588, wrote over a thousand lines of an epic based on Ariosto's *Orlando Furioso*.

Lope's theatrical output was so vast as almost to defy categorisation, but, if I had to pick out one masterpiece from his socio-political plays about peasant honour, it would be *Fuenteovejuna*, which was first published in 1619. As the story of a community taking the law into its own hands to rid itself of a brutally rapacious military commander, it has become an iconic protest play. In 1933 Lorca's touring troupe, La Barraca, famously staged it in modern dress, turning the feudal overlord into a wealthy landowner against whom the people rebelled. In 1936, when civil war broke out in Spain, a young Joan Littlewood played the female lead and directed a production for a newly formed Manchester group called Theatre Union (the forerunner of Theatre Workshop, which revived the play at Stratford East in 1955). And, for obvious reasons, Lope's play became a staple of Soviet theatre.

Yet, although *Fuenteovejuna* clearly shows that honour is not the exclusive property of the privileged and that the community is ultimately stronger than the individual, it is more than a piece of Spanish agitprop. It celebrates the rise of the people against seigneurial feudalism while ultimately endorsing the central authority of monarchy. In that sense, it is shot through with Shakespearean ambivalence. The commander is a tyrant who brutalises the villagers, rapes the heroine Laurencia and savagely punishes her husband Frondoso. After the commander has been killed, the peasants are individually tortured to disclose the name of his murderer and declare, 'Fuenteovejuna did it.' It is a turning point in world drama: a momentous demonstration of the power of collective action. In the end, the peasants seek pardon from Ferdinand and Isabella and, in Adrian Mitchell's translation, the king ominously announces that the community will be placed under monarchical rule: 'And we'll watch you carefully, Till we can find a new Commander Who's fit to govern such a town As Fuenteovejuna.'

Mitchell's text was used by Declan Donnellan in his tremendous revival at the National Theatre in 1989. The brilliance of Donnellan's production lay in the way he brought the Andalusian community to life: this was a working town in which the women pounded the earth with their washing, the men ground corn and the sexes joined forces in scenes of drum-beating festivity. James Laurenson's ramrod-backed commander was no stereotypical sadist but an insecure tyrant who craved to be liked by the very people he abused. But Donnellan and his designer, Nick Ormerod, also shrewdly split the Cottesloe in two to create a traverse stage on which Ferdinand and Isabella were permanently enthroned at one end. To remind us that the play is more than a pre-Marxist parable, a programme note told us that, after the historical rebellion, the monarchy had the principal buildings of Fuenteovejuna razed to the ground as if to obliterate the memory of the uprising.

In short, Lope's play is more equivocal than it first seems. It celebrates natural justice while backing monarchical power. It also – and this is a major part of its greatness – demonstrates that even collective action is sparked by individual courage: something, Lope suggests, more likely to come from women than from men. When the commander interrupts the wedding of Laurencia and Frondoso by dragging off the bride and groom, the menfolk bleat helplessly, reminding us that the town's name translates literally as The Sheep-Well. A later meeting of the town's impotent all-male council advocates caution in the face of military might. It is only with the entry of the ravaged, dishevelled Laurencia, who dismisses the council as 'Ancient cockerels, loafing around the dunghill While other men screw your wives', that the men are spurred into action. And when the men march off to assassinate the commander in his country house, Laurencia urges the women to follow them ('Form up in ranks and take part in an action Which will shake the world'), turning it into an act of communal resistance.

There is, of course, much more to Lope's astonishing play: songs and dances, arguments about the nature of love, debates on the power of post-Gutenberg printing and offstage battles in which the commander aligns himself with the Portuguese against the Spanish monarchy in the War of Succession. But what endures is Lope's ferocious ability to show the unstoppable force of popular protest without denying the need for social order and harmony. Like many great plays, Lope's is both radical and conservative, suggests that happy endings are tinged with irony and leaves posterity to debate its ultimate meaning.

19

Punishment without Revenge

LOPE DE VEGA
(1562–1635)

This is late Lope dating from 1631 and, arguably, an even greater play than *Fuenteovejuna*. It resurfaced in a season of Spanish Golden Age drama at Bath's Ustinov Studio in the autumn of 2013. The season was the brainchild of Laurence Boswell, who had curated others at London's Gate Theatre in 1991 and Stratford-on-Avon's Swan in 2004 and who had lived to see a resurgence of interest in Spanish classics fizzle out. As he said in one interview: 'The British theatre welcomes these Golden Age visits like comets – everyone gets very excited and then it goes back into orbit and everyone waits for the next comet to come into view ten years later.' Seeing Meredith Oakes's new translation of *Punishment without Revenge* (*El castigo sin venganza*) in performance, I didn't feel inclined to wait that long: this work, I passionately believe, should be part of the standard repertory.

For a start, it deals with an archetypal situation: the forbidden love between a stepson and stepmother. It was one which Euripides had tackled in *Hippolytus* and Seneca in *Phaedra* and which Racine would go on to explore in his own variation on the theme, *Phèdre* (1677). But there is no suggestion in Lope's work, as in that of his predecessors, that the characters are the playthings of the gods. They are the victims of their unstoppable passion, of the Spanish code of honour and, on the male side at least, of a dubious genetic inheritance.

Lope's play begins, rivetingly, with the disguised Duke of Ferrara out on the night-prowl looking for new flesh to appease his insatiable itch. The man is clearly an habitual lech. But although the duke has fathered a bastard son in Federico, he knows the city-state requires a legitimate heir if civil war is to be avoided after his death. So he has arranged to marry Cassandra, daughter of the Duke of Mantua, and has sent Federico to collect his bride. And when Federico gallantly rescues a broken-down carriage containing his future stepmother, the sparks fly, and their fate is sealed.

The greatness of Lope's play lies in its sense of postponed ecstasy. Far from falling into each other's arms, Federico and Cassandra are restrained by religious, moral and political sanctions. In Catholic law sex between a stepmother and stepson is classified as incest. The code of honour also prevents a son usurping his father's bed. To make the situation even more complicated, Lope shows that Federico has a prior attachment to the adoring Aurora and that his father, after a single night of conjugal bliss, quickly resorts to his old street-cruising habits.

Out of the main couple's self-denial, Lope creates an almost unbearable erotic tension. The great scene, as Laurence Boswell's production proved, comes at the end of the second act, when Federico and Cassandra confront each other in a state of despair: as played by Nick Barber and Frances McNamee, it was like watching two souls in torment because of their refusal to submit to the body's demands. What you also saw was drama's capacity to make you believe in the power of religious imperatives. We may not accept those rules today: the point is that Lope's characters undoubtedly did. So when Federico accusingly cries to Cassandra, 'I've lost my God because of you And you've become my god instead,' you glimpse the terrifying abyss into which he had fallen. And when Cassandra retorts that she trembled, 'Knowing what the power is of human and divine displeasure' you feel she too is fiercely conscious of mortal sin. At the end of the scene, Lope has the two characters touch hands, knowing that, in the duke's absence fighting papal wars, this gesture will lead both to a consummation devoutly to be wished and a death impossible to avoid.

But this is no straightforward morality play. Lope creates a work of infinite irony and ambiguity and one shot through with reflecting images. An earlier translation by Adrian Mitchell was called *Lost in a Mirror*, the duke himself says that 'the theatre is a mirror', and Aurora witnesses Federico and Cassandra making violent love through the clouded surface of a distorting mirror. In the end, this is a play about the insufficiency of even the strictest religious and moral codes when confronted by natural laws and genetic legacies.

One of Lope's bitterest ironies is that the duke returns from the papal wars a religious convert and penitent monogamist only to learn, through an anonymous letter, of Federico and Cassandra's incestuous passion. Honour demands that the guilty lovers be punished. Yet public acknowledgement of their sins would cause dishonour. This leads towards a tremendous climax in which the duke arranges for Federico to inadvertently murder the disguised Cassandra and then have his son killed for treason.

All this is prefaced by a long speech by the duke that can be, and has been, interpreted in many ways. On one level, it can be taken as a piece of intellectual sophistry in which the duke claims he is dispensing divine justice and 'Punishment without revenge For a sin beyond all shame'. It can also be viewed as a critique of the honour code in that the duke seems concerned that a vengeful slaughter would be bad PR. But the duke is also a tragic figure in that, through marriage, he has effectively disinherited the son he loves and seen his own dissolute behaviour passed on to the next generation: an idea that Ibsen would later explore in *Ghosts*. In Oakes's translation, as the duke surveys his murdered son, he cries:

> He has paid for what he did:
> As we sow, so shall we reap.

But the lines are rich in ambiguity since they apply as much to the speaker as to the person spoken of. They also provide a fitting end to a play of enormous moral complexity and shifting perspectives that invokes the force of Catholic religion and Spanish honour while exposing their fallibility in the face of unstoppable passion.

20

Life Is a Dream

PEDRO CALDERÓN DE LA BARCA
(1600–81)

Lope de Vega is one of the twin giants of Spanish drama: Calderón is the other. The latter's life was turbulent and productive, if not quite as harum-scarum as that of his predecessor. His father, a government official, died when Calderón was fifteen. Disinherited and dispossessed, he left university, abandoned a clerical calling and became a poet and playwright with a reputation for drink and duelling. In the course of a long life, he wrote spectacles for Philip IV's court, plays for the public theatre, and *autos sacramentales* (sacred works) for street festivals at Corpus Christi. He later became a soldier, had an affair with an unnamed woman, took holy orders but never lost his love for the theatre. He even wrote the script for his own funeral, insisting that his coffin be kept open so his corpse would be visible as it was dragged through the Madrid streets.

In Britain, he's taken a long time to gain acceptance. I first heard of him at Oxford in the late 1950s, when there was talk of a production of his most famous play, *Life Is a Dream* (*La vida es sueno*) so bad it quickly became known as 'Life's a Scream'. Since then I have seen three productions that have shown me Calderón's 1635 play is both seminal and stageable. One was John Barton's 1983 RSC revival in an Adrian Mitchell version. Then in 1998 the supposed Catalan bad-boy Calixto Bieito directed a sensational revival at the Edinburgh Festival in John Clifford's translation. And in 2009 Dominic West starred in a Jonathan Munby production and a Helen Edmundson version at the Donmar Warehouse. These three productions, along with close study of Gwynne Edwards's published translation, have taught me several things: that Calderón's play is a masterpiece; that it contains an important lesson for all drama; and that its final message is something that, for reasons I will explain, can help to change one's life.

Like so many great plays, *Life Is a Dream* looks back to the past and forwards to the future. It is, of course, of its time – the Spain of Philip IV – and fulfils what the great historian Jacques Barzun calls 'the Baroque desire for size and convolution'. Set in Poland, its main plot concerns Segismundo, who has been imprisoned in a tower since birth by his father, King Basilio. The reason? Prophesies that Segismundo would grow up to be a tyrant and overthrow his father. But when his son is twenty, Basilio has a change of heart. In a controlled experiment, he releases a drugged Segismundo and grants him unchecked power. The result is a disaster. Segismundo defenestrates a servant, reviles his father and tries to kill his tutor, Clotaldo. So Basilio imprisons him once more and orders Clotaldo to kid him that his moment of freedom was simply a dream. But, during a popular uprising, Segismundo is again set free and defeats his father's forces. He finally forgives his father, learns the art of moderation and promises to be a wise ruler.

It's a story that has many sources, including *The Arabian Nights*. But it's hard not be reminded of Sophocles' *Oedipus Rex* in that Basilio's attempt to thwart prophecies of disaster merely confirms them. It is also a play full of Shakespearean echoes, above all of *The Tempest*, in the pervasiveness of dreams and the ultimate triumph of virtue over vengeance. Yet the play also looks forwards in time. In particular, it anticipates Pirandello's twentieth-century obsession with appearance and reality, permanence and flux and the illusoriness of existence.

But we need to be clear what Calderón's play is really about. It is not simply saying life is a dream and therefore we should passively surrender to changing circumstances. In fact, it is arguing the exact opposite: that man's will is free and his destiny lies in his own hands. Segismundo – one minute occupying a prison, the next a palace – exists in a state of understandable confusion. Thrown into the slammer a second time, stripped of fine robes and clad in animal-skins, he articulates his bewilderment. In the words of Gwynne Edwards's translation, he asks:

> What is this life? A fantasy?
> A prize we seek so eagerly
> That proves to be illusory?
> I think that life is but a dream,
> And even dreams are not what they seem.

But this is not the play's final statement. We have to remember that Segismundo's sudden reversals of fortune are not simply a dream: they are the result of Basilio's political strategy. By the end of the play, shedding his dream-self, Segismundo has also learned a crucial lesson: how to exercise free will. He actively chooses civilisation over barbarism, mercy over vengeance, and even decides which of two women to marry. But free will, Calderon shows, provokes moral dilemmas. In a labyrinthine sub-plot, Clotaldo, Segismundo's tutor, is faced with a tough choice: should he seek revenge on a Muscovite prince who has dishonoured his daughter but coincidentally saved his own life? 'Who can advise,' he asks, 'when in the end the arguments are contradictory?'

Calderón's devastating play reminds us of a fundamental point about drama: that nothing is more exciting than the spectacle of a character confronted by an impossible moral choice. Obviously Calderón did not invent this. It happens in Greek drama. It recurs throughout Shakespeare. It goes on to form a basis of modern drama from Ibsen and Shaw to Brecht and Arthur Miller. But what Calderón teaches us is that drama is at its best when characters are forced to make a moral decision in the living moment, and the more evenly balanced the arguments, the richer the work becomes.

On a more personal note, I'd say that Calderón's play also proves that drama can provide spiritual comfort. The idea that the work is a reflection of our own situation was illustrated by Bieito's Edinburgh production. Above the stage, which in Carles Pujol's design resembled a giant cinder-track, hovered a vast mirror. Crazily tilted, it at first symbolised the disordered world of Segismundo. But when angled to show the audience gazing at itself, it reminded us that we too, like Calderón's characters, inhabit a changeable and transient universe.

The point came home to me forcefully when I found myself rereading the play shortly after receiving a potentially disastrous piece of medical news: on an ordinary working Friday I had a call telling me that a sizeable tumor had been detected on one of my kidneys. This is not, I hope, the arrogance of narcissism. I can only state, in all honesty, that I found genuine consolation in Segismundo's final meditation on life's swift reversals of fortune:

It is enough
To know that our joy today
May by tomorrow be our lasting
Sorrow, and from this lesson learn
To use as best we can the time
Still left to us. Let each man seek
Forgiveness for his sins, and others learn
That they do best to pardon him.

In a moment of crisis, I found practical wisdom in Calderón's philosophy. I was also reminded that, like all fine art, great drama has an irredeemable sanity and can provide us not just with aesthetic pleasure but also with guidance on how to live.

21

The Illusion

PIERRE CORNEILLE
(1606–84)

It's a small leap from Calderón's late Spanish masterpiece to
Corneille's brilliant French *jeu d'esprit* written in 1636 when he
was only thirty. One critic said of *The Illusion* (*L'Illusion comique*)
that 'the play is completely Spanish in taste'. One of the key
characters, Matamore, has a Spanish name (literally 'the killer of
the Moors'), and his kind of fantasising braggart is a familiar figure
in Hispanic literature as well as in Plautine comedy. Beyond that,
however, Corneille's remarkable play chimes with a seventeenth-
century preoccupation with the illusory nature of existence.
'We are such stuff as dreams are made on,' says Prospero in *The
Tempest*. Calderón's *Life Is a Dream* weaves elaborate variations
on the same theme. And then along comes Corneille with a work,
both philosophical and playful, that has a dream-like structure
and turns into a robust defence of theatre itself.

But all this from Corneille? In the nineteenth century he was
dubbed 'the Father of French Tragedy'. Insofar as we think of
Corneille at all, it is usually as the precursor of Racine and as a
severe classicist who wrote such austere tragedies as *Le Cid*, *Cinna*
and *Polyeucte*. In reality, a large number of Corneille's thirty-three
plays are comedies, and he ran into trouble with both the French
Academy and Cardinal Richelieu for his flagrant breach of the

classical proprieties. *The Illusion*, which Corneille himself dubbed a 'strange monster', was, in particular, seen as a wild aberration until Louis Jouvet staged it at the Comédie Française in 1937. Today, it has come into its own. Giorgio Strehler did a magical production at the Paris Odéon in 1984 that, in the words of Irving Wardle, 'offered an unearthly sequence of shimmering and dissolving stage pictures, giving the sensation of having wandered into Plato's cave'. In 1990 Ranjit Bolt's vivacious English version was given a highly inventive production by Richard Jones at the Old Vic. And in 2012 Tony Kushner's free adaptation, turning the play from a passionate apologia for theatre into a debate about the illusion of love, reached London's Southwark Playhouse. A play that looks back to Shakespeare and Calderón now seems to be a precursor of Pirandello.

What is startling is Corneille's imaginative freedom as he operates on three different levels of reality. He starts with a grief-stricken father, Pridamant, resorting to a magicican, Alcandre, for news of his missing son, Clindor. Instantly we are into a world of Prospero-like wizardry as we learn that the magician can make 'the winds rise in stormy ranks against his enemies'. But Alcandre can also conjure up spirits and he goes on to show Pridamant how his son, having been a shape-shifting Parisian Proteus, is now a Bordeaux-based sexual go-between.

This ushers us into the second level of reality: one in which we follow the amorous adventures of the duplicitous Clindor. Employed as an intermediary by the insanely puffed-up Matamore in his pursuit of the beautiful Isabelle, Clindor falls in love with the girl himself. At the same time, he protects her from a second suitor, the fiery Adraste. As if this weren't enough, this cut-price Casanova keeps his options open with Isabelle's maid, Lyse, who sees through him but secretly fancies him. All this comes to a head when Clindor is imprisoned for killing Adraste and, thanks to the self-sacrificing Lyse, gets out of gaol and makes his escape with the devoted Isabelle.

A romantic imbroglio? Possibly so, but in the final act Corneille introduces yet another level of reality. Two years have passed. We are in some Arcadian kingdom. Clindor and Isabelle, now known as Theagene and Hippolyte, are the guests of Prince Florilame. But when it is discovered that Clindor has cuckolded his host, he is swiftly killed, prompting Isabelle to expire on the spot. 'My son's been murdered and all hope is past,' cries Clindor's despairing dad, only for Alcandre to reveal that he has all along been watching not, as he assumed, a recreation of real events but a popular Parisian play. To underline the point, we have the unromantic spectacle of Clindor and his fellow actors divvying up the night's box-office takings.

You could hardly have a better demonstration of the interaction of illusion and reality. We know theatre is a controlled dream; yet we ourselves surrender to it in the moment. Here Corneille is at pains to remind us that we are witnesses to a fantasy by having the anxious Pridamant comment on the unfolding action: a point brilliantly underscored by Strehler, who had the father stand in the front stalls and vainly reach out to his son locked behind the proscenium arch. Yet we too become naive spectators engrossed in the action, wondering how Clindor is going to escape from the corners into which he has painted himself. Dramatists in the twentieth century, Brecht especially, would go to great lengths to dismantle the apparatus of illusion; yet the essence of theatre is that we temporarily abandon ourselves to the dramatic moment. We know the actor playing Gloucester in *King Lear* is not really being blinded, yet we still cry out in horror at the simulated cruelty.

Corneille plays, with great sophistication, on this duality. In every sense this is a witty play, one that not only shows Pridamant (and us) believing in illusions but one that also portrays the characters in the play-within-a-play as victims of fantasy. The most extreme example is Matamore: not just a descendant of the *miles gloriosus* in Roman comedy but a man who contrives his own self-concocted charades so that a fake 'ambassador' presents a spurious missive from the Queen of England purely so that Matamore can publicly spurn her. To a lesser degree, Clindor rejoices in his trickster-like cunning and Isabelle in her untarnished loveliness. Possibly the only fully alert character is Lyse, who has the pert self-awareness of the servants you find in Marivaux's eighteenth-century comedies.

You can see the play as looking back to Plato's cave or forwards to the techniques of modern cinema. But in the end it is a glorious tribute to the labyrinthine deceptiveness of theatre itself. It climaxes in a rousing speech by Alcandre that, in Bolt's translation, combines royal flattery with a hymn to drama:

> The king himself, less man than meteor,
> A Jupiter in peace, a Mars in war,
> Whose laurel crown proclaims his awesome power,
> From time to time will pass a carefree hour
> At the Théâtre français. Parnassus there
> Unfolds it many marvels, rich and rare.

This transcends mere sycophancy or self-congratulation. What Corneille's coruscating comedy shows is how theatre depends simultaneously on a heightened self-consciousness and the willing absorption in a visionary dream.

22

Tartuffe

MOLIÈRE
(1622–73)

Without lapsing into fawning Francophilia, one has to admit that much of the best seventeenth-century drama came out of Paris. And that was thanks to three theatrical giants: Corneille, Molière and Racine. Martin Turnell in *The Classical Moment* makes a crucial distinction between them. Corneille's big theme, he suggests, was the Man of Honour: the imposition of a moral order on the chaos of human desires. Racine, in contrast, wrote about the Man of Passion: the collapse of order before the unruliness of love. Turnell sees Molière as standing midway between them. 'The centre of his world,' he writes, 'is the Natural Man and he studies the way in which perverted natural instincts may become a danger to the community.'

That's a good enough description of *Tartuffe*, although it raises the key question of just whose instincts are the more dangerous to society: those of the pious hypocrite (Tartuffe) or those of the blinkered zealot (Orgon)? In its day, of course, the play was taken as an assault on religion per se. In its first three-act incarnation, in May 1664, Molière's play, although admired by Louis XIV, unleashed a storm of abuse. The *Gazette de France* declared the play 'extremely harmful to religion and likely to have a most dangerous effect'. A priestly tract dubbed Molière 'a devil clothed in human flesh' and the single most sacrilegious figure in history. The Archbishop of Paris forbade the faithful to attend a performance of *Tartuffe* on pain of excommunication. For the next five years, the play was effectively banned from the public stage, and it was only in 1669 that the version we know today had its Parisian première. It played to packed houses and has ever since become a staple not just of the French but of the international repertory.

Over the years I've seen eight or nine productions. At one extreme was the magnificently apocalyptic tragi-comedy that Roger Planchon's Théâtre National Populaire brought to London in 1976: at the other end was the broad-bottomed farce that Roxana Silbert treated us to at the Birmingham Rep in 2013. But one question has always intrigued me. What is it that Molière is really attacking?

In the course of the play we see that not only the credulous Orgon but also his mother, Madame Pernelle, have fallen under the sway of the seemingly devout Tartuffe. This is signalled early on in a magnificent comic passage where Orgon, on returning home, learns that his wife, Elmire, has succumbed to a terrible fever. Three times Orgon enquires, in the original, 'Et Tartuffe?' These antiphonal responses are interspersed with the information that Tartuffe meanwhile looks well, has dined heartily and slept soundly. And each time Orgon reacts with a cry of 'Le pauvre homme!' Thus Molière rhythmically reveals the extent of Orgon's delusion. And the point is reinforced when we see that Orgon is prepared to vouchsafe to Tartuffe his daughter, his property and incriminating documents. Only when Orgon, hidden under a table, hears Tartuffe making love to Elmire is he finally persuaded that he has a viper in his domestic nest.

Molière's theme looks straightforward enough: an attack on religious charlatanism. In fact, it is much more complex in its portrait of the danger of blind faith. It strikes me that Orgon – the role Molière himself chose to play – is the main character, and what Molière shows us is a man who is totally in thrall to a pious intruder. Eric Bentley put it succinctly when he wrote in *The Life of the Drama*: 'The ferment of the play comes largely from Orgon: Molière's real target is not religious hypocrisy but religious zeal.' The more astute productions have grasped this instinctively. In Tyrone Guthrie's oddly underrated version for the National Theatre in 1967 John Gielgud's Orgon gazed at the palms of Robert Stephens's Tartuffe as if searching for signs of stigmata. Planchon went even further in his 1976 production by having Guy Trejan's Orgon, on arriving home, divest himself of perruque, ruffs, boots and finery to don sackcloth and ashes in order to become Tartuffe's willing slave.

It's part of Molière's mastery that there is no end to Orgon's complexity. On one level, his surrender to Tartuffe is patently sexual as well as religious. In Ranjit Bolt's witty translation, used for Lindsay Posner's National Theatre production in 2002, the commonsensical maid, Dorine, says of Orgon:

A libertine could not adore
His very favourite mistress more.

And there is a sense in which Molière prefigures a standard French adultery play where the complaisant husband welcomes his wife's lover into the home. But Orgon also represents another theatrical archetype: the naive architect of his own, his house's and possibly society's destruction, an idea which Max Frisch took to its logical conclusion in his great 1958 black comedy *The Fire Raisers*, where the middle-class Biedermann plays host to a pair of palpable arsonists.

But if Orgon can be seen in many ways, so too can Tartuffe.

You can treat him as an outright villain, as Anthony Sher did in a 1983 RSC revival: with his black locks, demonic eyes and capacity to creep into a chair as if about to rape it, Sher presented us with a dry run for his Richard III. A year later, in Stratford Ontario, I saw Brian Bedford play Tartuffe as a plausible, smooth-tongued figure who looked truly shocked when a member of Orgon's household cried 'Damn'. This not only makes the whole play more fascinating but strikes at a crucial psychological truth: even the charlatan may be a victim of self-delusion. Martin Turnell observes, 'In spite of his viciousness, Tartuffe is in his way genuine – genuine in that his hypocrisy is an integral part of his character.' Eric Bentley also asks of Tartuffe: 'Is he a hypocrite at all? Might he not believe in religion quite sincerely and, like other religious persons, fall knowingly into sin? Certainly, he is conscious of the way he deceives people. Does he not deceive himself in a way he is not conscious of?'

That is a brilliant observation. Instead of a simple comedy about a knave and a fool, we are confronted by an immensely subtle play about two different forms of self-delusion. In an age like our own, when religion has frequently been invoked as a motive for acts of terrorist violence, Molière's play seems as pertinent as ever. Of course, one should never forget that it is wildly funny. The scene where Tartuffe all but seduces Elmire, while Orgon significantly hides beneath the two of them, is one of the best pieces of farce ever written. Even as I write that, I remember how in Planchon's production the table was covered by a vast blue altar-cloth suggesting something more than the household gods was being violated: a potent reminder of how, in Molière's play, sex, religion and self-deception are inexhaustibly intertwined.

23

The Misanthrope

MOLIÈRE

(1622–73)

As a critic, one sometimes gets things spectacularly wrong. I certainly remember doing so when I first saw Tony Harrison's translation of *The Misanthrope* at the Old Vic in 1973. It struck me initially that John Dexter's smoothly chic production and Alec McCowen's gift for hilarious apoplexy turned the scales against Molière's hero, Alceste: that, in short, we were invited to laugh at Alceste's scorn for social conformity rather than to admire his civil disobedience. A second viewing, and closer study, convinced me I had grossly underestimated one of the finest translations of modern times. But my biggest error was to approach Molière's play in a doctrinaire spirit. You can't say that Alceste is wholly right in his bruising sincerity, but nor you can say that he is totally wrong. He is a brilliantly contradictory character who, like many of Chekhov's later creations, is comic outside and tragic inside. His dazzling inconsistencies also leave open the question of how far the individual should go to obey the rules of a society he or she may detest.

Even Molière's title raises an awkward question. Is Alceste a true misanthrope, like Shakespeare's Thersites, or simply a prickly individual with a built-in bullshit-detector? A misanthrope hates all mankind. But what is striking about Alceste is that, although he fires off verbal fusillades and is subject to what Harrison's version calls 'black rage' ('une humeur noire'), he is not without a sense of reality. 'The world's not going to change because of you,' he is reminded by his moderating friend, Philinte. And even Alceste is not quite the all-or-nothing figure his furious tirades suggest.

You see this in Molière's dazzling first act (and, if I use Harrison's version set in the Gaullist Paris of the 1960s as my benchmark, it is because it finds a modern equivalent for the wit and vigour of Molière's alexandrines). The first crisis comes when a creepy Elysée insider, Oronte, asks for Alceste's opinion of a poem he has written. Twice Alceste tries to back off, saying that, since frankness is his forte, he might give offence: a reminder, in the words of Joseph Wright, 'how implicated he remains in social practices' and also a prophetic hint of how other great dramatic nay-sayers (Shaw's Saint Joan, Brecht's Galileo, Arthur Miller's John Proctor) seek to avoid confrontation. But it doesn't work. Oronte virtually provokes a showdown by insisting on reciting his paltry verses. Even when Alceste tries to camouflage his criticism by pretending it applies to an imaginary third person, he is goaded by Oronte into expressing the truth:

Jesus wept!
It's bloody rubbish, rhythmically inept,
Vacuous verbiage, wind, gas, guff.
All lovestruck amateurs turn out that stuff.

If Alceste circuitously seeks to avoid the inevitable showdown with Oronte, he is even more contradictory in his relationship with Celimène. She is, as the play goes on to show, a flirty coquette who likes to keep her suitors dangling on a string. She also has a capacity for feline bitchiness that enables her to discomfort her chum, Arsinoé, by quoting what people say about her friend's fake rectitude:

She'd daub a fig leaf on a Rubens nude
But with a naked man she's not a prude.

On the surface, you'd expect Alceste to reject Celimène out of hand since she represents everything he deplores. She is capricious, vain, inconstant. She is also, to us as well as to Alceste, irresistible. Kenneth Tynan put it well in reviewing a French production in 1962:

Alceste's devouring love for Celimène is the love, in all
the ages, of the intellectual perfectionist for the clever,
disarming, imperfect doll; she lives in the world as it is,
he in the world as it ought to be and that way friction lies.
Did we not say as much when Mr Miller married Miss
Monroe? And was not a similar disparity noted between
Molière himself and Armande Béjart, the pretty coquette
he took to wife?

Molière's understanding of masculine enslavement is perfect. Even when Alceste discovers that Celimène has been making overtures to his detested rival, Oronte, and even when he sees the extent of her duplicity towards a pair of camp followers, he can't shake off the erotic chains that bind him to her. In the superb final act, he makes one last offer to Celimène:

But I'm willing to forget these painful scenes,
concoct excuses for your crimes and say
the vicious times and youth led you astray,
provided that, on your part, you consent
to share my self-inflicted banishment.

The prospect of shunning society is, however, too much for the twenty-year-old Celimène, so Alceste is left to face the prospect of rural exile in self-vindicating solitude.

So where does Molière stand in all this? What is his play actually saying? I think its power lies in the author's humane ambivalence. Molière doesn't judge his characters, he simply dramatises an eternal dilemma: how does the individual stay true to his or her ideals in a corrupt society? Rather than sanctify or demonise Alceste, Molière presents him, in the round, as a tragi-comic figure who pays a high price for his unsullied frankness. Even Celimène is not condemned: I recall how, in John Dexter's 1973 production, a beautiful Diana Rigg was left ruefully alone to ponder Alceste's departure and the possibility of herself one day turning into the kind of frustrated sourpuss she saw in Arsinoé. The suave *raisonneur*, Philinte, is not totally idealised: there is more than a hint that his kind of adjustment to society's rules leads only to a comfortable hypocrisy. I'm rather with Martin Turnell when he says that 'Eliante [Celimène's cousin] is the only wholly sympathetic character in the play.' She sees something admirable in Alceste's frankness, yet she is wise enough to reject his offer of love when he turns to her to avenge himself on Celimène:

All lovers' tiffs blow over pretty soon,
hated this morning, loved this afternoon.

Like the maidservant Dorine in *Tartuffe*, Eliante sees things as they really are, stands on the sidelines offering mature comment, and, in her case, pricks Alceste's vanity while respecting his courage. But this is not a play with a straightforward message. This is, in fact, for Molière a new kind of comedy: one that neither ends in social harmony nor with a sense, as in *Tartuffe*, that wrongs have been righted through an ironic *deus ex machina*. If the play feels very modern, it is because of its deliberately open ending. As Alceste heads off for a life of internal exile pursued by Philinte and Eliante, we are left to ponder whether society will ever be able to accommodate the man or woman of outspoken principle. It is, supremely, a play that asks questions rather than supplies answers.

24

Andromache

JEAN RACINE
(1639–99)

Molière we can cope with in English, but for much of my lifetime there has been a rooted prejudice against the neo-classical tragedies of Racine. We are reminded at school – or at least I was – that Shakespeare employed a dramatic vocabulary of 20,000 words whereas Racine uses only a tenth of that number. Hazlitt claimed that, where Shakespeare's genius is dramatic, Racine's is didactic and that he gives us 'the commonplaces of the human heart'. And George Steiner, in a brilliant passage in *The Death of Tragedy*, suggests that Racine is ultimately untranslatable because 'the crises which reverberate through the muted air are crises of syntax'. He cites a scene in *Phèdre* where Hippolyte shies in horror from the queen's declaration of love. Up to that point the characters have addressed each other as *vous*. Suddenly Phèdre says:

Ah, cruel! tu m'as trop entendue.
Je t'en ai dit assez pour te tirer d'erreur.

Which translates as

Ah, cruel one! Thou hast understood me all too clearly.
I have told thee enough to dispel thy error.

As Steiner notes, 'the entire shock of revelation lies in the shift from the formal *vous* to the intimate *tu*'.

And yet, for all the obstacles, Racine *can* work in English. I've lived long enough to see productions of the major plays by Declan Donnellan for Cheek by Jowl, Jonathan Kent for the Almeida and Nicholas Hytner for the National. Ted Hughes, Robert David Macdonald and Tony Harrison have also found ways of rendering Racine in English. And audiences have learned to love *Phèdre*, the main role of which has been played by an array of dazzling actresses including Glenda Jackson, Diana Rigg and Helen Mirren.

Yet, although *Phèdre* has a formal perfection, I find *Andromache* a more intemperately exciting work. For a start, it's a young man's play: Racine wrote it in 1667, when he was only twenty-seven and the author of two previous minor tragedies (*The Thebaid* and *Alexander*). *Andromache* also destroys all one's Anglo-Saxon preconceptions about Racine. It is fast-moving, far from static and filled with a grim, ironic humour in its portrait of the destructive zeal of love. It also plays superbly. I saw it bravely done by Cheek by Jowl in 1985. Even more memorable was a Jonathan Miller production at the Old Vic in 1988 which had a cast led by Penelope Wilton, Kevin McNally and Janet Suzman and which used a direct and fluid translation by Eric Korn, which I shamelessly plunder.

What instantly strikes one is the speed with which Racine lays out the central dilemma. Within the four short scenes that constitute the first act we see the pattern of unrequited passion that will ultimately detonate the catastrophe. We are in the palace of Pyrrhus, the son of Achilles, at Epirus after the Trojan War. Pyrrhus' problem is that he is hopelessly in love with his captive, Andromache, whose son, Astyanax, is regarded as a potential threat by the Greeks. But, just as Pyrrhus is emotionally enslaved to Andromache, he, in turn, is loved by Hermione, the daughter of Menelaus and Helen, who has spent six months hanging around Pyrrhus' court, waiting for him to honour his promise of marriage. To complicate matters further, Hermione herself is loved by Orestes, who has been sent to Epirus by the Greek kings to demand the death of Andromache's son. With masterly economy, Racine sets up a situation where everyone is in love with the wrong person.

Chekhov in *The Seagull* would later explore the tragi-comic side of unrequited passion. What Racine gives us is a savage quadrille, an inexorable dance of death, but also one laced with multiple ironies. For a start we see how love induces a kind of madness in which reason goes out of the window. At one point Pyrrhus tells the stubbornly unresponsive Andromache: 'All that we did to Troy you've done to me.' Given that Troy was destroyed by fire, that Pyrrhus' dad killed Andromache's husband and that Pyrrhus himself slaughtered Hector's father and sister, the equation of private passion with cosmic calamity seems preposterous. But the idea of love as a disease which destroys all sense of proportion runs right through the action. In effect, love becomes inseparable from hate. As Martin Turnell sagely noted, 'The characters live, tragic or triumphant, in a perpetual state of oscillation between the two extremes, never knowing from one moment to the next at which pole they will find themselves.'

Pyrrhus, the supposed conqueror, is enslaved by Andromache. Orestes, blinded by love for Hermione, tells her how he has sought death at the hands of savage Scythian tribes to put an end to his torment: Hermione's brusque response is to tell him to 'stop chattering of Scythians or how cruel I am'. And Hermione, the richest character of them all, veers from one emotion to another. One moment she clings to the pathetic hope that she can persuade Pyrrhus to love her; the next, finding he is to marry Andromache after all, she prays for his death. This leads to one of the great moments in all classical drama. Who does Hermione engage to kill Pyrrhus during the marriage ceremony? None other than the devoted Orestes. And what does Hermione say when Orestes comes to report his mission is accomplished?

> What right had you
> To be his judge? Why kill him? For what crime?
> What had he done? What was he guilty of?
> Who told you to?

That last line ('Qui te l'a dit?') is one of the most resonant in Racine, and, although I remember it was greeted with barely stifled laughter when delivered by the great Penelope Wilton, I thought it was appropriate and proof of Racine's gift for sardonic humour.

In the end Pyrrhus is slaughtered, a distraught Hermione commits suicide, and Orestes goes mad. But Racine's supreme irony is that the one survivor of the play's central quartet is Andromache. You could say it's a close-run thing in that her initial plan, having married Pyrrhus to secure her son's life, was to kill herself. But she is forestalled by events and lives on. And why? Because, although she grieves for the dead Hector, she is immune from the destructive neurosis of love. And this seems to me very much Racine's point. In a play packed with psychological insight and dramatic intensity, Racine anticipates Strindberg in his depiction of love-hate and Freud in his exploration of the link between Eros and Thanatos. Forget the idea that Racine is decorous, stately and a bit dull. At his best, as here, he shows unchecked passion bursting through a geometrical framework like a tiger bounding out of a beautifully structured iron cage.

25

The Rover

APHRA BEHN

(1640–89)

At last, a play by a woman dramatist! Not before time, you may say. But the truth is that, prior to Mrs Aphra Behn and the Restoration of Charles II, there is little choice. Behn, in fact, is in iconic figure in many respects. She was the first recognised professional woman writer in English. She also led a life crowded with incident. She spent her early years in Surinam, which later inspired her novel *Oroonoko*. She served as a spy in Antwerp, was imprisoned for debt, saw the first of her twenty plays, *The Forced Marriage*, staged in Lincoln's Inn Fields in 1670, went on to write anti-Whig lampoons, short novels and erotic poems and was buried in Westminster Abbey in 1689. Unsurprisingly, she was long a figure of controversy.

In her day she was satirised as a vile 'punk and poetess', in the eighteenth century was attacked for her literary presumption, and that old sobersides William Archer, in 1922, dismissed her plays as 'the most worthless stuff that ever pretended to take rank as dramatic literature'. Yet in the twentieth century she found new champions. Virginia Woolf in *A Room of One's Own* (1929) writes:

> Masterpieces are not single and solitary births; they are
> the outcome of many years of thinking in common, of

thinking by the body of the people, so that the experience of the mass is behind the single voice. Jane Austen should have laid a wreath on the grave of Fanny Burney, and George Eliot done homage to the robust shade of Eliza Carter . . . All women together ought to let flowers fall upon the tomb of Aphra Behn . . . for it was she who earned them the right to speak their minds.

But do I put *The Rover* in my top 101 because it's an historic landmark or because it's a first-rate play? In truth, a bit of both. The play was certainly popular when first produced at Dorset Garden in 1677, was regularly revived until 1790 and was given a new lease of life by John Barton in a dashing RSC version in 1986. Barton cut 550 lines, added 350 from Behn's source (*Thomaso or The Wanderer* by Thomas Killigrew) and transposed the action from Naples to a Spanish colony. But his production, starring Jeremy Irons as the rakehelly rover and Imogen Stubbs as a potential nun anxious to acquire new habits, preserved Behn's essential point: that, since men invent moral laws for their own convenience, women are fully entitled to all the sex they can get.

The play is not, however, a straightforward feminist tract. Behn sets the action in Naples during the Interregnum, when the Caroline court was in exile and when the king's followers were forced to become soldiers or sailors of fortune. That is the situation faced by the play's protagonist, Willmore, and it is fascinating to see how Behn, as a royalist and a Tory, refuses to condemn his freebooting sexual and economic opportunism. At the same time, she creates two strong women characters who are rivals for his affection: the mischievous, man-hunting Hellena, who refuses to be confined to a convent, and the high-class courtesan Angellica Bianca, who shows both independence of mind and an appetite for revenge when wantonly discarded.

The plot, I admit, is a convoluted affair. No fewer than three different English exiles are on the loose in Naples and end up wed to local beauties. There is even a sub-plot involving a rustic booby who goes in hot pursuit of a Neapolitan whore: 'one night's enjoyment with her,' he says, 'will be worth all the days I ever passed in Essex'. Since he ends up robbed of his clothes, his money and his dignity, it suggests the Essex joke was current in the seventeenth century. But the nub of the play lies in the encounters between the wavering Willmore and the high-spirited Hellena. Simon Trussler, in the Methuen/RSC edition, sends our hearts to the right place when he says their wooing is in the tradition of Benedick and Beatrice and anticipates Congreve's Mirabell and Millamant and Shaw's Jack Tanner and Ann Whitefield. What Behn shows us is a man and woman of comparable wit and vigour. Willmore professes his inconstancy: Hellena shows she can match it. 'I am as inconstant as you,' she tells him, 'for I have considered, captain, that a handsome woman has a great deal to do whilst her face is good, for then is our harvest-time to gather friends; and should I in these days of my youth catch a fit of foolish constancy, I were undone; 'tis loitering by daylight in our great journey.' Hellena, who spends much of the play's second half dressed as a man, is more than a match for Willmore; you feel Behn admires her sexual pluck as much as his piratical zest. When Willmore tells Hellena 'thou hast one virtue I adore, good nature', it is Mrs Behn's way of giving both of them her benediction.

The one character who escapes the marital pattern is Angellica Bianca. She is, in many ways, the play's most complex figure. As a courtesan, she betrays her principles by falling in love with Willmore. Accused by him of being mercenary, she is quick to point to masculine double standards: 'when a lady is proposed to you for a wife,' she says of men in general, 'you never ask how fair, discreet or virtuous she is, but what's her fortune'. Angellica speaks good sense and ends the play, having lost the affection of both Willmore and the local viceroy's son, aggrieved, vengeful and stubbornly alone. She is almost too rich a character to be contained by a vivacious intrigue-comedy, and many commentators have seen parallels between Angellica and Aphra Behn herself. As Maureen Duffy pointed out, the play is a celebration of Mrs Behn's Cavalier childhood heroes. 'But I believe,' wrote Duffy, 'that though her identification with the cavaliers is intense, she was at the same time AB, the courtesan Angellica Bianca. Her trade was words and it was impossible that she shouldn't have noticed those initials.'

In the end, that gets close to the heart of the play's strength. Ambiguously famed both for her 'female sweetness' and 'manly grace', Mrs Behn has the imaginative capacity to embrace a multiplicity of viewpoints. She is simultaneously on the side of the randy rover and the sexy heroine while secretly sympathising with the lone outsider for whom marriage is a sacrifice. If Mrs Behn was a pioneer, it wasn't because she was an explicit feminist but because she embodied the value of androgyny to the true artist.

26

Venice Preserv'd

THOMAS OTWAY

(1652–85)

There is a strong link between Thomas Otway and Aphra Behn. As a scapegrace young man just down from Oxford, Otway was drawn to the stage and in the early 1670s made his acting debut in Mrs Behn's *The Jealous Bridegroom*. Not, according to a contemporary, with very happy results: 'He, being not us'd to the Stage, the full House put him to such a Sweat and Tremendous Agony, being dash't, spoilt him for an Actor.' Perhaps just as well since, in his brief career, Otway produced some fine plays. Having begun with adaptations of Racine and Molière, he wrote an excellent comedy in *The Soldier's Fortune* (1680) and in 1682 produced the masterly *Venice Preserv'd*, once described by Kenneth Tynan as 'the last great verse play in the English language'.

Set in the Venetian republic, it deals with a plot by two impoverished malcontents, Jaffeir and Pierre, to overthrow the Senate. But their motives are nothing if not personal. Jaffeir's bride, Belvidera, has been cruelly disowned by her senatorial father. And Pierre's adored mistress, Aquilina, is kept by a kinky old senator, Antonio. What is striking about the play, however, is its propulsive narrative, vigorous verse and opportunities for actors, which is partly why it held the stage virtually uninterrupted from 1682 to the 1840s. It was a big success when first seen at the Duke's Theatre, Dorset Gardens with

Thomas Betterton as Pierre and Elizabeth Barry as Belvidera. The performances of David Garrick as the knife-wielding Jaffeir and Mrs Cibber as Belvidera in 1748 are preserved in a famous Zoffany painting. John Philip Kemble and Mrs Siddons proved an equally lustrous partnership in the late eighteenth century. However, although the play proved an inspiration to British revolutionaries, it gradually fell out of favour and has been revived only sporadically in the last 100 years. Peter Brook famously directed it in 1953 with John Gielgud as Jaffeir, Paul Scofield as Pierre and Eileen Herlie as Belvidera. And Peter Gill came up with a thrilling revival at the National in 1984 that matched Michael Pennington's Jaffeir with Ian McKellen's Pierre and Jane Lapotaire's Belvidera. Since then the play has fallen into inexplicable neglect.

Several things about Gill's production, reinforced by subsequent readings, convinced me I was in the presence of a masterpiece. One is Otway's ability, consciously drawing on Shakespeare's Brutus and Cassius, to create two great figures in Jaffeir and Pierre. Jaffeir is the eternal romantic, driven to betray the revolution when his wife is threatened by a rapacious co-conspirator: Pierre is the more cynical and hard-headed man of action. Although they are classic opposites, they remind me of a line from Tom Stoppard's *The Real Thing*, which appeared only two years before the Gill revival. 'Public postures,' says Stoppard's Henry, 'have the configuration of private derangements.' For all their supposedly high-minded fervor about the iniquity of the Venetian Senate, you feel that both men are strongly motivated by a sense of personal pique.

Gill's production also reminded us that something else binds the two men together: a strong homoeroticism. The most intense relationship in the play is clearly between Jaffeir and Pierre. You see that clearly when Jaffeir, having betrayed the planned revolution, is struck in the face by Pierre and condemned as a coward. His response?

No, thou shalt not force me from thee,
Use me reproachfully, and like a slave,
Tread on me, buffet me, heap wrongs on wrongs
On my poor head; I'll bear it all with patience,
Shall weary out thy most unfriendly cruelty,
Lie at thy feet and kiss 'em though they spurn me,
Till, wounded by my sufferings, thou relent,
And raise me to thy armes with dear forgiveness.

This is the language of a rejected lover. Lest we miss the point, at the climactic moment when the captive Pierre is about to be executed, Jaffeir offers to sacrifice his wife and slit his child's throat in order to appease him. In the end, Jaffeir stabs Pierre before killing himself, but I think we get the message about the unbreakable bond between the two men.

If there is a strong element of masochism in Jaffeir's relationship to Pierre, that theme is presented even more vividly in the extraordinary sex scenes between the old senator, Antonio, and Aquilina. History tells us that Antonio was based on the Earl of Shaftesbury, who was leader of the Whig opposition to Charles II and who in 1681 was committed to the Tower for high treason. But these scenes, invariably cut in performance until the twentieth century, are of importance to us today because they represent the first portrayal of sado-masochism on the British stage. Antonio gets his thrills by using baby-talk to his mistress, whom he addresses as 'Nicky, Nacky', and by getting her to spit on him, whip him and beat him like a dog: 'do kick, kick on, now I am under the table, kick again – kick harder – harder yet,' cries the old man before uttering canine barks. Far from being some tawdry excrescence, these scenes – memorably played by a grovelling Hugh Paddick and a sumptuous Stephanie Beacham at the National – are integral to Otway's play. Greatly admired by Goethe, they not only establish a time-honoured link between political power and sexual perversion, they also remind us of the masochistic self-destructiveness at the very heart of Otway's play: when Pierre is on the scaffold, Jaffeir asserts that 'stripes (from a whip) are fitter for me than embraces'.

In its own time, Otway's play was seen as a comment on the supposed popish plot of 1678 and as an endorsement of the way popular opinion, fearing a new civil war, rallied to the Tory, Royalist cause. A hundred years later Otway's play, by showing a libertarian uprising against a decadent oligarchy, was adopted by radicals aroused by the revolutionary movements in France and America. As with so many great plays, its meaning shifts with time. If it deserves revival today, it's because it appeals to our own cynicism about political establishments and revolutionary extremists. And, of course, because it combines great roles with the surging, visceral excitement of a Verdi opera.

27

Love for Love

WILLIAM CONGREVE

(1670–1729)

And so to Restoration Comedy, a convenient, hold-all term that has come to be associated with brocades and spaniel wigs, fluttering fans and mannered acting. Only in recent years have we begun to grasp the vital distinctions within the genre. Congreve, for instance, was born ten years after the restoration of Charles II, saw little of court life and wrote the five plays that made his name in the years from 1693 to 1700 during the reign of William and Mary. What is startling about Congreve is his youthfulness: he gave up writing plays at the age of thirty. He is also justly famed for the grace and beauty of his style, described by Hazlitt as 'the highest model of comic dialogue'. Most agree this reached its apogee in Congreve's final play, *The Way of the World*. But, although that play has great scenes, no one ever fully understands the plot. *Love for Love*, on the other hand, is not only comprehensible but vigorous, witty, touching and eminently theatrical. It was highly popular at its 1695 première, in a converted tennis court in Lincoln's Inn Fields, held the stage for much of the eighteenth century and enjoyed a vogue in the twentieth century in revivals by Tyrone Guthrie, John Gielgud and Peter Wood. It is Wood, who directed the play for the National in 1965 and 1985, who is generally credited with injecting a new note of social realism into a genre that had become associated with bandbox prettiness and stylised artifice.

But what kind of play is *Love for Love*? In part a satire written, as Congreve makes clear in his Prologue, at a time when the form had grown harmlessly mild 'or only showed its teeth as if it smiled'. Money, as much as passion, spins the plot; Congreve paints a vivid picture of a late-seventeenth-century society where material gain governs human transactions. As G. M. Trevelyan wrote of the period: 'While religion divided, trade united the nation and trade was gaining in relative importance. The Bible had now a rival in the ledger.'

Congreve makes us instantly aware of the power of money. We discover the play's hero, Valentine, living as a putative poet in the genteel poverty long associated with the literary life, a point underscored in Wood's production by the sight of John Stride holed up in a vast panelled library surrounded by the decaying paraphernalia of the bookworm. Gradually we learn that Valentine has squandered his income in 'pleasurable expense', is up to his eyes in debt and is being forced by his father to sign a bond agreeing to renounce his inheritance in favour of his younger brother, Ben. To make matters worse, Valentine fears he has lost the love of his adored Angelica, who happens to be a wealthy heiress.

I wouldn't say that Valentine is the most admirable of heroes. In the first scene when a nurse from 'Twitnam' (Twickenham) comes to the door begging money for one of Valentine's bastard children, his response is 'she might have overlaid the child a fortnight ago if she had had any forecast in her'. While railing against money, Valentine also spends much of the play trying to trick his father into restoring his inheritance even, at one point, feigning a Hamlet-like madness. But Congreve's satirical vision of the power of money – or lack of it – is balanced by human warmth. At the play's climax, when Valentine is gulled into believing that Angelica is about to marry his father, Sir Sampson, he agrees to sign the crucial bond forfeiting his legacy: 'I have been disappointed of my only hope,' says Valentine, 'and he that loses hope may part with anything. I never valued fortune, but as it was subservient to my pleasure; and my only pleasure was to please this lady.' Through his act of renunciation, Valentine gets the girl. Far from being sentimental, this shows the hero has been subjected to a moral test to see whether he prizes love above wealth. It also reminds me of Bonamy Dobrée's observation that Congreve's particular quality is 'an expression of longing to find the world finer than it really is'.

But Congreve's satirical eye is seen in a rich gallery of minor characters who exude the robust vitality you find in Ben Jonson. Best of all is Tattle, a sexual predator who prides himself on his secrecy while bragging of his conquests. It's a role that attracted Charles Laughton – at once 'coy and servile, male yet mincing' – in Guthrie's 1934 Old Vic production and Olivier in Wood's 1965 revival. My chief memory of Olivier is of his outrageous skittishness, his sly glances into the wings as he confided his amours and his bulging calves subtly hinting that there was something fake about Tattle's virility. In a famous moment Olivier tiptoed along a narrow wall like a drunken tightrope walker and, coming to a wide gap, closed his eyes and jumped across with feline delicacy. But what's fascinating is how Olivier, in highlighting Tattle's sexual ambivalence, anticipated modern feminist criticism: Pat Gill in *The Cambridge Companion to English Restoration Theatre* tells us that Tattle's 'comfortable residence in both gender categories makes him a disturbing gender anomaly'. It is something Olivier, and Laughton before him, found out through pure actors' intuition.

Tattle, however, is only one of a number of exuberantly theatrical characters. Sir Sampson is not just the heavy-handed father but a sprightly lecher and Epicurean traveller. His seafaring son Ben talks exclusively in nautical metaphors, so that he tells his prospective bride, the ingenuous Miss Prue, 'I was commanded by father, and if you like of it, mayhap I may steer into your harbor.' Angelica's uncle Foresight is an astrological buffoon who suspects his young wife on the grounds that not only was she born under Gemini but also 'has a mole upon her lip, with a moist palm, and an open liberality on the mount of Venus'. And in Mrs Frail Congreve provides a classic portrait of the calculating adventuress who tells Ben, when she thinks he will come into money, that 'marrying without an estate is like sailing in a ship without ballast'.

In the end one comes back to Hazlitt's praise of Congreve and his argument that 'every sentence is replete with sense and satire, conveyed in the most polished and pointed terms'. Congreve observes the way of his world and reports on its follies, absurdities and excesses with a verbal precision that is not just an aesthetic pleasure but also a moral instrument.

28

The Recruiting Officer

GEORGE FARQUHAR

(1678–1707)

Like Congreve, Farquhar was educated at Trinity College, Dublin. Like Congreve, he was also a young dramatist: indeed Farquhar was tragically dead by the age of twenty-nine. Whatever the superficial resemblances, however, the two men were very different. Congreve was an impeccable stylist; Farquhar was a supreme realist. Congreve's natural territory was London; Farquhar took English comedy out into the provinces, setting *The Recruiting Officer* (1706) in Shrewsbury and *The Beaux' Stratagem* (1707) in Lichfield. While both men were shrewd observers, Farquhar at his best has a radical edge. Leigh Hunt rather loftily wrote of Farquhar that 'he felt the little world too much and the universal too little . . . his genius was entirely social'. But it is that ability to record the supposedly little world of regional England that makes *The Recruiting Officer* a remarkable play, and one that has had its influence on later writers such as Brecht, John Arden and Timberlake Wertenbaker.

Farquhar's own life was short, fraught and jagged. He was born in Derry at a time when it was a stronghold of Northern Protestantism. After graduating from Trinity College, he briefly became a Dublin actor and then moved to London, where his early plays failed, his debts mounted, and he married a penniless woman in the belief that she was an heiress. In 1704, during the War of Spanish Succession, he was rescued by being given a commission as a lieutenant of Grenadiers but, instead of joining Marlborough's troops at Blenheim as he had hoped, he was sent on a recruiting mission to Shrewsbury, which gave him the material for an autobiographical play. It is our good luck that, in the words of Bonamy Dobrée, 'he projected his disappointments in life onto the stage in the form of light-hearted comedy'.

But just how light-hearted is *The Recruiting Officer*? It is certainly brisk, funny and inventive. But what marks it out from other comedies of the period is its nose for corruption and eye for injustice. Consider the opening scene. Captain Plume and Sergeant Kite arrive in Shrewsbury with a simple mission: to muster men by any means possible. And within a few lines Farquhar establishes the unscrupulousness of their tactics. Kite presses money on a couple of credulous locals, Pearmain and Appletree. Plume is shown to have previously sired a bastard on 'Molly at the Castle': both mother and son are to be entered in the lists and Kite given a man's pay for the boy's subsistence. And when Kite announces that his roster of recruits already includes 'the strong man of Kent, the king of the gipsies, a Scotch pedlar, a soundrel attorney and a Welsh parson', Plume hits the roof and orders that the lawyer be discharged on account of his literacy. 'A fellow that can write,' he nervously says, 'can draw petitions.'

This establishes a theme that runs right through the play: that recruitment was a dirty, dishonourable business. In a brilliant scene, which palpably attracted Brecht, Farquhar shows how Captain Plume, having berated and beaten Kite for using dodgy impressment tactics on Pearmain and Appletree, himself ensnares them by playing on their greed and lust for violence.

Later Plume tells the rakish 'Jack Wilful' – not realising that he is addressing Silvia, a local justice's daughter whom he adores –

that sex is a great recruiting stratagem: 'kiss the prettiest country wenches and you are sure of the lustiest fellows'. Even more tellingly, Plume reveals that he doesn't want any gentlemen in his company on the grounds that 'those who know the least obey the best'. And Farquhar rounds off his portrait with a fifth-act courtroom scene where we see how a bent judiciary works hand-in-glove with the army and how a corrupt constable, Falstaff-like, takes bribes to release men from the muster-roll.

William Gaskill, who reclaimed the play for a modern audience with a brilliant production for Olivier's National Theatre company in 1964, got it right when he wrote: 'Farquhar saw the ruthlessness of the officers who were sent to beat up for Marlborough's army. He saw all this accurately but he was not indignant (he was one of the officers)'. And it is true that the play's exposure of military deviousness and judicial malpractice is leavened by Farquhar's own complicity in the business. He records what he knows and leaves it to us to draw our conclusions. He also very neatly dovetails the recruiting scenes with the love intrigue. As Irving Wardle observed in reviewing Gaskill's production: 'On the one side it is natural for the gallants to pursue their girls as if conducting a military campaign and on the other it is equally natural for them to ensnare their recruits with the tactics of seduction'. This interweaving of the two strands reaches its climax – or possibly doesn't – in the hilarious morning-after-the-night-before scene where the rural Rose can't hide her disappointment at having slept with the supposedly male Silvia. 'I can give you as many fine things as the captain can,' claimed Maggie Smith as Gaskill's breeches-clad heroine. A visibly dejected, sex-denied Lynn Redgrave brought the house down with her lugubrious 'But you can't, I'm sure.'

Farquhar may not have the satirical sting of Jonson or the stylistic suppleness of Congreve. But he belongs in the great line of English comedy because he sets down what he knows in bright, vivid colours. The play, which drew the town throughout the eighteenth century, has also had an astonishingly long afterlife. Brecht, transferring the action to the American War of Independence, heightened its social criticism in *Trumpets and Drums*. John Arden used the image of a group of recruiting redcoats arriving in a country town in *Serjeant Musgrave's Dance*. And Timberlake Wertenbaker's *Our Country's Good* is a brilliant hymn to the redemptive power of theatre that artfully capitalises on the fact that Farquhar's comedy, performed by naval officers and transported convicts, was the first play to be presented on Australian soil in 1789. But you only have to look at modern TV army-recruitment commercials – with their false promise of a life of Boys' Own adventure untarnished by violent death and Post Combat Stress Fatigue – to see why Farquhar's play has lost none of its potency in today's world.

29

The Game of Love and Chance

MARIVAUX
(1688–1763)

Can Marivaux – or, to give him his full name, Pierre Carlet de Chamblain de Marivaux – survive translation? It's a moot point. His supposedly precious, mannered dialogue was dismissed by unfriendly contemporaries as 'marivaudage' and Voltaire famously lampooned his style as 'the art of weighing flies' eggs on scales made from a spider's web'. A more charitable critic pointed out that in Marivaux 'language is no longer the sign of the action, it becomes its substance'. Yet, given sufficient tact and delicacy, the plays can be rendered in English, as Timberlake Wertenbaker skilfully proved with a trio she translated for Shared Experience in the 1980s. Against that one has to say that Neil Bartlett overlaid this exquisite play, *Le Jeu de l'amour et du hazard*, with a veneer of camp when he updated it from 1730 to the 1930s in a production at the Cottesloe in 1993. Even a much better production of the same translation at Salisbury Playhouse in 2012 couldn't disguise the superfluity of the approach.

Yet it is eminently worth perservering with Marivaux in English for a number of reasons: the perfect symmetry of his plays; their understanding of human psychology; and their acute awareness that love is almost impossible without the infliction or the reception of pain. In many ways, Marivaux's plays seem strangely modern, which is why since the 1970s they have been in constant revival in France. They reject the Greek classical models. The characters have none of the monomaniac obsessiveness you find in Molière. And there is something deliciously Mozartian about the way Marivaux combines formal perfection with understanding of the human heart.

You certainly see that in *The Game of Love and Chance*, for which I've relied on John Walters's translation. It starts with a neat set of parallel disguises. Silvia is informed by her father that a marriage has been arranged with a man called Dorante: to give herself time to examine her prospective husband, Silvia decides to swap places with her maid, Lisette. What Silvia doesn't realise – although both her father and brother do – is that Dorante also plans to change roles with his valet, Harlequin. So both Silvia and Dorante, instantly attracted to each other, find themselves falling for people they assume to be social inferiors. Equally Lisette and Harlequin, while secretly relishing their social promotion, are instantly drawn to the other's lack of affectation and downright sexiness.

At first glance, Marivaux's play may seem like a snobbish endorsement of the status quo: a reminder that class will out. And it is true that Marivaux observes eighteenth-century decorum by not showing too much interaction between the social opposites. Harlequin has a faint fancy for Silvia, whom he assumes to be the chambermaid, but it never goes much further than that. We also never see Dorante alone with Lisette, who is meant to be his future bride. What Marivaux focuses on is the turbulent battle between reason and passion: in particular, Silvia's distress at the conflict between her social and amatory instincts and her determination to test to the very limits the man who has so poleaxed her. This is not just a play about status. It's also about the sado-masochism of love.

Silvia, in fact, is a genuinely complex character. She begins with a salvo against husbands in general for putting on a polite mask for the world and saving their savagery for their wives. Having adopted a mask of her own, she then gets furious with her maid, Lisette, when the latter starts questioning Dorante's integrity: 'I'm still shaking from what I heard her say,' cries Silvia. 'How insolently servants treat us in their minds.' Silvia, the upstairs lady, is also baffled and bewildered by her fixation with the downstairs male. But the real moment of truth comes when Dorante reveals his true identity. Instead of rushing into his arms, Silvia decides to let the charade continue. For her the real test of Dorante will be whether he still loves her in spite of her supposed inferiority. 'I think his soul is in torment and I pity his suffering,' says Silvia's brother of Dorante. 'What it is costing him to make up his mind only makes him more estimable in my eyes,' replies Silvia. In other words, Silvia has suffered. So she decides to leave Dorante on the rack. For a supposedly decorous dramatist whose plays embody the picturesque harmony of a Watteau canvas, Marivaux shows a sharp awareness of romantic agony.

In short, he's much tougher than he looks. I'm not sure that even Silvia's father, Monsieur Orgon, is quite the benign patriarch he seems: it is he who allows this dual deception to go on much longer than it needs. And Marivaux's fascination with social experiments is seen at its fullest in a later play, *La Dispute* (1744). It concerns the idea of four children, two girls and two boys, being brought up in isolation until adulthood in order to discover which of the sexes is more fickle. It can seem a perfectly playful and harmless device. But the late, great Patrice Chereau did a production for the Théâtre National Populaire in 1976 that turned Marivaux into a contemporary of the Marquis de Sade, and that suggested the play was more a study in dubious eugenics than a piece of speculative humanism.

That, I think, is pushing things too far. But at least Chereau's production – like an earlier one by Roger Planchon for the TNP of *La Seconde Surprise de l'amour* that unequivocally placed a bed centre stage – helped to rescue Marivaux from decorative prettiness and the notion that he is all fancy style and little substance. He is rich and complicated. His plays are about sex, class and money, show that servants have an instinctive passion denied to their employers and prove that, in love, there's no gain without pain. Marivaux's comedies may look like delicate minuets, but there is always a trace of blood on the parquet.

30

The Servant of Two Masters

CARLO GOLDONI

(1707–93)

Where does one start? It all begins in 1746 with Goldoni's *Il servitore di due padroni*, which takes the stock characters and situations of commedia dell'arte and invests them with a new psychological truth. The Milanese maestro Giorgio Strehler then came up with a famous post-war production which the Piccolo Teatro endlessly toured with Ferruccio Soleri as a legendary Arlecchino. Various attempts have since been made to adapt Goldoni's original to suit British tastes. The worst I remember is a 1969 West End revival that starred Tommy Steele acting in a style I dubbed 'commedia dell hearty'. Lee Hall created a new, highly successful version for the Young Vic and the RSC in 1999 which restored something of Goldoni's realism. And then in 2011 came Richard Bean's *One Man, Two Guvnors*, which took Goldoni's basic plot, updated it to 1963 and gave the National Theatre one of its most durable comic hits.

Whichever version you opt for there are certain constants. You have a servant – Truffaldino in the original – who finds himself contracted to two masters: one is a woman disguised as her dead brother, the other is the brother's killer, with whom the woman herself is passionately in love. Unwittingly the two lovers find themselves staying at the same inn, and Truffaldino is obliged to serve them two separate meals in two different rooms at the same time. At the lovers' climactic reunion, the perpetually hungry and materialistic Truffaldino finally gains – like Papageno in Mozart's *The Magic Flute* half a century later – a partner of his own.

We know – because all the textbooks tell us so – that Goldoni took a traditional form and gave it new truth. It's also an established fact that the original commedia companies, because they were touring Italian states that all had different dialects, were obliged to create a highly visual theatre that relied heavily on improvisation. Goldoni knew all that and used it. But as a realist at heart, he gave a tired form fresh life. *The Servant of Two Masters* hinges on a murder. It shows the victim's sister, with the insouciance of a Rosalind or Imogen, becoming a proactive adventurer in male attire. And the whole plot is pervaded with a sense of loss and longing. As Lee Hall said of the play: 'It is impossible to realize its true value as a comedy without exploring its melancholy and its melancholy is not sufficient meat without the sauce of commedia.'

That delicate balance was famously achieved in the Strehler production. The great Soleri, sporting the black half-mask of the Venetian commedia, was athletically astonishing in the dinner scene, where he would hurtle from one side of the stage to the other, catching airborne items of food with his left hand and dispatching them again with his right. But there was a touch of Buster Keaton-like gravity about the moment where, as he tried to swat an imaginary fly, his head would busily rotate only to find the fly eluding him just as he was about to pounce. Even as we laughed Soleri would stare at us in silent reproof before inviting the scoffers in the gallery to come and try for themselves.

If the Strehler production, played on a fit-up stage with footlight candles and a traverse curtain, was as close as the modern world can get to Goldoni's original, Lee Hall came up with a very persuasive English facsimile. He never let us forget that Truffaldino is driven by a desperate desire for grub and money. I remember Jason Watkins, in a dazzling performance, going through agonies trying not to swallow the fragments of bread with which he was sealing an opened letter. Even in the double-meal scene Truffaldino's hunger became more important than circus acrobatics: at one point Watkins immersed his face in a bowl of pasta only to emerge with what looked like a severe skin rash.

But Goldoni was one of theatre's pioneering realists as well as a comic master. You see this after Truffaldino has mixed up the trunks of his two 'masters' – Beatrice and Florindo in Hall's version – leading each to presume that the other is dead. The situation is a cunning contrivance: the emotional consequences are devastating. The male-attired Beatrice, in particular, is driven to suicidal despair. 'It was torture enough to lose a brother,' she cries, 'but now a husband too? If I am the cause of this, let heaven tear me limb from limb and rip my heart out of my body as it is useless to me now.' This is authentic grief of a kind that transcends commedia dell'arte. Like Marivaux, Goldoni also suggests that servants have a grasp of life's realities that often eludes their masters. Upstairs, people suffer the agonies and ecstasies of love. Downstairs, the needs are sharper and the language cruder. Smeraldina, an earthy servant told at one point by a male superior that all women are hysterics, rounds on her accuser with a cry of 'Listen, the only reason we get all this stick is because we haven't got a dick.'

Goldoni, however, is an obliging writer in that his play is capable of endless adaptation. A work that starts as revivified commedia winds up in One Man, Two Guvnors as rollicking farce. Richard Bean wittily shifts the action from Venice to Brighton – a town that, as Keith Waterhouse said, 'always looks as if it is helping police with their enquiries' – and to a time, 1963, when the air was filled with sexual promise. Truffaldino also turns into

Francis Henshall, a failed skiffle-player who finds himself working simultaneously for a snooty toff and his transvestite lover. There wasn't much trace of Goldoni's underlying melancholy in Bean's version. But the comedy was, if anything, even funnier, with verbal jokes supplementing the visual. At one point a cynical gangster announced that 'love passes through marriage quicker than shit through a small dog', and when the hero, originally played by James Corden, was asked whether he preferred eating or making love, his features contracted into a puzzled frown as he replied 'Tough one that, innit?' But the masterstroke of both Bean's script and Nicholas Hytner's production was to add to the dinner scene an octogenarian waiter whose palsied hand quivered as he clutched a tureen of soup and who revealed an amazing capacity to fall backwards down stairs and bounce back like a rubber ball.

In the end, however, it all comes back to Goldoni: a would-be tragedian, a sometime lawyer and a writer who realised that comedy, at its best, bursts with contradictions. For over two and a half centuries audiences have been roaring at the predicament of a servant working simultaneously for two masters. At the same time Goldoni recognises, in more serious vein, the power of economic imperatives over human action: Beatrice, for instance, raises enough money in Venice to pay the fines her lover may incur for the murder he committed in Turin. This is proof that Goldoni was a realist who was among the first in world drama to chart a decisive and long-lasting shift from aristocratic to bourgeois values.

31

La Triologia della Villegiatura

CARLO GOLDONI

(1707–93)

I've opted for the Italian title: the English equivalent, *Trilogy on Holidays in the Country*, sounds too banal. But this is one of the true masterworks of modern theatre. We saw how in *The Servant of Two Masters* (1746) Goldoni purged commedia of much of its crudity and gave it a new realism. In this trilogy, written in Venice in 1761, Goldoni observes middle-class life with a wit, perception and sense of heartbreak that shows him to be a precursor of Chekhov. Shortly after writing these plays, Goldoni left his native Venice to live in Paris, where he was to die a pauper in 1793. But he was not unappreciated by the French. Voltaire wrote to him 'Here is an honest and good man who has purified the Italian stage, who conceives with imagination and writes with wisdom. You have delivered your country from the clutches of Harlequin. I would like to call your comedies Italy liberated from the Goths.'

I first became aware of *Villegiatura* when I attended the 200th anniversary celebrations of the Vienna Burgtheater in 1976. The highlight, for me, was seeing Giorgio Strehler's production of the Goldoni trilogy. I was stunned by the physical beauty of the staging: coffee, cards, music and flirtation on elegant balustrades in a gathering twilight. But it was the emotional desperation and Goldoni's awareness that a man, or woman, can be both tragic and a buffoon at the same time that instantly put me in mind of Chekhov. Back in London Ken Tynan, as the National's Literary Manager, told me that the trilogy was high on his wish-list of plays for the company to present. The Glasgow Citz and the Lyric Hammersmith did shredded versions in the meantime, but it was 1987 before Mike Alfreds staged his own translation, *Countrymania*, in a five-hour production in the Olivier. It didn't have Strehler's visual magic but it told you this was a landmark in world theatre: the starting point for the realistic prose drama that was to come to fruition in the nineteenth century. There were also superb performances from Mark Rylance as the distraught Leonardo, Siân Thomas as his fetishistically fashion-conscious sister Vittoria and Philip Voss as the bumptious freeloader Ferdinando. But I'd almost given up hope of seeing the plays again until I chanced upon a show called *There and Back* at RADA in the summer of 2014. This was Edward Kemp's version of the second and third parts of the trilogy (I'd missed the first part, called *Mad to Go*), directed by Simona Gonella, who had briefly worked under Strehler at the Piccolo Teatro in Milan. Her production updated Goldoni's trilogy to the 1980s, yet, even if not faithful to the letter, it was true to its spirit of anguished elegance.

The trilogy began from Goldoni's observation of the country houses on the banks of the Brenta in northern Italy. 'In former times,' he wrote, 'our ancestors frequented these spots for the purpose of collecting their revenue while their descendants go there merely to spend theirs.' That establishes a key theme of the trilogy: money. We see a group of Livorno citizens planning their annual retreat to the country like a military campaign and returning with hearts broken, tempers ruffled and pockets significantly emptied.

Each section of the trilogy also has its distinct tone. In the first part, *Country Fever* – to adopt Mike Alfreds' title – there is a mad frenzy as people plan their summer retreat to Montenero much as Jane Austen characters might organise a trip to Bath. And who travels with whom becomes a major issue. The real problem is that the debt-ridden and pleasure-loving Leonardo is insanely jealous that Giacinta, on whose dowry he hopes to get his hands, is planning to share a carriage with his detested rival, Guglielmo.

In the second play, *Country Hazards*, the summer holiday becomes a source of rancid tension. On one level, it's all coffee, cards and gaiety. But Leonardo anxiously fumes at Giacinta's waywardness. She, meanwhile, falls hopelessly in love with Guglielmo. He, in turn, is promised to Leonardo's ratty sister, Vittoria. Yet another character, Ferdinando, sets out to fleece an elderly maiden aunt with merciless rapacity. Among the parasitic hangers-on, the hard-up Constanza sees her niece being pursued by a total booby. Under the surface elegance lies a world of greed, temper and heartbreak.

But it is in the third play, *Country Harvest*, that we grasp the elegant savagery of Goldoni's rueful satire. We are back once more in Livorno and, as in traditional comedy, the play ends in multiple marriages. Of the five pairings, however, only one looks remotely happy. The bankrupt Leonardo and the coquetteish Giacinta are joined together more by financial necessity than love and face the prospect of running a pasta factory in Genoa. The bitchy Vittoria is teamed up with the morose Guglielmo. The fluttery Ferdinando reluctantly accepts the role of toy-boy to the elderly aunt. Costanza's niece is hitched to a blinking idiot. It is only the servants, as so often in Goldoni wilier than their masters and mistresses, who look to have a hope in hell: it is rather as if, at the end of *As You Like It*, Touchstone and Audrey were the sole emblems of future happiness.

This is something new in comedy: an awareness that marriage is dictated more by economics than by emotion. But I would pin down two moments, both from the final play, that reveal Goldoni's genius. In one Giacinta tries to convince herself that she can overcome her obsession with Guglielmo by force of reason and by opening the brain-cells 'containing duty, honesty and reputation': no sooner has she done so than she goes weak at the knees on hearing he is at the door.

The other supreme moment comes at the climax, when Ferdinando reads out in public a letter from the maiden aunt, Sabina, in which she reveals her emotional desperation: 'since your departure, I have not eaten, I have not drunk, I have not slept, I scarcely recognise my own reflection'. The whole company laughs uproariously at the old woman's pathetic dependence while failing to acknowledge that they themselves are all heading to the arctic hell of a loveless marriage.

But Goldoni has one more twist of the knife in store. We ourselves have found guilty amusement in the sight of so many mismatched couples bound together by social convention or potential bankruptcy. At the end, however, Giacinta (Sylvestra le Touzel in Mike Alfreds' production) turns to us and says, 'If we have given you occasion to laugh at the poor behaviour of others, go home comforted by your own prudence, your own moderation, your own well-regulated lives.'

This is lethally sardonic mockery; for what Goldoni, a supremely unsentimental realist, has done is hold a mirror up to the middle classes and show us our own capacity for muddle, mess and self-wounding compromise.

32

She Stoops to Conquer

OLIVER GOLDSMITH
(*c.*1730–74)

Mistaken identity lies at the root of much comedy. A is mistaken for B, and complications ensue. But could anyone really confuse a private house for a public inn, as happens in this imperishable comedy? Goldsmith always claimed it could and that his play, which enjoyed an unexpected Covent Garden triumph in 1773, was based on a true incident in his childhood.

He was making his way home on horseback from his Irish secondary school in Edgeworthstown to the family manse in Lissoy. Taking his time, he found himself at nightfall in Ardagh and asked a local to direct him to 'the best house in the village'. With a certain Irish whimsy, a wag sent him to the residence of the squire, a Mr Featherstone, who was unperturbed when the schoolboy summoned up wine and victuals and invited his hosts to join him for dinner. Only the next morning, when the young Noll asked for the bill, did he discover his mistake.

If you think this could happen only in eighteenth-century Ireland, you are wrong. A few years ago an American friend took a stroll with my wife along the towpath at Chiswick and they dropped in at a riverside establishment whose front door was open and from whose parlor emerged the sound of merry laughter. Seeing the half-timbered interior and wine and beer being dispensed to a large party of people, our American guest assumed she was in a peculiarly informal English pub. Only later did she realise, to her acute embarrassment, that she was in a private home.

So Goldsmith's comedy, in which Marlow and Hastings are led by the mischievous Tony Lumpkin to mistake Mr Hardcastle's house for an inn, is not wholly implausible. But Goldsmith, who subtitled his play 'The Mistakes of a Night', builds on that simple deception to create a series of dazzlingly escalating misunderstandings. You could call it a one-joke play except that Goldsmith, who was determined to provoke mountains of laughter in audiences drenched in the warm bath of sentimental comedy, provides endless variations on his main theme. Like all good comedy, his play is about the multiplication of misfortune.

For a start, Marlow is kept in the dark until the last possible moment. In contrast, his friend Hastings quickly learns from his lover, Constance, that they are really in Hardcastle's house. Hastings's deception, however, rebounds brilliantly when he entrusts to Marlow the jewels stolen from Mrs Hardcastle to fund his own romantic elopement with Constance. But, believing he is still in an inn, Marlow immediately hands the jewels back to their rightful owner for safe keeping.

That same circularity is seen in the last act, when even topography acquires a dizzying unreliability. Determined that Constance should marry her son Tony, Mrs Hardcastle decides to whisk the girl off to a remote rural aunt far away from the predatory Hastings. But Tony, anxious for his own reasons that the lovers should marry, takes his mother and Constance on a nightmarish, forty-mile journey round the houses until they end up 'with a circumbendibus' in the horsepond at the bottom of the Hardcastle garden. Nothing in Goldsmith's world is quite what it seems. A home can be mistaken for an inn. Mrs Hardcastle believes her husband, emerging out of their own darkened garden, to be a murderous highwayman.

It seems to be a comedy of pure plot; yet there is also psychological acuity under the mathematical ingenuity. This is seen most clearly in the character of Marlow, who is painted as a palpable victim of the English class system. His dilemma is that he is a tongue-tied wreck amongst women of his own class but brimming with sexual bravura with a barmaid or college bedmaker. He himself expresses his dilemma with painful clarity:

> MARLOW: My life has been chiefly spent in a college or
> an inn, in seclusion from that lovely part of the creation
> that chiefly teach men confidence. I don't know that I was
> ever familiarly acquainted with a single modest woman
> except my mother. But among females of another class
> you know
> HASTINGS: Ay, among them you are impudent enough of all
> conscience.

Marlow himself rightly calls this 'the English malady': a paralysing fear, resulting from a monastic education, of women of his own class and an ability to be at ease only with social inferiors whom he can bully, dominate or treat as purchasable commodities. It took an observant Irishman to pin down the damage done to the English male psyche by a punitive educational system.

But it's part of Goldsmith's genius to make theatrical capital out of his perception. Marlow's duality becomes, in fact, a vital part of the play's misunderstandings. He treats Hardcastle, apparently a rural innkeeper, with arrogant condescension. Confronted by Kate Hardcastle, however, he is all timorous bashfulness. The result? When father and daughter compare notes, they seem to be talking of two different people. To Hardcastle, Marlow seems 'a bouncy, swaggering puppy'.

MISS HARDCASTLE: Surprising! He met me with a respectful
    bow, a stammering voice and a look fixed on the ground.
HARDCASTLE: He met me with a loud voice, a lordly air and a
    familiarity that made my blood freeze again.

And there is further evidence of Marlow's split personality when Kate accosts him in the guise of a household drudge. Marlow the psychological wreck turns into a brazen lech who, within seconds, is asking to taste the nectar of Kate's lips. Not only that. He is soon bragging of his sexual exploits at a louche London club attended by the likes of Mrs Mantrap, Lady Betty Blackleg, the Countess of Sligo, Mrs Langhorns and old Miss Biddy Buckskin. That lust for the chase came out nicely in Jamie Lloyd's boisterous 2012 revival at the National Theatre, where Harry Hadden-Paton's Marlow pawed the ground like an impatient stallion while Katherine Kelly's Kate archly reared her rump in readiness for goodness knows what.

But that was merely the latest in a long line of revivals of a play that has always captivated audiences for its inventiveness, humanity and warmth. Folly is punished in that Mrs Hardcastle gets her just deserts for spoiling her son Tony. But at the end Marlow seems miraculously cured of his sexual hang-ups, Hastings has his beloved Constance, and Hardcastle proposes to invite 'the poor of the parish' to supper.

Yet two weeks before the play opened in March 1773 Dr Johnson wrote in a letter to an American cleric that 'Dr Goldsmith has a new comedy in rehearsal at Covent Garden to which the manager predicts ill success.' George Colman, the playwright impresario who ran Covent Garden, had in fact dithered over putting the play on, given it no new sets or costumes, allowed his actors to refuse parts and chosen an unpropitious time for the première. Above all, Goldsmith's play seemed to fly in the face of popular taste, which at that time demanded sentimental comedy. In fact, the permanently penurious author, depending on the play's success, was so nervous that he walked apprehensively round St James's Park on the first night. Hastening back in time for the curtain-calls, Goldsmith joined Colman in the wings and asked if he had just heard some hissing. 'Pshaw!' replied Colman. 'Don't be fearful of squibs when we have been sitting almost these two hours upon a barrel of gunpowder.' It is one that has kept exploding for well over two and a half centuries.

33

The School for Scandal

RICHARD BRINSLEY SHERIDAN
(1751–1816)

Another great comedy by another great Irishman. Like Goldsmith, Sheridan was Dublin born. Like Goldsmith, he used laughter to satirise sentiment. But there were also considerable differences. Garrick said of Goldsmith that 'he wrote like an angel but talked like poor Poll'. Sheridan, on the other hand, devoted the bulk of his life to politics, once spoke for five hours in the Commons on the impeachment of Warren Hastings and in 1809, as he stoically watched the burning of Drury Lane Theatre, of which he was manager, had the wit to remark, 'A man may surely take a glass of wine by his own fireside.'

Sheridan's playwriting career blazed like a comet but was virtually abandoned by the time he was thirty. He left us, however, two exhilarating comedies which made direct use of his own experience. In the early 1770s Sheridan left Bath, where his family was based, to elope with a beautiful singer, Eliza Linley, on whose behalf he fought two duels with an overwrought suitor. The duels provided him with material for his first successful play, *The Rivals* (1775), which also bequeathed us the immortally word-mangling Mrs Malaprop. The hysterical rumour-mongering that followed the escapade with Eliza also fed into *The School for Scandal*, which was first seen at Drury Lane on 8 May 1777 and which has scarcely been off the stage since. In a lifetime of theatregoing I recall a host of cherishable revivals. My first was a star-studded Haymarket affair in 1962 with Ralph Richardson, Anna Massey and John Neville. Ten years later Jonathan Miller directed a characteristically revisionist production, steeped in scruffy-wigged Hogarthian squalor, for Olivier's National Theatre company at the Old Vic. And in 1983 the play was back at the Haymarket in a John Barton production spearheaded by Donald Sinden as a robust Sir Peter Teazle, who treated the audience as his intimate confidants.

So what is the secret of the play's success? It depends on the timeless comedy of an elderly man, Sir Peter, fractiously married to a youthful bride in the sparkish figure of Lady Teazle. It shows the unmasking of an unctuous hypocrite, Joseph Surface, and the corresponding confirmation of the good nature of his younger brother, Charles. And in the college of scandal-mongers, led by Lady Sneerwell, Snake, Sir Benjamin Backbite and Crabtree, Sheridan shows how all societies breed malicious tittle-tattle. It is a big mistake, however, as a misconceived production by Deborah Warner at the Barbican in 2012 proved, to update the play to our own era of 'celebrity culture'. It needs no such modernising and has, in fact, two important lessons to teach us about the nature of period comedy.

The first is that a play may simultaneously be topical and timeless. And I should admit straight away that I am deeply indebted to Fintan O'Toole for opening my eyes in his masterly biography of Sheridan, *A Traitor's Kiss*, to the political resonances of *The School for Scandal*. O'Toole brilliantly makes the point that Sheridan's play shows how the cult of sensibility – 'the capacity for intense and authentic feeling' – which had begun in the writing of Rousseau and Diderot as part of the Enlightenment critique of the *ancien régime* had dwindled into a front for prudery and hypocrisy. Sir Peter Teazle, who is proved to be wrong about most things, roundly declares, 'there is nothing in the world so noble as a man of sentiment!' But much of the action of the play is concerned with exposing the bogus sentiments of Joseph Surface, who professes altruistic charity but who is driven by self-seeking cupidity.

Sheridan, however, wasn't just dealing with the degradation of a philosophical idea: the decline of sensibility into hypocritical sentiment. Only after reading O'Toole did I grasp that Drury Lane audiences would have seen the play as a topical satire. The opposition of Joseph and Charles Surface was clearly intended to reflect the contest between Benjamin Hopkins and John Wilkes for the office of Chamberlain of the City of London. Hopkins was a respected banker and merchant who was accused of being a usurer and whose ostentatious morality was a front for fraudulence. Wilkes, on the other hand, was a dissolute rake and heavy drinker but also a constant champion of freedom and open supporter of the American Revolution. The parallels between the Surface brothers and Hopkins and Wilkes were sufficiently clear for the play almost to be refused a licence by the state censor. Yet the play's explosive political immediacy in no way prevents Joseph and Charles being seen as psychological archetypes.

Sheridan's play not only shows how comedy can exist in two dimensions at once, it also yields a broader lesson based on the famous 'screen scene'. The situation is that Joseph entices Lady Teazle to visit his library in order to seduce her. When her husband turns up, Joseph hides Lady T behind a screen and later pretends to Sir Peter that he is concealing 'a little French milliner'. With the equally unexpected arrival of Charles Surface, Sir Peter is persuaded to hide in the closet. And when Joseph is briefly called away, Sir Peter and Charles converge and, at the latter's insistence, throw down the screen, leading to the famous antiphonal lines:

CHARLES: Lady Teazle, by all that's wonderful!
SIR PETER: Lady Teazle, by all that's damnable!

There are many other aspects to this beautifully plotted imbroglio. It is only while she is hiding, for instance, that Lady Teazle learns of her husband's intention to give her a generous financial settlement, something that paves the way to their reconciliation. But the broader theatrical lesson of the scene was provided in the refutation of an argument by a Sheridan commentator, Mrs Oliphant. She bizarrely claimed that the scene would have been much better if we'd been as surprised as the participants that it was Lady Teazle behind the screen.

An American professor, Brander Matthews, effectively dismissed this absurd proposition by saying, 'The playgoer's interest is really not so much as to what is to happen as the way in which this event is going to affect the characters involved.' William Archer, in his 1938 book *Play-Making*, takes the argument a stage further by suggesting that all drama depends on a degree of omniscience. 'Curiosity,' claims Archer, 'is the accidental relish of a single night; whereas the essential and abiding pleasure of the theatre lies in foreknowledge. In relation to the characters in the drama, the audience are as gods, looking before and after.'

In a nutshell, that is why Agatha Christie's *The Mousetrap* is eminently forgettable and Shakespeare's *Hamlet* is not. The idea of foreknowledge is especially applicable to comedy. To take a classic example, the fun in *The Comedy of Errors* depends precisely on our being able to identify which twin is which: get one set of actors to play the Antipholuses and the Dromios, as I've seen done, and the audience ends up just as confused as the Ephesian residents. In the twentieth century Brecht also exploited the point made by both Matthews and Archer: that theatre depends less on momentary suspense than on seeing how characters are affected by a given situation.

I have overlooked many other aspects of Sheridan's play such as its stylistic felicity and mastery of intricate detail. The two are nicely joined in a passage where one of the scandal-mongers, Crabtree, describes an imagined pistol duel between Charles Surface and Sir Peter. The latter's shot, we are told, missed, 'but what is very extraordinary, the ball struck against a little bronze Shakespeare that stood over the fireplace, grazed out of the window at a right angle and wounded the postman, who was just coming to the door with a double letter from Northamptonshire'.

There are many lessons to be learned from Sheridan's *School*, but not the least of them is that writing of that texture induces a delight bordering on ecstasy.

34

The Marriage of Figaro

PIERRE-AUGUSTIN CARON DE BEAUMARCHAIS

(1732–99)

Well did it or didn't it? Did Beaumarchais's play help to ignite the French Revolution? Or is it simply a sublimely delightful comedy? It's a complex issue, but there is plenty of evidence that in France in the 1780s it was seen as a potentially explosive work. As Louis XVI himself remarked, with uncanny prophetic insight, 'For this play not to be a danger, the Bastille would have to be torn down first.'

It should be said that Beaumarchais himself was more a libertarian individualist than a downright revolutionary. Born in 1732, he gained fame as a Parisian watchmaker of such skill that he invented a timepiece that was both accurate to the second and small enough to fit inside a signet ring. As a litigious journalist, he successfully pursued a notoriously corrupt Paris magistrate, Goezman, through the courts. And in 1777 he assisted the French government's support of the revolt in Britain's American colonies by organising the shipment of guns and ammunition for 25,000 men.

But it is on his plays, and the operas they inspired, that Beaumarchais's reputation rests. *The Barber of Seville*, first performed in 1775, shows Figaro helping his master, Count

Almaviva, to secure the hand of a beautiful young heiress. *The Marriage of Figaro*, written in 1778 but not publicly performed for another six years, is that rare example of the sequel that both capitalises on and outdistances its source (maybe you have to wait another couple of centuries for Francis Ford Coppola's *The Godfather Part 2* to find a comparable example). By now Figaro is working against, rather than with, Almaviva to deny the master his ancient feudal right to sleep with his own future bride, Suzanne. The opera is sometimes rechristened *Figaro's Wedding*, and, although the play remains a comedy, it is about a nuptial day darkened by the shadow of *droit de seigneur* and threatened infidelities.

The spectacle of an articulate servant outwitting his aristocratic master was obviously fraught with danger. Louis XVI vetoed the play outright when it was first accepted by the Comédie Française in 1781. Beaumarchais retaliated by organising a number of private readings. Finally the play was sanctioned, with suitable cuts, for public performance on 27 April 1784 and was an immediate sensation. Noblemen camped out in artists' dressing rooms on the eve of the première in order to be sure of a seat. The first night was punctuated with spontaneous bursts of applause. And the play was performed an unprecedented sixty-seven times in a period when a twenty-night run was deemed a big success.

But what precisely was it that made the play so potent? The answer is usually thought to reside in Figaro's long climactic speech, which begins with his ringing assertion that the count shall not enjoy Suzanne.

'What,' asks Figaro of the count in John Wood's Penguin Classics translation, 'have you done to deserve such advantages? Put yourself to the trouble of being born – nothing more! For the rest – a very ordinary man! Whereas I, lost among the obscure crowd, have had to deploy more knowledge, more calculation and skill merely to survive than has sufficed to rule all the provinces of Spain for a century! Yet you would measure yourself against me.'

As a justification of the meritocracy in a world of rank and privilege, the speech has obvious incendiary qualities. Yet two things should be remembered. The rest of the speech is an account of Figaro's ramshackle career as playwright, journalist, banker and barber, in which his high spirits have more than compensated for his periodic failures: in short the speech is less a revolutionary manifesto than a hymn to the joys of a carefree existence. While Figaro declares that he is every bit as good as the count, we should also recall that this speech comes in the final act. At this point in the plot, Figaro is being as extensively gulled as Almaviva. The count woos his masked wife in a darkened chestnut grove, believing her to be Suzanne. At the same time Figaro imagines he is being cuckolded by the count on his wedding day. The play is as much about the superiority of women to men as it is about the primacy of the servant over the master.

I'd suggest the play's real subversiveness lies in its preceding scenes, where Almaviva is shown to be an impotent booby: as vain as he is jealous and constantly outwitted not just by Figaro but by Suzanne, the countess and even that randy boy-woman, Cherubin. In the first act the predatory Almaviva is reduced to hiding behind an armchair. In the second act he is made to look as big a chump as the frantic Ford in *The Merry Wives of Windsor* when he invades the countess's dressing room in pursuit of her supposed lover. In the third act he is outwitted by Figaro when he claims, 'The servants in this house take longer to dress than their masters,' to which Figaro replies, 'Because they have no servants to assist them.' In the fourth act the count is shown to have made overtures to his gardener's daughter. In the final act he is not only tricked into seducing his wife but also into handing over the gold intended to compensate for the exercise of a feudal fuck. It is the exposure of Count Almaviva's strutting futility that gives the play its political power.

But did Beaumarchais's play really help overturn the social order? Was it, as Napoleon Bonaparte famously said, 'the Revolution in action'? That's a hyperbolic claim. What the play did, through subversive laughter, was hold up a mirror to society. John Wells, who did a good translation for a so-so Jonathan Miller National Theatre production in 1974, compared Louis XVI, vacillating over liberal reforms that might have led to constitutional monarchy, to Almaviva illicitly trying to re-establish his absolute power. And Thomas Carlyle, in his masterly book *The French Revolution*, while sniffily dismissing Beaumarchais's 'thin, wire-drawn intrigues', also sees the power of a play 'wherein each, as was hinted, which is the grand secret, may see some image of himself, and of his own state and ways'. That is the real point. Beaumarchais may, in his own life, have been a fortune-hunting adventurer and raffish opportunist. But in *The Marriage of Figaro* he wrote a play that undermined the hereditary principle, echoed reformist sentiment and asserted the right of the individual against the constraints of social privilege. Beaumarchais may not actually have fathered the French Revolution but he showed the power of drama to create an intellectual climate in which it became possible.

35

Nathan the Wise

GOTTHOLD EPHRAIM LESSING

(1729–81)

Why is this masterly play so little known in Britain? Maybe because it's German, written in verse and would take over four hours to perform in its full text.

Suitably adapted, however, it's eminently stageable and rivetingly topical. Edward Kemp did a brilliantly lucid prose adaptation which the late Steven Pimlott directed at Chichester's Minerva in 2003 and which Anthony Clark revived at Hampstead Theatre in 2005. On each occasion I felt I had encountered a great play that eloquently argued the case for religious tolerance.

But who exactly was Lessing? He was the son of a Lutheran pastor, a leading figure in the Enlightenment and a mix of critic, literary manager and playwright. He was a passionate champion, and translator, of Shakespeare; worked with the Hamburg National Theatre 1767–8, which led him to write an influential theoretical volume called *Hamburg Dramaturgy*; and wrote a number of fine plays. *Miss Sara Sampson* (1755) owes much to the English Sentimentalist tradition, and *Minna von Barnhelm* (1767) echoes Farquhar's *The Beaux' Stratagem*. But it is on *Nathan the Wise*, written in 1779 but not performed until after his death, that Lessing's reputation rests. Eric Bentley makes a good point when he says, echoing Georg Lukács, that before the eighteenth century drama arose naturally out of the theatre. It is only towards the end of the century with men like Lessing and Schiller – and Bentley might have added Beaumarchais – that the 'play of ideas' begins to take root.

Nathan the Wise is emphatically a play of ideas, one that challenges prevailing Germanic anti-Semitism and puts the case for Christianity, Judaism and Islam to peacefully co-exist. It may sound slightly preachy or propagandist. But behind its plea for mutual tolerance lies a passionate belief in the quest for truth and a critique of Christianity as practised in the late eighteenth century.

Lessing, for obvious reasons of censorship, could not place his play in contemporary Germany. Instead his setting is Jerusalem in 1192. An uneasy truce exists between the Muslim forces of Saladin and the Western Crusaders. The focus, however, is on Nathan, a rich, wise Jew who, at the start of the play, returns from a trip to Babylon to find that his house has suffered a fire and that his supposed daughter, Rachel, has been rescued from the blaze by a Christian Knight Templar. The play pivots on a crucial meeting between Nathan and Saladin. Nathan presumes the subject will be a request for money. In fact Saladin wants to know which, out of Islam, Judaism and Christianity, is the 'true religion'.

Nathan answers with a parable. He tells the story of a family which possessed the Ring of Truth that had the power to make its owner loved by all men. The ring eventually fell into the hands of a father who loved his three sons equally and gave each of them a ring without revealing which was the genuine article. The three sons quarrelled and took their case to a judge, who declared that each son must have faith that his ring was the true one. 'Vie with each other,' he tells them in Nathan's version of the story, 'to prove the power of your ring through gentleness, tolerance, charity and a deep humility before the love of God.' The logic of Nathan's story is not that all three rings – or all three faiths – have an equally good pedigree but that the origin of each may be equally uncertain. Better, therefore, to judge by results rather than by origins.

That is easily said. But the greatness of Lessing's play derives from the way it shows the practical problems of achieving the prescribed tolerance. Saladin is shown as a beneficent ruler who frees the Knight Templar from captivity. Nathan is a humane figure who withstands the insults heaped upon his race. The problem lies with the Christians. The Knight Templar, having instinctively rescued Rachel from burning, avoids contact with Nathan himself, proclaiming, 'a Jew's a Jew'. Later he tells Saladin that we never lose the superstitions of our race: 'We drink them in with our mother's milk and we may mock them but they are bred into our bones.' To make matters worse, when it is discovered that Nathan has, out of charity and goodness of heart, adopted Rebecca and reared her as his own daughter, the Catholic Patriarch firmly declares: 'A Jew found guilty of leading a Christian into apostasy must be burnt at the stake.' The character of Daya, who acted as Rebecca's surrogate mother, is even described as 'the kind of Christian who believes she alone knows the true path'.

Lessing knew a good deal about Christian rigidity and Germanic anti-Semitism. As Edward Kemp points out, Lessing's early play *The Jews* was attacked for its creation of an upright, noble hero. Lessing's good friend Moses Mendelssohn (grandfather of the composer) was known as the 'German Socrates' but had to enter Berlin through the Rosenthal Gate, designated for Jews and cattle. But, having shown the Christians in such a bad light, Lessing faced the problem of how to end a play that was a plea for tolerance. He did it through a conclusion that you could take as either an echo of late-Shakespearean romance or a cunning piece of dramatic algebra: Rebecca and the Knight Templar prove to be long-separated siblings and Saladin their uncle. It looks suspiciously neat, but at least it ends the play on a note of concord.

Lessing's play was, of course, too much for the Nazis, who banned it in 1933 but today it is played throughout Germany. It was also very moving to see it staged in Britain in 2003, when the West was once more involved in a Middle East crusade and when Islamophobia was in danger of becoming as ingrained as our residual anti-Semitism. I still remember, from Pimlott's production, the spiritual poise of Michael Feast as Nathan, the massive dignity of Jeffery Kissoon as Saladin and the intemperate callowness of Geoffrey Streatfeild as the Christian knight. But what struck me most was the cleansing quality and permanent topicality of a play that attacks prejudice, endorses our common humanity and suggests no religion has a monopoly on wisdom.

36

Don Carlos

FRIEDRICH SCHILLER

(1759–1805)

In the unlikely event of a Hollywood movie being made of Schiller's play, you can easily imagine the posters. 'Love. Passion. Power. An Epic Study of the Spanish Golden Age,' they might proclaim. Or perhaps 'He Risked His Life for an Illicit Love. He was . . . Don Carlos.' And the posters might have a point. There is something inordinate, melodramatic and romantic about Schiller's play, qualities that Verdi was quick to spot in one of the grandest of grand operas composed in the late 1860s. But this is a play of ideas as well as of grand passions and high theatricality. Written over a long period from 1782 to 1787, during which, as Schiller himself said, 'a great deal had changed in myself', it even switches its prime focus as it progresses.

As a five-act tragedy in blank verse, it was for a long time greeted by the British theatre with the studied indifference reserved for major European drama. But in 1987 Nicholas Hytner directed an exciting version by James Maxwell for the Royal Exchange, Manchester, dominated by Ian McDiarmid's brutally solitary Philip II. The Glasgow Citizens came up with a fuller version of the text, translated by Robert David MacDonald, for a Schiller–Verdi season at the 1995 Edinburgh Festival. But the ultimate reclamation came when Michael Grandage, who'd played the title role in Hytner's production, made it the final show of his Sheffield Crucible tenure in 2004. A potential theatre-emptier turned into a massive box-office hit that transferred to London in 2005. Audiences may have been drawn by Derek Jacobi's Lear-like Philip II. What they saw was a spellbinding production which, with its swinging thurible and high-barred windows, evoked the idea of Spain as a religious prison but which also reflected Schiller's intersection of private and public passions.

On one level, the play seems high romantic drama about lost love and heroic self-sacrifice. Don Carlos, son of Philip II of Spain, nurses a none-too-secret passion for his stepmother, Elizabeth of Valois. Various intrigues ensue, mostly involving Princess Eboli, a lady-in-waiting, who steals from the queen the letters which Carlos had written to Elizabeth before her marriage and shows them to the king. Eventually Carlos is arrested until a last attempt is made to save him by his friend the Marquis of Posa, who nobly but vainly tries to draw suspicion to himself.

Interwoven with the love tragedy is the struggle of the Netherlands to free themselves from the Spanish imperial yoke. It is a belief in this cause, as well as an implicitly homoerotic attachment dating back to childhood, that unites Carlos and Posa. But their passionate commitment to freedom for Flanders leads them into fierce contention with Philip II. So you have son pitted against father and subject against king. What complicates the issue is that Carlos's opposition to Philip's imperialist policies is inextricably tied up with his love for his stepmother. But with Posa revolutionary fervour is the product of a pure libertarian idealism that has strong echoes of Rousseau. And it is the Act 3 confrontation between Posa and Philip that yields what Eric Bentley calls 'one of the greatest scenes of ideas in dramatic literature'.

But why is it so great? For this reason: because it is not simply a contest between an idealistic hero and an autocratic villain. It is great because, as Bentley says, 'the author is on both sides: both, not neither'.

Schiller, who had created politically intemperate heroes in previous plays such as *The Robbers* and *Passion and Politics*, enters into the heart and soul of Posa. Rejecting royal-politik and speaking truth to power, Posa urges Philip not just to give Flanders its freedom but to usher in a new age of enlightenment. As he says in Robert David MacDonald's translation:

All the kings of Europe
Respect the name of Spain. March at the head
Of Europe's sovereigns! One stroke of the pen
From your hand and the world will be as
Created new. Give men the right to think!

It is a stirring rallying cry and one that excited freedom fighters all over late-revolutionary Europe. But Schiller also shows us a Posa who is intoxicated by his own rhetoric and who naively assumes that you can move from sixteenth-century absolutism to nineteenth-century liberty with 'one stroke of the pen'. Philip, for his part, sees in Posa 'a strange man and a visionary' and recognises his oratorical power. At the same time, he is a practical politician who knows that an empire cannot be dismantled overnight. Our sympathy for Philip is intensified by an earlier scene in which we have seen him as a sleepless monarch, very like Shakespeare's Henry IV, in this case racked by doubts about his wife's fidelity. But the climactic confrontation is a great scene precisely because Schiller enters into the spirit and soul of both characters: the Utopian Posa and the pragmatic Philip. And even if Posa finally lays down his life for the sake of Carlos and the cause, Philip remains the play's most tragic figure.

It is a play of multiple layers and, in the end, Schiller shows us that in sixteenth-century Spain temporal power was subordinate to the Catholic Church. The dramatist's masterstroke is to introduce, at a late stage, the Grand Inquisitor: an old man of ninety, blind, supported by crutches and, as played by Peter Eyre in Grandage's production, resembling a scarlet stick insect. Philip seeks absolution from the Grand Inquisitor for the murder of Posa and salvation for his son, Don Carlos. On both counts he is chillingly rebuffed. The Church, keeping tabs on all of Posa's movements like an ecclesiastical MI5, wanted him kept alive 'to manifest the vanity of Reason'. In the case of Carlos, Philip is reminded that the son of God died on the cross to make atonement and that the life of his own aberrant offspring is now at the disposal of the church.

You could easily make a case against *Don Carlos*. Schiller himself admitted it was 'much too broadly tailored'. It is over-stuffed with echoes of Shakespeare, including *Hamlet* and *Othello*. It leaves us puzzled, in the final act, about Posa's motives. Yet it remains a towering play, one that combines sex, politics and religion and that uses the framework of historical drama to reflect the burning issues of a Europe aflame with revolutionary ideals.

37

Mary Stuart

FRIEDRICH SCHILLER
(1759–1805)

This is the one Schiller play that has taken root in British theatre. In my theatregoing lifetime there have been revivals at the Old Vic (1958), Greenwich Theatre (1989), the National Theatre (1996) and the Donmar Warehouse (2005). Schiller's play is especially popular in Scotland. It was seen at the Glasgow Citizens in 1988 and again in 2006 in a David Harrower version by the newly formed National Theatre Scotland. And it was staged at the Edinburgh Festival in 1958 (the Old Vic version), 1987 and again in 2002 in a wonderful production by Andrea Breth imported from the Vienna Burgtheater.

It is not hard to work out why the play, written in 1800, has become Schiller's calling-card in Britain. It deals with a slice of our own history. It also offers golden roles to two great actresses: something rare enough in world drama. At the National in 1996 Isabelle Huppert's volatile, vixenish, headstrong Mary confronted an Elizabeth, in Anna Massey, who seemed steeped in solitude. And in Phyllida Lloyd's Donmar production, which later moved to the West End and Broadway, Harriet Walter's regally entrapped Elizabeth was opposed by Janet McTeer's Mary, who grew in grace and dignity as the play progressed. The famously invented encounter of the two queens at Fotheringay is a theatrical masterstroke that adds to the play's excitement. But for all the psychological depth of Schiller's portrait of the two women I'd argue the play's greatness also resides in its study of the intricate manoeuvres of power politics, something that Schiller wrote about with a detail no other dramatist can match.

One has to start with the double tragedy of Mary and Elizabeth, and George Steiner hit the nail on the head when he wrote that 'the action dramatizes at every moment the exact balance of doom'. At first, the two queens seem antithetical figures. Mary is sensual, passionate and, although imprisoned at Fotheringay, idolised by her followers: Elizabeth is political, pragmatic and, although enthroned at Westminster, surrounded by double-dealing. And in the unhistorical but magnificent confrontation in the park at Fotheringay you see the depth of their animosity. Elizabeth initially greets Mary with a cold indifference that turns to outright contempt as she turns to her favoured courtier and asks, in Peter Oswald's Donmar version, 'Is this the beauty, Leicester, dangerous for a man to glimpse, disaster for any woman to be near?' Mary, meanwhile, starts the scene in kneeling supplication and ends defiantly on her feet impugning her rival's origins ('We all know for what crime Anne Boleyn was killed'). As Elizabeth angrily departs, Mary claims moral victory, crying, 'I plunged a knife into my enemy's heart!' What she has actually done is to make her own execution inevitable.

It is superb theatre. But when Steiner writes of 'the exact balance of doom' he touches on Schiller's underlying theme: the strange kinship between the warring cousins. Both are, in different ways, imprisoned: Mary's confinement is physical while Elizabeth's is metaphysical. Both women are also plagued by their past. Mary is guiltily tormented by her implication in the murder of Darnley, from which only Catholic Communion can release her. Elizabeth is agonised, given her reputation for justice, by the prospect of signing a death warrant from which there can be no escape. When Elizabeth says, 'The pattern of my past actions is my condemnation,' she might be speaking for both women. And the parallels between them have been intriguingly highlighted by female directors. In Andrea Breth's Viennese production Corinna Kirchoff's Mary and Elizabeth Orff's English queen were both imperious, highly sexed figures conscious of being solitary women in a masculine world. Phyllida Lloyd, in her Donmar revival, emphasised their isolation even further by putting Walter and McTeer into period costume and their conspiring male followers into modern dress.

But part of the play's greatness lies in Schiller's ability to use romantic tragedy as a means of analysing the processes of power. You see this in the play's second act, set in the Palace of Westminster. It starts with Elizabeth being manoeuvred into a possible marriage with the King of France: a reminder of the way diplomacy trumps personal instincts. We then see Elizabeth beset by contradictory arguments about the fate of her imprisoned rival. Lord Burleigh argues for immediate execution, saying of Mary that 'the tantalising fact of her existence' is a stimulus to Catholic assassins. Talbot, the Earl of Shrewsbury, counters this by claiming that clemency will enhance England's global reputation. But the prize moment comes when Leicester, Elizabeth's favourite and Mary's clandestine lover, is put on the spot. With Machiavellian subtlety, he argues that Mary's death sentence, for which he voted in council, should still stand but that she should be allowed to live 'in the shadow of the axe'. This is the essence of drama in that each case has validity while at the same time reflecting the temperament, or tactical position, of the speaker.

Political theatre and tragedy may sound like opposites. In *Mary Stuart*, Schiller shows they can be combined. And this becomes apparent in the play's final stages. Mary goes to her death with an heroic grandeur: Schiller even invents the idea that her steward, Melvil, has been secretly ordained, which allows him to grant her absolution and give her Holy Communion. Elizabeth, however, is both the slave of political circumstance and inherently tragic. Told by her secretary of state, Sir William Davison, that the people are rising in rebellion and demanding Mary's head, she signs the death warrant. Elizabeth then hands the warrant over to Davison, leaving him to decide whether to act upon it. After it has been seized by Burleigh and Mary has been duly executed, Elizabeth then rounds on both Burleigh and Davison, threatening the former with banishment and the latter with beheading.

Does this make Elizabeth contemptible? Not at all. If anything, it stirs memories of Shakespeare's *Richard II*, where Bolingbroke, at the play's end, attacks Sir Piers of Exton for carrying out his deepest desire by killing the king. As Bolingbroke says to Exton:

They love not poison that do poison need.
Nor do I thee. Though I did wish him dead,
I hate the murderer, love him murdered . . .
With Cain go wander through the shade of night
And never show thy head by day nor light.

Both *Mary Stuart* and *Richard II* end with a regal death, a banishment and a guilt-haunted survivor. While Schiller may not have Shakespeare's poetic eloquence, he understands equally well the haunted solitude of monarchy. Eric Bentley says that, while *Mary Stuart* is a good play, one does not find in it 'an experience of chaos'. For me that's exactly what one does find: the chaos of a tortured soul in Elizabeth's final tragic loneliness. It's an unforgettably resonant image.

38

The Broken Jug

HEINRICH VON KLEIST

(1777–1811)

We may have come to terms with *Mary Stuart*. But the British theatre has never learned to love Kleist's *The Broken Jug* (*Der zerbrochene Krug*). Yet it's a near-perfect play: on one level a comic *Oedipus*, on another, a religious study of man sitting in judgement on his own fall. It famously failed on its première at the Weimar Court Theatre in 1808 – one courtier was even placed under house arrest for hissing – but that, one suspects, was because Goethe, as director, fatally divided a headlong play into three acts. Today it's a staple of German theatre. Thomas Langhoff brought a brilliant production from Berlin's Deutsches Theater to the Edinburgh Festival in 1993. I've also seen a fine Peter Stein production from the Berliner Ensemble steeped, like Langhoff's, in the microscopic realism of a Dutch interior. In Britain the play's only been seen of late in a version by Blake Morrison called *The Cracked Pot*, staged by Northern Broadsides in 1995 and transferring the action from a Dutch village in the late seventeenth century to Skipton in 1810. By all accounts, it was very jolly, but it still leaves one hungering to see a version capturing Kleist's combination of rural comedy and moral mayhem.

Kleist's own life was short, sharp and tragic. He was born in 1777 into a Prussian military family, resigned his commission at the age of sixteen and thereafter led a life of neurotic restlessness. At different times he worked for the civil service, tried to join Napoleon's army as it prepared to invade England – even though he was a former Prussian officer – and was briefly imprisoned by the French as a spy. But his great crisis came after reading the works of the philosopher Immanuel Kant. Kleist had believed since he was a child that the purpose of life was to attain perfection. However, in a letter to his long-suffering fiancée in 1801, Kleist revealed that he was shattered by the Kantian argument that no truth is discoverable here on earth. 'My highest and only goal,' he wrote, 'has sunk and now I have none.' He nevertheless went on to write seven plays as well as important essays, stories and poems. But he always suffered what his excellent translator David Constantine calls 'a fundamental unease' and in 1811 shot himself and his lover, Henriette Vogel, in a suicide pact on the Wannsee, Berlin.

Out of a chaotic life came some magnificent plays, and few better than *The Broken Jug*. Its starting point was a painting by Jean-Baptiste Greuze that Kleist had seen in a friend's house in Bern. Called *La Cruche cassée*, it shows a pretty girl holding a broken jug on her right arm. There is clearly an allusion to a sexual fall, but that was only the mainspring for a comedy that combines a secular robustness with a spiritual aura.

Kleist's ability to work on two levels – or more – is evident from the opening exchanges. Adam, a judge in a village near Utrecht, is bandaging a badly damaged leg when Licht, the clerk of the court, enters. In the words of Constantine's version:

> LICHT: Now, what in hell's name, tell me, brother Adam
>   Has happened to you? Look what a sight you look.
> ADAM: Yes, look. All a man needs for slipping up
>   Is feet. Everything's level here

But here I tripped, for every man carries

The cursed stumbling block in him himself.

LICHT: Pardon me, brother? Every man carries . . .

ADAM: The stumbling block in him.

LICHT: The devil he does.

The situation is village comedy: the language is theological. Adam is a rustic judge. He is also, in every sense, a fallen man. Even his clerk Licht (or Light) talks of hell and the devil. And when Adam falsely declares that he injured his left foot while clambering out of bed and singing hymns, Licht adds another element to the mix by calling him, in Constantine's translation, 'Clubfoot': a pre-emptive reference to Oedipus or 'swollen foot'.

All this comes together, with tragic hilarity, in the succeeding action. Adam is asked to preside over a case brought by the voluble Frau Marthe against a peasant lad, Ruprecht. She accuses the boy of breaking a treasured jug while secretly visiting her daughter, Eve. Ruprecht, however, protests his innocence, claiming he caught Eve with a nocturnal intruder who broke the jug while escaping through a window. As the case unfolds, under the suspicious eye of a judicial assessor called Walter, it is clear where the guilt lies. Adam's damaged foot, bruised features, lost wig and determination to incriminate Ruprecht confirm what we have already guessed: that Adam himself was the rapacious night visitor who broke the earthen jug synonymous with Eve's chastity.

The parallel with *Oedipus Rex* is, you might say, blindingly obvious: the investigator who is guilty of the original crime. Of even greater fascination is Kleist's seamless mix of the holy and the secular: of spiritual fall and civic corruption. Adam judges his own crime and bears false witness against others: he is also a rustic old lech who uses the exemption of Ruprecht from threatened military service as a means of getting into Eve's knickers. But the corruption doesn't stop with Adam. Licht may be a source of light; he is also eminently bribable. Even Walter, the austere assessor who views the shambolic court proceedings with mounting horror, is an equivocal figure. I remember how in Langhoff's production the moment when he shared bread and wine with Adam had strong religious echoes. Yet at the end Walter seems prepared to cover up Adam's sin rather than jeopardise the entire legal system.

It's an amazing play that, like so much great drama, looks backwards and forwards simultaneously. It has strong echoes of Sophocles. But it anticipates Brecht's *The Caucasian Chalk Circle*, where Azdak, a drunken village scribe, is elevated to the judicial bench. It even foreshadows Pinero's Victorian farce *The Magistrate*, in which the amiable Mr Posket is obliged to try a case in which he is personally implicated. At its heart there is also an attention to what Blake called 'the holiness of the minute particular'. Frau Marthe has a magnificent speech in which she expatiates on the decorative detail of the broken jug ('Right on this hole, where there is nothing now All the provinces of the Netherlands Were handed over to Philip of Spain') that makes it sound like the Holy Grail. I just hope one day to see a British revival that does justice to Kleist's vigorous rural comedy and sense of encroaching moral chaos.

39

The Prince of Homburg

HEINRICH VON KLEIST

(1777–1811)

Kleist's last play, written shortly before his suicide in 1811, has fared much better on the British stage than *The Broken Jug*. Tom Courtenay starred in a stirring production that opened Manchester's Royal Exchange in 1976. Neil Bartlett directed a compelling new version by himself and David Bryer that played at Stratford's Swan and the Lyric Hammersmith in 2002. I got less joy out of a Dennis Kelly version that the Donmar Warehouse did in 2010, which put a modern, anti-militaristic spin on Kleist's original ending. In so doing Kelly undermined the ambivalence at the heart of this weird masterpiece.

Search through world drama and it is hard to find a more arresting opening than the one to Kleist's play. We are in a castle garden. The time: the late seventeenth century. The place: Fehrbellin in Brandenburg (later Prussia). The sleepwalking prince, who's gone missing from his military duties, is making a laurel wreath, an emblem of the victories of which he fervently dreams. The elector, his commander-in-chief, takes the wreath away from him, winds his chain of office through the wreath and hands it to his niece, Natalie. As the courtiers depart, the somnambulistic prince declares his love for Natalie, snatches at the wreath and instead grabs her glove. As his entourage exits, the elector says to the prince in Bartlett's version:

When next we meet the struggle will be real!
No battle's won upon the field of dreams.

The beauty of the play is that the final scene echoes the first. It is again midnight in the moonlit garden, and a solitary prince is encircled by courtiers. As Neil Bartlett writes in his introduction: 'These two scenes are an extraordinary trick of theatre; although the stage picture in both scenes is identical, the meaning of the image is utterly different at the end of the play both for the characters and the audience. Everything looks the same; everything is different. What, then, can be trusted? What can be known?'

But Kleist's genius lies in the fact that these philosophical questions – the ones that haunted Calderón in *Life Is a Dream* and that were to recur in the work of Strindberg and Pirandello – are presented in compellingly concrete terms. Indeed the plot has a propulsive, edge-of-the seat excitement. Having established the prince as a sleepwalker, Kleist shows him still only half-awake the next morning when he receives his battle orders for the attack by the Brandenburg troops on the invading Swedes. Disregarding orders, the prince launches his assault too early and, although he routs the Swedes, is condemned to death for insubordination. At first the prince cannot believe that the elector, his adoptive father, will carry out the execution. In response to pleas for mercy, the elector says that he will offer a reprieve only if the prince can prove that the sentence was unjust. Accepting his fate, the blindfolded prince is led once more into the garden, expecting death, only to find Natalie preparing to crown him with a laurel wreath. He falls unconscious and, on being roused, asks, 'Tell me, is this a dream?'

I describe the plot in detail to hint at the play's rich ambivalence and to show how it occupies a pivotal place in world drama. Like Schiller, Kleist consciously echoes Shakespeare. In the battle scenes, a surrogate elector is slain exactly as happens in *Henry IV Part One* to the king's lookalike at Shrewsbury. Even more pertinently, the imprisoned prince is filled with a terror of mortality. Having glimpsed the open grave where he expects to lie next day, the prince hymns life's loveliness and begs, 'Don't let the black shadows close over me.' It is the same thought, expressed more eloquently, by the doomed Claudio in *Measure for Measure*, with his vision of his spirit residing 'in thrilling region of thick-ribbed ice'.

Yet, while looking back in time, Kleist anticipates many of the recurrent motifs of modern drama. The equivocal nature of reality, the power of the subconscious, the sense of the individual alienated from society: all are there in Kleist's play, which inhabits a strange world between nineteenth-century romanticism and our own age of anxiety.

But what does it all mean? The glory of the play is that one can never be quite sure. Notoriously, the Nazis appropriated the play and turned it into a parable on the need for strict military obedience, but to condemn it for that reason is like boycotting *The Mastersingers of Nuremburg* because it was Hitler's favourite opera. In Germany the play was decontaminated by a famous Peter Stein revival in 1972 for the Berlin Schaubühne, one that treated the piece as a dream-creation embodying Kleist's own yearning for recognition and rescue from a state of restless isolation. Seeing the Bartlett revival, I was struck by Kleist's emphasis on the enigmatic nature of responsibility and the idea that every action has an infinite number of possible causes, which is precisely what makes life a dream. If I questioned the Kelly version, it was because it turned the play into a glib assault on Prussian militarism: there was an orgy of heel-clicking, Ian McDiarmid as the elector became a barking autocrat shrieking, 'I want rules and order,' and, at the end, the prince unequivocally died while the elector's cry of 'Death to the enemies of Brandenburg' was greeted with stony silence.

Kleist was a subtler writer than that: a tormented individual who was neither endorsing nor satirising the Prussian military code. He is one of drama's great misfits: a natural outsider who combined an inherited romanticism with a modernist sense of apprehension, a product of the military caste with a deep awareness, as he showed in *The Broken Jug*, of institutional corruption. It is this divided nature that makes him so fascinating. On one level, *The Prince of Homburg* can be seen as a parable of resurrection. 'In the dream garden,' wrote George Steiner, 'the Prince partakes both of the fall of man and of his redemption.' Expecting execution, he has a tremendous speech beginning:

> Oh, Immortality, now you are mine!
> I can see a light, though my eyes are blind
> And it shines brighter than a thousand suns.

What makes this glimpse of the divine so moving is the knowledge that, within a few months of writing it, Kleist himself, the dramatist of unfulfilled dreams, would be dead by his own hand.

40

The Government Inspector

NIKOLAI GOGOL

(1809–52)

In 1835 Nikolai Gogol wrote to his mentor, Pushkin: 'Send me an authentically Russian anecdote. My hand is itching to write a comedy . . . Give me a subject and I'll knock off a comedy in five acts – I promise, funnier than hell.' Pushkin obliged with a story, which he had himself experienced, of an incognito traveller being mistaken in a provincial town for an important official. Out of that came a comedy, written in a white heat in a couple of months, that had its première in St Petersburg in April 1836. The play was an instant, if controversial, success, and it has been a standard part of the world repertory ever since.

But just what kind of play is it? Even in Gogol's own lifetime there were fierce debates on the subject. Radical critics seized on it as a scathing portrait of Tsarist corruption. Gogol, a timorous conservative with a penchant for mysticism, was so alarmed by this that in 1846 he wrote a dramatic dialogue interpreting the play as a religious allegory: Khlestakov, the St Petersburg clerk mistaken for a top official, became man's corrupt conscience made flesh, while the genuine government inspector, whose arrival is announced at the end of the play, symbolised the awakening of our spirit at the Day of Judgement. And in the Russian theatre the play has been performed in wildly varying ways. Stanislavsky did a realistic production for the Moscow Art Theatre in 1908 based, as he said, on 'deep psychological investigation of the characters and the rediscovery of direct, simple speech'. In total contrast, the anti-naturalist Meyerhold directed a famous production in 1926 that highlighted Gogol's grotesquerie and showed the town's bombastic mayor and his feather-brained wife as they imagined themselves in their social-climbing dreams.

So is the play realism or fantasy? Is it a scathing social satire? Or was Vladimir Nabokov right when he described it as the product of Gogol's fancy in which 'his private nightmares are peopled with his own incomparable goblins'? I would suggest that, like so many of the world's great plays, Gogol's work inhabits several dimensions at once. Maurice Baring, in his 1910 book *Landmarks in Russian Literature*, says that Gogol combined a love of the grotesque with the keenest power of observation – something you see in his short stories. 'The Nose' is about a nose which gets lost and takes on a life of its own. On the other hand, there is a vivid realism to 'The Overcoat', in which a clerk buys the warm overcoat of which he has always dreamed only for it to be stolen on the first day he wears it. What makes Gogol's work so fascinating – and *The Government Inspector* is a prime example – is its ability to be realistic and fantastic at the same time.

One big influence on the burgeoning Russian theatre of the early nineteenth century was Molière, and you see something of the Frenchman's satirical eye in the opening scene. The news that a government inspector is about to arrive reveals the depths of corruption and decay in Gogol's chosen provincial backwater. The local judge, we learn, accepts bribes in the form of greyhound pups. The charity commissioner and the physician (who doesn't speak a word of Russian) treat the patients in their care with a cavalier disregard for human life ('Man is a simple creature: if he is going to die, he'll die; if he's going to recover, he'll recover').

The schools superintendent presides over a bunch of cranks and drunks. The postmaster routinely opens everyone's letters. But the biggest offender is the mayor himself, who pockets public money, sanctions violence among the constabulary and allows rubbish to pile up behind rickety shops. His immediate solution to the last problem is to demolish the buildings themselves. As he says, in one timelessly topical line, 'The more things we pull down the better, it shows the administration's active.'

This is comedy fulfilling one of its traditional purposes: exposing the abuse of power. But with the citizens' assumption that Khlestakov, a scavenging pen-pusher who can't even pay for his next meal, is a St Petersburg bigwig, the play spirals into delirium.

For a start Khlestakov himself is revealed to be a wild fantasist suffering delusions of grandeur. In the great third act, fawned on by the mayor and spectacularly pissed, he lets his imagination rip: he claims to have written *The Marriage of Figaro*, *Robert le Diable* and *Norma*, brags of the size of his St Petersburg balls and boasts of counts and princes buzzing around his soirées. A play that starts as civic satire turns into an exhibition of dementia: something far more extreme than, for example, Malvolio's fantasies of social promotion in *Twelfth Night*. And Gogol's wildness was well caught in David Harrower's version and Richard Jones's no less sprightly 2011 Young Vic revival, one in which Kyle Soller's ginger-haired beanpole of a Khlestakov drunkenly climbed onto a mantelpiece to pose alongside a portrait of Tsar Nicholas.

But what is striking is how Khlestakov's delusional dreams quickly become infectious. After the fake inspector has proposed to the mayor's daughter before beating a hasty retreat, his appetite for fantasy is virally transferred to the town's inhabitants. And this has two immediate consequences. Not only do the mayor and his wife imagine themselves mixing in high St Petersburg society, but the mayor also turns with sadistic fury on the shopkeepers with whose swindling he was previously complicit. With great skill, Gogol subtly returns us to the origins of the comedy and its portrait of entrenched corruption: once again realism and fantasy are not opposites but symbiotically merged.

When it comes to staging, the play is susceptible to many possibilities. I've seen it pushed, at Moscow's Satire Theatre of all places, in the direction of broad-bottomed farce. Peter Hall did a famous production for the RSC in 1965, with Paul Scofield as a magnificent Khlestakov, that was the Russian equivalent of a Jonsonian comedy of humours. Richard Jones at the Young Vic leaned towards expressionism. The one thing the play doesn't need is updating. David Farr did an ill-advised version at the National in 2005 called *The UN Inspector*, in which a Balham estate agent was taken for a global power-broker by the inhabitants of an ex-Soviet satellite: in the age of instant communication, an improbable premise. Gogol's play is universal precisely because it is so local: a portrait of graft and dreams in a provincial Russian hellhole that shows drama's great gift for combining the mundane and the mythic.

41

Woyzeck

GEORG BÜCHNER
(1813–37)

All the plays I've examined so far are rooted in their historical period but speak to us today: a basic definition of a great play. But *Woyzeck*, a bleeding torso left incomplete on Büchner's death in 1837 at the age of twenty-three, is something else altogether. This is a work so far ahead of its time as to represent a new beginning. Both in its form and content, it feels like the birth of modern drama. It is also so magnificently elusive as to have been claimed by everyone: for realists and expressionists alike, it is the *fons et origo* of their respective movements.

As with Kleist, Büchner's life was brief, productive and marked by the stigmata of genius. He was born into a military-medical family in Hesse-Darmstadt in 1813, studied natural science (zoology and comparative anatomy) and became involved in revolutionary student politics. But it was between 1835 and his premature death from typhus in 1837 that he wrote the plays that were to have a lasting impact. *Danton's Death* is an historical drama that both charts Danton's disillusionment and reflects Büchner's own detachment from the idea of blood-letting revolution. *Leonce and Lena* is a dream-play suffused by ironic romanticism. Then came the unfinished *Woyzeck*, which exists in variant texts and which, in twenty-four elliptical scenes, tells the story of a military barber who, through vividly portrayed social exploitation, is driven to murder his common-law wife Marie.

Although Büchner was a theatrical pioneer, it is vital to recall that his plays did not surface until long after his death: the first critical edition of the *Complete Works* did not appear until 1879, and *Woyzeck* only received its stage première, in a corrupt text, in Munich in 1913. One result is that his work's impact was long delayed. 'What would have happened in the theatre,' asks George Steiner in *The Death of Tragedy*, 'if *Woyzeck* had been recognised earlier for the revolutionary masterpiece it is? Would Ibsen and Strindberg have laboured over their unwieldy historical dramas if they had known *Danton's Death*?'

Because *Woyzeck* embraces multiple styles and there is no definitive text, it also provides open season for experimental directors. In 2002 London audiences saw a version by Robert Wilson, with songs by Tom Waits and Kathleen Brennan, that was the embodiment of international avant-garde chic. Two years later Daniel Kramer gave Büchner's play the full expressionist works at London's Gate Theatre. In 2005 Iceland's Vesturport brought their characteristic physical exuberance to the play in a sensuous, water-filled production. And in 2013 *Woyzeck* was the source – though not many would have guessed it – of Punchdrunk's *The Drowned Man* and of a production at the Lyric Hammersmith staged as part of a season of 'Secret Theatre'. Amid the welter of *Woyzeck*s I've seen only one production that, for reasons I hope will become clear, got close to the heart of Büchner's play. Significantly that was staged at London's Gate Theatre in 1997 by Sarah Kane, another tragically short-lived dramatist whose own formal experiments testified to the lasting influence of Büchner.

But what is it that makes *Woyzeck* so sensationally modern? Firstly, the fact that it deals with a working-class hero. You can rake through the history of world drama, from the Elizabethan *Arden of Faversham* to Lessing's *Minna von Barnhelm*, to find plenty of forerunners of the bourgeois protagonist. Wily servants are also a staple of comic drama from Plautus to Molière and Marivaux. But Woyzeck is the first true example of the proletarian hero. What's more, Büchner uses naturalistic detail to chart his exploitation. To supplement his meagre pay Woyzeck acts as guinea-pig to a doctor who for three months has made him eat nothing but peas. And when Woyzeck is accused of lack of morality by the captain whom he daily shaves, his reply is unequivocal. In John Mackendrick's Methuen translation, he says: 'You see, people like us don't have any virtue, they only have what's natural to them. But if I was a gentleman and I had a hat and a watch and a big coat and all the proper words, I'd be virtuous alright. Must be a great thing, sir, virtue. Only I'm just a poor man.' Or, as Brecht was to put it in *The Threepenny Opera*: 'Food comes first, then the morals.'

On one level, Büchner's play is a naturalistic tragedy about a victimised hero whose descent into madness is a direct consequence of poverty and near-starvation. But on another level, Büchner anticipates the focus on psychological essences and bold physical outlines that came to be the hallmarks of theatrical expressionism. The drum-major who seduces Marie, the doctor who regards human beings as expendable experiments, the captain who preaches morality while being susceptible to 'a pair of white stockings twinkling down the street' are all governed by a single, dominating characteristic. As is the showman, who, anticipating Wedekind's *Lulu*, introduces us to a menagerie that blurs the distinction between animals and humans.

Formally, Büchner's play is like nothing seen before. In their fragmentation and substitution of isolated points for linear development, Büchner's scenes anticipate Brecht. As Michael Paterson has pointed out, in place of Aristotelian theatre ('One scene leading to another: Growth') we get something closer to Brecht's Epic Theatre ('Each scene on its own: Montage'). Büchner's language is also hypnotic: jagged, poetic, elliptical yet with echoes of the Bible and Shakespeare (the touchstone for all German dramatists). Steiner puts it brilliantly when he says that Büchner 'shaped a style more graphic than any since *Lear* and saw, as had Shakespeare, that in the extremity of suffering, the mind seeks to loosen the bonds of rational syntax'. Seized with rage as he sees Marie dancing with the drum-major, Woyzeck cries, 'Flesh, filth, man, woman, human, animal – They all do it in the open day, do it on the back of a human hand like flies. Slut!! She's hot, hot.' It is as if Lear's disgust with procreation were combined with Othello's frenzied jealousy, and in Woyzeck's broken phrases we hear a mind on the verge of disintegration.

Reading this amazing play, we feel we are witnessing the birth of a new dramatic sensibility, even if it took nearly a century to become fully known. It is also a play that deserves to be treated as something more than an avant-garde plaything, which is why I so admired Sarah Kane's 1997 production. She grasped Büchner's essential point that man's fate is determined by environment: as he himself wrote, 'I despise nobody, least of all because of their intellect or education, because nobody can determine not to become a fool or criminal.' Kane's production also mixed realism and stylisation: as the doctor placed electrodes over the emaciated body of Michael Shannon's Woyzeck we heard the nerve-grating sound of a cello-string being rawly scraped. You felt an important figure in late twentieth-century drama was paying homage to a pioneering forebear who had rearranged the theatrical landscape.

42

An Italian Straw Hat

EUGÈNE LABICHE
(1815–88)

While Büchner was carrying out an unacknowledged revolution in Germany, in France the drama continued on its familiar path. And if the nineteenth century was, as so often claimed, the bourgeois century, no one was better equipped to become its prime entertainer than Eugène Labiche. He was the son of a wealthy Parisian manufacturer. His popularity coincided with the rise to power of Napoleon III, nephew of the great emperor and chief architect of the Second Empire (1852–70), famed for its material progress and economic prosperity. In a busy career, Labiche turned out 175 plays, nearly all of them written with collaborators and belonging to the French genre of vaudeville, in which song is combined with fast-moving, comic action. But if Labiche was heavily indebted to Eugène Scribe (1791–1861) and his belief in the 'well-made' play, he was also more complex than he first appears. Labiche married the mechanics of farce to shrewd social observation, and nowhere is this more apparent than in his early masterpiece, *An Italian Straw Hat* or *Un Chapeau de paille d'Italie*, written in collaboration with Marc-Michel in 1851. I've read it in a lively English translation by Lynn and Theodore Hoffman but I long to see it one day given the production it richly deserves.

Over the years it seems to have been treated largely as a madcap romp. W. S. Gilbert did two free adaptations in one of which a young Franklin D. Roosevelt appeared while a student at Groton. Intriguingly it was for the Federal Theatre Project – inspired by Roosevelt's New Deal – that Orson Welles did his own version in 1936 known as *Horse Eats Hat*; Simon Callow in his masterly biography of the great Orson makes it sound like an archetypal Welles farrago based on collapsing scenery and hair-raising stunts. In Britain the play is rarely, if ever, done: I missed a Ray Cooney Theatre of Comedy revival in 1986 which replaced its original director at the eleventh hour and which was universally condemned ('what is on offer at the Shaftesbury is not farce but fiasco,' wrote Peter Kemp in the *Independent*). And although I raced eagerly to a production at the Comédie Française in 2014, I emerged disappointed. The director, Giorgio Barberio Corsetti, not only updated the play to the 1970s but encouraged a style of coarse overacting. To appreciate the play best one should look at the 1927 René Clair film, which, as David Thomson points out, is funnier than much of Chaplin or Keaton and rooted in precise observation. That hits the nail on the head: Labiche's original play is a farce filled with real people.

The premise itself is very funny. On the day of his marriage a wealthy young man, Fadinard, is forced to go in hectic pursuit of a straw hat which his horse has inadvertently eaten. The hat itself belongs to a married woman, a Mme Beauperthuis, totally unknown to Fadinard, who, at the time of its consumption, was herself busy in the bushes of the Bois de Vincennes consuming an ardent lieutenant. So you have the neat idea of a prospective groom forced to cover up adulterous hanky-panky. But that is only the start of what René Clair dubbed a 'vaudeville-cauchemar' (a nightmare vaudeville). Fadinard's quest for a replacement hat takes him to a milliner's, where he embarrassingly encounters an ex-lover, to a baroness's party, where he is mistaken for a visiting Italian tenor, and even to the home of the cuckolded Monsieur Beauperthuis. Fadinard, however, is not only the pursuer. What adds to the play's momentum is that he is also the pursued. Everywhere he goes he is followed by a large wedding-party headed by his future bride, his apoplectic father-in-law and his profoundly deaf uncle. It's a play about flight and pursuit: a basic idea of farce later exploited by the Keystone Cops.

Like Scribe, Labiche was a master of the ingenious plot. As in all the best farce, nothing is wasted. The first scene, lasting barely a minute, shows Fadinard's valet trying to get off with a chambermaid who just happens to work for the Beauperthuis family, a complication that pays rich dividends. The equally brief second scene shows Fadinard's uncle arriving with a hatbox containing a wedding present; only at the end do we learn that it's an Italian straw hat of exactly the kind Fadinard has spent the day sweatily pursuing. But Fadinard's nightmare is compounded by the fact that identities are mistaken and places confused. When Macbeth says, 'Nothing is but what is not,' he might have been describing the essence of farce. Arriving at the milliner's, the wedding-party mistake it for a registry office and the astonished bookkeeper for a civic official. Even funnier is Fadinard's forced assumption of the role of a famous Bolognese tenor at the baroness's rout. In farce, the fragile sense of self is always a matter for momentary negotiation.

But where Labiche really scores is that he creates characters rather than demented marionettes and subtly punctures the buoyant materialism that was a feature of mid-nineteenth-century Paris. Fadinard's whole dilemma starts from the fact that he stopped his carriage in the Bois de Vincennes to retrieve his whip because 'it's got a silver handle on it'. When the adulterous couple whose coitus was so rudely interrupted turn up at his apartment to demand a new hat, Fadinard seems more concerned at the damage the soldier may do to his furniture than at the threat to his impending marriage. Labiche also uses the wedding party to satirise the money-mad bourgeoisie. Nonancourt, the future father-in-law, was ready to throw Fadinard out of the house when he first learned he had an income of twenty-five francs: only when he discovered that was per day did he invite him to stay. And Hélène, whom Fadinard hastily marries in the course of the flight-and-pursuit, is horrified when her father tells her they are going home. Ignoring the loss of a husband, she cries, 'But Papa, I don't want to leave my jewellery and my wedding-gifts behind!' In the words of a French critic, Philippe Soupault, the play is 'a document which allows us to find again an epoch, a class, a milieu, a world'.

By modern standards of political correctness, the play may seem faintly cruel. Every reply the deaf uncle makes to a question is a startling non-sequitur. The cuckolded Beauperthuis, first seen taking a footbath, has scalding water poured on his exposed legs. But I see no malice in Labiche. Instead he is one of the great entertainers and the first modern writer to explore the rich potential of farce. He shows that this most theatrical of all forms can be a vehicle not just for dizzying frenzy but also for social observation and examination of character. In Labiche's masterly hands, it becomes a study of disgrace under pressure.

43

Brand

HENRIK IBSEN
(1828–1906)

'It's like a very long Bruckner symphony; you either like its spiritual strength and clarity or you don't.' Those were Peter Hall's words in his *Diary* when Ibsen's play was revived at the National in 1978. And Hall was right. First published in 1866 and conceived more as dramatic poem than actable play, *Brand* is bound to divide opinion. I first came across it when a landmark production was staged by Michael Elliott at the Lyric Hammersmith in 1959 starring Patrick McGoohan. Incredible as it may seem today, the production was re-created for television, and I watched it spellbound. Since then I've seen the play on stage several times – at Nottingham Playhouse in 1973 with Brian Cox, at the National in 1978 with Michael Bryant, at the Haymarket in 2003 with Ralph Fiennes – and always been mightily impressed. Others find it daunting, exhausting and – that favourite word of British critics for Scandinavian drama – 'gloomy'.

What can't be denied, however, is that *Brand* is a bank on which Ibsen was to draw for the rest of his life. I'd go further and say that its confrontation of the ideal and the real reverberates through modern drama.

Before offering proof, I should briefly sketch out the plot. Ibsen's Brand is a Calvinist pastor and uncompromising idealist whose creed is 'All or Nothing'. This brings him into conflict with the materialist trimmers who govern the local community. But Brand's Mosaic certainty extracts a high price from himself and others. He refuses to attend his dying mother and is morally responsible for the death of both his son and his loving wife Agnes. In the last act Brand is stoned by the villagers as he attempts to lead them into the mountains to found a new church and is finally buried under an avalanche. Before he dies, he cries out, 'If not by Will, how can Man be redeemed?' to which a heavenly voice answers through the thunder, 'He is the God of Love'.

Brand is the man of fixed principle: Peer Gynt, who comes a year later, is the man of no principle. Between them they provide Ibsen with a rich storehouse; part of the fun of seeing or reading *Brand* – and I'd recommend the Geoffrey Hill translation – lies in spotting its influence on the later work. In its satire on civic mediocrities, whom Brand fiercely opposes, it anticipates *An Enemy of the People*: the mayor, proposing to build a Philanthropic Hall with a workhouse, gaol and an extra wing 'to accommodate Culture, that sort of thing' was played by Robert Stephens in the 1978 production with the gleaming rapacity of a politician for whom power was the ultimate aphrodisiac. The pompous ceremony attending the opening of a tall-towered church of 'awe-inspiring size' prefigures *The Master Builder*. Brand's final ascent into the mountains leads eventually to *John Gabriel Borkman*. But the conflict between the real and the ideal, central to Ibsen's play, recurs time and again in twentieth-century drama, not least in the work of the great Americans O'Neill, Miller and Williams.

But just how great a play is *Brand*? Even an Ibsen admirer like William Archer was tempted to say there was no psychology in *Brand* and that the hero was 'a mere incarnation of intransigent idealism'. If that were so, the play would be monotonous. But the American critic and director Harold Clurman was wiser than

Archer when he wrote: 'Brand's "sin" is that he rejects his own tenderness, yet it shines through the armor of his inflexibility.' Exactly so. Like Molière's Alceste and future protagonists such as Brecht's Galileo and Miller's John Proctor in *The Crucible*, Brand is the uncompromising hero who momentarily yields: only circumstance drives him back into a posture of unflinching rigidity.

As evidence, I would cite the third act of Brand – as overwhelming as anything in the whole Ibsenite canon – where the hero is subjected to a succession of temptations. Brand is thrice asked to attend his dying mother but each time refuses because of her unwillingness to surrender all her earthly goods. Then Brand refuses to budge when the mayor urges him to pack his bags and go. But the final temptation is the greatest: a doctor tells Brand his child will die unless he's moved to a warmer clime. And what is Brand's reaction? He instantly agrees. But the peripateia, exactly midway through the play, comes when the doctor says:

For a man without remorse
you're quick to compromise
when the lamb to be slain
is yours, your own first-born.

And Brand's doubts about his concession to instinctual tenderness are confirmed when he is accused of betrayal first by a parishioner and then by Gerd, a wild mountain-girl. We may not empathise with Brand's eventual, Abraham-like sacrifice of his son: what makes it great drama is that Brand does not come to his decision without a titanic struggle.

This raises the obvious question: where does Ibsen stand in all this? Does the play ask us to admire Brand in his heroic solitude and assault on a morally blemished world? Or is it intended as a warning against fanaticism and the elevation of human will above divine love? Different people have different answers. Time is also a factor: it was noticeable that, when the play was revived by Adrian Noble in 2003 in a post-9/11 world, several critics saw Brand as the epitome of a toxic religious fundamentalism. Yet the greatness of the play rests, as so often in world drama, on its ambivalence. Is Brand hero or villain?

The answer is that he is both – and neither. There is an element of nobility and moral grandeur in Brand's burning zeal: this, after all, is a man who early in the play risks his life by crossing a storm-ridden fjord to shrive a dying sinner. Yet, in Shaw's words, Brand 'caused more intense suffering by his saintliness than the most talented sinner could possibly have done with twice his opportunities'. Ibsen was a master of theatrical dialectic, and all his plays constitute an argument being carried out with himself. If *Brand* stands high among his finest works, it is because it is so many things at once. Brand is the kind of visionary Utopian and radical romantic without whom civilisation would wither. He is also a tragic figure who embraces the absolutism of the Old Testament without acknowledging the clemency of the New. Like him or loathe him, you cannot but feel that he is the centre of a momentous play.

44

The Forest

ALEXANDER OSTROVSKY

(1823–86)

'Too Jewish?' That was the question the American comedian Jackie Mason used to ask midway through his act. And 'too Russian?' is the question people constantly pose about Alexander Ostrovsky. Even Fyodor Dostoevsky noted of Ostrovsky in 1873 that 'at the very least three-quarters of his comedies remain completely beyond European understanding'. But is it really true?

For a start one has to look at the lasting influence Ostrovsky has had on modern theatre. As the son of a wealthy Moscow lawyer, Ostrovsky quickly abandoned his university studies to devote himself to theatre: between his first prentice effort in 1847 and his death he turned out some forty-eight original plays and twenty translations. His views on acting technique (especially the importance of individual memory), scenic design and production fed directly into the theories of Stanislavsky. His microscopic realism had a huge influence on Chekhov. He even in January 1886 achieved a long-cherished dream by being appointed director of repertoire for the Moscow Imperial Theatres, the equivalent of running a National Theatre. 'I have never been so happy in my life,' he wrote enthusiastically to his wife. Five months later he was dead.

In the words of the critic and translator Margaret Wettlin, 'Alexander Ostrovsky *was* the Russian theatre of his day'. Yet, although his work is endlessly performed at home, it's had only a spasmodic impact on the British repertory. *Artists and Admirers* was lovingly revived by David Leveaux, in a version co-translated by Hanif Kureishi, at the Riverside Studios in 1982. Richard Jones's 1988 production of *Too Clever by Half* at the Old Vic won Olivier awards for himself, Alex Jennings and designer Richard Hudson. The Almeida did a decent revival of *The Storm* in 1998. And I caught a fringe production of *Larisa and the Merchants*, in a lively Samuel Adamson version, at the Arcola in 2013. But if any of Ostrovsky's plays has penetrated the British theatre's suspicion of Russian drama outside Chekhov, it is *The Forest*. It was given a gorgeous production by Adrian Noble, with Alan Howard and Richard Pasco unforgettable as a pair of strolling players, at Stratford's The Other Place in 1981. The National Theatre countered with a production of its own in 1999, which, although sluggishly directed, had the advantage of a sparky text by Alan Ayckbourn, which I have used as my source.

So what is it that makes *The Forest* so attractive? Partly, its theme, which is the triumph of generosity of spirit over a crabbed and miserly meanness. More specifically, it shows two nomadic and impoverished actors – Gennadiy the tragedian and Arkadiy the comedian – coming to stay with the former's aunt on her country estate: in the course of the action, Gennadiy wrests a large sum of money, to which he is legally entitled, from the miserable old matriarch and hands it over to a destitute relative and her young suitor so they can run away and get married. As in so many of his plays, Ostrovsky was on the side of the free-spirited actors as against the tightwad landowners and the materialist merchants.

But first-rate comedy, which this is, depends on social detail, and you feel Ostrovsky gets this exactly right. Moreover, he doesn't just observe his two actors, he clearly loves them. Like all provincial actors, they constantly swap stories of past performances and have a deep distrust of civilians. Gennadiy, while being instinctively generous, also has a touch of the hauteur of the high tragedian and peppers his conversation with quotes from *Hamlet* and *King Lear* and finally rounds on his hosts with a passage from Schiller's revolutionary tragedy *The Robbers*: 'Where is love? Where is love to be found here? Oh, if only I were a wolf, I'd set about these heartless forest rodents and tear them limb from limb!' Arkadiy, meanwhile, has the earthiness, pragmatism and booziness of the born low comedian. As a pair, these actors evoke the barnstorming beneficence of Dickens's Vincent Crummles in *Nicholas Nickleby*; as played by Michael Feast and Michael Williams at the National, they also suggested the tattered dignity of Didi and Gogo in *Waiting for Godot*.

Ostrovsky is as precise in his observation of the landowners and merchants as he is of the actors. Raisa, the matriarch, is a magnificent creation: wealthy, widowed, rapacious and frivolously selfish in her willingness to sell off her real and symbolic forest to satisfy her sexual desire; her weakness is that she is helplessly smitten by a foppish young wastrel. The love of cash and sex are intricately interwoven in her character: I've never forgotten the sight of Barbara Leigh-Hunt, in the RSC production, flashing her money-box at people as if it were a form of physical enticement. Ostrovsky anticipates Chekhov in that Raisa combines the foolishness of Ranevskaya with the meanness of Arkadina, but she also exists in her own right as a vicious voluptuary.

An even more vivid example of a pre-Chekhov character is Vosimbratov, a wealthy wood-merchant who is attempting to buy off Raisa's forest at a knockdown price. Ostrovsky, writing in 1870, barely a decade after the emancipation of the serfs, reflected the changing social structures of his times: in particular, the decline of the gentry and the emergence of a new capitalist class. Vosimbratov has much of the entrepreneurial vigour that you find in Chekhov's Lopakhin in *The Cherry Orchard*. But he is also a cheating rogue, and nothing is funnier than the scene where he caves in before Gennadiy's theatrical bombast and hands back the money he has diddled out of Raisa.

Ostrovsky was a sharp observer of an evolving Russia, 'the Shakespeare of the merchant class', according to Turgenev. But he also had the inventive élan of the natural comic writer, and his work is susceptible to different directorial styles. Stanislavsky staged a realistic production of *The Forest* in Moscow in 1887; Meyerhold in 1923 came up with his own riotously revolutionary version. He rearranged the text according to the principles of cinematic montage. Raisa brandished a whip, spoke in a gruff, drink-sodden voice and sang sentimental romances off key. The two travelling actors were a conscious evocation of Don Quixote and Sancho Panza. All this was in confirmation of the Meyerholdian creed that 'A play is simply the excuse for the revelation of its theme on the level at which that revelation may appear vital today.' Without the genius of a Meyerhold, that principle can easily lead to the directorial excess that characterises a lot of contemporary German theatre. But Ostrovsky's play was strong enough to withstand expressionist treatment. One can only hope that one day British theatre will warmly embrace a dramatist who wasn't merely the nominal father of modern Russian theatre, he virtually created it.

45

A Doll's House

HENRIK IBSEN

(1828–1906)

'Why?' is the big question. Why, in the second decade of the twenty-first century, are we still so haunted by a play written towards the end of the nineteenth? In 1879, to be precise. Is it because we have made so little progress towards gender equality? Is it because so many marriages are still based on a lie and depend on sexual, economic and emotional subservience?

The easy answer is to say that Ibsen's play, like his entire oeuvre, is about so much more than women's rights. Everyone quotes a famous speech he made in 1898 at a gala evening in his honour organised by the Norwegian Association for the Cause of Women. 'I have been,' said Ibsen, 'more of a poet and less of a social philosopher than one generally appears inclined to believe. I must decline the honour consciously to have worked for the cause of women. I am not even quite clear what the cause of women really is. For me it has appeared to be the cause of human beings ... My task has been to portray human beings.'

All that is true and was clearly Ibsen's response to reductive readings of his work as social propaganda. Yet it seems disingenuous to deny that *A Doll's House* had enormous impact in empowering women: as a play, it overturns the Hegelian notion of a traditional, patriarchal, sexist family structure. I'm with the critic Toril Moi when she says (invoking the entire Ibsen canon): 'Read in this light, *A Doll's House* becomes an astoundingly radical play about women's historical transition from being generic family members (wife, sister, daughter, mother) to becoming individuals (Nora, Rebecca, Ellida, Hedda).' If Ibsen's play transcends its historical origins, it is because of its astounding psychology, plot and theatrical poetry – not that, this being Ibsen, you can easily separate the three.

My own reading of the play has been deeply influenced by two specific performances and productions: one was Janet McTeer's Nora in Anthony Page's 1996 revival at London's Playhouse Theatre; the other was Hattie Morahan's Nora in Carrie Cracknell's 2012 Young Vic production. Prior to those, I had always seen Nora as the role-playing doll-wife who undergoes a sudden awakening in the final scene. What McTeer and Morahan revealed was something more potent: the idea of Nora as a borderline hysteric who finally stumbles towards self-realisation. In other words, Ibsen's play was less about a violently gear-changing volte-face than about a woman coming to terms with the source of her sickness. As so often with theatrical revelations, the clues were all there in the text.

Trace Nora's development through the play and you find Ibsen offers several pointers to her wildness. What, for instance, was she like as a young girl? She tells her devoted admirer Dr Rank that she would escape the parental clutches and 'always thought it fun to hide down with the maids', a brilliant image that anticipates Strindberg's *Miss Julie*. Nora's friend, Mrs Linde, also sharply observes, in the Frank McGuinness version used in the Page production, 'even in school you spent money like water'. But these are mere harbingers of the recklessness we see in the adult Nora. We know that when faced, like Brand, with the crucial need to save a loved one's life, she found the money to take her husband

Torvald to the healing south by forging her father's signature on a credit loan.

Within the action of the play we also see a Nora who, under the joint pressure of Krogstad's blackmail and Torvald's sexual imperiousness, is going virtually mad. She seems to have a death-wish that leads her to talk openly to Krogstad, and later to Torvald himself, of suicide. Famously, at the end of Act 2 she dances a tarantella (so named, because it was thought to be a cure for a deadly tarantula bite) with a whirling frenzy that leads Torvald to observe, 'Nora, my love, you dance as if your life depends on it,' to which she replies, 'It does.'

The tarantella is the key moment when Ibsen's psychology, plot and theatrical poetry perfectly coalesce. Toril Moi is right when she says that 'dancing the tarantella, Nora's body expresses the state of her soul': a soul in extreme anguish. In plot terms, the dance is a strategy to distract Torvald's attention from the mailbox, where a crucial letter lies that will expose the truth about Nora's forgery. But the tarantella is also a rebuke to the idea that Ibsen's career fits neatly into three strands: the early verse dramas, middle-period naturalism, late symbolism. Even Ibsen's naturalistic dramas depend on poetic effects, and in Nora's frenzied dance of death we see the spirit of the trolls enter the drawing room.

This is not to deny the impact of Nora's final confrontation with Torvald or the power of her exit: 'the slam of the door behind her,' wrote Shaw, 'is more momentous than the cannon of Waterloo or Sedan'. My point is that Nora's self-realisation stems from everything that has gone before and even depends on her inherent recklessness. Look closely in the text at what Nora actually hoped for: that Torvald would tell Krogstad to go to hell, that he himself would accept the moral responsibility for Nora's disgrace and that Nora would, to redeem her husband's reputation, commit suicide. None of this actually happens. But what it reveals to me is that

Nora retains the instinct of a wild idealist who is brought face to face with pragmatic reality. Her idealised image of Torvald lies in ruins, and she has no alternative but to quit the family home.

The beauty of the play is that it exposes the shams of marriage and is not without sympathy for Torvald, who is a tormented figure in his own right: a social puritan with an overpowering sexual urge. It is significant that, in the two modern productions I've mentioned, Janet McTeer and Owen Teale and Hattie Morahan and Dominic Rowan left us in little doubt as to the Helmers' mutual physical attraction.

If we continue to respond so warmly to the play when many overtly propagandist pieces are forgotten, it is because of the aesthetic grace of its interlocking plot and because of the complexity of its heroine. Ibsen's Nora is not simply a trophy wife who suddenly sees the light but a tortured, romantic soul who, at great personal cost, achieves a precarious sanity and who exits into an unknown future.

46

The Wild Duck

HENRIK IBSEN

(1828–1906)

Ibsen had an unrivalled capacity for arguing with himself. In *A Doll's House*, written in 1879, he shows the danger of a domestic life based on a lie. In *The Wild Duck*, written in 1884, he shows the value of sustaining illusions. Intriguingly, doors are crucial to both plays. Nora emphatically slams the door behind her in *A Doll's House*. And what is the pivotal moment in *The Wild Duck*? It comes when Hjalmar Ekdal is playing a Bohemian folk-dance on the flute with his wife Gina and their daughter Hedvig sitting alongside him. 'It may be modest and cramped under our roof, Gina,' says Hjalmar. 'All the same, it's home. And I'll tell you one thing: it's a good place to be.' At that moment there is a knock at the door, one that signals the arrival of the crusading idealist Gregers Werle, whose admittance will destroy the household's happiness. The parallels are hardly exact but, when I saw *The Wild Duck* at London's Donmar Warehouse in 2005, I couldn't help seeing in Gregers, the torch-bearing missionary who brings disaster in his wake, more than a hint of Tony Blair.

Simply because it imposes so many demands – a cast of over twenty, two different sets, the careful placement of an onstage loft – *The Wild Duck* is the least revived of the major Ibsens, yet it seems to me his greatest work in its blend of pathos and comedy, its psychological depth and the intricacy of its plotting. Harold Clurman says, 'I find the first-act exposition with the guests at the elder Werle's house somewhat stiff and awkward.' I'd argue that nowhere does Ibsen more ingeniously plant the clues to the later events and point the way to the coming cataclysm.

What do we learn from Werle Senior's party? For a start that Werle helped to ruin his erstwhile business partner, Old Ekdal. Driven by a mixture of guilt and self-interest, Werle has also done a number of favours to Ekdal's son Hjalmar: he has set him up in business as a photographer and contrived his marriage to his own former housekeeper, Gina Hansen. But we also learn a lot more: that Gregers is a mother-fixated figure with a hatred of his father, that Werle Senior (not unlike Captain Alving in *Ghosts*) is a respected pillar of society with a goatish appetite and that he suffers from weak eyesight. All this bears fruit in the great central section of the play, where Gregers persuades his old friend Hjalmar that his marriage is based on a lie and that his home is built on shaky foundations. Even the paternity of the fourteen-year-old Hedvig, suffering a premature form of macular degeneration, is fatally brought into question.

The plotting is brilliant. But then so too is Ibsen's psychology. Gregers Werle is neither wicked nor evil, he is supremely well-intentioned, which makes his destructiveness all the more terrible. We also learn a lot about Gregers in the course of the play. We discover that, as an idealist, he is hopelessly impractical (he causes stinking chaos in the room he rents from the Ekdals: a sublime case of the real merging into the symbolic). We also learn that he idealises Hjalmar, failing to see that he is a workshy dreamer. We also perceive, in a point brilliantly and extensively argued by Toril Moi, that he debases language by talking in pseudo-profundities. 'Gregers's metaphors,' says Moi, 'are so obscure as to become, at least in the mind of many critics, deep symbols. The alternative is to wonder whether they mean anything at all.'

If Gregers is depicted with clinical accuracy, Hjalmar Ekdal is one of the great tragi-comic characters in modern drama: a supremely self-deluding fantasist. The link between Gregers and Hjalmar is also crucial. If the language of the former is based on metaphysical obscurity, that of the latter, as Moi points out, derives from histrionic exaggeration. One minute Hjalmar sees himself as 'a man weighed down by a mountain of troubles', the next as a paradigm of domestic bliss. Too grand to take portraits of ordinary people, he vaingloriously vows to raise photography to 'the status of both an art and a science'. My favourite moment, however, comes when Hjalmar, having declared he can't stay a moment longer in a house tainted with lies, sits down to his breakfast and then complains there's no butter on the table. This is superbly serio-comic in a way that anticipates Chekhov. Over the years I've seen Hjalmar excellently played by Stephen Moore, Alex Jennings and Paul Hilton; in my mind's eye, however, I envisage him being performed by Michael Redgrave with something of the baffled self-deception he brought to *Uncle Vanya*.

Some people admittedly find the symbolism of the wild duck itself oppressive. What, after all, does it mean? Everything. Or possibly nothing. Rather than precisely define it, I would say it subtly infiltrates the play and alters according to circumstance. It can stand for Hjalmar's father, Old Ekdal, who is emotionally devastated by serving his prison sentence; or it can embody the fragile innocence of the wounded Hedvig; or it can be a symbol for Hjalmar himself, who, like the duck in her basket, has happily adjusted to straitened circumstances. The wild duck has the potency of a poetic image. The only mistake is to take it literally, as I once saw in a production at Washington's Arena Theatre, where duck's eggs periodically descended from the flies and landed on the stage with a resounding plop.

The greatness of *The Wild Duck* is that it eludes easy categorisation. It has moments that steer close to melodrama, as when the climactic pistol-shot in the loft is assumed to come from Old Ekdal, only for him to suddenly appear elsewhere: a moment comparable in its effect to that in Victor Hugo's *Le roi s'amuse* (or Verdi's *Rigoletto*) when the jester mistakenly believes the murdered body in the sack to be that of the detested duke. But then Ibsen's play is suffused with wild comedy, as when Hjalmar seeks to piece together the handsome financial settlement on Hedvig that he has so ostentatiously torn up. At the same time, the play is a tragedy rooted in the world of the everyday: easily the play's sanest character is Hjalmar's wife Gina, who has to take portraits, retouch photographs, cook meals and clean rooms while all around her a belief in the ideal is wreaking havoc. In the end, Ibsen is not arguing that idealism itself is destructive. What he shows, with masterly control of the medium, is what happens when abstract principles take precedence over people. As Ibsen wrote in his notebooks: 'Liberation consists in securing for individuals the right to free themselves, each according to his particular need.'

47

The Power of Darkness

LEO TOLSTOY

(1828–1910)

Tim Crouch, a British experimental play-maker, attacked in a newspaper article in 2014 a theatre 'mired in realism'. It's a familiar enough charge: theatre's supposed denial of the conceptual experimentalism of the visual arts. But to my mind this shows an historic blindness to the massive achievements of the movement more familiarly known as naturalism. Its origins are often dated to the prefatory manifesto that Emile Zola wrote in 1873 to his stage version of *Thérèse Raquin*. And if we accept Eric Bentley's definition of naturalism as 'the candid presentation of the natural world', its impact has been enormous, varied and long-lasting. Bentley went on to point out that: 'Naturalism has presented the facts of man's life and environment in a quite new and rich explicitness. It signifies the conquest of a great area of human experience previously ignored, understressed, if not altogether taboo in art.' In drama, it gave us Ibsen, Chekhov and Strindberg. In fiction, it led to the masterpieces of Tolstoy, Dostoyevsky and Proust.

But although Tolstoy is revered for *War and Peace* and *Anna Karenina*, too little attention has been paid to his plays, most specifically *The Power of Darkness*, on which he began work in 1886 but which was not licensed for public performance in

Russia until 1895. The work post-dated Tolstoy's conversion to what Isaiah Berlin called 'a programme of Christian anarchism' and his immersion, on his estate at Yasnaya Polyana, in the life of the peasants. Although Tolstoy is often seen as their champion, what is startling about *The Power of Darkness* is his portrayal of the peasants as rapacious, drunken, greedy and murderous. It is a truly shocking play, one that contains an act of infanticide even more brutal, because more calculated, than that in Edward Bond's *Saved*. Tolstoy's play is also a significant landmark in naturalist theatre, one that was picked up by André Antoine for his Théâtre Libre in Paris and Erwin Piscator for his Proletarian Theatre in Berlin but one that, aside from a stunning revival by Sam Walters at Richmond's Orange Tree Theatre in 1984, remains almost unknown in the English-speaking world.

Tolstoy's story, based on a real-life case, is both gruesome and engrossing. Its central figure is Nikita, a twenty-five-year-old peasant who is shiftless, vain and lecherous. He first of all discards the orphaned girl he has casually ruined. He then marries the widowed Anisya, with whom he's long been having an affair and in ignorance of the fact that she has poisoned her husband. But Nikita's problems don't stop there. Once installed as Anisya's husband, he squanders her money and seduces her deaf, mentally undeveloped stepdaughter Akoulina. And when Akoulina is found to be bearing his child, Nikita is forced to take the baby and crush it to death before burying it in a cellar. At the end, as Akoulina is about to be married, Nikita first tries to kill himself and then publicly confesses his crimes.

This is Russian village life rendered with unsentimental realism. It also anticipates a brilliant Chekhov short story, 'Peasants', which was published in 1897 and which offers a similar picture of barbarism and brutality. Yet Chekhov, with characteristic generosity, finally offers a justification for peasant behaviour: 'there was nothing in their lives,' he writes, 'which did not provide some excuse: killing work which made bodies ache all over at night, harsh winters, poor harvests, overcrowding, without any help and nowhere to find it' (translation by Ronald Wilks). Tolstoy takes a different line. He doesn't so much find a social explanation for peasant brutality as suggest that it is offset, and even redeemed, by a Christian conscience. Tolstoy's peasants are capable of great evil; they are also alert to good.

Actually one figure is unrepentant. This is Nikita's mother Matryona, who conspires in robbery and murder and tries to thwart her son's confession. She is part of a long line of tyrannical matriarchs you find in Russian drama going back to the towering figure of Kabanova in Ostrovsky's *The Storm*, on which Janáček based a famous opera. But Tolstoy contrasts Matryona's villainy with the primitive Christian virtue of her peasant husband Akim. In a touch wholly characteristic of a great novelist Tolstoy makes Akim helplessly inarticulate except when fired by moral zeal. Disowning Nikita for his financial and sexual greed, Akim tells his son that he is 'stuck fast in sin'. And in the great scene where it is explained to Akim how both banks and rich peasants lend money and charge extortionate interest, the old man proclaims, in the Arthur Hopkins translation, 'It's filthy, that's what I call it; it's not right.'

Even in the scene – one of the most horrifying in world drama – where Akoulina's baby is first smothered and then buried, Tolstoy shows how the worthless Nikita has a conscience that rebels against the deed. There is nothing grand or heroic about Nikita's initial resistance. In many ways, he is a cringing coward who blames his wife, his mother and even Akoulina for his plight. But there is a heart-stopping moment when Nikita first discovers that the child he is to bury is still alive. After he has done the terrible deed, he rushes up from the cellar, haunted by the baby's whimpering cries like some village Macbeth.

Unsurprisingly, that scene was revised and slightly toned down when Stanislavsky directed the play for the Moscow Art Theatre in 1902. But that production yields a wonderful story, recounted in *My Life in Art*, which says a lot about theatrical naturalism. Stanislavsky and his wardrobe mistress visited the estate in the Tulska district where the original murder had taken place and came back laden with shirts, coats, pots and pans and accompanied by a peasant couple to advise the Art Theatre on local manners and customs. The woman turned out to be a natural performer, and at one point it was suggested she take over the role of Matryona. She was dropped because she kept improvising her own dialogue and using unspeakably foul language. But Stanislavsky was loath to lose her entirely and first gave her a place in the crowd scenes and then had her crossing the stage humming a song. In the end, however, her presence seemed so anachronistic that she was simply reduced to an offstage voice. The lesson Stanislavsky learned from this is that 'Naturalism on the stage is only naturalism when it is justified by the inner experience of the actor.' It is not enough, in other words, simply to reproduce the external world by getting a peasant to play a peasant. In the theatre you don't merely represent reality, you re-create it with all the imagination, empathy and skill at your disposal – which is precisely what makes naturalism such a potent and durable weapon.

48

The Father

AUGUST STRINDBERG

(1849–1912)

Like Tolstoy, Strindberg was a pioneer of theatrical naturalism – indeed far more so, since he was a dedicated dramatist and expounded the principles of naturalism in his preface to *Miss Julie* (1888). Not that Strindberg had any great love for Tolstoy as a literary figure. 'Have been reading *War and Peace*,' he wrote to a friend in 1886. 'Can anyone endure this unending female chatter?' Four years later, he wrote again: 'Have read *Kreutzer Sonata*. Fine observations but rubbishy reasoning; above all, I don't think the old man understood the philosophy or philogyny of love-hatred.' But even if the Swede deplored the Russian's doctrine of sexual abstinence, the two men are linked by their late-nineteenth-century belief in a theatre that advocated psychological and social realism.

Strindberg was to change in later life as his plays became more symbolic and expressionist. But in the 1880s he was a pioneer of the new naturalism, and this motivated his first major work, *The Father* (1887). Today the later *Miss Julie* is more widely revived, but I find it has little of the shattering dramatic power of its predecessor. What *Miss Julie* does have is a brilliant preface that establishes many of the principles of modern theatre. Strindberg wanted swift, natural dialogue in which the talk is sent 'spinning in a thousand directions', no act divisions, interval breaks or footlights and, above all, 'a small stage or a small house where perhaps a new kind of drama would arise'. If today we spend much of our time watching ninety-minute plays in intimate spaces, we have Strindberg to thank for it.

But it is in *The Father*, whatever problems it raises, that we see Strindberg at his demonic best: it has a touch of madness and makes uncomfortable viewing for the modern liberal spectator but leaves you in no doubt you've encountered a neurotic genius. It presents us with a duel to the death between a figure simply known as The Captain and his wife Laura. The initial conflict is over their daughter Berthe and The Captain's decision to remove her from a house 'filled with women' to the calm of a nearby town. To counter The Captain's decision, Laura casts doubt on whether Berthe is really his child. Suspicion on The Captain's part grows into a fixation that aids Laura's scheme to have him certified insane. In the end The Captain is coaxed into a straitjacket by his old religious nurse and suffers a fatal stroke, leaving Laura claiming Berthe as 'My child! My own child!'

The stock charge against Strindberg is one of misogyny, and it's fair to admit that the play sprang out of Strindberg's own disintegrating marriage to the actress Siri von Essen. Laura herself is also presented as a calculating schemer. She intercepts The Captain's letters to hinder his mineralogical studies. She sows totally unwarranted doubts about Berthe's origins and her own fidelity. She also tells a barefaced lie to the doctor in claiming that it was her husband who first had the 'wild notion' that Berthe wasn't his child. Whichever way you look at it, Laura wages a tactical campaign to propel The Captain towards madness.

It would be reductive to label the play simply as a display of virulent anti-feminism. John Osborne wrote a perceptive introduction to the version he did for the National Theatre in 1988 in which he claims: 'The ferocity of the battle between The Captain and Laura apprehends far more than an isolated account of the battle between the sexes. His [Strindberg's] constant reversion to lyricism of agonizing power, his astonishing modernism, his sense of the nineteenth century receding and, with it, the disintegration of structures of faith, moral philosophy and accepted notions of romantic love, put him, as the director of the present revival said to me, "in the Great and Unreasonable camp of the humanists".'

That's pitching it strongly, but Osborne has a valid point. For a start the play is clearly about a world where science is superseding religion and faith is breaking down. When the nurse encourages The Captain to acquire a divine humility, he retorts, in Osborne's version, 'It's a funny thing but every time you talk about God and love, your voice becomes hard and your eyes fill with hatred.' But Strindberg also makes it clear that loss of faith creates an agonising vacuum. As The Captain says: 'For me, without a belief in the life to come, my child was my afterlife. She made me immortal. She was my ultimate reality. Take that away from me and I am nothing.'

Osborne also hits the nail on the head when he says that Strindberg both questions and radically revises our notions of romantic love. The big encounter between The Captain and Laura charts, with uncanny pre-Freudian insight, the complexity of sexual relationships. At first The Captain sought in Laura the tender comfort of a surrogate mother. The marriage soured at the point where The Captain, thinking he was despised for weakness, forcibly asserted his conjugal rights. 'Yes,' says Laura, 'and that was your mistake. The mother was your friend. But the woman was your enemy.' That may not be the whole truth about marriage, which is, ideally, a partnership of equals. But what Strindberg precisely anatomises is the quasi-incestuous nature of a certain kind of marriage which depends on a re-enactment of the mother–son relationship.

However much one may theorise about the play, and however disquieting it may seem in the age of gender equality, the blunt fact is that it has a ferocious emotional intensity on stage – one reason why I prefer it to the later, drawn-out, love-hate duel in *The Dance of Death* (1900). I would dearly love to have seen Michael Redgrave's Captain, in a 1949 revival, which Tynan described as 'a large, elemental piece of acting: we watch the blind, frightened animal slowly succumbing to the hypnotic power of his mate'. Wilfred Lawson gave a famous performance in 1953, which Michael Meyer described as 'the greatest individual Strindberg performance I have seen'. Although I missed that, I did see the David Leveaux revival at the National in 1988 and, like most critics, was transfixed by the play and the performances. Alun Armstrong's Captain, with his rimless specs and hair like a nest of snakes, was particularly memorable in his calm acceptance of the fatal straitjacket, while Susan Fleetwood lent Laura a bruising sardonic comedy and hinted there was something sadly Pyrrhic about her ultimate victory. More recently, I caught an excellent 2012 revival at the Belgrade, Coventry, where Joe Dixon's Captain was a mix of soldierly arrogance and intellectual voracity, while Katy Stephens played Laura, from her own point of view, as a woman forced to adopt devious strategies to redress the imbalance of a patriarchal society. I'm not denying Strindberg presents a problem. But dramatists should be judged by the quality of their imagination and their ability to establish their own idiosyncratic world. Even if we don't automatically subscribe to Strindberg's beliefs, *The Father* remains a work of unremitting theatrical power.

49

Spring Awakening

FRANK WEDEKIND
(1864–1918)

I hope I've made clear my admiration for naturalism, a movement that turned drama and fiction away from the purple excesses of romanticism and allied them to a Darwinian spirit of scientific enquiry that proved to be the dominant mode of the future. But naturalism not only takes many forms, it also breeds opposition. One of the finest flag-bearers for the anti-naturalist cause was Frank Wedekind, a disciple of Büchner, a forerunner of Brecht and a revolutionary writer-performer who left behind a handful of extraordinary plays including *Spring Awakening* (1891), *Earth Spirit* (1895) and *Pandora's Box* (1902). The last two have been conjoined as the 'Lulu' plays. If I give pride of place to *Spring Awakening* (*Frühlings Erwachen*), it is because it offers a still-shocking portrait of the way an oppressive society deals with puberty. Nothing quite like it had been seen before in terms of its sexual candour, and far from being a straightforward thesis-play about the need for sexual education, it combines stark tragedy with wild humour. Indeed Wedekind himself wrote: 'I believe that the play is more gripping the more harmless, sunny, laughing the performance.'

It was clearly the work of an original spirit: indeed his whole life reads like an adventure story. For an excellent summary of Wedekind's career, read the potted account by Elizabeth Bond-Pable which provides the preface to her husband Edward's translation. In a nutshell, Wedekind was conceived in California, where his left-liberal father had fled after the failure of the 1848 revolution and where he married a San Francisco opera singer. But the young Frank was born in Germany in 1864, schooled in Switzerland, where his father bought a castle, and in his late teens wrote copious letters on love, sex, education, religion and death, all subjects at the heart of *Spring Awakening*. Sent to Munich to study law, Wedekind spent much of his time going to the circus, playing the guitar and hanging out with the German Zolaists, whose embrace of naturalism he grew to detest. In later years he became a cabaret singer, actor and journalist, eventually jailed for his contributions to the magazine *Simplicissimus*. But it was in Munich in 1890 that he sat down to write *Spring Awakening*, knowing that it had little chance of being publicly staged.

But why? For a start it deals with the conflict between adult repressiveness and adolescent urges in a provincial German town. Melchior impregnates the fourteen-year-old Wendla after a lovemaking experiment in a hayloft: Melchior is later sent to a reformatory, while Wendla dies after a clumsy abortion. Haunted by his academic failure and sexual ignorance, Melchior's friend Moritz kills himself. Wedekind also wickedly satirises boneheaded schoolteachers, shows two boys tenderly kissing and depicts solo and communal masturbation – in the solo case with a boy assiduously poring over a portrait of a Renaissance Venus while he squats on a lavatory seat.

Baldly described, the play sounds sensational. But what is striking is Wedekind's sympathy with these hapless adolescents. Melchior is a restless young intellectual who preaches self-interest while offering Moritz help with his homework and practical sexual guidance; it is typical of Wedekind's mordant irony that Melchior is expelled from school not for impregnating Wendla but for providing Moritz with a graphic guide to sexual reproduction. In a scene equally full of pathos and comedy, Wendla begs her mother to give her instructions about how babies are born, only to be fobbed off with stories of storks flying through windows. But the most complex figure is Moritz, a boy aflame with desires he doesn't understand, paralysed by fear of failing his exams and dogged by prophetic dreams of a headless queen.

Wedekind presents all this in scenes that alternate jagged, poetic dialogue with long, discursive speeches. He deals with real emotions in a non-naturalistic form and a lack of linearity that echoes Büchner's *Woyzeck*. The play also gets wilder as it goes along. In a staffroom the assembled teachers discuss a teenage suicide epidemic while agonising over the opening and closing of a window. As the mourners gather at Moritz's graveside, one teacher spouts pietistic nonsense: 'as the most unimaginable violation of the moral code, suicide is at the same time the strongest possible confirmation of its existence' (in the Ted Hughes translation). Finally, Wedekind goes all out for expressionism, a movement that relies heavily on a distortion of reality and that was to have a significant impact on all the arts in Germany in the early twentieth century. You see Wedekind's expressionist tendencies in the last scene, which takes place in a moonlit cemetery where Melchior is on the run from the reformatory. He is confronted by Moritz (with 'his head under his arm'), who invites him to join the massed ranks of the dead. But he also meets a masked gentleman who tempts him with the prospect of the life to come, however 'insatiable, overwhelming, doubtful' it might be. It is a scene of stunning power in which Wedekind draws on operatic and literary tradition. Moritz is like the commendatore in Mozart's *Don Giovanni* offering death; the masked gentleman resembles Goethe's Mephistopheles tantalising Faust with hope. There is little doubt where Wedekind himself stands in all this: as an anti-bourgeois Bohemian and a rebel with a cause, he is on the side of life in this humane, progressive play. Unsurprisingly, it's had a long history of trouble. In Germany it had to wait until 1906 before getting a public performance at the Berlin Kammerspiele. Even then the director, Max Reinhardt, evaded police censorship only by making cuts and claiming that, since the theatre seated only 300 and charged high prices, the play wouldn't reach a broad public. In Britain the play has had an equally chequered history, as Nicholas de Jongh excellently records in *Politics, Prudery and Perversions*. In 1963 the play was given a Sunday-night club production at the Royal Court after an examiner in the Lord Chamberlain's Office had declared, 'This is one of the most loathsome and depraved plays I have ever read.'

After an attempt by Olivier's National Theatre to stage the play in 1964 had been blocked by the Board, the Court did a full-scale, diplomatically cut production in 1965 – a very good one, as I recall, with Derek Fowlds and Richard O'Callaghan as Melchior and Moritz. Finally, Bill Bryden did the full text for the National at the Old Vic in 1974, proving that audiences were unfazed by communal masturbation and homosexual kisses. Tim Supple also staged the Ted Hughes version for the RSC in 1995 in a production that showed a surprising sympathy for the confused parents as well as their tormented children. Finally Wedekind's play achieved the ultimate accolade of modern theatre: it was turned into a Broadway musical which ran over two years in New York but had a more limited shelf-life in London's West End in 2009. Some adored it. I felt it neutered the anger and frustration of Wedekind's play by showing the kids empowered by music. But at least it reminded us just why fearless Frank was such an important figure in the history of drama: an experimenter with form, a pioneer in his attack on life-haters and a man who anticipated Freud, D. H. Lawrence and Henry Miller in showing the danger of demonising sex.

50

The Importance of Being Earnest

OSCAR WILDE
(1854–1900)

The scene: a wine bar next door to the Harold Pinter Theatre. The time: July 2014. Two critics are engaged in conversation. One, whom we'll call Michael, is a rheumy-eyed veteran who has been reviewing plays for over forty years. His companion, Helena, is a bright-eyed newcomer just down from Oxford who writes fiercely intelligent critiques for her own website. They have just emerged from a revival of *The Importance*, presented as if it were a country-house, am-dram production. The advantage, if such it can be called, of the device is that it allows two senior actors to play Jack and Algernon as they did thirty-two years earlier at the National Theatre.

Michael: Well! What rubbish that all was! I know one sign of a classic is that it is indestructible, but that seemed to be testing the theory to its limits.

Helena: Oh dear, I actually rather enjoyed it. I thought it reminded us that Wilde's play is a delightful piece of fun that owes a lot to the nonsense tradition of Lewis Carroll and W. S. Gilbert. And surely you'd agree it's important to see the great classics reimagined?

M: Reimagined but not subverted! Wilde's play is one of the greatest comedies in the language, and you muck about with it at your peril. You're dead right that, at one level, it is sublimely absurd. You couldn't have anything much dottier than a plot that hinges on two women who will only marry a man called Ernest, on a baby deposited in a handbag and on the discovery that all the characters are intimately related. But the play also offers a coherent attitude to life.

H: Aren't you being a bit over-earnest? Wilde himself called the play 'a delicate bubble of fancy' and a work 'written by a butterfly for butterflies'. After those society melodramas like *Lady Windermere's Fan* and *An Ideal Husband*, which are all about Victorian hypocrisy, he's here letting his hair down and allowing his imagination to take wing.

M: Up to a point. But we can sit here all night long and quote Wilde against himself. In the same letter where he talked about 'a bubble of fancy' he also said the play had a 'philosophy'. I don't want to get heavy-handed, but you can also see in it a premonition of the disaster that was about to overtake Wilde's own life. Much of the action rests on a calculated duplicity. Jack Worthing creates a fictive brother in town so that he can escape the monotony of country life, Algernon invents an ailing friend, Bunbury, in order to flee the routine of the London season and, in a classic line, he tells Jack, 'You don't seem to realize that in married life three is company and two is none.' Given Oscar's oscillations between his wife Constance and Lord Alfred Douglas and the tragedy about to befall him, those lines take on an ominous ring.

H: But you're falling into the classic trap and searching the play for retrospective, biographical clues. We don't go to *The Importance* – or, at least, I don't – looking for metaphors for Wilde's sexuality but to be transported into an imaginary world and to laugh at those famous scenes: Lady Bracknell's forensic examination of Mr Worthing's parental background or the moment when he enters the manor-house garden in deep mourning for a brother who never actually existed. That's pure ecstasy. You're trying to pin a moralistic label on Wilde when his great gift was for eluding definition. You remember how he once wrote to his friend, Whistler, telling him that 'to be great is to be misunderstood'.

M: But Whistler also once described Wilde as 'le bourgeois malgré lui', meaning, I think, that Wilde's flair for subversion was accompanied by a hunger for acceptance. Look, I'm not claiming that Wilde was a sententious moralist, simply that *The Importance*, like all great comedies, offers a subliminal commentary on life. Just take the opening, where we hear an offstage piano before Algernon enters and addresses his manservant. Algernon says, 'Did you hear what I was playing, Lane?' and Lane replies, 'I didn't think it polite to listen, Sir.' Instantly that tells us a lot about the master–servant relationship. Algernon expects instant appreciation while Lane implies either that high art is outside his province or that Algernon's playing was so atrocious that comment would be superfluous.

H: OK. But you don't sit there in the theatre making a mental note of the shrewdness of Wilde's observations. You simply surrender to the joy of the moment.

M: I think that takes us close to the heart of Wilde's genius. He makes us laugh almost unstoppably. At the same time, without our being fully aware of it, he is offering a running commentary on class, money, marriage, economics, social hypocrisy, the decline of the aristocracy and the rise of commerce. And just look at the character of Lady Bracknell. I suppose because Edith Evans once played her with incomparable hauteur the idea has grown up that she is an old, upper-class battle-axe. But Wilde's text makes it clear she is a social upstart who was penniless when she married Lord Bracknell. She has the parvenu's fear of any form of revolutionary upset and warms to Cecily Cardew the second she learns she has a substantial private fortune.

H: I hear what you are saying. But look at the play in the larger context of Wilde's life and career. He tells us, in the preface to *The Picture of Dorian Gray*, that 'all art is quite useless' and consistently preached the idea that aesthetics belong to a higher spiritual realm than ethics. In *The Importance* he creates a flawless comic construct that sets out to delight rather than instruct.

M: I can see you're not an ethics girl but I don't accept your antithesis. I can't think of any comedy ever written that doesn't express some vision of the world. To me it's a sign of Wilde's greatness that he takes us into a Gilbertian fairyland, where muffins and cucumber sandwiches acquire monumental importance, while showing us a society that depends on deceit, duplicity, doubleness and pretence.

H: But, Michael, you need to be careful about pinning Wilde down too precisely. You remember that Richard Ellmann in his biography remarked that, given a choice of alternatives, Wilde always managed to choose both.

M: My point exactly. Wilde is not an either/or man. There is a character in Scott Fitzgerald who is described as 'dynamically humorous, fundamentally serious'. That fits Wilde exactly. In an age that expected artists to be either escapist entertainers or utilitarian moralists, he creates in *The Importance of Being Earnest* a supremely great comedy in which style is married to substance and from which we emerge elated but also surreptitiously enlightened. And now, can I top you up?

H: I thought you'd never ask.

51

Le Dindon

GEORGES FEYDEAU

(1862–1921)

Shaw's basic objection to *The Importance of Being Earnest* was that it was nothing but a piece of Gilbertian absurdity. 'It amused me, of course,' he wrote, 'but unless comedy touches me as well as amuses me, it leaves me with a sense of having wasted my evening. I go to the theatre to be moved to laughter, not to be tickled or bustled into it; and that is why, though I laugh as much as anyone at a farcical comedy, I am out of spirits before the end of the second act and out of temper before the end of the third.'

One sees Shaw's point: a play needs to be more than an industrial laughter-machine. But all the best farces, from Plautus to Shakespeare to Molière and Labiche, engage us with human beings who arouse our curiosity, sympathy and interest. I would argue that is even true of Georges Feydeau, who is often regarded as the most heartlessly accomplished of all farce-writers. His plays are written about as if they were simply geometric constructs created to a precise formula: two outer acts of domestic disquiet and a middle act in which all the characters converge on a louche hotel. But his plays are much more varied than that and obliquely reflect the sadness of his own life. Having made a fortune as a young dramatist and married an heiress, Feydeau gambled recklessly on the stock exchange, lost both his money and his wife and was forced to sell his valuable art collection. He went to live in solitude at the Hotel Terminus (near the Gare St Lazare), contracted syphilis, lost his reason (he announced he was Napoleon III) and died in a sanatorium.

However, he left behind a number of imperishable farces, of which the best, for me, is *Le Dindon*, written in 1896 and excellently translated by Kenneth McLeish as *Sauce for the Goose*. If it works beautifully, it is because it introduces us to a set of recognisable people, projects them into a nightmarish world and then returns them to a reordered reality. You could say it follows the format of the well-made play. But Feydeau's genius was that he combined clockwork precision with an understanding of human waywardness, mocked marriage while also celebrating it and mixed compassion with what now seems politically incorrect cruelty.

Plot and character fuse perfectly in the opening act of *Le Dindon*, a reminder that exposition itself can be funny. It starts with a cut-price Don Juan called Pontagnac pursuing the lovely Lucienne Vatelin to her home only to discover that she is the wife of a friend and colleague. Confronted by her amazed husband, Pontagnac is instantly thrown into that state of fluster and panic that is the essence of farce. Matters get worse when Pontagnac's own wife unexpectedly turns up (no one in farce arrives expectedly). Since she is supposedly a semi-paralysed victim of illness living in Switzerland, more frantic explanations are required. But although it is Pontagnac (the turkey-cock or fall-guy of the title) who sets the plot boiling, Feydeau's real focus is on the marriage of the Vatelins. M. Vatelin is the archetypal complaisant husband. Lucienne is the desirable wife who says she will only betray her husband if she ever catches him in flagrante. So it becomes imperative for Pontagnac and a rival admirer, Redillon, to arrange for Vatelin to be caught with his trousers down.

You'd need a diagram to explain the ingenuity with which Feydeau gets the principal characters – and several new ones – to converge on Room 39 of the Hotel Ultimus in the central act. But Feydeau's masterstroke is to make the genuine occupants of this much-visited room a lecherous old military doctor and his profoundly deaf wife, Mme Pinchard. Props are always crucial in farce, but none is more brilliantly deployed than the pair of alarm-bells that Pontagnac places under the bedroom mattress to signal any sign of adulterous hanky-panky. Needless to say, the bells continually go off at the wrong moment and lead to a mass invasion of the room just as the elderly Pinchards are settling down for a night's slumber. I shall never forget, in Sam Walters's 2013 production at the Orange Tree, the look of aghast horror on the face of Auriol Smith's Mme Pinchard as total strangers poured into her room and rudely rummaged under her night-dress to stifle a ringing sound she herself could not hear.

Like Labiche in *An Italian Straw Hat*, Feydeau uses deafness as a comic device, which may be totally contrary to our notions of good taste but which also induces helpless laughter. My defence would be twofold. We only cry 'bad taste' when things are unfunny: Shakespeare's jokes about sand-blindness in *The Merchant of Venice*, for example. Feydeau is also not ridiculing the deaf, he is asking us to empathise with a woman whose disability is callously exploited by her goatish husband and who awakes to find herself in a mad world where pop-eyed figures are fumbling under her nightwear.

Feydeau is often seen as the desecrator of the household gods. What is surprising about *Le Dindon*, for all its orchestrated mayhem, is just how moral, and implicitly feminist, it is. The unsympathetic figures are all men who are uniformly vain, lecherous and deceitful. Pontagnac, a suburban satyr, never gets the sex with Lucienne he is after. Redillon, admittedly, does have a night of pleasure with an upmarket whore but is too physically spent to offer Lucienne any satisfaction when she comes calling. Even M. Pinchard, a dirty-minded old bottom-pincher, is roundly slapped by a chambermaid and has a night of torment in a Paris hotel. The real victors of the play are Vatelin and Lucienne. He learns that the wages of long-ago sin in a foreign hotel with a woman called Brunnhilde lie in being stalked by her mad husband. Lucienne resolves to forgive and forget and banishes her spaniel-like pursuers. Far from being destroyed, marriage is reaffirmed. While you could say this is Feydeau appeasing his Palais-Royal audience, it is also evidence of a wistful admiration for a domestic stability the author himself never knew. Feydeau was much more than a supreme theatrical carpenter. He created farce out of real people: their uncontrollable itches, their self-incriminating lies and, above all, their urge to restore order out of the chaos they themselves have created.

52

Uncle Vanya

ANTON CHEKHOV
(1860–1904)

I've measured out my life in *Uncle Vanya*s. I first saw Chekhov's play in a legendary production by Laurence Olivier at the Chichester Festival Theatre in 1962. At the time I was a slightly unhappy, self-absorbed twenty-two-year-old working in a repertory theatre in Lincoln. I was filled with sexual frustration, the pangs of despised love and a feeling that my life was going to waste. To my astonishment, I found in Chekhov's play echoes of my own predicament. I even identified strongly with the forty-seven-year-old Vanya, superlatively played by Michael Redgrave, who gave what Olivier, not always known for his charity to fellow actors, described as 'the best performance I've ever seen in anything'.

I've seen a dozen or more productions since then, and my love for the play has never diminished. It always, in my experience, evokes strong emotions in audiences. While it may lack the symphonic richness of *Three Sisters* and *The Cherry Orchard*, it is audaciously radical in its structure and shows Chekhov redefining the possibilities of drama. Chronologically it comes after *The Seagull*, which, for all its beauty, has residual touches of melodrama and a too overt symbolism. But when Chekhov sat down to write *Uncle Vanya* in 1896, he was effectively reimagining a work he had written ten years earlier, *The Wood Demon*, and in the process revealed the nature of his genius. Read *The Wood Demon* and you will find many of the same characters and situations that are in *Uncle Vanya*. But the differences are crucial. In the earlier play Vanya shoots himself: in the later version he fires at the professor and misses. Yelena, who originally runs away from her husband, is now tethered to him in permanent exile. Where Astrov and Sonya are happily paired off at the end of *The Wood Demon*, in *Uncle Vanya* they are doomed to irreconcilable solitude.

The Wood Demon is a conventional drama: one that ends in resolution. *Uncle Vanya* is totally unconventional: a play that shows life has no fixed solutions. The play has emotional momentum and progress from ignorance to knowledge in that the visit of the professor and Yelena to the country estate induces self-recognition. But Chekhov's theme is the need for endurance and survival. In the words of Michael Frayn, one of its finest translators, *Uncle Vanya* is about 'the tragedy not of death but of continuing to live after life has been robbed of hope and meaning'. What is fascinating is how quickly that was understood by the play's earliest critics. In one of the finest Chekhov reviews ever penned, Desmond MacCarthy, writing of the first British production in 1914, described the impact of the final act. It was, he said, full of that dreariest of all sensations:

the beginning of life again on the flat, when a few hours before it has run shrieking up the scale of pain till it seemed the very skies might split. If I were a painter and painted the animated features of Tragedy, I should not forget the puffy, sodden-eyed familiar who peeps from behind her with a smile, something kind if it were not so vacantly meaningless; I should not forget the heavy Goddess, Anticlimax.

No ending in world drama is more moving than that of *Uncle Vanya*. Sonya, kneeling before her weeping uncle, wipes away his tears and offers him the vain consolation that, in some future life, 'we shall rest'. But Chekhov intensifies the moment with a musical orchestration of sound and image. As the last words are spoken we hear a watchman knocking and Telegin quietly strumming his guitar while we see Vanya's mother still obsessively writing notes in the margins of her pamphlets and the old nurse, Marina, winding her wool. Chekhov not only overturns the existing canons of drama by ending with an anticlimax, he also creates an aching sense of the poignancy of existence: it is like seeing a Dutch interior infused with real pain.

Chekhov teaches us how drama can exist without the visible buttress of exposition, complication, denouement. He structures the play like music: look at the endless reiteration of the words 'they've gone' as the visitors finally depart. He counterpoints the diurnal realities of life with a sense of a wider imagination: it's there in Astrov's ecological fervour and vision of a future Russia. But rather than murder the play by analysis, I would like to indicate how particular productions have enriched my understanding of it.

Viewing the magical 1963 Olivier production again on DVD, I was struck by the close kinship and irreparable distance between the characters. Redgrave's Vanya and Olivier's Astrov are united by their cultivation, their drinking, their fascination with the beautiful Yelena; yet that last also marks the crucial distinction between them. Olivier's cynical Astrov bids farewell to Yelena with unsentimental finality: Redgrave's romantic Vanya gazes after her departing figure in rapture merely because she has rewarded him with a kiss. A similar complex duality is present in Rosemary Harris's Yelena and Joan Plowright's Sonya: both, at different points, gaze at their hands after Astrov has courteously kissed them, but Harris does so with a languorous delight while Plowright exhibits the ecstasy of the totally lovelorn. The production offers a masterly display of psychological realism down to the kindly tenderness shown by Sybil Thorndike's old nurse to Max Adrian's gout-afflicted professor, separated by class and background but united by the physical punishments of old age.

In 1996 Peter Stein directed an Italian production, which came to the Edinburgh Festival and which swathed the action in richly atmospheric Stanislavskian detail. Reminding us that the play was subtitled 'Scenes From Country Life', Stein filled the stage with birch trees that were in full flower in the sultry first act but which had achieved the coppery tint of autumn by the close, thus echoing the emotional transition of the characters. Maddalena Crippa's Yelena and Elizabetta Pozzi's Sonya were also beautifully played as spiritual soulmates and physical opposites. There was a heartstopping moment in the second act when the bodies of Remo Girone's Astrov and Pozzi's Sonya were almost touching, and he leaned intimately towards her – only to reach over her shoulder to retrieve a vodka bottle from the drinks cupboard.

More recently, there have been two fine British productions that offered their own illuminations. In Sam Mendes's 2002 Donmar Warehouse version, using a Brian Friel translation, Emily Watson's Sonya had a latent sensuality that made you realise just what Astrov was sacrificing through his emotional indifference. And in Jeremy Herrin's 2012 Chichester revival, an act of homage to its ancestor, Roger Allam's Vanya unconsciously picked the petals off a bouquet of roses – one he had previously intended for Yelena – as a symbol of his wasted life. But that is merely a reminder of the play's inexhaustibility, of its openness to interpretation and of Chekhov's capacity to induce in all of us a sense of recognition as we contemplate the disappointments of our own lives.

53

The Cherry Orchard

ANTON CHEKHOV

(1860–1904)

It seems unfair that one of the greatest plays of the twentieth century – some would argue, the greatest – is also one of its earliest. Chekhov spent three years working on *The Cherry Orchard* before it had its première at the Moscow Art Theatre on 17 January 1904. Six months later Chekhov was dead. But his final play sent its ripples through the succeeding decades, has spawned countless productions – five alone in the first fifty years of Britain's National Theatre – and has been endlessly imitated. Yet, even now, the debate continues as to what kind of play this elusive, poetic masterpiece actually is. A comedy? A tragedy? A nostalgic portrait of a declining, landowning class? A prophetic study of the coming revolution?

Chekhov himself initiated the debate by saying he was writing 'a four-act vaudeville'. Later he wrote to Stanislavsky's wife that 'what has emerged in my play is not a drama but a comedy, in places even a farce'. And to his wife Olga Knipper, who played Ranyevskaya, he revealed that 'the last act will be cheerful – in fact the whole play will be cheerful and frivolous'. Stanislavsky, as the play's first director, categorically disagreed: 'This is not a comedy nor a farce you have written. It is a tragedy whatever prospect of a better life you hold out in the last act.'

The argument was never fully resolved. Attending rehearsals, although desperately ill, Chekhov objected to the battery of sound effects, to confusion and vagueness amongst the actors and to an over-elaboration that caused the final act to run for forty minutes instead of an improbably brief twelve.

So who was right? Both were. It is not a case of defining *The Cherry Orchard* as either comedy or tragedy. It is both comedy *and* tragedy. Maxim Gorky was correct to observe that Chekhov, as a doctor, wrote like a clinician and was objective about his characters, noting signs and symptoms. Chekhov sees the comic absurdity of Ranyevskaya and her brother Gayev, who live in a world of illusions, who refuse to acknowledge the reality that their estate will have to be sold and who depart having learned little: Ranyevskaya leaves for Paris and a fatal romantic attachment while the cossetted Gayev, having secured a minor post in a bank, preposterously announces 'I'm a financier.' Yet there is also something indisputably tragic about their blinkered nostalgia – in the sense of a rooted attachment to place – and about the waste that makes it impossible, even when offered the perfect opportunity, for the prosperous businessman, Lopakhin, to propose to Ranyevskaya's adopted daughter, Varya, a scene of heartbreaking poignancy that echoes the irreconcilable separation of Sonya and Astrov in *Uncle Vanya*.

What makes *The Cherry Orchard* Chekhov's supreme masterpiece, however, is its elevation of realism to a symphonic level. Every detail in the play is concrete and precise, yet the total effect is musical. You see this in the astonishing first act, where Chekhov introduces all the crucial motifs: the fecklessness of Ranyevskya and Gayev, Lopakhin's mix of exasperation and adoration in his dealings with Ranyevskaya, Varya's bustling efficiency, Anya's wounded innocence, the impatient outsiderishness of Trofimov, the wandering student. All this, and much more, is established with almost invisible economy. Yet a stage direction, late in the act, tells us 'a long way, beyond the orchard, a shepherd plays on a reed pipe'. That's a tiny but classic example of Chekhov's organic approach to theatre in which sound as well as design, props and dynamic movement are as important as dialogue in creating meaning. An even more famous example occurs in the open-air second act, where 'suddenly there is a distant sound, as if from the sky: the sound of a breaking string – dying away, sad'. Even to the characters on stage, it means different things. For the pragmatic Lopakhin it is probably the snapping of a mining cable, to the fanciful Gayev it suggests a heron, to the edgy Ranyevskaya it portends something 'horrible'. But it's a measure of Chekhov's mastery that he extends the boundaries of realism by introducing an open-ended, sonic symbol.

Precisely because Chekhov's play is so multi-faceted it uncannily reflects the needs of a particular, historical moment. British productions of the 1940s and 1950s were often accused of turning the play into a wistful lamentation for a lost country-house culture. In 1977 Trevor Griffiths did a new version for Nottingham Playhouse that turned Trofimov into a blazing revolutionary prophet while conveniently playing down the absurdity of a character who tells Anya that 'we're above such things as love'. And in accord with the blunt spirit of our own age, Andrew Upton's translation for a 2011 National Theatre production had Lopakhin, asked yet again to outline his plans for the estate, declare, 'I've told you a thousand, bloody, frigging, bloody, frigging times.'

Of the myriad productions I've seen it was Peter Stein's for the Berlin Schaubühne in 1989 that best caught the tragi-comic richness and theatrical poetry of Chekhov's play. There was a moment in the first act when the shutters of Christophe Schubiger's set were suddenly flung open, sunlight flooded the stage, and we saw a profusion of white cherry blossom extending into the distance; for the first time I fully understood why the family couldn't bear to part with the estate. Stein also brought out, better than any other director, Chekhov's seamless blend of realism and symbolism. In the second act Jutta Lampe's Ranyevskaya hurled herself into a huge haystack with a wilful childishness, yet the sound of the breaking string was accompanied by a distant prospect of industrial chimneys and Kremlin domes. And the third act party scene combined Gogolian grotesquerie, as short, fat men danced with needlessly tall women, and vindictive triumph, as Michael Konig's Lopakhin returned from the sale of the estate on a manic high. Stein even reverted to one of Chekhov's original images by showing, as Firs sat dying in the abandoned house, the lopped branch of a cherry tree crashing through the shuttered window as if to symbolise the break-up of the old order.

The Cherry Orchard remains elusive, mysterious, defiantly uncategorisable. Like *Hamlet*, it reflects both the temperament of its interpreters and the tenor of the times in which it is produced. If it is the greatest play of the twentieth century, it is not only because it has a perfect dramatic structure, but also because it allows each of us to find in it what we are searching for. It allows us to identify with the revolutionary zeal of Trofimov or the purposeful optimism of Anya. Equally it permits us to empathise with Ranyevskaya and Gayev and what Michael Frayn calls their 'inertia and helplessness in the face of truly desolating loss'.

But we don't have to make a choice. The beauty of *The Cherry Orchard* lies in its openness, abundance and multi-dimensionality.

54

Summerfolk

MAXIM GORKY
(1868–1936)

Chekhov's play ends with the thud of axes as Lopakhin's workmen destroy the trees of the cherry orchard. In their place will come villas for summer visitors that will be 'gay with life and wealth and luxury'. Gorky's *Summerfolk* – rejected by the Moscow Art Theatre but receiving its première in St Petersburg a mere ten months after Chekhov's play – shows a different reality. Wealth and luxury there may be among Gorky's vacationers, but there is also idleness, disillusion, tetchiness and triviality offset by an awareness of the need for profound change. Gorky does not possess Chekhov's symphonic mastery of form; he nevertheless offers a profoundly realistic study of the volatility of Russia in 1904 and creates a play that cries out for great ensemble acting.

You can't banish the memory of Chekhov while reading or watching *Summerfolk*. Bassov, a shady lawyer, has invited a group of fellow professionals to his summer dacha. They drink, gossip, quarrel, fall in and out of love. There is also a visit by a celebrated writer, Shalimov, whom Bassov's wife, Varvara, once idealised. There is an aborted suicide, picnics, plays, the sounds of nature and the whistles of the surrounding watchmen. Pure Chekhov. And yet there is a crucial difference. Gorky had a commitment to social action. As the son of a boatyard carpenter, Gorky had left school early, done a vast range of jobs from cabin-boy to clerk, had mixed with students, tramps and prostitutes, been arrested for his involvement in radical politics. But Gorky was also a passionate autodidact, had made pilgrimages to the homes of Tolstoy and Chekhov and, by the time of *Summerfolk*, had written two novels and seen two plays (*Philistines* and *The Lower Depths*) successfully produced. In short, Gorky was a working-class writer who combined an attachment to Chekhovian realism with a detestation of Russia's educated intelligentsia. In 1902 Gorky had spent the summer, with his wife, at a dacha not far from his birthplace of Nizhny Novgorod and been appalled by the rusty tins and wastepaper left by the previous year's holidaymakers. 'The summer visitor,' he concluded, 'is the most useless and perhaps the most harmful individual on earth: he descends on a dacha, fouls it up with rubbish and then leaves.' Out of that disgust with the physical, and moral, detritus left by seasonal visitors sprang the astonishing play that is *Summerfolk*.

It is a play that takes its time. The first act, with its vast mix of characters, can seem a bit bewildering. But gradually you get to know and understand Gorky's gallery of middle-class drifters. Several figures stand out. There is Varvara, the discontented wife of the smugly wealthy Bassov. Then there is Bassov's bluestocking sister Kaleria, who has pretensions to poetry, and his brother-in-law Vlass, who hides his unhappiness under a mask of antic buffoonery. Even the arrival of the writer Shalimov does little to appease their sense of futility: if anything, his presence makes it worse, since he is just as rootless as the rest of them. He no longer knows who he's writing for, can't fulfil the prophetic role demanded of the writer in Russia and turns out to be staggeringly chauvinist: it is when Varvara overhears him remarking that 'Women are an inferior species – we must never allow them to convince us otherwise' that her disillusion with him becomes total.

Gorky does, however, provide a counterpoint to all this misery in the figure of Maria Lvovna: an impassioned thirty-seven-year-old idealist who delivers a stinging rebuke to her fellow holidaymakers that, in Nick Dear's version, runs:

We're the children of cooks and laundry-women and decent working people. We have a duty to be different! Never before has our great country had an educated bourgeoisie with direct blood ties to the working class. Those ties should feed us, should plant in us a burning desire to improve and regenerate and illuminate the lives of our own people – people who toil and toil, till the day they die, trapped in dirt and darkness . . . But we've lost our way. And we've abandoned them. And we've created our own bitter isolation, and filled it with anxiety and little private wars.

Stirring stuff! But does this prove, as some claim, that Gorky the dramatist turns into Gorky the propagandist? I don't think so. Gorky may endorse everything Maria Lvovna says. But he has sufficient objectivity to show her as a faintly absurd figure who harries everyone with her views and who cannot accept the love that Vlass unequivocally offers her. Although the play shows the self-preoccupation of the intelligentsia and their indifference to a country in crisis (3,000 factories had closed at the start of the century, strikes were erupting, anti-Semitic pogroms were taking place), Gorky was able to give dramatic life and colour to a class he basically despised.

Confirmation of that has come from the four productions I have seen in the past four decades. In 1974 the RSC gave *Summerfolk* its British première in a version by Kitty Hunter-Blair and Jeremy Brooks and directed by David Jones with an outstanding cast that included Ian Richardson, Susan Fleetwood and Norman Rodway. At the time, Martin Esslin drew attention to the similarity between the Russian intelligentsia of 1904 and that of seventy years later equally concerned with status and protection of privilege rather than the plight of the oppressed. Then, in 1977, Peter Stein's magnificent Berlin Schaubühne version became the first foreign-language production to visit the new National Theatre. My abiding memory is of the moment when the summerfolk, returning from a day's picnic, moved forwards to the front of the Lyttelton stage silhouetted against the white back-light like children lost in a forest. It was not only pure visual poetry, it was a comment on a class living in a dream world. Sam Mendes, who had studied with Stein, did a production at Chichester in 1989 that faithfully replicated many of the Schaubühne effects.

But it was Trevor Nunn, in his 1999 production at the National, who showed that the British could achieve the molten ensemble style demanded by Gorky. His production captured the definable Russianness of a play in which the characters drink like fishes and fish like drinkers. It highlighted Gorky's embryonic feminism and faith in women as moral touchstones: it is Marya and the husband-deserting Varvara who, at the end, lead a mini-exodus from this world of reckless hedonism. And a cast that included Patricia Hodge as the fiery Marya, Jennifer Ehle as the unhappy Varvara, Roger Allam as her oafish husband and Henry Goodman as the coarse-grained novelist proved that Gorky, while lacking Chekhov's musical genius, was his match when it came to exploring the personal tensions within a self-regarding group. Joseph Conrad in *Under Western Eyes*, published in 1911, sees cynicism as the key to the Russian character. For Gorky, like Chekhov, it was egotism, and in this fine play he explores its consequences with an unflinching realism.

55

Peter Pan

J. M. BARRIE

(1860–1937)

In 1904 Chekhov and Gorky both wrote plays about adult Russians unable to face up to life's responsibilities. *The Cherry Orchard* begins, symbolically, in the nursery, and Gorky's bourgeois drifters seek refuge from reality in booze, talk and sex. In that same fertile year for new drama, a diminutive Scotsman, J. M. Barrie, also wrote a play about the pleasure and penance of permanent immaturity: *Peter Pan or The Boy Who Would Not Grow Up*. Notice, it's 'Would Not' rather than 'Could Not': there is an element of wilfulness about the hero's, and arguably Barrie's, state of arrested development.

Ever since its première at the Duke of York's in 1904 Barrie's unnerving masterpiece has been a staple of Christmas entertainment. It has also been endlessly adapted, animated, musicalised, vulgarised and Disneyfied. Scan the entertainment listings in Britain for a typical year such as 2013 and you find at least five variations on Barrie's original play. In the author's native land there were two jolly travesties including one entitled *Peter Panto and the Incredible Stinkerbell*. In Birmingham there was a £10 million Belgian spectacular kitted out with songs by Madness, Rod Stewart and Duran Duran. At London's Pleasance Theatre children were subjected to *Peter Pan Goes Wrong*, in which the play was staged with cod ineptitude. Meanwhile in Stratford-on-Avon, the RSC offered a more thoughtful adaptation by Ella Hickson, *Wendy and Peter Pan*, which became a study in female empowerment and which had Mrs Darling briefly deserting her Ibsenite doll's house to join the suffragettes.

Barrie's play survives all this revisionism because it does something only a handful of works (including *Alice in Wonderland*, *The Jungle Book* and *Treasure Island*) have ever managed to do: it effortlessly transcends the generation barrier. It would be easy to say that it appeals to children because it contains pirates, crocodiles, fairies and what we now call Native Americans. Adults meanwhile are confronted with Barrie's sombre vision, in which you either exist in a state of eternal boyhood like Peter or accept maturity and lose your imaginative freedom. But part of Barrie's peculiar genius is that he demolishes this polarised response. Children, in my experience, are as alert as anyone to Peter's tragic isolation, while parents relish the magical adventure and Barrie's knowing allusions in his portrait of Captain Hook to Richard III: the old tradition in which Peter himself was played by a leggy lady (Phyllis Calvert was my first Peter) was also a none-too-subtle way of ensuring that fathers were part of the jolly family outing.

But my point is that Barrie's play appeals to all of us for one basic reason: it is a spectacular about a sense of loss. It also depends on a dramatic formula which runs through all Barrie's work: two slices of reality enclose one of dream. In *The Admirable Crichton* (1902) the decorous butler blossoms on his island fling before returning to the Edwardian hierarchy. In *Peter Pan* (1904) the exotic adventures in Never Land are framed by scenes in the Darlings' Bloomsbury nursery. And in *Dear Brutus* (1917) and *Mary Rose* (1920) excursions to a magic wood and a Hebridean island are bookended by domestic realism. It is, when you think about it, the same pattern that Shakespeare used in *A Midsummer*

Night's Dream with which Barrie's play has certain parallels. Indeed Max Beerbohm, reviewing *Peter Pan*, remarked, 'Credible and orderly are the doings of Puck in comparison with the doings of Peter Pan.' Puck is also an immutable part of fairyland, whereas Barrie's Peter opts for a life of permanent exclusion.

That element of choice is crucial. Peter is not a lost boy, he is in flight from reality. Early on he tells Wendy that he ran away the day he was born 'because I heard father and mother talking of what I was to be when I became a man. I want always to be a little boy and to have fun.' Barrie's skill lies in showing the gains that entails: playing games, fighting pirates, rescuing drowning maidens, being a gang-leader. But Peter is also, in many ways, a tragic figure. He doesn't understand sex: he mistakes a thimble for a kiss, chillingly cries 'no one must ever touch me' and sees Wendy as a surrogate mother rather than a loving girl. His mother-fixation even leads him into acts of emotional cruelty: a little-noticed aspect of Barrie's original is that Peter, in Act 5, is the first to return to the Bloomsbury nursery and urges Tinkerbell to fasten the window. 'Now,' says Peter, 'when Wendy comes she will think her mother had barred her out and she will have to come back to me!' But possibly Peter's most resonant line is his boyish vaunt of 'To die will be an awfully big adventure.' Barrie offers his own comment on that in his concluding stage directions. As Peter finally rejects Wendy's wish that she could take him up and 'squdge' him, Barrie writes that Peter only half understands what she means. 'It has something to do with the riddle of his being. If he could get the hang of the thing his cry might become "To live would be an awfully big adventure!"' That epitomises the play's pervasive sense of loss: you either remain trapped in eternal boyhood like Peter or mature into a conformist adulthood.

I mustn't make Barrie's play sound too Beckettian because it also ripples with fantasy and humour. In the early scenes there is the demolition of the father figure, Mr Darling, who is choleric, cowardly and ineffectual. The flying, which we now take for granted, must have seemed eye-opening in the confines of the modestly sized Duke of York's. And Captain Hook – always played by the same actor as Mr Darling – is, by any standards, a magnificent creation: a comic villain, a suave dandy with 'a touch of the feminine as in all the greatest pirates' and a man who ends up ignominiously swallowed by a crocodile while crying 'Floreat Etona'. Of the many Hooks I have seen, Ian McKellen was the finest because he caught the role's Shakespearean dimensions.

But what is finally astonishing about Barrie's play is its air of exuberant melancholy. It is the work of a man who vainly tried to supersede a dead brother in his mother's affections, whose marriage was eventually wrecked by his impotence and who became possessively absorbed in the lives of the five sons of the Llewelyn Davies family. But you don't need to know Barrie's biographical background to understand the play. It touches something inside all of us, whether we are parents or children and whether we are instinctive escapists or victims of the workaday world. Barrie's masterpiece thrillingly embodies a sense of exclusion and loss. And that is something we can all understand.

56

Waste

HARLEY GRANVILLE BARKER

(1877–1946)

At first, there may not seem any obvious connection between Barrie, the shy Scotsman, and the pioneering Harley Granville Barker, a man who, as actor, playwright, director, manager and critic, helped to create the British theatre as we know it today. In fact, Barrie and Barker were close friends. Barrie took a kindly interest in *Prunella*, 'a play for grown-up children', that Barker co-wrote and which opened four days before *Peter Pan*. Barrie also attended rehearsals of the Shaw plays which Barker, in partnership with J. E. Vedrenne, presented at the Court Theatre in three famous seasons from 1904 to 1907. And Barrie joined Barker and a host of other writers, including Shaw, Galsworthy, Hardy, Conrad, Yeats and Henry James, in signing a letter to *The Times* in October 1907 protesting against the arbitrary power of the Lord Chamberlain as a theatrical censor.

Barker had more reason than most to attack censorship: his play *Waste*, intended for production at the Savoy in the autumn of 1907, had just been banned. The ostensible reason, according to a letter from the Lord Chamberlain's office, was 'the extremely outspoken reference to sexual relations'. And it is perfectly true that much of the action hinges on the fact that Henry Trebell, a radical reformer who wants to bring in a parliamentary bill to disestablish the Church of England, impregnates a married woman, Amy O'Connell, who dies in a backstreet abortion. But a play written in the same year as Barker's, *Votes for Women* by Elizabeth Robins, was no less explicit in dealing with extra-marital relations and yet was licensed for performance. So what was it about Barker's play that so offended the censor? Reading and seeing it today, it's not hard to conclude that it was Barker's cynicism about politics and willingness to put on stage – in a way no one in Britain had done before – the shabby, backstage manoeuvres that shape parliamentary life. Barker had previously written brilliantly about financial fraud in *The Voysey Inheritance* (1905). In *Waste*, by combining sex, politics and religion, he virtually invented what came to be known as the 'state of the nation' play.

Mae West once enthusiastically hymned 'a guy who takes his time'. Barker certainly falls into that category. His first act offers a leisurely introduction to the kind of country-house party where, while the men are in the smoking room, the women reveal their influence on public affairs. Even William Archer, one of Barker's keenest advocates, thought the opening scene too long, and Barker himself drastically rewrote it in 1927. But the second scene of that act, where Trebell ('my time for love-making is so limited') briskly seduces the married Amy O'Connell, reveals a lot about the cold-hearted compartmentalisation of his existence. Trebell reserves his passion for politics. And the play really catches fire in the second act, where Trebell, an independent MP ready to switch his allegiance from the Liberals to the Conservative government-in-waiting, outlines his plans to disestablish the Church of England and devote the income from its ancient endowments to education. Seeking the support of Lord Charles Cantelupe, an aristocratic Anglican, Trebell displays his missionary zeal and belief in the inspirational power of knowledge. 'A man's demand to know the exact structure of a fly's wing,' he tells Cantelupe, 'and his assertion that it degrades any child in the street not to know such a thing, is a religious revival . . . a token of spiritual hunger. What else can it be?' But it is typical of the man that, when Amy turns up between his appointments to announce that she is bearing his child, Trebell's reformist fervour is replaced by emotional indifference.

But Barker's masterstroke is the third act, in which he shows the incoming Tory prime minister, Lord Horsham, dealing with the implications of the news of Amy's death. In world drama only Schiller has dealt as vividly with the shifting nature of political alliances. In *Waste*'s three major post-war revivals – John Barton's for the RSC in 1985, Peter Hall's at the Old Vic in 1997 and Samuel West's for the Almeida in 2008 – it is this act that has proved compulsively gripping. Initially it shows Horsham and his future ministers trying to buy the silence of Amy's husband about the cause of her death: this is the politics of the cover-up, in which a scandal has to be buried in order to save both Trebell's public reputation and a prospective parliamentary bill. The only people who cut through the cant are O'Connell and Trebell himself, who tells a wavering colleague, 'You know we're an adulterous and sterile generation. Why should you cry out at proof now and then of what's always in the hearts of most of us?' But even after news has reached the cabinet-in-waiting that O'Connell plans to keep silent we see the anxious jostling for power among the future ministers, who seize the opportunity to ditch both Trebell and his uncompromising bill. As Lord Horsham, wearied after a night of political haggling, tells Cantelupe, 'I have never sat in a cabinet yet that didn't greet anything like a new idea in chilling silence.'

In the last act we see the consequences for Trebell of having lost both his actual child and his surrogate one in the form of the parliamentary bill: he commits suicide. I share William Archer's reservations about whether this is wholly consistent with the character Barker has created. But it certainly underscores the play's governing idea. As Dennis Kennedy, the most sympathetic modern editor of Barker's work, puts it 'The central theme of the play is sterility'. And it is astonishing how often this is underlined by verbal motifs. The implacably Catholic O'Connell, who desperately wanted children of his own by Amy, asks the nocturnal meeting of ministers, 'Is the curse of barrenness to be nothing to a man?' Trebell's doctor tells his patient, 'I can talk cleverly and I've written a book . . . but I'm barren.' And Trebell finally says to his loving but stoically unmarried sister, 'I could still do more work outside the cabinet than the rest of them, inside, will do. But suddenly I've a feeling that the work would be barren.'

The insistent hammer-blows of this word are revealing. This is not just a play about the political process. It is also the tragedy of a man who, for all his public zeal, ends up without the consolation of either living progeny or a tangible public legacy. It is tempting, in fact, to wonder how much of himself Barker poured into Trebell. Barker was married twice: first to the actress Lillah McCarthy and then to a wealthy American heiress, Helen Huntington, who took him away from the world of the London theatre. But Barker had no children and never lived to see the causes he so ardently championed – the ending of censorship, the building of a National Theatre, the establishment of a vibrant, non-commercial theatre – come to fruition. Barker had retired from the theatrical scene by the time he was forty. Although we are all the beneficiaries of Barker's campaigning fervour, I suspect that much of the power of *Waste* stems from his identification with the brilliant but unfulfilled Trebell.

57

Professor Bernhardi

ARTHUR SCHNITZLER
(1862–1931)

There are fascinating parallels between *Waste* and Schnitzler's *Professor Bernhardi*. Both feature a young woman who dies of a botched abortion. Both reveal the backstabbing process of politics, dominated by place-seeking men. Both plays suffered censorship problems. Schnitzler was not thanked for exposing the anti-Semitism behind the glittering surface of Viennese life: *Professor Bernhardi* was initially banned in his native Austria and had its première in Berlin in 1912. But the similarities between Barker and Schnitzler do not end there. Both employed a naturalistic form to tell disquieting truths about their society and used a particular fact-based episode to explore big issues: in Schnitzler's case, the conflict between science and faith.

Schnitzler certainly knew what he was writing about. His father was a successful Viennese laryngologist, his mother was a doctor's daughter, and he himself studied at Vienna's medical school and worked in his father's private clinic. His career seemed set from the start. But, while never totally abandoning his work as a physician, Schnitzler was, like Chekhov, primarily a writer. In *Anatol* (adapted by Granville Barker for the British stage in 1911), in *Liebelei* (translated by David Harrower as *Sweet Nothings* in 2010) and, most famously, in *Reigen* (filmed by Max Ophüls as

La Ronde and rewritten by David Hare as *The Blue Room* in 1998) he explored the sexual mores of *fin de siècle* Vienna with unerring sophistication: one abiding image of his early work is of 'das süsse Mädel' (the sweet girl) casually destroyed by heartless males. But Schnitzler's later novels and plays, including the 1908 *Das weite Land* (which became *Undiscovered Country* in Tom Stoppard's 1979 adaptation), deal more extensively with the corruption and latent violence behind the baroque façade of imperial Austria. Like his contemporary and sometime acquaintance Sigmund Freud, Schnitzler was fascinated by individual psychology. He also brilliantly chronicled the anti-Semitism that was working its way through the Viennese body-politic like a virus. We tend to think of Schnitzler as a writer about sex; *Professor Bernhardi* shows that he was a major social dramatist.

In Britain the play is scarcely known. In 1936 it was briefly seen in an English version directed by Schnitzler's son Heinrich. In 2005 Mark Rosenblatt directed a first-rate production at London's Arcola Theatre in a new version by Samuel Adamson. Since Adamson's version contained several cuts, I've gone back to the full translation by J. M. Q. Davies for the Oxford World's Classics. And, my God, the play is long! But you come away from the Davies version feeling you've encountered a work that puts a vast section of Viennese society on stage and that, although billed as a comedy, has a tragically prophetic quality.

The action starts in a private clinic, the Elizabethinium, very like the one run by Schnitzler's father. And the first act allows us to see the events that will propel the play's moral debate. A young woman is dying after a failed abortion. Professor Bernhardi, head of the clinic, thinks it best that she dies in a state of camphor-induced euphoria. However, a Catholic priest is summoned by a nurse to administer the last rites. Bernhardi bars the priest, Reder, from the sick room: he doesn't want the girl to expire in terror. But neither Bernhardi nor Reder achieves his wish: the girl dies anyway in a state of fear without being granted the sacraments. But what seems like a minor clash between a doctor and a priest escalates into a national scandal. The clinic's trustees resign, its professors are divided on racial lines, questions are asked in parliament, Bernhardi faces a trial, and, after his release from prison, various factions compete to turn him into a martyr. Bernhardi starts out as a doctor trying to do what he thinks best; he ends up being dubbed a 'medical Dreyfus'.

Schnitzler leaves us in little doubt that it is anti-Semitism that drives Bernhardi's opponents. A medical success for Bernhardi's team is sarcastically said to prompt 'rejoicing in Israel'. Pressure is put on Bernhardi to support a not over-competent Gentile rather than a talented Jew for a crucial medical post. Indeed, it's suggested the whole case against him will be dropped if he agrees. During a vehement boardroom battle, Bernhardi's main opponent points out that eighty-five per cent of the clinic's patients are Catholic, while the majority of the doctors are Jewish. 'The fact is,' he says, 'that this creates bad blood in certain circles.' Bernhardi is undoubtedly punished for being Jewish. But it's part of the play's rich irony that he makes singularly little fuss about his faith. In the end, Bernhardi stands less for orthodox Judaism than for a secular humanism fighting both religious certainty and political opportunism. There are two great scenes in the play: one where Bernhardi has an intellectual ding-dong with the priest who caused him so much vexation and another where he confronts a trimming politician and ex-doctor who argues it's worth sacrificing Bernhardi for the sake of the greater good.

In one way, you can see Bernhardi as part of a long line of uncompromising dramatic heroes: a disciple of Molière's Alceste, Shakespeare's Coriolanus and Ibsen's Dr Stockman in *An Enemy of the People* (which Schnitzler's play closely resembles) and a forerunner of Shaw's Saint Joan, Brecht's Galileo and Miller's John Proctor in *The Crucible*. But, like all the great dramatists, Schnitzler empathises with his protagonist while seeing the opposition's point of view. Bernhardi is naive in his disdain for politics, willful in his rejection of press support, arrogant in his belief in the unassailability of truth. He has right and justice on his side. But when he says, 'I'm in the business of curing people – or at least trying to persuade them that I can' you feel that he is guilty of treating medicine as if it were sacrosanct and ignoring the social context in which it inevitably operates.

Schnitzler himself said of politics, in a diary entry for May 1896, 'It is the lowest thing and has the least to do with the essence of humanity.' But he was far from indifferent to public life. He eloquently recorded his disgust with anti-Semitism, was horrified by a Jesuit priest's call in 1918 for the extermination of the Jews because of their alleged failure of patriotism and in 1922 was himself the victim of violence when a group of National Socialists broke up a public reading he was giving. And what Schnitzler does in *Professor Bernhardi* is to portray, in intricate detail and with prophetic insight, one of the great evils of the twentieth century without either sanctifying his hero or endorsing his apolitical stance. It's a big play on a big issue that shows Schnitzler, even when writing about the corrosive poison of anti-Semitism, never sacrificed the irony that was his forte.

58

The Daughter-in-Law

D. H. LAWRENCE
(1885–1930)

Schnitzler and Barker had to endure the myopic interference of theatrical censorship. But with D. H. Lawrence the case is slightly different. Although his fiction, poetry and paintings were sometimes subject to publishers' panic and police raids, his plays were largely kept off the stage in his lifetime by iron-clad convention. Put simply, the British theatre was not yet ready for Lawrence's brand of luminous, working-class realism often couched in strong Nottinghamshire dialect. Lawrence was undoubtedly a dedicated playwright. By 1912 he had published three novels but had also written six plays including the mining trilogy of *A Collier's Friday Night*, *The Widowing of Mrs Holroyd* and *The Daughter-in-Law*. Yet it was not until the late 1960s, over thirty years after Lawrence's death, that the plays were rediscovered by Peter Gill, first singly and then collectively, in a ground-breaking season at the Royal Court. I remember John Osborne, in handing over an award to Gill for his revelatory productions, astringently remarking that 'they were so good that even critics couldn't fail to see their quality'.

Of the three plays, it is *The Daughter-in-Law*, written in 1912, when Lawrence had abandoned his teaching job in Croydon to flee to the continent with Frieda Weekley, that now looks like his masterpiece. 'It is neither a tragedy nor a comedy – just ordinary,' said Lawrence in a letter to Edward Garnett. But that supposed 'ordinariness' now looks extraordinary. It offers a portrait of a marriage, between the 'stuck-up' Minnie and her miner husband Luther, that in its love-hate intensity rivals anything in Strindberg. It articulates the familiar Lawrentian theme, famously explored in *Sons and Lovers*, of men caught in a tug-of-war between rival female claimants: 'how is a woman,' asks Minnie in the play's most resonant line, 'to have a husband if all the men belong to their mothers?' But Lawrence sets the domestic conflict against the background of the 1912 miners' strike and suggests that Minnie and Luther's marriage can only survive when they meet on terms of economic equality and when Luther has asserted his manhood by successfully thwarting the blacklegs. Lawrence's theme is the intersection of sex and class in British life, portrayed with blistering realism in authentic Nottinghamshire dialect. Given the middle-class bias of the British theatre, it's not surprising the play had to wait so long for public performance.

But what is fascinating is the way the play's ideas grow organically out of the action: Lawrence is not advancing a thesis but exploring a set of complex relationships. In the opening scene you instantly see the dependence of Luther's live-in bachelor brother Joe on their domineering mother Mrs Gascoigne. When Joe, a miner refused compensation for a workplace accident, talks of emigrating to Australia or seeking consolation in marriage, he is quickly squashed on both counts: 'marriage,' his mother asserts, 'is like a mousetrap, for either man or woman. You've soon come to th' end o' th' cheese'. But with the arrival of a neighbour, Mrs Purdy, the action shifts up a gear. Mrs Purdy announces that her daughter Bertha was impregnated by Luther before his recent marriage to the la-di-da Minnie. How is this to be dealt with? In a conventional drama you'd expect a head-to-head collision between Mrs Purdy and Mrs Gascoigne. In Lawrence's play they disagree only over tactics. Mrs Purdy would be happy to accept a discreet settlement of forty pounds on her daughter without Luther's wife ever knowing. It is Luther's mother who insists that Mrs Purdy makes Minnie aware of the unwelcome news. 'It'll take her down a peg or two,' she claims, 'and, my sirs, she wants it, my sirs, she needs it.'

Without raising his voice, Lawrence tells us an enormous amount about the interdependence of sons and mothers in a single scene. And when the action shifts to Minnie and Luther's cottage, furnished in the Arts and Crafts style of the modestly affluent, we quickly grasp the truth about this six-week-old marriage. Lawrence leaves us in no doubt about its erotic power. Minnie at first protests about Luther sitting down to supper still clad in his collier's gear. At the same time, she is clearly turned on by his unwashed state: 'you don't look nearly such a tame-rabbit in your pit-dirt,' she says, kissing him passionately. The sex is clearly still good between them. Yet Minnie and Luther scratch away at each other's nerves, suggesting the class and economic tensions between them have never been resolved. Minnie has a small nest-egg from her years in domestic service. Luther, in her eyes, is lazy, proletarian and molly-coddled. 'That's what your mother did for you,' says Minnie, 'mardin' you up till you were all mard-soft.' You don't need a dialect dictionary to see the power of her insult.

Lawrence's instinctive dramatic intelligence lies in the way he tackles the situation. In the second act, when Minnie learns that Luther has fathered an unwanted child, you might expect violent hysterics. In fact, Minnie accepts the reality of the situation and, to Luther's chagrin, offers to pay the forty pounds required in hush money. And even though Minnie leaves Luther for a fortnight to go to Manchester, her return offers further proof of Lawrence's theatrical craft. Private and public worlds seamlessly intertwine as the threatened miners' strike, which has rumbled in the background, becomes a means of resolving the marital gridlock. There's more than a touch of wild comedy – not a quality Dr Leavis ever perceived in Lawrence – to the suggestion by Joe that, since Minnie has effectively gone on strike by her absence, one of Luther's old flames should be brought in to do the housework. Luther's intemperate gesture, in hurling into the fire the £90 worth of prints that Minnie has bought in Manchester, also at last puts them on an equal economic footing. And when Luther and Joe risk death, at the hands of the imported redcoats, by stopping the scabs taking over the mines, Luther graduates into manhood. Lawrence is too good a dramatist to suggest that the final reconciliation between Luther and Minnie is anything but uneasy. Indeed, when Minnie takes Luther in her arms and he begins to cry, you wonder if he has simply swapped one mother for another. But in the theatre the scene is as powerfully affecting as the close of *Uncle Vanya*. In Peter Gill's 1968 Royal Court production that final moment was beautifully played by Judy Parfitt and Michael Coles. So too in David Lan's 2002 Young Vic revival, where Anne-Marie Duff's Minnie had the strength of tempered steel and Paul Hilton's Luther proved 'a disarming mix', as Robert Shore wrote in the *TLS*, 'of gawky vulnerability and pride'. Lawrence himself, declaring his dramatic intentions in a letter to Edward Garnett, said, 'I am sure we are rather sick of the bony, bloodless drama we get nowadays.' In *The Daughter-in-Law* he countered that by writing a play full of sinew, blood and theatrical viscera.

59

Pygmalion

GEORGE BERNARD SHAW
(1856–1950)

On the surface, it's hard to think of two more antithetical dramatists than D. H. Lawrence and Bernard Shaw. Indeed in the letter to Edward Garnett quoted above Lawrence goes on to say, 'It is time for a reaction against Shaw and Galsworthy and Barker and Irishy (except Synge) people – the rule and measure mathematical folk.' Shaw, for his part, was more generous, saying, after reading *The Widowing of Mrs Holroyd*, 'I wish I could write such dialogue – with mine I always hear the sound of the typewriter.'

Yet, for all their differences of style, method and temperament, Shaw and Lawrence were not as far apart as they seem. Around the time in 1912 that Lawrence was working on *The Daughter-in-Law* Shaw was writing *Pygmalion*. Both are socialist plays dealing with class, sex and economics. And both show the stifling effect of mother-love on the English male. Lawrence's Luther is still secretly tied to Mrs Gascoigne's apron-strings, and Shaw's Professor Higgins, in a revealingly Freudian passage, tells his mother, 'Oh, I can't be bothered with young women. My idea of a loveable young woman is somebody as like you as possible.' And Shaw expands on this idea in his epilogue, when he explains that one reason why there could never be any romantic attachment between Eliza and Professor Higgins is that 'she could never obtain a complete grip on him or come between him and his mother (the first necessity of the married woman)'.

That is one of the many reasons why Shaw's play is vastly superior to the musical, *My Fair Lady*, which has supplanted it in the public's affections. In the Lerner and Loewe musical, for all its melodic grace, Professor Higgins claims he's just 'an ordinary man' (something you could never say of Shaw's truculent hero), and the ending implies a romantic alliance between him and Eliza. But the whole point of Shaw's play is to offer an ironic inversion of standard romance and to raise provocative questions about the class system's dependence on income, accent and posture as much as genetic inheritance.

Behind the play, of course, lies a famous myth: that of a Cretan king, Pygmalion, who fell in love with his own sculpture, which was transformed by Aphrodite into the flesh-and-blood Galatea. In the legend, a statue was turned into a human being. In Shaw's play a human being is turned into a statue, a mechanical doll who resembles a duchess. That is why one of the funniest scenes in modern drama is that in which Eliza, 'speaking with pedantic correctness of pronunciation and great beauty of tone', reveals to Mrs Higgins's astonished guests the murkiness of her origins and the suspicion that her aunt was murdered: 'Them she lived with would have killed her for a hat-pin, let alone a hat,' claims Eliza with cut-glass precision. The scene is a confirmation of Henri Bergson's theory that comedy derives from human beings behaving like automata. It also proves that supposed class distinctions are a sham, in that you can manufacture a plausible facsimile of an upper-class Englishwoman.

But Shaw's play is even more subversive than that. It doesn't just demonstrate that a flower-girl can be passed off as a duchess, it goes on to show Higgins's artificial creation rebelling against her creator by becoming an independent woman. That is why Shaw found the idea of a romantic liaison between Higgins and Eliza 'disgusting' and why his last scene is so thrilling. It offers, as Eric Bentley says, the most dramatic of situations: 'two completely articulate characters engaged in a battle of words on which both their fates depend'. But it is more than an intellectual battle. It shows that Shaw, so often caricatured as a bloodless polemicist, was capable of deep emotion. Higgins is torn between his intellectual delight in having created 'a consort battleship' and his emotional desire to retain Eliza 'for the fun of it'. Eliza, for her part, is as determined to make an exit as Ibsen's Nora in *A Doll's House*, while simultaneously wondering, 'What you are to do without me I cannot imagine.' It is a brilliant scene full of human contradictions. I've never seen it better played than in Peter Hall's 2007 production, where Michelle Dockery's mettlesome Eliza confronted Tim Pigott-Smith's confused Higgins, who was left laughing with suspect hilarity at the idea of Eliza's impending marriage. This was a deeply moving image of the loneliness of the creator outstripped by his own creation, a reminder of how many of Shaw's plays, famously including *Saint Joan*, end on a note of autobiographical solitude.

Eliza's transition from screeching flower-seller to imitation duchess and putative shop-owner shows that class is an artificial construct: the fate of her father, Alfred Doolittle, shows it can also be an entrapment. When we first see the dustman Doolittle he is a workshy cadger determined to extract money from Higgins for the latter's takeover of his daughter. This leads to a classic exchange in which the outraged Colonel Pickering asks, 'Have you no morals, man?' To which Doolittle replies, 'Can't afford them, Governor.' This, written in 1912, is every bit as subversive as a famous line from Brecht's 1928 *The Threepenny Opera*: 'Erst kommt das Fressen, dan kommt die Moral,' or 'Food comes first, then morals.'

That's why I call the play socialist: Shaw, like Brecht, understands that economics and morality are ultimately inseparable. For me the point is somewhat overstressed in the final act, when we see Doolittle transformed by a gift of £3,000 a year from an American philanthropist. The former buccaneering free spirit has now been turned into a victim of middle-class morality: forced to marry, pestered by parasitic relatives, badgered by bloodsucking doctors. It's a neat ironic joke, but it shows Shaw's occasional surrender to pattern-making: even the name of Doolittle's beneficiary, Ezra D. Wannafeller, strikes a note of whimsical jocularity.

But this remains a great and extraordinary play. It is one that invokes a whole variety of myths: not just Pygmalion and Galatea, but Frankenstein and the monster, Svengali and Trilby and, in its portrait of Marylebone bachelordom, Holmes and Watson. At the same time, it is a play of strong and powerful emotion: the post-ball scene in which Eliza hurls the slippers at Higgins and dents his negligence by returning the borrowed jewels in case she is accused of theft should bury for ever the idea that Shaw was incapable of creating real characters. And while the play offers a critique of society, it is also filled with Shaw's own particular verbal music. Just listen to the rhythms and cadences of that final scene:

> ELIZA: Oh, you are a devil. You can twist the heart in a girl as easy as some could twist her arms to hurt her. Mrs Pearce warned me. Time and again she has wanted to leave you; and you always got round her at the last minute. And you don't care a bit for her. And you don't care a bit for me.
> HIGGINS: I care for life, for humanity; and you are a part of it that has come my way and been built into my house. What more can you or anyone ask?

With writing as exquisitely harmonious as that, who needs the gilded romanticism of *My Fair Lady*?

60

Heartbreak House

GEORGE BERNARD SHAW

(1856–1950)

The debate about Shaw himself is never-ending. Some years ago I sat on a literary panel where Michael Holroyd and I were asked to propose the case for Shaw while two others argued the case against. It was a stimulating evening at the end of which Michael Holroyd, with characteristic insight, remarked that we could all easily have swapped sides. This was, in fact, confirmed when a totally different Michael, the septuagenarian hack we last encountered talking about Oscar Wilde, and Helena, the bright-eyed Oxford graduate, enjoyed one of their periodic, post-show chats. They met in a café just after the latest revival of *Heartbreak House*.

Helena: Well, what about that?

Michael: What indeed?

H: Three and a half hours of clever dialogue and debate but with no real plot and leaving you, at the end, with nothing more than a vague sense of Shaw's nihilistic despair at the prospects for the human race.

M: You could say that. But I remember when David Hare directed *Heartbreak House* at the Almeida in 1997 he called it 'the century's original state-of-England play'. Don't forget Shaw was writing it over a long period, from 1913 to 1916, and he brings together, under one roof, a cross-section of society: Bloomsbury bohemians, horse-and-hound colonialists, a captain of industry, an ineffectual idealist, a naive romantic, all presided over by the Lear-like figure of Captain Shotover. What more could you ask?

H: A great deal! You say it's a state-of-England play. But Shaw draws large conclusions from a limited selection of characters. The suburban middle-classes are missing. And, as so often, Shaw treats the working classes as little more than comic relief. There's a servant, Nurse Guinness, who turns out, somewhat improbably, to have been married to an ex-pirate and so-called burglar whose main aim is to get caught so he can bribe the householders into taking up a collection for him. What on earth does that tell us about the state of the nation?

M: With respect, I think you're being unfair. This is a play of mood and atmosphere that movingly captures the pervasive disillusion of the thinking classes at a crucial period in world history. Shaw even suggests they have a collective death-wish which is why, in that extraordinary conclusion, they turn on all the lights in Shotover's house as the bombers fly overhead. Even if the play wasn't produced in England until 1921, that strikes me as extraordinarily daring in its image of a civilisation inviting its own destruction. And one that retains its power in the nuclear age. But don't forget Shaw also called the play 'a fantasia in the Russian manner on English themes'. Wouldn't you agree that *Heartbreak House* is deeply Chekhovian?

H. Not as I understand Chekhov. I accept that Shaw was influenced by *The Cherry Orchard*. He also borrows the Chekhovian externals: the country-house setting, the dislocated conversations, the distant sound effects. But Chekhov's characters all have their own internal dynamic. They exist as real people. Shaw's characters, however, all stand for something. Michael Holroyd admits as much in his excellent biography, where he lists their symbolic attributes.

Shotover, he says, represents religious concentration of thought, his daughters Ariadne and Hesione power and culture respectively, while Boss Mangan is capitalism, and Ellie Dunn, who ultimately rejects marriage to Mangan, embodies will.

M: I take your point. But what you miss out is the comic vitality of his characters and what Borges called 'the flavor of liberation' that animates Shaw's work. Shaw's approach to character is also prophetic in that, like Pirandello and Genet, he peels away the pretence to expose the reality beneath. That's precisely what Boss Mangan objects to when he says 'we've stripped ourselves morally naked'. The great capitalist is revealed to be at the mercy of a syndicate, Hesione's ladykiller husband is shown to be a posturing fantasist, Ellie Dunn a manipulative schemer and even Captain Shotover is no more than a rum-soaked dreamer. *Heartbreak House* is actually a House of Illusions.

H: Nice phrase. But I'd still argue that drama depends on a forward-moving narrative, on a constructive philosophy, on the ability to engender emotion. One of the play's early critics called it 'Jawbreak House'. Shaw leaves us without a shred of hope. And I, as a young woman, find it difficult to connect to any of the characters: even Ellie moves, with improbable speed, from romantic naivety to heartbroken stoicism to salvation through a spiritual marriage to the eighty-eight-year-old Shotover. I ask you!

M: I can see we'll never agree on Shaw's capacity to make disquisition dramatic. As for philosophy, a dramatist is entitled to his despair. I've noticed, whenever I've seen the play, how the audience always responds to Shotover's image of England as a ship heading onto the rocks. But I must pick you up on the question of emotion. Just look at Hesione's description to Ellie of the power of love: 'How delightful it makes waking up in the morning! How much better than the happiest dream! All life transfigured! No more wishing one had an interesting book to read, because life is so much happier than any book! No desire but to be alone and not to have to talk to anyone: to be alone and just think about it.' Doesn't that get to you?

H: Only up to a point. I accept that the cadences are seductive. But it's an old man's fantasy, an eloquent description of love rather than its embodiment. Shaw tells rather than shows. He's a dramatist of ideas, of witty talk, of clever manipulation of character. But for me there is always something missing: the sense that the characters have escaped the author's control and are leading him in unexpected directions.

M: A fair point. But it's a matter of fact that Shaw was partly inspired to write the play by sitting with the Woolfs and the Webbs in a Sussex garden in summertime and had little idea where his imagination would take him. And I think *Heartbreak House* is a turning point in that it shows Shaw shedding some of his earlier didacticism and heading towards a more intuitive theatre. Eventually that leads him, in *Too True To Be Good*, towards an Ionesco-like absurdism. As for his lack of theatricality, it's hard to beat the moment at the very end when Randall Utterword plays 'Keep the Home Fires Burning' on his flute even as the bombs descend.

H: Ah, but that appeals to your own sense of nostalgia and your long theatrical memory. But I am young and live in a different world.

M: I can't argue with that. And it's perfectly true that we are both coming at Shaw from different angles: I'm more like Shotover, you're more like Ellie.

H: Except, I don't see us entering into a spiritual marriage!

M: Quite so. But I suspect neither of us is quite as certain of our viewpoints as we seem and, on another day, we could easily take opposite sides. That is the beauty of Shaw.

H: Or possibly the problem!

M picks up the tab, and they go their separate ways.

61

Exiles

JAMES JOYCE

(1882–1941)

James Joyce dismissively branded Shaw 'a born preacher'. Shaw was more appreciative of his fellow Irishman, describing *Ulysses* as 'a literary masterpiece'. It also seems a total myth, fostered by Joyce himself, that his play *Exiles* (written in 1915 after *A Portrait of the Artist as a Young Man*) was initially rejected by the Stage Society in London because of a Shavian veto. It is true that one of the Stage Society's Reading Committee described *Exiles* as 'Reminiscent of Strindberg at his worst. Putrid'. But Shaw, while requesting a few excisions, hailed 'a considerable youthful talent'. And *Exiles*, having been premièred in Munich in 1919, eventually got a Stage Society production in 1926. Sadly, it made little impact.

We had to wait until 1970 for the reclamation of this astonishing play. Just as Peter Gill rescued D. H. Lawrence's plays from oblivion, so Harold Pinter lovingly restored this forgotten work in a brilliant production first seen at the Mermaid and then absorbed by the RSC into its Aldwych repertory. As Irving Wardle wrote at the time, 'what Pinter offers is the kind of insight which only one creative artist can perform in the service of another'. But Joyce had long been part of Pinter's intellectual landscape. As a Hackney teenager, he had written an article about *Ulysses* for his school magazine, claiming, 'This enormous work, which depicts a day in the life of a Dubliner, stands supreme among twentieth-century literature.' In rediscovering *Exiles* for the stage, Pinter revealed his instinctive affinity with Joyce: they shared a preoccupation with betrayal, memory, guilt and the sado-masochistic intricacy of sexual relationships as well as a belief that drama often lay in the interstices of everyday conversation. Like so many of Pinter's plays, Joyce's was also triggered by an intensely recollected personal experience.

Joyce had left Ireland for Italy in 1904 with the adored Nora Barnacle, and a year later they had an illegitimate son. But it was thanks to Richard Ellmann's indispensable biography that we discovered the extent to which Joyce was haunted by doubts about Nora's fidelity. On a return visit to Ireland in 1909 he was tormented by the allegations of an old university friend, Vincent Cosgrave, that the latter had slept with Nora while Joyce was courting her. And back in Trieste two years later, Joyce was shocked to learn that an admiring Venetian journalist, Roberto Prezioso, had sought to become Nora's lover. What is significant is that Nora kept Joyce fully informed of the situation, thereby allowing him to study Prezioso's activities, in Ellmann's words, 'for secrets of the human spirit'.

All this feeds into *Exiles*. Both formally and in its ability to show how the past shapes the present the play demonstrates Joyce's devotion to Ibsen. In its focus on the uncertainty of ever fully knowing one's partner, on the idea of sex as a battleground and on the ambivalence of male friendship, it anticipates the Pinter of *The Collection*, *Old Times* and *Betrayal*.

The action revolves around the return of the writer Richard Rowan to Ireland from Italian exile in the company of his common-law wife Bertha and their child Archie. From the start Joyce makes it clear that Richard has found in the letters of his intellectual confidante, Beatrice, an inspiration his wife cannot provide. But the real action stems from the sexual advances made by Robert Hand, a leading Dublin journalist and Richard's oldest friend, to Bertha. The first of many dramatic shocks comes when Bertha reveals to Richard every stage of Robert's amorous attack: even now I can recall the persistent, hammer-blow note in John Wood's voice, in the Pinter production, as he repeatedly enquired of Bertha 'And then . . . And then? . . . And then?'

But the husband–friend–wife relationship is taken several stages further in the remarkable second act set in Robert's cottage. Robert has made an assignation with Bertha, deviously timed to coincide with an academic appointment he has arranged for Richard with the university vice-chancellor, one that will hopefully lead to Richard taking up a post in Dublin as a lecturer in romance languages. But it is Richard who first turns up at the cottage in place of Bertha. In a conventional play you'd expect an angry confrontation between the potential cuckold and the would-be seducer. Instead Joyce explores the labyrinthine complexity of Richard's nature. A part of him espouses the idea of sexual freedom; another part is a tortured masochist who tells Robert he longs to be betrayed. When Bertha herself turns up at Robert's hideaway, Joyce extends the erotic complications. At one point Richard, speaking of Bertha's putative seducer, tells her, 'I cannot hate him since his arms have been around you. You have drawn us near together.' This is exactly what René Girard called 'triangular desire', with all its homoerotic implications, which Pinter went on to explore so subtly in a number of plays. And the very fact that we never know exactly what takes place between Robert and Bertha in the cottage, after Richard's departure, haunts the final act. The next morning Robert offers a suspiciously circumstantial account of his night's activities – including writing an opinion piece for the paper, celebrating Richard's return from exile – while Richard himself tells Bertha, 'I have a deep, deep wound of doubt in my soul.' As for Bertha, she seems to have acquired a new power over Richard as well as an intensification of her profound and unswerving love.

Joyce, in his extensive notes on *Exiles*, says 'the play is three cat and mouse acts'. But who is the cat and who are the mice? At first, one assumes that Richard Rowan, whose predicament so closely echoes Joyce's own, is the cat. But I suspect it is really Bertha, wiser in spite of her supposed intellectual inferiority to Richard, Robert and the coldly inspirational Beatrice, who is the controlling force. And it is she who speaks the movingly poetic final invocation, 'O, my strange, wild lover come back to me again.'

But for all the play's hermetic intensity and psychological insight Joyce never lets us forget that its unspoken subject is Ireland itself. Explaining his title, Joyce writes in the notes, 'A nation exacts a penance from those who dared to leave her, payable on their return.' Joyce also, in a series of deft touches, sketches in the social background of his native land, a place where vocal Catholic certainty confronts 'the asthmatic voice of protestantism', where reputation is often dictated by journalistic opinion-formers and where, in Robert's own prophetic words, 'Some day we shall have to choose between England and Europe.' Intensely erotic personal relationships are tied to politics and religion with a scarcely visible thread. And while the play will always be a treasure-trove for Joyce scholars seeking intimations of *Ulysses*, it stands on its own as a lacerating portrait of the battle between a belief in sexual freedom and the desire to possess the object of one's love.

62

The Verge

SUSAN GLASPELL
(1876–1948)

I once dubbed Susan Glaspell 'American drama's best-kept secret'. It's fair to say that today that is no longer strictly true. Feminist critics write books and articles about her. In 2003 an International Susan Glaspell Society was formed. And Sam Walters ardently championed her work in his tenure at Richmond's Orange Tree. In his time, five of Glaspell's full-length plays and three of her one-act pieces were presented. Of the former, *The Verge* (1921) proved outstanding: a strange, compelling piece that showed Glaspell, like her friend Eugene O'Neill, was seeking to push American drama in new directions.

Glaspell's own story is fascinating. Like her exact contemporary, the novelist Willa Cather, she was a product of the American Midwest. Glaspell was born in rural Iowa, was a bright star at Drake University and excelled in local journalism. But it was her meeting with, and eventual marriage to, George Cram Cook that helped transform her from an admired novelist into a prolific playwright and key figure in American theatre history. Cook was a flamboyant figure and ardent Hellenophile who inveighed against the rampant commercialism of American theatre. In personality, Glaspell seemed his diametric opposite: 'private and reclusive', as Arthur and Barbara Gelb say in their biography of

O'Neill, 'she possessed a steely steadiness inherited from the pioneering women who had settled the Iowa prairies'. But Cook and Glaspell, who married in 1913, were united in their desire to create a new form of theatre. In 1915 they were founding members of the Provincetown Players, a group of like-minded artists who converted a fisherman's shack at the tip of Cape Cod into a summer theatre. Eventually, this yielded a winter operation in Greenwich Village which marked the birth of Off-Broadway. But what is astonishing is the work produced by the Players in their first seven years, which included O'Neill's *The Emperor Jones* and *The Hairy Ape* as well as plays by Theodore Dreiser, Wallace Stevens, Edna Ferber and eight pieces by Glaspell herself. She, even more than O'Neill, was the company's house-dramatist and no less experimental.

But just how good was she? The crustily dogmatic George Jean Nathan in his idiosyncratic *Encyclopedia of the Theatre* (published in 1940) devotes an entry to Women Playwrights in which he notes the emergence of a new generation including Rachel Crothers, Zoë Akins and Glaspell herself. But Nathan makes two criticisms of women dramatists. One is that they're no good at writing men, whom they see 'either as romantic heroes or childlike and blundering oafs, either as intellectual and emotional giants or as goats and blockheads'. Nathan's other claim is that 'it seems to be impossible for a woman playwright to stand aloof and apart from her central character and not identify herself, in however slight a degree, with her'. Ignoring the obvious point that male playwrights throughout history have similarly projected themselves into their heroes, it's worth applying the Nathan test to Susan Glaspell's *The Verge*.

The first thing to say is that Glaspell clearly puts a lot of herself into her protagonist, Claire Archer. At the same time, she is deeply critical of the way Claire subordinates her compassion to her campaigning zeal. Claire is a plant scientist who is trying to create a new species. One plant, the Edge Vine, fails her, and she tears it up by the roots. As a result, she pins her faith in another plant, Breath of Life, accurately described by Christopher Bigsby in an essay on Glaspell as 'delicate, strange, too fragile to exist outside a hothouse environment'. It is clear that Glaspell identifies with Claire's desire to create new forms through cross-fertilisation: exactly what the dramatist herself is doing through her blend of American realism and European expressionism, her mix of surface accuracy and psychological essences. But when Claire says to her husband, Harry, 'We need not be held in forms moulded for us,' it is clear that the plant experiments symbolise the need to create new social and sexual relationships.

Glaspell's play is a cry of despair at the return to traditional gender patterns after the liberation induced by the 1914–18 war. But, while identifying with Claire's plight, Glaspell also views her heroine objectively. Claire behaves with extreme cruelty to her daughter Elizabeth, who returns home from her conventional college education and offers to help her mother in producing 'a new and better kind of plant'.

Claire not only rejects the word 'better' but, having savagely uprooted the Edge Vine, ferociously turns on her daughter and says, 'To think that object ever moved my belly and sucked my breast'. Claire treats her sister with similar, if somewhat wittier, contempt, claiming, 'You haven't any energy at all, Adelaide. That's why you keep so busy'. And when Claire is offered the chance of escape by her would-be lover, Tom, she simply sees his passion as another form of imprisonment. It would be too reductive to say, as several characters do, that Claire is mad. But what Glaspell charts, with painful acuteness, is the desperation of a woman driven to the verge by her desire not only to create new plant-forms but also to deny the conventional demands of domestic life.

Invoking Melville's *Moby-Dick*, Christopher Bigsby says, 'she is Ahab defying the world through challenging it'.

Claire, memorably played by Isla Blair in Auriol Smith's Orange Tree revival, is a richly complex character. But what of Nathan's charge that women dramatists are no good at writing men? It is perfectly true that the men in Glaspell's play are, as in so many expressionist plays, typified by dominant characteristics: significantly they are called Tom (the idealistic lover), Dick (the Platonic admirer) and Harry (the perplexed husband). But that doesn't mean they are mere stooges; Harry, in particular, is a three-dimensional figure. He is the protective second husband who, in wartime, was a daredevil aviator but who in peacetime has lapsed into country-club respectability. But his devotion to Claire is unstinting, and his bewilderment at her transition into an obsessive plant-scientist genuinely touching. Glaspell doesn't just tell, she shows. In the richly amusing opening scene we see Harry driven from his arctically cold dining room into the hothouse in order to eat his breakfast and then denied salt on his egg for fear that reopening the door would interfere with the room temperature. Where a later play like Enid Bagnold's *The Chalk Garden* (1955) uses horticultural symbolism as a form of arch window-dressing, Glaspell makes it integral to her play: one where form and content perfectly coalesce and where we hear, for the first time on the American stage, the despairing frustration of a woman seeking to shatter stale conventions but destroying a vital part of herself in the process.

63

Henry IV

LUIGI PIRANDELLO
(1867–1936)

Albert Finney, Rex Harrison, Richard Harris: a lot of big actors have been to drawn to Pirandello's play. As Irving Wardle wrote in *The Times*, reviewing Harrison in 1974, 'Henry IV is a part that gratifies the ultimate acting fantasy: control over other people within a self-created private world.' But it was only when I saw Ian McDiarmid play the part in Tom Stoppard's translation at the Donmar Warehouse in 2004 that I felt I really got a handle on this brilliantly perplexing play, one that combines philosophical ideas with playful theatricality.

One definition of a great play is that it absorbs the past while intimating the future. Pirandello's play, written in 1922 shortly after his wife's confinement to an asylum, does just that. You could easily make a list of its main themes: the interplay of illusion and reality, madness and sanity, inherited and constructed identities. But these were the stuff of drama long before Pirandello. Hamlet is a Pirandellian play *avant la lettre* and leaves us in constant doubt as to whether the hero's 'antic disposition' has merged with an unfeigned madness. Segismundo in Calderón's *Life Is a Dream* is driven to conclude that all existence is an illusion. And Kleist's Prince of Homburg, reprieved after a mock-execution, immediately asks, 'Tell me, is this a dream?' *Henry IV*, in short, confirms a point made by the American critic Harold Bloom: that great art has the capacity to subsume what has gone before. But it is also defined by its prophetic instinct. And what, for me, marks out Pirandello as a great dramatist is his poetic grasp of one of the key themes of twentieth-century literature: the entrapped isolation of modern man. Pirandello looks back to Shakespeare. He also anticipates Beckett and Camus.

It is, however, not so much Pirandello's philosophy as his ability to give it theatrical flesh that makes his drama fascinating. Nowhere is that more evident than in *Henry IV*. We are in a private asylum in the 1920s. Its principal occupant is an Italian nobleman who, while playing the eponymous eleventh-century German emperor in a pageant, was thrown off his horse, badly concussed and has spent the last twenty years believing himself to be the historical Henry IV. The charade is maintained by a group of suitably costumed 'courtiers'. But the precariousness of the fiction is exposed when a group of visitors arrive, all with multi-layered motives. Matilda, the woman the hero loved before his concussion, is drawn by an unresolved curiosity. Her buffoonish follower Belcredi has come mainly to mock. Meanwhile a shrink, Dr Genoni, believes he can administer a shock that will restore the hero's sanity.

I admit Pirandello takes his time setting up the fake-historical background and explaining Henry's journey to Canossa to seek papal absolution. But from the moment of Henry's entry late in the second act the play becomes riveting. For a start there is the absurdity of 1920s Italian visitors pretending to be a medieval duchess or Benedictine monks in order to persuade Henry of their authenticity. There is also the curious sense that Henry, while wearing a penitent's sackcloth, is playing a cat-and-mouse game with his guests. He talks of the 'duchess's' masquerade in attempting to arrest time by colouring her hair. He adopts an accusatory tone to a Cluniac monk who is, in reality, the Belcredi who has stolen the Matilda he once loved. And he also shows piercing moments of revelation: 'we inhabit,' he says at one point, 'the self we have chosen for ourselves and don't let go'.

This is the clue to the shock moment that comes midway through the play when Henry, bidding farewell to his visitors, cries, in the Stoppard version used at the Donmar, 'What a bunch of wankers! I played them like a kiddy-piano with a different colour for every key.' Rex Harrison, in the 1974 production, underscored the transition by humming the toreador song from *Carmen* and pulling a cigar out of his eleventh-century tunic. This is what I mean by Pirandello's innate theatricality: our sudden awareness that Henry's reason was restored eight years earlier, that he has ever since been sustaining an elaborate fantasy and that he has been toying with his visitors in a spirit of cryptic revenge. With Pirandello, the ideas are not separate, easily extractable propositions, they are expressed through the physical action.

But the great thing about Pirandello is that his answers breed ever more questions, and that the conundrums go on multiplying. Why did the 'sane' Henry not seek his freedom? Is it a sign of insanity to sustain the fiction of one's madness? Has the mask of 'Henry IV' now supplanted the face of the real man? What I learned from watching Ian McDiarmid's hypnotic performance in the 2004 Michael Grandage production is that these questions, however fascinating, are almost beside the point.

What Pirandello is really writing about is the quintessential loneliness of mankind and the absurdity of our existence. Even the buffoonish Belcredi understands 'You're dying the moment you're born . . . those who started first are beating the path for those who follow.' And Henry, recalling the moment when he was thrown from the horse, says, 'What I saw when I came round was solitude, bleak and empty, and I decided to deck it out in all the colours and splendour of that long-gone carnival day.'

All this came out strongly in McDiarmid's performance. Whether displaying foxy irony or withering disdain, whether surrendering to the fiction of his historical persona or sending it up, he always seemed a tragically unreachable figure. Paul Taylor put it well in the *Independent* when he said that for McDiarmid's Henry the carapace of 'insanity' became 'a shelter, a gun tower and a prison', in other words, a protection, a tactical weapon and a permanent incarceration.

There are earlier Pirandello plays, especially *Right You Are (If You Think So)* and *Six Characters in Search of an Author*, that play similar games with illusion and reality. But it is in *Henry IV* that I hear the resonant solitude that characterises modern literature. The play was first seen in 1922, the year of T. S. Eliot's *The Waste Land* and Joyce's *Ulysses*. It preceded by a mere three years Kafka's *The Trial*. And it is intriguing to note that Beckett's first attempt at full-length drama, *Eleutheria*, contained a spectator who climbed onto the stage to comment on the vagaries of the dramatic action in a manner that was distinctly Pirandellian.

No one has ever questioned the influence the Sicilian master has had on modern drama with his exploration of appearance and reality, mask and face, permanence and flux, though, as I suggested earlier, these themes had been explored prior to his arrival. What I find more moving is Pirandello's realisation, most vividly expressed in *Henry IV*, that we are all sentenced to solitude inside our own skins.

64

Juno and the Paycock

SEAN O'CASEY

(1880–1964)

A great play, indisputably. But what kind of play is it? O'Casey himself called it 'A Tragedy in Three Acts'. Yet there has always been a debate about its form. W. J. Lawrence, reviewing the original 1924 Abbey Theatre production in the *Irish Statesman*, said that O'Casey 'flouts all the precepts of Aristotle'. James Agate, writing about the first London production in 1925, said that there was twenty minutes of tragedy and that the remaining two-and-a-half hours was 'given up to gorgeous and incredible fooling'. Of the many fine revivals I've seen, the one that best conveyed the tragic weight of O'Casey's masterpiece was that directed by Howard Davies for the National Theatre and the Abbey in 2011. Sadly, it was never fully appreciated by the majority of British critics.

I suspect you have to relate the play to its historical context to understand what O'Casey is up to – something that Declan Kibberd does brilliantly in his book, *Irish Classics*, which changed my own perception of the play. Before that, I'd always approached it with a hazy appreciation of its background. I knew, obviously, about the Easter Uprising of 1916, the War of Independence that raged from 1919 to 1921 and the 1922–3 Civil War, which I always thought of as providing the bloodshot backcloth to O'Casey's play. Except that it is much more than a backcloth: it is woven into the very fabric of the text. As Kibberd points out, it is a popular misconception that the Civil War was simply a battle between diehard Republicans and partitionist Free Staters who accepted the ceding of six northern counties to the United Kingdom. Of more immediate concern was the Oath of Allegiance to the Crown demanded of all political representatives of the Free State. 'The legacy of all this,' says Kibberd, 'was a distinct conservatism in public life' which turned yesterday's rebels into today's conformists and which led to the triumph of middle-class morality over genuine independence of thought.

All this informs O'Casey's play, which is not just a study of the troubled Boyle family but a metaphor for Ireland itself. On one level, the play looks relatively straightforward: a jaunty account of the vain, bombastic 'Captain' Jack Boyle and his stoically enduring wife Juno that, as Agate claimed, turns to tragedy in its final section. The key plot-point comes when the perennially hard-up Boyles believe they have inherited a small fortune. But not only does the fortune turn out to be a fake, leaving the Boyles debt-ridden after a riot of spending, their daughter Mary is pregnant by the lover who has deserted her, and their son Johnny is shot by the Diehards for his betrayal of a republican colleague.

The legacy that turns out to be a will o' the wisp is a stock dramatic device. But in the context of the times it acquires a rich metaphorical resonance: it becomes a symbol of the dubious inheritance of a nationalism that, as Kibberd says, 'had promised workers reconquest of Ireland but delivered no more than green flags and green postboxes'. Boyle himself is also transformed by the fake will from a saloon-bar rebel into a mouther of conventional pieties, something vividly caught in Olivier's 1966 revival, where Colin Blakely changed from a drunken dreamer into a mock-capitalist encased in tweeds and watch-chain. But the clues are all there in O'Casey's text. In the first act Boyle fiercely attacks the clergy's historic power over the Irish people, claiming, 'If they've taken everything else from us, Joxer, they've left us our memory.' In Boyle's case, that's precisely what they haven't left. Believing himself newly enriched, Boyle totally contradicts his earlier anti-clerical defiance, declaring, 'As far as I know the History o' me country, the priest was always in the van of the fight for Irelan's freedom.' Even domestic relationships are shaped by the historical context. When Boyle, asserting his male rights, boldly declares, 'Today, there's goin' to be issued a proclamation by me, establishin' an independent Republic an' Juno'll have to take an oath of allegiance,' there is a clear equation between the family and the Free Staters.

I'm not denying O'Casey's rich vein of comedy: Jack Boyle, bragging of his seagoing exploits on the basis of working as a collier on a Liverpool-bound ferry, is very funny, and his relationship with his weasely buddy Joxer is a venomously accurate study of a braggart's need for an audience. I also detect in the minute recall of day-to-day detail by a neighbour, Maisie Madigan, that same brand of comic garrulity I heard in Shakespeare's Mistress Quickly and Dickens's Mrs Nickleby. But for all its humour I would argue the play is imbued with tragedy from the start. It is there in Johnny's violent reaction to the news of the death of a neighbour's son in the republican cause. It is there in Mary's chilly rejection of a fellow trade-unionist who fervently adores her. Above all, it is there in the figure of Juno, who is both a symbol of long-suffering Irish womanhood and a richly complex character in her own right.

Juno is the lynchpin of the Boyle family: a loyal Catholic, a teeth-gritting breadwinner, a chastening critic of her workshy husband. I remember Judi Dench in Trevor Nunn's 1980 RSC production raising her eyes to heaven whenever her husband spouted his seafaring nonsense and finding a bulwark against despair in domestic routine. Yet it would be a mistake to see Juno as some kind of plaster saint. In the second act she too succumbs to the selfish irresponsibility of the seemingly prosperous Boyle household: she happily plays the gramophone as a funeral passes her door and says of the grieving mother, Mrs Tancred, 'In wan way, she deserves all she got; for lately she let the Die-hards make an open house of th' place.' But Juno shows a capacity for moral growth and, after the death of her own son, comes to regret her earlier callousness. In a powerful moment that often seems to stand as the play's epigraph, she echoes Mrs Tancred's appeal to the Sacred Heart of Jesus: 'Take away this murderhin' hate, and give us Thine own eternal love!'

In the end O' Casey leaves us with an image of a bare tenement room stripped of its furniture and of characters similarly reduced to their meagre essentials. Juno has gone to live with her sister, accompanied by her pregnant daughter. Meanwhile Boyle and Joxer drunkenly return to the desolate room, bound together only by a fragile co-dependence and a shrinking vocabulary that uncannily anticipates Beckett. But the climax is not simply a coda to a boisterous comedy. The tragedy is implicit throughout in a play that begins with Mary reading a line from a newspaper: 'On a little bye-road, out beyond Finglas he was found.' There's melancholy in the cadence, but the line refers to a republican fighter's death, caused by the treacherous Johnny, and invokes the betrayal of personal dreams and national aspirations that informs every line of O'Casey's magnificent play.

65

The Front Page

BEN HECHT

(1894–1964) and

CHARLES MACARTHUR

(1895–1956)

Frank Rich once shrewdly observed that *The Front Page* is the one play that will never receive a negative newspaper review. It has a whiff of nostalgia in that it harks back to a time – 1928 to be precise – when a city like Chicago had eight competing daily papers. More importantly, it appeals to journalists' romantic self-image of themselves as men – and in the 1920s they were almost always men – as fast-talking rogues engaged in a never-ending battle against civic corruption.

But *The Front Page* is much more than an effective laughter-machine offering a hymn to hacks. It is a phenomenal play that is both a product of its times and a reminder that satire, at its best, is rooted in observant realism. Harold Clurman, a legendary American director-critic, has pointed out that 'In the hysterically prosperous twenties we had the energy and wit to poke fun at ourselves and to confess our nightmares – if only as a corrective to our creeping complacency.' Energy is the right word for *The Front Page*. But it also reflects a time when a heedless nation was heading towards crisis. In the autumn of 1928 the New York Stock Exchange actually had to close down for a day to clear a backlog in trading of nearly 7 million shares. A year later no fewer than 400 banks had gone bust.

If Hecht and MacArthur's play catches something of the hysteria of the times, it is also that rare thing: a farcical comedy with a realistic base. Hecht had worked for the *Chicago Daily News* and MacArthur for the City News Bureau, and both knew that journalists were more mountebanks than crusaders. The action takes place in the press room of the Chicago Criminal Courts Building on the eve of an execution. What is startling, especially in the first act, is the portrayal of the journalists as a hard-bitten bunch of sexist, racist, domestically screwed-up hacks. One of them, resenting the early-morning hanging of the prisoner, asks, 'Why can't they jerk these guys at a reasonable hour, so we can get some sleep?' They play poker to pass the time and pooh-pooh psychological explanations for the crime. And when the star reporter, Hildy Johnson, announces he is leaving to marry and take a steady job as a New York ad man, their scorn is total: 'You'll be like a firehorse tied to a milkwagon,' one of them crisply remarks. But Hildy retaliates in a speech that damns his old trade in language that shows Hecht and MacArthur's mastery of the vernacular:

Journalists! Peeking through keyholes! Running after fire engines like a lot of coach dogs! Waking people up in the middle of the night to ask them what they think of companionate marriage. Stealing pictures off old ladies of their daughters that get raped in Oak Park. A lot of lousy, daffy buttinskis, swelling around with holes in their pants, borrowing nickels from office boys! And for what? So a million hired girls and motormen's wives'll know what's going on.

Michael Blakemore, whose dazzling production for the National Theatre in 1972 confirmed the play's classic status, eloquently describes his own initial reaction to it in *Stage Blood*. It was, as he says, rooted in a close observation of the world Hecht and MacArthur knew, and his mission was to stage it 'with as much realism and persuasive detail as we could muster, starting with a set so authentic you could almost smell the stale tobacco-smoke, a place where men's hats rarely left their hair-oiled heads'.

This, in short, is a farce about real people. But it is subtler and more complex than it first seems. For a start, while portraying journalism as a trade for grubby sensation-seekers, it also shows the fourth estate provides a necessary corrective to corrupt politicians. Time and again the point is made that the hanging of Earl Williams, who has shot a black policeman, is motivated less by a passion for justice than by electoral convenience. Even though Williams is a self-confessed anarchist, the local sheriff is campaigning for re-election on the crude slogan 'Reform the Reds with a Rope'. And when a messenger arrives from the state governor with a reprieve for Williams, the mayor and sheriff suppress the information. The mayor even bundles the messenger off to a specified address with the information 'It's a nice homey little place and you can get anything you want': in other words, a whorehouse. Everything, Hecht and MacArthur imply, is relative: in a world of graft and corruption even scandal-seeking hacks exercise a vital function.

Social history combines with farcical energy. In addition Hecht and MacArthur offer us a genuine tug-of-war for the body and soul of Hildy Johnson. To whom is he really married? To his old profession, in the bullying shape of his managing editor, Walter Burns? Or to his intended bride, Peggy, with whom he's supposed to catch the 11.18 train to New York? The crisis is triggered by the fact that the fugitive prisoner falls into the hands of Hildy and

Burns, who conceal him in a roll-top desk. Hildy is torn between the urge to record the scoop of the decade and the longing to escape into a life of marital respectability. It's an extreme example of a classic journalistic dilemma: whether the job takes precedence over the life.

What is extraordinary, however, is the way Hecht and MacArthur maintain their interest in character even as the action gathers a furious, Feydeauesque momentum. Burns, who doesn't appear until two-thirds of the way through the play, is a great comic creation, an obsessive monster who will sacrifice anything for the sake of a story. He sadistically manipulates the versifying hack who owns the roll-top desk, detains the deserting Hildy by tossing him on the floor ('At a time of war, you could be shot for what you're doing!') and shows scant concern for the possible death of Hildy's future mother-in-law. You might say he had stepped out of a comedy by Ben Jonson except that he was based on a real-life Chicago editor. Although he was memorably played by Walter Matthau in an otherwise indifferent 1974 Billy Wilder Hollywood film, I still treasure Alan MacNaughtan's iron-clad assurance in the Blakemore revival.

Britain sometimes tends to patronise Broadway success. But this is a play that shows American farcical comedy at its best: attentive to character, constructed with Swiss-watch precision and, at the same time, endowed with a social conscience in its protest at politicised excecutions, artificial anti-Red scares and Town Hall chicanery. As a farce, it is both of its time and sublimely durable.

66

Machinal

SOPHIE TREADWELL
(1885–1970)

Even in a supreme farce like *The Front Page* American drama is conspicuous for its observant realism. This, it seems to argue, is how life is. But there have always been divergent tendencies in American theatre, and in the 1920s this divergence took the form of expressionism. The term itself was first used, around 1900, as an antithesis to impressionism in painting. It heavily influenced the German drama of Georg Kaiser and Ernst Toller. It quickly spread to America and was seen in plays such as O'Neill's *The Emperor Jones* (1920) and *The Hairy Ape* (1922), Susan Glaspell's *The Verge* (1921) and Elmer Rice's *The Adding Machine* (1923). I suspect its sudden popularity had many causes: an awareness of European experiment, resistance to Broadway commercialism, a protest against the mechanisation of society. What is fascinating is that women writers such as Glaspell and Sophie Treadwell, especially in her 1928 play *Machinal*, embraced it so eagerly.

Like Glaspell, Treadwell began life as a journalist. She had a long, richly fulfilled career in which, as a newspaper writer, she covered everything from theatre to baseball for the *San Francisco Chronicle*, interviewed the Mexican revolutionary Pancho Villa and worked as a reporter in the First World War. But she also had a passion for theatre, which led her to write over thirty plays, of which *Machinal* (the French term for 'mechanical' or 'automatic') was far and away the most successful. It had a good run on Broadway in 1928, when Brooks Atkinson in the *New York Times*, while noting its debt to Elmer Rice and Theodore Dreiser's *An American Tragedy*, called it 'a triumph of individual distinction, gleaming with intangible beauty'. Frank Rich similarly acclaimed a New York Public Theater revival in 1990. And in 1993 the play got a sensational production at Britain's National Theatre, directed by Stephen Daldry, for which Ian MacNeil designed a virtuosic set that showed a massive iron platform weighing down on the characters and deployed a vast variety of hydraulic lifts and giant trucks. The critical consensus was that a dazzling production had helped to rescue a partial and thinly written play. I believe the exact opposite: a tremendous play that, like so many great works in this book, acknowledges the past while anticipating the future, was overlaid by a self-advertising production.

Examine the text, and Treadwell's purpose is clear: to show how a woman, not unlike the heroine of Glaspell's *The Verge*, is driven to murder by a sense of entrapment. The big difference is that Glaspell gives Claire Archer a sense of missionary zeal as a plant-scientist. Treadwell's heroine, whose married name we finally learn is Helen Jones, is mostly described as Young Woman: a name as anonymous as that of Rice's Mr Zero in *The Adding Machine*. And Treadwell's whole point is that her heroine, like so many women at the time, felt herself driven by irresistible social and economic forces. The murder is not the point of the story: it is simply the inexorable outcome of a sense of imprisonment.

What is astonishing is how swiftly Treadwell captures the essence of her heroine's dilemma. In *From Morning to Midnight* (1912) Georg Kaiser showed his hero passing through seven 'stations' that resembled those of a contemporary Christ. Treadwell's Helen is seen in nine separate scenes that, as Judith E.

Barlow has pointed out, echo the nine months of gestation.

In the number-crunching world of business – pure Elmer Rice – she is simply a stenographer who fatally attracts the attention of her boss, George H. Jones. At home, she is pressured into marriage by her mechanised drudge of a mother. On her honeymoon, she is the terrified plaything of a husband who treats her as his doll-wife, playfully putting her on his knee. And, having given birth, she finds herself in a maternity ward subjected to a biological determinism that demands she breast-feed her baby and patronised by a male doctor who asks, 'How's the little lady today?' At every stage of her life, Helen is expected to fulfil a pre-existing role. Ironically, it is only when she breaks the pattern and takes a lover, who gives her a vision of a life of freedom beyond the Rio Grande, that she is driven to an act of murder.

Treadwell was not the first writer to record the claustrophobic entrapment felt by American women. Her originality lies in her polyphonic use of theatre's possibilities and in her prophetic gift for language. For a start she deploys a dazzling array of sounds – whether it be of typewriters, telephones, footbeats, electric piano or hand organ – to evoke particular settings. She also gives Helen a series of interior monologues that express her jagged resistance to oppression: in the maternity ward she cries, 'Let me alone – let me alone – let me alone – I've submitted to enough – I won't submit to any more – crawl off – crawl off in the dark.' But Treadwell's greatest triumph is to create patterned dialogue that reminds us that, in 1928, the overweening business of America was business, and that uncannily anticipates Pinter and Mamet. This is Helen and her husband in their sterile sitting-room discussing his latest deal:

YOUNG WOMAN (*by rote*): Did you put it over?
HUSBAND: Sure I put it over.

YOUNG WOMAN: Did you swing it?

HUSBAND: Sure I swung it.

YOUNG WOMAN: Did they come through?

HUSBAND: Sure they came through.

YOUNG WOMAN: Did they sign?

HUSBAND: I'll say they signed.

YOUNG WOMAN: On the dotted line?

HUSBAND: On the dotted line.

YOUNG WOMAN: The property's yours?

HUSBAND: The property's mine.

This type of musically repetitive dialogue was employed by T. S. Eliot, to similar effect, in his 1932 Aristophanic fragment 'Sweeney Agonistes', and Eliot, like Treadwell, was a theatrical pioneer who anticipated the staccato rhythms of modern drama.

It was typical of the National Theatre's overblown production that, in the scene just quoted, the couple conversed from opposite ends of a sofa that had been sliced down the middle. But the distance is in the dialogue, where Helen mechanically questions a husband who smugly represents the mercantile values famously embodied by Sinclair Lewis's Babbitt. And that in itself is characteristic of a play that brilliantly conveys the de-individualising tendencies of a supposedly burgeoning capitalism and that uses all the expansive possibilities of theatre to show the narrowing choices available to a distressed Everywoman.

67

Tales from the Vienna Woods

ÖDÖN VON HORVÁTH

(1901–38)

Great drama springs from a variety of sources: individual temperament; theatrical circumstance; 'the form and pressure of the time', as Shakespeare puts it. And it is no accident that, from the mid-1920s onwards, much fine drama is characterised by a feverish restlessness. In America that can easily be related to the hysteria surrounding a stock market on the verge of a momentous crash. In central Europe the big bogies were mass unemployment and soaring inflation. Aside from Brecht, the dramatist who best captured the resulting instability was the Austro-Hungarian Ödön von Horváth, and nowhere better than in *Tales from the Vienna Woods*, which had its première at the Deutsches Theater, Berlin, in 1931 with a cast headed by Carola Neher and Peter Lorre.

There is one fact about Horváth that everyone remembers: the manner of his death. On 1 June 1938 he was in Paris to meet the film producer Robert Siodmak. After the appointment, he dropped into a cinema on the Champs-Elysées to see *Snow White and the Seven Dwarfs*. Leaving the movie, he was on his way to a rendezvous with some friends when he sheltered under a chestnut tree opposite the Theatre Marigny during a violent storm. A branch broke off the tree and struck him on the back of the head, killing him instantly. The bitter irony is that the superstitious Horváth had, a week before, consulted a clairvoyant in Amsterdam, who had urged him to go to Paris, where the greatest adventure of his life awaited him.

If we know all this, it is largely because Christopher Hampton, who has done more than anyone to promote Horváth in English, used it as the starting point for an excellent play, *Tales from Hollywood* (1982), that imagined Horváth surviving and joining a group of European exiles, including Brecht and Heinrich Mann, in Los Angeles.

It was, though, Hampton's fine translation of *Tales from the Vienna Woods* that put Horváth squarely on the British map in a spectacular production by Maximilan Schell at the National in 1977. If I suggest Horváth's work is characterised by restlessness, it is hardly surprising, given his background. As the son of a Hungarian diplomat, he had a peripatetic childhood depending on his father's postings. He chose for himself, however, the identity of a German dramatist and openly declared his central aim: 'to record', as Hampton says, 'the decay of a society haunted by inflation and lurching towards Fascism'. The evidence was all around him. Even in the 1920s Berliners had carried off milliard-mark notes in carts as soon as they were printed. As unemployment topped 3 million in Germany in 1930, the National Socialists increased their number of MPs to 108. As Trotsky noted, in the 1930 German elections 'counter-revolutionary despair embraced the petty-bourgeois mass with such force it drew behind it many sections of the proletariat'.

That is the background to *Tales from the Vienna Woods*, a play that brilliantly uses the crises in a petty-bourgeois community to show a society in turmoil and implying that out of chaos will come a terrifying hunger for order. But what is startling is the form Horváth uses: that of the *Volksstück*, which roughly translates as 'people's play'. It is a form that harks back to the popular comedies of the Viennese Johann Nestroy, who wrote the seminal work that inspired Thornton Wilder's *The Matchmaker* and ultimately *Hello Dolly!* Its main ingredients are recognisable characters, lively dialect and seductive melodies. Reading the text of *Tales from the Vienna Woods*, you constantly have to imagine, in your head, a sound-score made up of lilting Strauss waltzes and popular Viennese ballads. The play's content is bitter: the music is sweet. It was exactly the kind of counterpoint that Joan Littlewood was to use to such devastating effect in *Oh! What a Lovely War*.

The focus of Horváth's play is on the character of Marianne, memorably played at the National by Kate Nelligan in 1977 and Nicola Walker in a 2003 production. The daughter of a toyshop owner, Marianne starts out as a simple, uneducated girl – almost a variant of the *süsse Mädel* you find in Schnitzler's plays – who ends up a racked, tormented woman. First she abandons her fiancé, a devoted butcher called Oskar, to run off with a no-good gambler, Alfred, by whom she has a child. She farms out the child to Alfred's mother, is disowned by her father and deserted by Alfred. To survive, she becomes a naked dancer in a sleazy cabaret, a career that ends with her falsely accused of theft. Finally, she is reconciled with Oskar but, when she goes to reclaim her child, she discovers he is dead. As she does so, a string orchestra plays the haunting Strauss waltz that gives the play its title.

Baldly summarised, the story sounds sensational. But Horváth roots it firmly in a middle-class milieu: the world of shopkeepers, tradesmen, lottery-playing pensioners. He also deftly portrays a society where jobs are scarce, money tight, women second-class citizens and the church strict and unforgiving: in one of the most poignant scenes, Marianne is abruptly rejected by a Catholic confessor for her refusal to repent of her sin in bearing a child out of wedlock. But Horváth never lets us forget that such a society provides the perfect soil for fascism. One of the key characters is Erich, a young law student who becomes the lover of the forty-nine-year-old Valerie, who owns a newspaper and tobacco shop. In his intolerance, anti-Semitism and rigid adherence to Prussian military values, Erich is a symbol of the Nazi future. Even in the cabaret where Marianne works, one of the tableaux symptomatically consists of three naked women forming the shape of a Zeppelin, while the audience sings 'Deutschland über Alles'.

Much has been made, not least by Christopher Hampton, of the contrast between Horváth and Brecht. Brecht is seen as a didactic dramatist, Horváth as a descriptive writer who provides the audience with the social evidence. I find it an exaggerated contrast that omits Brecht's irony, contradiction and pioneering genius. But I still admire Horváth hugely for his ability to combine personal crises with a panoramic vision and a political sub-text. There's one particular scene in *Tales from the Vienna Woods* that always haunts me. The main characters repair to the woods for a summer picnic full of whirling parasols, idle flirtations, *La Bohème* on a wind-up gramophone and distant echoes of Strauss waltzes. It seems breathtakingly idyllic and reminds one of similar scenes in Goldoni, Chekhov and Gorky. Yet when Erich starts to do target-practice with an airgun, in preparation for a cadet corps contest, Horváth makes you chillingly and suddenly aware of the serpent lurking in this vision of a Viennese Eden.

68

The Suicide

NIKOLAI ERDMAN

(1900–70)

Satire has a strong place in Russian literature: think of Gogol, Bulgakov, Mayakovsky. 1924 even saw the opening of the Moscow Theatre of Satire. It was launched with a comic revue, *Moscow from a Point of View*, one of whose contributors was a young sketch-writer called Nikolai Erdman. He went on to write a play, *The Mandate*, produced by Meyerhold in 1924 and satirising both the petty-bourgeoisie and card-carrying political opportunists. But it is with *The Suicide*, written in 1928 but decisively banned in 1932, that Erdman finally pushed the Soviet authorities too far. Although riotously funny, Erdman's play shows the planned suicide of its jobless hero, Semyon Podsekalnikov, mercilessly exploited by the intelligentsia, business, the church and anyone who wishes to protest against society.

What is fascinating is how close the play actually got to production. Both the leading directors of the time, Stanislavsky and Meyerhold, competed to stage it. Stanislavsky, to forestall trouble, even sent the play to Stalin to get his approval. Stalin's reply, dated 9 November 1931, is intriguing in that it registers his dislike of the play without actively seeking to stop it. 'My closest colleagues,' wrote Stalin, 'consider it empty and even harmful ... Nevertheless I am not against the theatre experimenting and showing its skill. Provided that the theatre achieves its aims.' In the event, the play passed to Meyerhold's Vakhtangov Theatre and went into rehearsal only to be banned on the eve of production by the Central Licensing Board.

Erdman himself precariously survived. After three years of 'free confinement' in Siberia, he returned to Moscow to work on film scripts until his death. But *The Suicide*, like its hero, obstinately refuses to lie down. It had its world première in Sweden in 1969. It soon became an international hit and was produced by the RSC, in Peter Tegel's lively translation, at Stratford's The Other Place in 1979. This was an exhilarating affair, vigorously directed by Ron Daniels, with Roger Rees playing Semyon as a Hamlet-like ditherer in outsize jacket and Buster Keaton hat. Moira Buffini also did a sprightly version, retitled *Dying for It*, for the Almeida in 2007 with Tom Brooke, of the extravagantly lunar profile, as the desperate hero. But the play didn't make its debut in Russia, at Moscow's Taganka Theatre, until 1989, the year that saw the dissolution of Soviet communism. It was directed by the Taganka's founder, Yuri Lyubimov, and marked his return after a period of exile. I visited the Taganka in the Soviet era and was astonished by the expressionist exuberance of Lyubimov's productions, most especially his version of Bulgakov's *The Master and Margarita*. According to the Russian critic Anatoly Smeliansky, Lyubimov, in staging *The Suicide*, had lost none of his desire to shock:

Lyubimov and his designer, David Borovsky, hung across the stage a huge sheet showing the face of Karl Marx. The leader of the world's proletariat took an active part in proceedings. Sometimes his eyes would sparkle: from his beard little suicide notes were retrieved. Upstage in front of Marx stood a railway handcar. A wooden monument, it was a tower on which were acted out not scenes from the play but from its author's life of exile in the camps.

Apparently Lyubimov was urging his actors to do the play in a way that would provoke the authorities into suppressing it. But, as Smeliansky wanly observes, 'there was no one around to close them down'.

Even if Lyubimov was pushing at an open door, Erdman's play retains its power. Mixing farce and satire, it has that feverish quality I've noted in the plays of Horváth and Treadwell. It also offers a timeless plea on behalf of the individual battling against an oppressive system. There is nothing heroic about its protagonist, Semyon: he's selfish, greedy and as bullying towards his wife and mother-in-law as Dickens's Quilp in *The Old Curiosity Shop*. But he has been out of work for a year and has reached a pitch of desperation. With insane glee, Semyon decides to teach himself the tuba in order to make his fortune. Devotedly following an instruction manual, he learns that 'the scale is the umbilical cord of music'. Unfortunately, the handbook goes on to say that the only way to master the scale is to buy yourself a piano.

By now at his wits' end, Semyon decides to shoot himself. But word of his planned suicide quickly spreads, and he finds himself besieged by people who wish to exploit it for their own ends. First on the scene is a discontented intellectual who urges him to leave behind a protest note on the grounds that 'nowadays only the dead may say what the living think'. But he is soon followed by a horde of others, one of whom is a determined ideologue: accused of peeping at Semyon's wife through a keyhole, he announces, in Tegel's translation, 'I am looking at her from the Marxist point of view.' Eventually a banquet is held by Semyon's exploiters to celebrate his impending suicide. But, having been placed in a coffin not so much dead as dead-drunk, Semyon rises up to articulate his own protest against Soviet communism. 'Why is it,' he says, 'I don't want to read the posters our government puts up? "For each and all." Because I know! For each and all, but not for me. Not that I'm asking for much. Our achievements, our success, our reconstructed society, you can keep it. I want a quiet life and a living wage.'

The audacity is breathtaking when you consider the context in which it was written. But the play outlives its period for a variety of reasons. It celebrates the will to live. It argues for the right to work. And it has a wild, madcap humour: as Robert Cushman wrote of the 1979 RSC production, 'the play becomes "to be or not to be" acted out as farce'. In fact, the play is full of *Hamlet* jokes. When it's suggested to the Marxist that he might begin his funeral oration by saying there's something rotten in the state of Denmark, he takes this to be a piece of hot news from 'comrade Marcellus' proving that 'the rottenness of capitalism cannot but reveal itself'.

Suicide, you may think, is no joke. But Erdman's play lives on as a testament to the survival instinct of the individual and also to his or her sense of impotence in the face of crushing external forces. At one point Semyon, with the fake bravura of someone who thinks he's going to die, decides to phone the Kremlin direct and let the top people know how he feels about his plight. We may laugh at the absurdity of a Soviet citizen believing he can harangue Stalin. But you only have to think of what might happen today if a jobless car-worker or steelmaker decided to ring Number 10 or the White House to protest to realise that Erdman is standing up, with a frenzied, farcical abandon, for the desperation of the dispossessed.

69

Design for Living

NOËL COWARD
(1899–1973)

The feverishness I've noted in drama of the late 1920s and early 1930s even finds its way into the work of Noël Coward, the most geographically restless of playwrights, who admitted he wrote much of his best work during periods of exhausting travel. *Design for Living* was no exception in that he penned it in 1932 in a small cargo ship at the end of a strenuous visit to Latin America. For years Coward had been mulling over the idea of a play for himself, Lynn Fontanne and her husband Alfred Lunt; they had first met when all three were young, hard-up actors in the early 1920s. The immediate stimulus to write the play came when Coward, travelling in the Argentine eleven years later, received a curt cable from the Lunts, saying, 'Contract with the Guild up in June – we shall be free – what about it?'

Coward wrote funnier plays than *Design for Living*: none, however, that so successfully catches the moral ambivalence at the heart of his work. I love Coward's early plays. After 1945, however, a serious decline sets in largely, I believe, because Coward could never reconcile himself to Labour's post-war electoral victory and the social and cultural changes that accompanied it. But if there is one constant factor in his work, it is his equivocal attitude to the idea of Bohemian freedom and sexual candour. Coward revered fame, success, wealth; he believed equally fervently in work, duty, self-restraint. It's no accident that Ernest, the token representative of propriety in the world of sexual ardour so vividly portrayed in *Design for Living*, tells the heroine, Gilda, 'Your life is so dreadfully untidy.' Tidiness is a key Coward concept. Reviewing a revival of his 1926 play *Semi-Monde*, set in the promiscuous world of the Paris Ritz, I wrote: 'He [Coward] was, by instinct, a puritan dandy with a dry Martini in one hand and a moral sampler in the other ... Even his attitude to homosexuality is not exactly encouraging: he seems to suggest it should be practised but not preached.' In this regard, it's worth noting that in 1953, when Sir John Gielgud was arrested for importuning, Coward's instinctive reaction, in a passage tactfully excised from his *Diaries*, was 'Poor, silly, idiotic, foolish, careless John.' No one could ever accuse Coward himself of carelessness in matters of sexual revelation.

Design for Living is as near as he ever got to a coming-out party. Even here, his stance remains shrewdly ambiguous. But let us first admire the play for its delightful symmetry. Act 1 shows the desirable Gilda living in a Paris studio with the painter Otto but enjoying a sudden, rapturous fling with their mutual friend Leo. By Act 2 the action has shifted to London eighteen months later: Gilda is now shacked up with Leo, a fashionable playwright, but, during his absence, goes to bed with Otto. In Act 3 we are in New York two years later. Gilda is now married to the wealthy art-dealer Ernest and is herself a successful interior decorator. But her quilted marital calm is upset when Otto and Leo arrive together, having jointly cruised the world. They immediately lay claim to Gilda, to the insensate fury of Ernest. The play ends with Gilda, Otto and Leo groaning with laughter as Ernest makes a clumsy, undignified exit.

It is perfectly possible to read this as a piece of silken sexual propaganda. John Lahr, in his perceptive study of the author, writes: 'Coward's comic revenge at the finale is the victory of the disguised gay world over the straight one.' The play also drops heavy hints as to the intensity of Otto and Leo's friendship. The second act ends, after Gilda has walked out on both of them, with the two men getting wildly drunk and sobbing 'hopelessly' on each other's shoulders. And there is an air of sustained camp, suggesting their relationship has gone way beyond fraternal chumminess, about their disruptive third-act arrival. When Sean Mathias revived the play at the Donmar Warehouse in 1994 he took these hints as a sign that the play was a paean to sexual freedom and, at the climax, showed Rachel Weisz, Paul Rhys and Clive Owen joyously intertwined as if on the verge of committing an act of spectacular troilism.

But Coward, I suspect, would have been quietly horrified at being enlisted as a card-carrying sexual campaigner. Indeed it is precisely his evasiveness that makes *Design for Living* such a richly tantalising play. On one level, it can be seen as an enactment of his long-standing relationship with the Lunts (for all three, it had been a case of fame at first sight) and a defence of love among the artists. As Leo says to Ernest, 'We have our own decencies. We have our own ethics. Our lives are a different shape from yours.' But while Coward mercilessly lampoons wealthy American philistinism in the final act, he also shows the central trio to be ruthlessly egotistical and understands the importance of being Ernest. In fact, much of the play hinges on how you interpret the character of the sexual outsider. Coward himself, in his preface, said if the final laughter is directed against Ernest, 'it was certainly cruel and in the worst possible taste'. And in Anthony Page's excellent 2010 revival at the Old Vic we were confronted by the memorable sight of Angus Wright's Ernest running around the stage with a frantic despair, suggesting that the price for the trio's self-fulfilment was pain for other people. Coward himself was one of the twentieth century's leading exemplars of the talentocracy, but in his two volumes of autobiography, *Present Indicative* and *Future Indefinite*, he repeatedly insists that celebrity is no excuse for unkindness or indifference to others.

However one interprets the play, it confirms that Coward, at his best, had a fastidious ear for speech. When Otto, Gilda's ex-lover, unexpectedly turns up in Act 2, the dialogue between them has just the right air of strained politesse:

> OTTO: I met an odd-looking woman going out. She opened the door for me.
> GILDA: That was Miss Hodge. She's had two husbands.
> OTTO: I once met a woman who'd had four husbands.
> GILDA: Aren't you going to take off your hat and coat?
> OTTO: Don't you like them?
> GILDA: Enormously.

Coward, as Tynan once said, took the fat off English comic dialogue: 'he was the Turkish bath in which it slimmed'. He also was a self-created sophisticate who admired style and elegance in others. In *Hay Fever*, *Private Lives* and *Blithe Spirit*, he wrote some of the funniest plays of the century. But inside the tirelessly cosmopolitan Coward there always lurked a hint of the pursed-lipped maiden aunts by whom he was surrounded in childhood. In *Design for Living* you see the man of the world and the moralist wrestling with each other in joyous combat and neither emerging victorious.

70

The House of Bernarda Alba

FEDERICO GARCÍA LORCA

(1898–1936)

Although written in 1936, it is only in recent times that Lorca's play has become a staple part of the international repertory. One obvious reason is that this story of a tyrannical matriarch and her five daughters provides a palpable political metaphor. Lorca completed the play on 19 June 1936. On 18 July General Franco initiated a military uprising against the democratically elected Madrid government. On 19 August Lorca himself was shot by Francoist thugs. Inevitably, our knowledge of this informs our vision of the play. Howard Davies's 2005 National Theatre production, using a new version by David Hare, left us in no doubt of the play's forewarning of fascism. A 2012 revival by Bijan Sheibani at the Almeida shifted the action from Andalusia to rural Iran. A year before that, I caught an Athenian production that inescapably evoked memories of Greece under the fascist colonels.

Like the bulk of the plays in this book, *The House of Bernarda Alba* exists in multiple time-zones. As Eric Bentley has said, its ultimate theme is 'the attempt to preserve honour in the face of the sexual instinct': Bernarda herself lives by a strict code that results in the sacrifice of her youngest daughter, Adela, to traditional values. And clearly Lorca is harking back to the honour plays of the Spanish Golden Age. Gwynne Edwards, whose excellent translation I have used as my text, reminds us specifically of Lorca's debt to Calderón's *The Surgeon of His Honour* (*c.*1645), a play in which a husband has his young wife murdered in order to avoid a public scandal about her suspected adultery.

But Lorca's obliging masterpiece is also rooted in the Spain he knew. Far more realistic than his earlier work such as *Blood Wedding* and *Yerma*, it was dubbed by him 'a photographic documentary'. It was subtitled 'A Drama of Women in the Villages of Spain' and loosely based on a particular case: the story of 'Doña Bernarda, a very old widow who kept an inexorable and tyrannical watch over her unmarried daughters' in a house that adjoined the rural property to which Lorca's parents repaired every summer. Recording the present and invoking the past, Lorca's play anticipates the future by using domestic tyranny as an image of political fascism.

The power of the play, however, lies in the fierce concentration of the writing. Some plays are baggy monsters; this is an Ibsenite work in that every line is freighted with meaning, and realism is coloured by symbolism. Look, for instance, at the play's opening. We see a startlingly white inner room in Bernarda's house. We hear the sound of church bells. Gradually, the room fills up with black-clad mourners, newly returned from the funeral of Bernarda's second husband. Bernarda herself, leaning on a stick, enters, accompanied by her five daughters, and admonishes a weeping servant with the word 'Silence!' (the same word ends the play after Bernarda has killed her youngest daughter, Adela). Relying on the practice of her father and grandfather, Bernarda terrifyingly proclaims, 'In the eight years this mourning will last the wind from the street shan't enter this house.' Within minutes of the opening, Lorca has established an atmosphere of oppression, entrapment, the dead weight of the past, the perverse denial of life:

even Adela's gesture in offering her mother 'a round fan decorated with red and green flowers' acquires a symbolic meaning in this sterile context.

Lorca's brilliance lies in showing sex as a force that destablises Bernarda's tightly ordered world. The plot hinges on the fact that Angustias, the oldest and least prepossessing of the daughters, is to be married off to Pepe el Romano, 'the best-looking man for miles around'. That itself seems a breach of nature. While supposedly paying nightly court to Angustias at her window, Pepe is, in fact, covertly wooing, and seducing, the youngest of the daughters, Adela. It is the eventual discovery of this that leads to Adela's death at her mother's hands and the pretence, in the interests of family honour, that she died a virgin.

Photographic realism is Lorca's method. To take a tiny example, I remember how, in Nuria Espert's superb 1986 production at the Lyric Hammersmith, Joan Plowright, as the servant Poncia, smoothed the nap of folded white linen in a way that evoked both her own lifetime's drudgery and Bernarda's obsession with purity. But Lorca's realism is countered by verbal and visual imagery that evokes the freedom that exists beyond Bernarda's domestic fortress. At one point Bernarda's daughters gather to listen to the sound of sun-bronzed male reapers singing, 'Open your doors and windows, You girls who live in the town' – the self-same windows that Bernarda wanted shuttered to exclude even the wind. Later a hot stallion is heard kicking against a stable wall – the same stable in which Adela loses her virginity to Pepe el Romano. And Maria Josefa, Bernarda's mad mother, periodically escapes from the room in which she is imprisoned: at one point she enters clutching a lamb, which symbolises both nature's creativity and religious rebirth.

Realism, in Lorca's hands, acquires a distilled poetry.

Without overt moralising, he also shows how honour is

inextricably tied up with money and class. Bernarda denies her daughters' suitors on the grounds that 'there's no one for a hundred miles that can match them'. When Adela yearns to join the men in the fields, her sister Magdalena retorts, 'Each class does what it must.' And when Poncia tries to warn her mistress of the impending tragedy, Bernarda reminds her that, as a prostitute's daughter, she is her financial slave. While Bernarda puts on airs and graces because she can afford them, Poncia is allowed no such luxury, 'because you know what your origins were!'

In short, this is one of those rare plays in which social, sexual, psychological and political ideas are seamlessly intertwined. And if the play is ultimately an attack on the destructiveness of an outdated honour code, it would be a mistake to see Bernarda herself simply as a melodramatic villain. She is undoubtedly a monster who, when the villagers turn on a girl who has buried her bastard child, urges her to be punished with 'a red-hot coal in the place of her sin'. But Bernarda, as both Glenda Jackson and Penelope Wilton have proved in performance, is also a profoundly tragic figure trapped in a dead belief system and enslaved by the dangerous seduction of power.

71

The Life of Galileo

BERTOLT BRECHT

(1898–1956)

A lot of rubbish has been written about Brecht over the years. In Britain especially he has been endlessly dubbed didactic, humourless, monumentally tedious. In reality, he is inquisitive, ironic, highly theatrical. The point has been proved in a wide range of productions from Michael Blakemore's landmark staging of *Arturo Ui* in 1967 to the various revivals of *The Life of Galileo* which have used fleet, light-footed versions by Howard Brenton, David Hare and Mark Ravenhill. If I have returned to earlier translations by Desmond Vesey and John Willett, it is because they stick loyally to Brecht's text.

But which text exactly? One of the problems with Galileo is that it exists, like Shakespeare's *Hamlet* or Verdi's score for *Don Carlos*, in various versions. In effect, it can be whittled down to two alternatives. *Galileo* 1 was written by Brecht in 1938, with help from Margarete Steffin, and was a defence of intellectual freedom against tyranny. *Galileo* 2 revised the original in the wake of the dropping of the atomic bomb on Hiroshima, was first presented in Los Angeles in 1947 and defended the social responsibility of science against the idea that the exploration of truth was an end in itself. The key difference lies in Galileo's final speech. In the second version he says 'the only purpose of science is to ease the hardship of human existence', foresees the rise of 'a race of inventive dwarfs who can be hired for anything' and attacks himself as a traitor who surrendered his knowledge to those in power. If Galileo's self-flagellation occasionally seems excessive, the speech still has enormous resonance today, which is why *Galileo* 2 is now the version most often used and the one to which I refer.

What Brecht does brilliantly in the body of the play is show the sly, sensuous Galileo as a man driven by a belief in the inviolability of reason and the implacability of scientific evidence. His researches in Padua and Florence in the early 1600s reinforce the Copernican argument that the earth is a planet that revolves round the sun: an argument that threatens both the Catholic church's belief in a divinely ordained universe and the established social order. After a period of enforced silence, Galileo pursues his researches, is threatened with torture by the Inquisition, recants and ends up an old, half-blind man kept under strict clerical supervision. But eventually a copy of his *Discorsi* is smuggled out of Italy by his former housekeeper's son Andrea, whom he once taught the basics of astronomy.

Brecht's line of argument is clear: as Galileo himself says, 'truth is the child of time, not of authority'. But it is unfair to suggest, as Christopher Hart did reviewing the RSC's 2013 revival, that the play boils down to a simplistic argument: 'Science good, church bad'. For a start Brecht's Galileo is a decidedly unheroic figure: he passes off a telescope easily available in Amsterdam as his own invention, sacrifices his daughter's marriage to his researches, recants under physical threats and ends up attacking scientific irresponsibility. As for the church, Brecht specifically shows it peopled not by gargoyled monsters but by men whose humanity is subject to hierarchical demands: in one of Brecht's most famous scenes Cardinal Barberini, himself a mathematician, only accedes to the Inquisitor's demand to interrogate Galileo as he dons the heavily ceremonial papal robes.

Brecht is often dismissed as a Marxist dogmatist; in fact, he has the great dramatist's ability to see contradictory arguments. In the magnificent Scene 8 Galileo, after it has been decreed that Copernican doctrine is heretical, engages in a conversation with a character called The Little Monk. The monk, who has studied astronomy, argues that there is true maternal compassion in the church's views: he cites the case of his peasant parents, who find consolation in Holy Writ and who have learned, through religion, to endure life's hardships. Galileo's counter-argument is that clerical orthodoxy is used to reinforce an oppressive feudal system and says, 'I perceive the divine patience of your people but where is their divine anger?' Brecht may ultimately be on Galileo's side but he has sufficient empathy, and dramatic acumen, to allow The Little Monk to make the case for the peace of mind and private consolations induced by religious belief.

Brecht, who rejected the Aristotelian principles of drama, was also a shrewd man of the theatre who used every weapon to hand, and one of those was dramatic suspense. Before Scene 13, set in Rome in 1633, we are told that 'Galileo recants his teaching about the movement of the earth'. Yet every time I see the play, the audience is inescapably caught up in the mechanics of his denial. The focus, in fact, is on Galileo's followers: Andrea, The Little Monk, the lens-grinder Federzoni. As they wait outside the palace of the Florentine ambassador, they express their faith that Galileo will never recant. If he does so, the great bell of St Marks will be rung at five o'clock. The appointed hour passes and they all, except Galileo's daughter, rejoice in the hero's obduracy. Suddenly their euphoria is cut short by the tolling of the bell, and the broken Galileo emerges. 'Unhappy the land that has no heroes!' says Andrea. 'No, unhappy the land that is in need of heroes,' replies Galileo. If that is not great theatre, I don't know what is.

But this is also a work that actively resonates today. Kirsten Shepherd-Barr, in her invaluable book *Science on Stage*, calls *Galileo* a watershed play. 'From hereon in,' she writes, 'science plays either directly or indirectly engage this notion of the responsibility of the scientist.' And it is true that just about everything which follows, from Dürrenmatt's *The Physicists* to Frayn's *Copenhagen* to Tom Morton-Smith's *Oppenheimer*, ultimately harks back to *Galileo*.

Brecht's play has been challenged on grounds of historic and scientific accuracy; it is nevertheless the masterwork that addresses still-unresolved issues about whether dedication to pure research should be tempered by a moral awareness of its consequences. Apart from being a seminal work, it also has the classic's ability to support different approaches. John Dexter's 1980 National Theatre production exuded the aesthetic grace that was a Brechtian hallmark and made a star of Michael Gambon. Jonathan Kent directed a slimmer, more fast-paced version at the Almeida in 1994 with Richard Griffiths. Howard Davies put the play into modern dress when he directed David Hare's version at the National in 2006 with Simon Russell Beale as a Galileo who strangely came to resemble Beckett's blind Hamm in *Endgame*. And Roxana Silbert's 2013 RSC production, with Ian McDiarmid as a scruffily obsessive Galileo, used a springy new text by Mark Ravenhill. If the play invariably works, it is partly because it deals with a man who, in a pungent phrase used by David Hare in a *Guardian* article, 'is ethically unequipped to deal with his own genius'. Not unlike Brecht himself, one surmises.

72

Mr Puntila and His Man Matti

BERTOLT BRECHT

(1898–1956)

When Brecht's exuberant comedy got its British premiere in a 1965 RSC production, there was a predictable reaction in some quarters. Bernard Levin in the *Daily Mail* described it as 'merciless rubbish full of half-baked Marxist trash' not to mention preposterous theories 'about alienation and other imbecilities' which he felt the work itself contradicted. It's a bit rich that the intemperate Levin went on to attack the shrillness of Brecht's supporters. Unwittingly, however, Levin put his finger on one of *Puntila*'s many charms: its subversion of Brecht's own theories. What might, in lesser hands, have been a work of Marxist dogma leaves the audience in two minds about its main character. As Eric Bentley said of *Galileo*, 'moral disapproval goes one way but human sympathy goes the same way'.

In outline, Puntila – written in Finnish exile in 1940 and partly based on a work by Brecht's host, Hella Wuolijiki – looks straightforward enough. Mr Puntila is a rich farmer who overflows with boisterous good humour when drunk: he throws his money about, gets engaged to four village girls simultaneously and encourages his daughter to ditch her foppish fiancé and marry his chauffeur, Matti. Once sober, however, Mr Puntila becomes brutal and businesslike: he accuses Matti of pinching his wallet, shows the four village girls the door and wants Eva hitched to the wimpish diplomat. The moral seems clear enough: the whole class system stinks, especially when masters prove unreliable. As Matti, who finally deserts Puntila after one *bouleversement* too many, puts it in a concluding song in the John Willett translation:

And if it's sad to find out in the end
That oil and water cannot ever blend
Let's waste no tears, there's nothing we can do:
It's time your servants turned their backs on you.
They'll find they have a master really cares
Once they're the master of their own affairs.

So that's all clear then? Overturn the system, give power to the people and never trust the fitful benevolence of liberal reformers. While that may be the Marxist message, it's not how the play works in performance. In the character of Puntila Brecht creates one of the great rogues in world drama: inordinate, overflowing with vitality and both a direct descendant of Shakespeare's Falstaff and a forerunner of Azdak in *The Caucasian Chalk Circle*. It's as if Brecht's creative energy is so unstoppable that it outstrips his political intention. You see that in the brilliant scene where Puntila, after a two-day drunken binge, goes to the village in search of more alcohol, which he can only get by pretending it's for his ailing cows. As with Falstaff multiplying the number of robbers at Gadshill, the quantity of sick cows exponentially increases every time Puntila speaks.

Having got his hooch, Puntila then finds himself, in a fit of sexual enthusiasm, offering to marry four different girls: a grog-peddler, a chemist's assistant, a milkmaid and a telephonist. This achieves its pay-off in the remarkable Scene 8, when the four girls, having been turned away from Puntila Hall, ruefully filter their experiences and the lessons learned through a series of folk-tales. This shows that Brecht can be didactic and humane at the same time: the most moving story involves a starving political prisoner who spurns the fish and butter his mother brings because she's soft-soaped the landlord's wife in order to get them.

We may deplore Puntila and what he stands for, but we also find his Jekyll and Hyde duality mesmeric. He has, in fact, the one quality that matters in a dramatic character: he overflows with life. With his man Matti, the fascination lies not so much in what he stands for – pragmatism, sobriety, suspicion of his superiors – as in his debt to a long line of theatrical forebears. Matti reminds me a lot of the suave butler in J. M. Barrie's *The Admirable Crichton*: he's omnicompetent, sexually attractive to the master's daughter and wary of too much easy familiarity with his boss. On the other hand, he's happy to play up to the highly sexed Eva in a manner reminiscent of Jean in Strindberg's *Miss Julie*: there's a wonderfully erotic encounter between Matti and Eva in the farm kitchen where their talk of catching slippery crayfish by hand ripples with innuendo. The scene where Matti tests Eva's suitability to be a working man's wife even suggests, as Stephen Unwin has pointed out, Petruchio's physical and psychological warfare in *The Taming of the Shrew*. You can see the point Brecht is making: the class divide is not easily bridged. All the same there is something a bit cruel in Eva's humiliation and Matti's exposure of her inability to souse herring, darn socks and know how to behave to a work-drained husband. If this were a good Marxist play, we'd like Matti a bit more; as it is, we find ourselves drawn to the reprehensible Puntila.

But Brecht's play is witty, vigorous, playful and eminently performable. Penelope Gilliatt, reviewing the 1965 production, was quick to point out the similarities with *Galileo*. In the earlier play a cleric's opinions visibly harden as he dons the papal vestments. 'In *Puntila*,' wrote Gilliatt 'there is a scene rather like it and just as theatrical, with the benevolent drunk undressing, going into a sauna bath, having cold water thrown over him and becoming with each bucketful a more sober and ungenerous man.' A later revival by Kathryn Hunter in 1998 at the Almeida also applied the talents of the Right Size duo, Hamish McColl and Sean Foley, to a play that cries out for physical comedy: one of its many forebears is Chaplin's 1931 film *City Lights*, in which a millionaire lavishly entertains the tramp when drunk and cruelly ignores him when sober.

For some, Brecht still presents a problem: specifically, how to reconcile his espousal of Marx with the collapse of Soviet communism and our own political scepticism. But, outside his early *Lehrstücke*, or 'teaching pieces', Brecht was a very individualistic Marxist for whom dogma was always subordinated to inquisitive irony. As for the alienation effect that so troubled Bernard Levin and others, it seems to me mainly a fireguard to ward off rhetoric and sentimentality in German acting and a means of protecting Brecht himself against his own powerful emotions. In the end, the dramatist is bigger than the theories. You see this in the extraordinary penultimate scene in this play, where the increasingly drunken Puntila climbs, with Matti's help, an imagined Finnish mountain made out of piled-up, broken furniture on top of a billiard table. The scene is lyrical, absurd, poetic, preposterous and *echt* Brecht in its ability to make us simultaneously look critically at Puntila's shaky grasp of human reality and laugh generously at his high-flying aspirations. But that is Brecht all over: a dramatist of infinite contradictions who refuses to be shackled by imprisoning theory.

73

Long Day's Journey into Night

EUGENE O'NEILL

(1888–1953)

I find it hard to dissociate O'Neill's great play, written in 1940 but posthumously produced in Stockholm and New York in 1956, from the various productions I have seen. It was the first truly big show I ever reviewed for the *Guardian* in December 1971 in a famous National Theatre production by Michael Blakemore. I remember rejoicing in the chance to write about Olivier's performance as James Tyrone: the sixty-five-year-old actor who is both a witness to, and a decisive factor in, his family's misfortunes exposed during a single summer's day in 1912. Olivier moved brilliantly from a nervy jocularity to a monumental despair at facing up to his wife's relapse into morphine addiction. But there was also wit and subtlety in his performance: one noticed how Olivier marked Tyrone's stinginess by sniffing at a diluted whisky bottle with both nostrils and, when he sweetly crooned, 'We are such stuff as dreams are made on,' he made you believe this compromised matinee idol had the makings of an Irish-American Kean. With Constance Cummings as Tyrone's disintegrating wife and Denis Quilley and Ronald Pickup as his two sons, this production woke me up to the fact that I was watching the great American tragedy.

That impression was confirmed forty-one years later, when I saw a West End revival directed by Anthony Page. David

Suchet allowed one momentarily to banish memories of Olivier by emphasising Tyrone's poker-backed dignity and sorrowful resignation as, confronting his wife's relapse, he helplessly cried, 'It is you who are leaving us, Mary.' Laurie Metcalf was no less astonishing as Mary: she charted, with compelling precision, the degrading process of the character's drug dependence and instinctively flinched when her husband went to caress her heavily injected left arm. Yet, as so often with this play, one emerged from the theatre moved by O'Neill's ability to confront his own past. Only bad art is depressing. Great tragedy always leaves you uplifted.

But what precisely is it that gives this play its power? Partly the fact that we know what it cost O'Neill to delve into his family history: beginning work on it, he described it as 'a play of old sorrow, written in tears and blood'. But the power also derives from the tension between the play's tight classical structure and picture of the erratic contradictions of family life. O'Neill spent much of his life trying to refashion Greek tragedy for the American stage: *Desire under the Elms* (1924) is heavily indebted to Euripides and *Mourning Becomes Electra* (1929–31) to Aeschylus and Sophocles. *Long Day's Journey* also strictly observes the classical unities: the action is confined to the living room of the Tyrones' summer home from 8.30 a.m. to midnight on a single day. Yet, if the form is classical, the passions on display are dizzyingly contradictory.

This is what never ceases to astonish me about O'Neill's play. From the beginning all the characters switch in a moment from a snarling vindictiveness to a forlorn love, from a confrontation with reality to a refuge in illusion. One moment Tyrone raspingly condemns his elder son Jamie for corrupting his brother Edmund with his own brand of cynical worldly wisdom; a second later Tyrone consolingly says 'I know you may have thought it was for the best, Jamie. I didn't say you did it deliberately to harm him.' Jamie himself sneers at Edmund's work on the local paper, describing him as 'a pretty bum reporter'. Two sentences later he's claiming that 'some of the poems and parodies he's written are damn good'. Even the maid, Cathleen, is affected by the zigzag emotions of the Tyrone family. Warning the consumptive Edmund against sneaking a quick, pre-lunch snort, she says, 'I'd never suggest a man or a woman touch drink, Mister Edmund. Sure, didn't it kill an uncle of mine in the old country. Still, a drop now and then is no harm when you're in low spirits or have a bad cold.' But the supreme example of contradiction is Mary Tyrone herself, who, for much of the time, inhabits a world of drugged delusion but who suddenly cuts through it by announcing it were better if Edmund had never been born because 'he wouldn't have had to know his mother was a dope fiend – and hate her!'

O'Neill's play is often seen as the ultimate domestic drama, the one in which a writer most nakedly puts himself, in the persona of the sickly Edmund, and his family onto the stage. Yet, while this may be true, there is even more to the play than that. Harold Clurman, as so often, hit the nail on the head when he wrote that the source of the Tyrones' tragedy is that they have lost their faith. 'Loss of faith,' wrote Clurman, 'is the main theme almost throughout O'Neill's work. For him it was more than a personal tragedy, it was *the* American tragedy.' And it is visible in all the characters in *Long Day's Journey*.

James Tyrone's dream was to be a great Shakespearean actor but, driven by memories of childhood poverty, he sacrificed it to exploit a box-office hit to the maximum. This exactly parallels O'Neill's father, who toured *The Count of Monte Cristo* for twenty-five years and who, after the 5,678th performance, told a Chicago journalist: 'I would like to bury Edmund Dantes so deep that he would never come to life again.' But if Tyrone has lost his artistic faith, the convent-educated Mary subordinated her religious belief to her attraction to a romantic actor. As she tells us in the play's resonant last line: 'I fell in love with James Tyrone and was happy for a time.' Meanwhile her elder son, Jamie, has become a hardened cynic, blaspheming against his mother's religion and his father's profession. Even Edmund, in a moment of drunken confession, tells his father that, as a writer, he can never recapture the ecstatic vision he felt as a young seaman when he felt he belonged to something greater than his own life – 'to God, if you want to put it that way'. Instead he has sacrificed poetic intensity to 'faithful realism'.

If that is intended as O'Neill's self-indictment, he does himself a grave injustice. For a start, there is a structural beauty, worthy of Ibsen, to his exploration of cause and effect and the unshakeable impact of the past on the present: it is the grinding poverty of Tyrone's immigrant upbringing that motivated his miserliness and led him to engage a quack doctor to attend his wife after Edmund's birth, thereby inducing her disastrous morphine addiction. And while O'Neill's play is steeped in a cauterising domestic realism, it also operates as a powerful social metaphor. Through his microscopic analysis of the Tyrones, O'Neill offers a portrait of a nation that has sacrificed spiritual coherence to temporary gain: 'What shall it profit a man if he gain the whole world and lose his own soul?' was O'Neill's text for his intended nine-play portrait of America. At the same time the play, filled with what Clurman excellently called 'the soulful poetry of despair and forgiveness', leaves us strangely fortified in the manner of great tragedy.

74

Men Should Weep

ENA LAMONT STEWART
(1912–2006)

Ena Lamont Stewart suffered a double disadvantage for a playwright of her generation. She was a woman and she was Scottish. Today there is a whole generation of Scottish women playwrights who have had organically developing careers and whose work is widely acclaimed: Rona Munro (*The James Plays*), Liz Lochhead (*Mary Queen of Scots Got Her Head Chopped Off*), Zinnie Harris (*Further than the Furthest Thing*), Sue Glover (*Bondagers*). For Stewart, as a playwright in the 1940s, life was much tougher, but at least she bequeathed us one magnificent, enduring work.

Stewart was a daughter of the manse: her father was a minister in one of Glasgow's poorest districts. She was also sent to work, as a young woman without higher education, as a receptionist in a Glasgow hospital. Her background certainly wasn't deprived, but Stewart had a sharply observant eye and ear and turned her experiences to good account. Her first play, *Starched Aprons*, written in 1942 but not produced at Glasgow's Unity Theatre until 1945, dealt with life in a big city hospital. But it was her second play, *Men Should Weep* (1947), depicting working-class life from a woman's viewpoint, that made people sit up and take notice. It was seen in Glasgow, Edinburgh and London and should have been the launchpad for a long career. Instead Stewart wrote little of substance thereafter, although she did live long enough to see *Men Should Weep* magnificently revived by Giles Havergal for the 7:84 Company in 1982.

What happened? Kenneth Roy, in a sympathetic profile of Stewart to accompany Josie Rourke's excellent production of *Men Should Weep* at the National in 2010, suggests she lacked encouragement from the Scottish male theatrical establishment: in particular he points an accusing finger at O. H. Mavor (better known as the playwright James Bridie) who, as founder of the Glasgow Citizens, patronised and dismissed Stewart. It is also difficult to exaggerate the prejudice of London managers against dramatists who used a Scottish dialect. Some playwrights, such as Barrie and Bridie, softened their Scottishness to suit English ears; others, such as Robert McLellan and Alexander Reid, made no such compromise and paid the price. Even the *Observer*'s Aberdonian critic, Ivor Brown, in 1954 pointed out the danger to young Scottish writers of their 'zeal for the aboriginal' and the difficulty of requiring non-Scottish playgoers 'to listen to strange words in a strange pronunciation'.

I'd say all that has radically changed. Southern audiences are now more hospitable to local dialect. The National Theatre of Scotland, established in 2006, has acquired an international reputation with Gregory Burke's *Black Watch* and John Tiffany's production of *Let the Right One In*. Scottish Nationalism, under Alex Salmond and Nicola Sturgeon, has also become a powerful political movement impossible to ignore.

Men Should Weep has played its part in all that. Its strength, however, lies not in its political crusading but in its social accuracy: it tells us exactly what it was like to live in an overcrowded tenement in Glasgow's East End during the Depression of the 1930s. More specifically, it pays tribute to the resilience, courage and tenacity of women struggling to bring up large families in the face of grinding poverty. In her ability to compensate for her husband's fecklessness, the play's heroine, Maggie Morrison, puts one in mind of O'Casey's Juno. When Maggie's daughter-in-law complains of the way her husband is tied to his mother's apron-strings, one also hears echoes of D. H. Lawrence. But, whatever the influences, Stewart's voice is utterly distinctive: she is the first dramatist to deal with working-class deprivation from a female perspective.

She tells the truth about women and their capacity for endurance. Maggie has to cope with five young children, one of whom is suffering from TB. Her husband John is a bookish, out-of-work socialist who has the impertinence to tell Maggie she needs to get 'a system'. And the couple's grown-up children are an endless source of trouble. Their daughter Jenny, her dad's pet, leaves home to go and live as a shop-owner's mistress. And Alec, a petty thief ruinously spoilt by Maggie, is married to a faithless good-time girl. As the family scratches and scrimps to survive, John impotently cries, 'Christ Almighty! A we've din wrong is tae be born intae poverty. Whit dae they think this kind of life does tae a man?' Stewart's real concern, however, is what it does to a woman who is left, through a mix of back-breaking toil and a residual optimism, to hold the family together.

For all the grimness of its subject, the play is shot through with a wild humour. Maggie's spinster sister is constantly mocked for her grudging hatred of men. When Maggie recalls how John was first drawn to her, in their courting days, by the red hat she wore, a neighbour retorts, 'Mines wouldna hae noticed if I'd met him at Simpson's Corner wi a floral po on ma heid.' Maggie also has to cope with a tetchily demanding old gran, who, given the rare treat of a digestive biscuit, moans, 'It's only chocolate on the wan side.'

Stewart's play is, on one level, a priceless social document. But in the final act, which Stewart rewrote for the 1982 revival, it turns into a resolutely feminist statement. Set on Christmas Day, it shows the Morrison family enjoying a modest upswing thanks to John getting work as a van-driver. They are still haunted, however, by the fact that their tubercular son Bertie has been forbidden by doctors to return to a damp slum. Dramatically, the crunch comes when a guilt-ridden Jenny returns, offering to finance the family's move to a healthy home by the park. Her father, John, adamantly refuses to accept what he calls 'a whore's winnins'. But Maggie both pragmatically accepts the money and turns on John, claiming he treated her as a whore in their youth and that, even today, he still grabs her for a quickie when excited by the sight of his daughter-in-law 'wi her breasts fa'in oot o her fancy claes'. By the end, you don't feel all the Morrisons' problems have been solved. But Maggie has saved her son, humiliated her husband and exposed the hypocrisy of a marriage contract where working-class women are treated as whores with 'nae winnins'. The result is a landmark play in British drama. If men should weep, it is because Ena Lamont Stewart was discouraged from writing a successor to a work that blends a savage indignation at the exploitation of women with an intoxicating theatrical exuberance. It is a true tenement symphony.

75

A Streetcar Named Desire

TENNESSEE WILLIAMS
(1911–83)

I have a cherished personal memory of Tennessee Williams. In 1978, when his play *Vieux Carré* was being produced in London, I was asked to interview Williams on a breakfast radio programme. As I summarised Williams's deeply autobiographical play about a struggling writer in a New Orleans boarding house, a loud, rumbling laugh came from across the table. At first, I took it to be a comment on my inept plot précis. Only later did I realise that it was the recollection of his own life that Williams found unutterably comic. This was the same man who was once asked to leave a London revival of *The Glass Menagerie* because his constant hilarity was thought to be disrupting the mood of this delicately sensitive play.

I always recall these incidents when I read phrases – which I've probably used myself – about Williams being 'the poet of the dispossessed' and a man who captures 'the martyred music of the truly solitary'.

These phrases have a measure of truth. But Williams was also a robustly comic writer who, especially in *Cat on a Hot Tin Roof*, showed a satirist's eye for greed, pretension and the vulgar excesses of wealth. His plays, while rich in empathy for the defeated, also show an understanding of the instinct for survival. And nowhere is that tension more evident than in *Streetcar*, a play that never ceases to fascinate and that, in recent years, has enjoyed a number of outstanding London revivals starring Glenn Close (2002), Rachel Weisz (2009) and Gillian Anderson (2014).

Inevitably, one focuses on Blanche DuBois, the refugee from the Old South who arrives at the New Orleans home of her sister Stella in a state of fragile dependence and who departs a few weeks later bound in a straitjacket. But Blanche's predicament creates polarised reactions. Harold Clurman, writing of the initial 1947 Broadway production, grasped the social resonances and metaphorical power of Williams's play. 'It would be far truer,' wrote Clurman, 'to see Blanche as the potential artist in all of us than as a deteriorated Southern belle.' Of Blanche's sensual and ultimately rapacious brother-in-law Stanley Kowalski Clurman also wrote: 'his mentality provides the soil for fascism, viewed not as a political movement but as a state of being'. John Osborne took a directly opposite line when reviewing a collection of Williams's plays for the *Observer* in 1958. Arguing that Williams's women cry out for defilement, Osborne wrote: '"You and me have had this date from the beginning," says Stanley. The female must come toppling down to where she should be – on her back. The American male must get his revenge sometime.'

You don't need to endorse Osborne's crude gender politics to realise that it is perfectly possible to entertain contradictory visions of Blanche. On the one hand, you can see her as a symbol of grace and the will-to-beauty in an ugly, materialistic world; that's very much how she sees herself when she urges her sister, 'In this dark march toward whatever it is we're approaching . . . Don't – don't hang back with the brutes!' Equally you can see in Blanche a self-deceiving fantasist whose attitude to Stanley is, from the start, one of patronising disdain. For me, the test of any Blanche is whether she can capture this duality. Glenn Close did it superbly in Trevor

Nunn's National Theatre production: she tripped through the shabby New Orleans apartment as if on her way to a governor's ball yet she also caught the aching desolation of a woman who cries, 'I don't want realism. I want magic.' Gillian Anderson, in Benedict Andrews's Young Vic production with its famous rotating set, showed us Blanche, in every sense, in the round: she gave us the alcohol-fuelled snobbishness of a woman who condemns the eavesdropping Stanley as sub-human while also conveying Blanche's emotional solitude, especially in the desperation with which she reached out to her nervous beau, Mitch.

As in so many great plays, we are not forced to take sides. Williams is not presenting us with a simple fable of beauty versus the beast. He sees the virtues and defects in both his main characters and in the values they represent. Blanche is in flight from the Old South where the veneer of refinement and grace was a mask for corruption. Explaining the fate of the ancestral family home, Belle Rêve (Beautiful Dream), Blanche tells Stanley 'our improvident grandfathers and father and uncles exchanged the land for their epic fornications'. Yet it was precisely from such a society that Blanche was hypocritically banished for her promiscuous liaisons in Laurel's Hotel Flamingo. Blanche is a refugee from the Old South but can find neither rest nor sanctuary in the urban melting pot of New Orleans.

Blanche, in short, is a shifting, multi-dimensional figure whose vanity, nostalgia and tantalising sexuality – I remember Anderson sensuously stroking Stanley's hairy forearms – is balanced by a terrifying vulnerability. But Stanley is also much more than the quasi-fascist brute described by Clurman. Stanley exudes a vitality, energy and Lawrentian sexuality untainted by puritan guilt. As Stella says, in one of the play's most potent lines, 'there are things that happen between a man and a woman in the dark that sort of make everything else seem unimportant'. It is also possible to understand the resentment of Stanley, a travelling salesman by profession, at overhearing Blanche tell his wife there is something 'ape-like' about him. But the dark side of Stanley lies in his domestic violence: he beats his wife and rapes Blanche although, without endorsing Osborne's macho bluster, it is fair to say that Stanley destroys his sister-in-law only by becoming what she has always accused him of being.

Williams offers no solutions. As Christopher Bigsby has written, his play shows 'a deep ambiguity' towards a past whose civilised veneer concealed real corruption and towards a present whose social banality is accompanied by a sexual directness. But Williams's play grows larger and richer the more you see and study it. There is undoubted comedy, as well as pathos, in the collision between Blanche's affectation and Stanley's earthiness. There are vast social implications in Blanche's pseudo-aristocratic attachment to the fine arts and Stanley's gung-ho endorsement of the demagogic populist Huey Long with his philosophy of 'Every Man Is a King'. Williams also echoes the over-arching theme of American drama which resounds through the work of O'Neill, Miller and Albee: the conflict between illusion and reality. Blanche clings in desperation to her beautiful dreams and duly perishes. Her sister Stella accepts a necessary life-lie ('I couldn't believe her story and go on living,' she says of Blanche's accusation of rape) and precariously survives. It's a measure of the play's greatness that it maintains a tension between mighty opposites until the very last and leaves us feeling a complex compassion for all its characters.

76

The Chairs

EUGÈNE IONESCO

(1912–94)

By now the basic qualities that I look for in a great play should be fairly clear. I seek the smell of reality, a clearly defined social context, vivacity of phrase, moral ambivalence, a fluctuating tragi-comic mood. Except in the last of these, Ionesco's *The Chairs*, first produced in Paris in 1952, is largely deficient. Ionesco, a French dramatist born in Romania, dubbed his play a 'tragic farce'. Yet it exists in its own eccentrically enclosed universe, mocks the clichés of daily existence and is, philosophically, unambiguous. Life, Ionesco suggests, is essentially meaningless, progress an illusion and the totality of our experience nothing but a piece of incomprehensible gobbledegook. I don't really believe any of this. But Ionesco has created such an arresting theatrical image and filled the stage with such antic activity that I am happy to call this a great play. Anyone lucky enough to have seen Simon McBurney's astonishing revival, jointly presented by Complicité and the Royal Court in 1997 and memorably starring Richard Briers and Geraldine McEwan, will know that the piece is infinitely more than a musty relic of 1950s absurdism.

Peter Brook argues in *The Empty Space* that the acid test of a theatrical experience is that it leaves behind an ineradicable image that contains the play's essential meaning. 'When years later I think of a striking theatrical experience,' writes Brook,

I find a kernel engraved on my memory: two tramps under a tree, an old woman dragging a cart, a sergeant dancing, three people on a sofa in hell – or occasionally a trace deeper than any memory. I haven't a hope of remembering the meanings precisely but from the kernel I can reconstruct a set of meanings. Then a purpose will have been served. A few hours could amend my thinking for life. This is almost but not quite impossible to achieve.

It is, however, exactly what Ionesco achieves in *The Chairs*. What, after all, is the image from it that remains? The spectacle of two old people rushing about in a manic frenzy filling the stage with chairs for a set of invisible guests. This, in itself, contains much of the play's meaning: the quintessential solitude of the old couple, the illusory nature of their guests, the idea of life itself as a purposeless rushing about. But the more closely you examine the play, the more you see how skilfully Ionesco builds up to, and leads away from, that central image.

Take, for instance, the resonant opening exchange in the Martin Crimp translation used by Simon McBurney. We are in a circular room surrounded by water. The Old Man is leaning on a stepladder looking out of a window. The Old Woman is lighting a gas-lamp:

OLD WOMAN: Please – poppet – shut the window. You're letting the stench of stagnant water in. Not to mention the mosquitoes.

OLD MAN: Don't bother me now.

OLD WOMAN: Please – please – poppet – come and sit down. Stop leaning out. You might fall in. Remember what happened to Henry the Seventh. You can never be too careful.

OLD MAN: Spare me your examples, petty-pie. I'm sick to death
of Tudor history. I like looking out. The little boats are like
sunspots.

OLD WOMAN: There aren't any little boats. There isn't any sun.
It's night-time, popsy.

OLD MAN: There's still the afterglow. (*He leans right out.*)

With remarkable economy, Ionesco sets the mood and establishes
his key motifs: the power of illusion, the mutual dependence of
the old couple, their deep nostalgia for a world about which they
cannot agree.

As the play develops, we discover that the couple are awaiting
the arrival of a swarm of guests who have come to hear the Old
Man's message to the world delivered by a professional orator. But
one of Ionesco's tragic jokes is that the old couple are indissolubly
bound together by seventy-five years of marriage but still at
odds about their experience. 'Alone together, so much shared'
is Beckett's later pithy encapsulation of marriage. But Ionesco's
couple are hilariously at variance. 'We had a son . . . very much
alive, yes,' the Old Woman tells a guest. 'I'm afraid we never had
children,' the Old Man informs another. And while the Old Man
remorsefully announces, 'I left mother to die alone in a ditch,'
the Old Woman describes him as 'A man who dearly loved his
parents'.

If we cannot make sense of our own experience, asks Ionesco,
what hope do we have of understanding the world beyond us?
So the invisible guests arrive, crowding the stage as if this were a
phantom version of the cabin scene in the Marx Brothers' *A Night
at the Opera*. The ultimate arrival turns out to be a mixture of
earthly emperor and divine saviour, to whom fawning reverence
is shown. And after the old couple have committed suicide by
leaping out of the window, the deaf and dumb orator chalks up an

indecipherable message on a blackboard, after which we are left with a whirlwind of emptiness.

You can take this as a symbol of the absurdity of the artist's plight or a comment on the meaninglessness of human experience. But even if I am not disposed to share Ionesco's philosophy, I love the abundant theatricality with which he expresses it. The play's poetry lies in the intensity of its vision and the thrill of its performance, and one will never see it better done than in McBurney's version. Richard Briers played the Old Man as a sulky overgrown child, swivelling his head in dismay at mention of the word 'geriatric' and petulantly stamping his foot at the need to deliver his message. Geraldine McEwan was an equally dazzling mixture of the deeply maternal and the sexually frisky, at one point feverishly caressing her body as she imagined herself seduced by one of the guests. McBurney's production, while respecting Ionesco's vision, also theatrically enhanced it. At the end the whole house blew away to reveal an aching, ruinous void and, as murmuring laughter and conversation welled up, a stationary chair suddenly turned in our direction. As John Lahr wrote in the *New Yorker*: 'In that one startling moment – not scripted by Ionesco – the production teases one final caprice from oblivion: a theatrical illusion within a universe that to Ionesco was all illusion.' It was a moment that also put the seal on a play that fulfils one of the definitions of great drama: it leaves behind an indelible image and reverberates in the mind long after one has seen it.

77

The Deep Blue Sea

TERENCE RATTIGAN

(1911–71)

It is hard to think of a playwright further removed from Eugène Ionesco than Terence Rattigan. In one corner you have a whimsical Romanian absurdist, in the other, a seemingly conventional English craftsman. Indeed in the introduction to his third volume of *Collected Plays*, published in 1962, Rattigan goes out of his way to list Ionesco among the 'anti-dramatists' whose work the public would eventually dismiss. Yet, whatever Rattigan's shortcomings as a prophet, he was an outstanding, profoundly misunderstood dramatist. Under the veneer of urbane sophistication lay a writer of whom David Rudkin once wrote: 'I detect in his plays a deep personal, surely sexual, pain which he manages at the same time to express and disguise.' While Rattigan's plays are formally conventional, they probe the inequality of passion and the sadness of the undernourished heart. They are also unequivocally on the side of the underdog: Crocker-Harris stands up to the bullying educational establishment in *The Browning Version* (1948), and the bogus, implicitly homosexual major, in the second half of *Separate Tables* (1954), triumphs over bigotry and prejudice.

But it is in *The Deep Blue Sea* (1952) that we see Rattigan at his accomplished best. It is a well-established fact, explored in Michael Darlow's superb biography of Rattigan, that the play was prompted by the suicide of the dramatist's former lover, Kenneth Morgan. Rattigan received the news of Morgan's death while on tour in Liverpool in 1949 with his latest play, *Adventure Story*. Although visibly shaken, Rattigan saw the dramatic potential in Morgan's death and apparently said to his director, Peter Glenville, 'The play will open with the body discovered dead in front of the gas fire.' Rumours of an early draft dealing with an intense relationship between two men persist, but the eventual version of *The Deep Blue Sea* conformed to the expectations of the time. The play does indeed open with the attempted suicide of Hester Collyer, a judge's wife who has sacrificed a life of ease and comfort to live with Freddie Page, a boyish ex-war hero who cannot meet her emotional and sexual needs. But in the course of an agonising day we see how Hester overcomes both Freddie's desertion and her husband's imploring request to return home and survives on her own terms.

The play is a brilliant psychological study – one of the best on the modern stage – of the destructive power of love. But it was Karel Reisz's 1993 production at the Almeida, starring a luminous Penelope Wilton, that brought home to me two important factors: Rattigan's ability to encapsulate the mood of post-war England and his capacity to generate overwhelming emotion through verbal restraint. By making transparent the grey-green walls of the play's Ladbroke Grove apartment block, Reisz's production suggested we were contemplating a modern *Heartbreak House*. At the same time it reminded us that the emotional inarticulacy Rattigan saw as the English vice was also his most powerful dramatic weapon.

I have argued in my book *State of the Nation* that Rattigan's play provides a resonant social metaphor for the England of the early 1950s. Hester, far from being a special case, stands for all those women who defy their class origins in their search for sexual and emotional fulfilment. Freddie embodies the tragedy of the character who had 'a good war' but who fits uneasily into a peacetime world where there is little call for their form of resilient bravery (a theme later explored by David Hare in *Plenty*). And every single one of Rattigan's supporting characters adds to the composite portrait of England. Hester's husband Bill is a reticent Establishment Englishman for whom love, as Hester says, is 'that thing you read about in your beloved Jane Austen and Anthony Trollope' rather than experience in life. Miller, the struck-off émigré doctor who acts as Hester's saviour, is clearly a persecuted victim of antiquated homosexual laws. Philip and Ann Welch, the young couple who live in the flat above Hester, embody a kindly incomprehension of love's physicality. Not least there is the landlady, Mrs Elton, who expresses a tolerant, working-class acceptance of people as they are. I don't believe for a moment that Rattigan consciously set out to write a state-of-the-nation play. But it is his instinctive empathy for characters of different gender and diverse backgrounds that gives his play a metaphorical weight.

What is often dismissively referred to as Rattigan's 'craftsmanship' – as if lack of craft were somehow an attribute – is also his way of surreptitiously inserting vital information about plot and character. Freddie abandons Hester because, in his words, 'we're death to each other, you and I'. The play's most bitter irony is that, in deserting Hester to ensure their mutual survival, Freddie almost certainly signs his own death warrant. He has already lost a job as a test pilot in Canada because his heavy drinking caused him to crash a plane. To escape Hester, he accepts a similar post in South America. 'Don't worry about my nerve and judgement, Hes,' he cheerfully says. 'A month or two on the wagon and I'll be the old ace again – the old dicer with death.' Hester's survival, one assumes, is achieved at the price of Freddie's life.

But it is in the play's final scene that Rattigan reveals his ability to generate profound emotion. Some dramatists achieve this though a verbal torrent; Rattigan, through sub-text. Freddie has been lured back to the flat for one last time to collect his belongings and is confronted by Hester:

> HESTER: How are you feeling now?
> FREDDIE: All right.
> HESTER: Thank you for coming.
> FREDDIE: I shouldn't have sent the kid anyway, I suppose.
> HESTER: Had any food?
> FREDDIE: Yes, I had a bite at the Belvedere. What about you?
> HESTER: Oh, I'll get myself something later.

This strikes me as dramatic writing of the highest order in that the strong emotion felt by the two characters is entirely at odds with the banality of their expression. Many years ago Lindsay Anderson, in one of a series of essays by members of the so-called Angry generation in a book called *Declaration*, inveighed against the understatement of British movies. He chose an example from *The Blue Lamp*, where a policeman's wife, on being told of her husband's death, says, 'I'll just put these flowers in water.' In fact, that always struck me as a very moving line. Rattigan shows a similar awareness that, however much we may regret the inarticulacy of the English at moments of extreme passion, it makes for unforgettably powerful drama. It is a measure of Rattigan's greatness that he perceived that the English vice contains its own singular virtues.

78

The Crucible

ARTHUR MILLER
(1915–2005)

Great plays change their meaning depending on time and circumstance. When Arthur Miller's historical drama about the Salem witch trials of 1692 was first produced on Broadway in 1953, it was inevitably treated as a topical parable: Senator Joe McCarthy's anti-communist witch-hunts were too fresh in memory for it to be seen any other way. As I watched Dominic Cooke's revival for the RSC in 2006, it then struck me as a play about unyielding intellectual rigidity: when Deputy-Governor Danforth, presiding over the witch-trials, cried 'a person is either with this court or he must be counted against it' he eerily anticipated a similar phrase by George Bush about opposition to the Iraq War. Yet seeing Yael Farber's astonishing Old Vic revival in 2014, in the wake of a spate of accusations of sexual exploitation of minors by TV entertainers and Catholic clerics, the play took on a whole new resonance: one was reminded that the action is triggered by an older man's abuse of his power over a young girl. A play once described as 'a rip-roaring melodrama' now seems to have the multi-dimensionality of great art.

The sexual element was very deliberately emphasised by Miller. Assiduously researching the Salem records, he discovered that the charges of witchcraft – leading to the hanging of nineteen adults and two dogs – depended heavily on the testimony of adolescent girls. But Abigail Warren, who testified against John Proctor and his wife, was only twelve at the time. By altering her age to seventeen, Miller was able both to give her a plausible sexual motivation and to make her an instrument for exposing Proctor's residual guilt. Miller's play is about many things: a repressive Puritan theocracy, the unreliabilty of enforced confession, the break-up of a fractious community. But at its heart lies the relationship between Proctor, his wife Elizabeth and Abigail. If the play is simply treated as the story of a good man undone by the machinations of a wicked girl, then it is indeed melodrama. Miller's skill, however, lies in suggesting that Abigail is herself a victim: what happens is that, in seeking vindictive retribution, she both forces Proctor to confront his self-loathing and helps to destroy an already divided Salem.

The evidence is all there in the text, but it was Farber's production, more than any other, that explored the play's moral complexity. Abigail, crucially, is an orphan: 'I saw Indians smash my dear parents' head on the pillow next to mine,' she tells Betty Parris, 'and I have seen reddish work done at night.' Proctor, as her employer and a man twice her age, breaks a double trust in having sex with her: as Abigail says, 'I know how you clutched my back behind your house and sweated like a stallion whenever I came near.' Proctor is also culpable in that, out of a desire to protect both Abigail and himself, he delays passing on vital information: that he knows, from Abigail, there was no real witchcraft in the Salem woods. Only when Elizabeth is arrested does he act, and by then it is too late to halt the momentum of hysteria. 'Is the accuser always holy now?' Proctor famously asks. Although it's a great line, it overlooks his own complicity in the torrent of false witness.

So what kind of man is Proctor? He's no shining beacon of virtue and, although he dies at the end, that doesn't automatically make him a tragic hero. I see him as following the dramatic trajectory once specified by Aristotle: 'the change from ignorance to knowledge'. Or, more precisely, from self-deception to self-recognition. At the start, he hides from the sins he actually has committed: by the end he refuses to confess to those he hasn't. But what is fascinating is his link with many of world drama's other celebrated nay-sayers such as Ibsen's Dr Stockman in *An Enemy of the People*, Shaw's Saint Joan and Brecht's Galileo: he is prepared to compromise up to a certain point. But there comes a crucial moment when defiance replaces submission.

At the climax, Miller's play subsides into rhetoric as defined by Yeats: 'the will struggling to do the work of the imagination'. But what it does brilliantly before that is provide a vivid portrait of both a marriage and a community. I never cease to be astonished at the opening of the second act, where the friction between John and Elizabeth is audible under every line of dialogue. Proctor sits at his farmhouse table, eats his rabbit supper, talks about buying a heifer and is urged by his wife to go to Salem and report to the court that Abigail told him the accusations were false. 'If the girl's a saint now,' says Proctor, 'I think it's not easy to prove she's a fraud and the town gone so silly. She told it to me in a room alone – I have no proof for it.' 'You were alone with her?' enquires Elizabeth. 'For a moment alone, aye,' says Proctor. 'Why, then, it is not as you told me,' says Elizabeth. As played by Richard Armitage and Anna Madeley in the Farber production, the air was thick with recrimination and pauses of Pinteresque potency.

As well as analysing a marriage, Miller shows how the seeds of the community's downfall lie within itself: in Salem a confession of personal guilt carries with it the bonus of accusation against others. And in the tumultuous first act, Miller shows neighbour pitted against neighbour. Proctor accuses the Reverend Parris of simony. Thomas Puttnam claims that Proctor is appropriating lumber from his land. The litigious Giles Corey has fought with Puttnam and his forebears over vital pasture. Mrs Putnam has lost seven of her eight children at birth and, resenting Rebecca Nurse's secure progeny, angrily says 'There are wheels within wheels in this village and fires within fires!' It is often overlooked that Mrs Putnam, in getting her Barbadian maid Tituba to carry out secret rituals to preserve her surviving child, is also condoning a form of black magic. Miller's point is that superstition, fear, guilt and acrimonious disputes over territory provide fertile soil for charges of witchcraft.

In its avoidance of moral melodrama and refusal to classify people as wholly good or wholly bad, it's a very Shavian play. Miller even follows the model of *Saint Joan* in preserving a balance between the zealous witchfinder (Judge Hawthorne), the rational authority figure (Deputy Governor Danforth) and the apostate cleric horrified at the consequences of his actions (Reverend John Hale). But Miller's play has one vital quality missing in the Shavian prototype: sexuality. And in this lies a vital clue to the play's longevity. Miller, in his prose, often resorts to lofty abstractions. But as a dramatist he understands perfectly how deeds beget consequences and how an act of animal passion behind a farm door can lead to the unravelling of a whole community.

79

Summer of the Seventeenth Doll

RAY LAWLER

(1921–)

So far I have focused chiefly on plays from Britain, continental Europe and America. But there is a world elsewhere, including Australia, a country whose drama we either ignore or patronise. When *Cloudstreet*, an epic family chronicle based on a novel by Tim Winton, opened in London in 1999, one Sunday critic began her column by saying: 'This week's starter for ten: list Australia's contribution to the contemporary theatre scene. I managed Dame Edna Everage, Rolf Harris and his digeridoo and Kylie Minogue before being told I was snooty.' I wouldn't say 'snooty'. My friend and colleague was simply overlooking a substantial body of post-war Australian drama.

For a start the work of David Williamson, Australia's leading commercial dramatist, has travelled widely: in plays such as *Don's Party*, *The Removalists* and *The Club* he has harpooned the rigidity of sexual relationships and the lurking authoritarianism in Australian society. Meanwhile Hannie Rayson in *Hotel Sorrento*, in which three sisters return to their family home after the death of their father, charted the predicament of women in a male-dominated society. And one could list a wide range of fine Australian dramatists. There is Michael Gow, who in *Away* wrote about Australia's need to discard its colonial inheritance; Louis

Nowra, who in *Cosi* explored the themes of manic depression and music; and the highly political Stephen Sewell, who in *It Just Stopped* analysed the fatal precariousness of our consumer-based civilisation. Visiting Australia, I've also admired the work of Dorothy Hewett, Patrick White and Wesley Enoch, who, in *The Sunshine Club*, dramatised a subject about which most of us know little: the prejudice facing Aboriginal soldiers as they returned home after serving in the Second World War.

But if there was one play that put Australian drama firmly on the international map, it was *Summer of the Seventeenth Doll*, which first appeared in Melbourne in 1955 and went on to enjoy success in London and New York. Ray Lawler's achievement was twofold. He pinned down, with merciless realism, defining aspects of 1950s Australia: the concept of 'mateship', the competitiveness of a macho culture, the dream of an itinerant life based on rural toil and urban recreation. At the same time, his play touched on issues everyone could recognise: fear of commitment, a refusal to accept the advancing years, a preference for romantic fantasy over unpalatable fact. Lawler's play was traditional in form. But Kenneth Tynan, in a glowing review in the *Observer*, pointed out just how radical it was in its content: it showed a respect for ordinary working people 'who were neither "grim" nor "funny", neither sentimentalized nor patronized, neither used to point a social moral nor derided as quaint and improbable clowns'.

Lawler's two male workers are Roo and Barney, sugar-cane cutters in their late thirties who habitually spend seven months a year in Queensland and then come down to Melbourne to enjoy the company of two women, Olive and Nancy, who are, in effect, their unmarried wives. And the regularity of the event is neatly marked by the kewpie dolls Roo has brought with him for the last sixteen summers and which adorn the walls of the house Olive shares with her mother.

But this year everything is different. Roo has lost his status as the lead 'ganger' among the cutters to a younger rival, has quit the plantation and arrived in Melbourne totally skint. Meanwhile Barney's old partner, Nancy, has left him to get officially married. A professed ladies' man, Barney finds himself trying to forge a new relationship with Olive's friend, Pearl, a widowed barmaid with a teenage daughter and a good name she is anxious to protect. What follows, over the course of a summer month, is the realisation that the past is past and cannot be retrieved as everyone faces up to devouring time.

What I find fascinating is Lawler's exploration of the peculiar intensity of Australian male friendship. In Britain hetero men tend to bond shyly, discussing everything in life except what really matters. In Australia 'mateship' implies a total and unflinching trust. That is why Roo and Barney are on edge even from the start of Lawler's play. Roo has stalked off the cane-cutting plantation prematurely, expecting Barney to follow him: Barney's failure to do so is regarded as an act of treachery. To make matters worse, Barney goes off boozing in Melbourne with Michael Dowd: the very youngster who has supplanted Roo. No wife could be more angry or jealous if her husband went off with another woman. In the end Roo and Barney are reconciled and depart together into an uncertain future. Lawler never implies there is anything sexual in the kinship between the two men, yet the rapport between them has a molten intimacy which you certainly don't see in the relationship between their partners, Olive and Pearl.

Lawler is writing of Australia in the 1950s, since when much has changed, although in recent memory Julia Gillard, as the country's first woman prime minister, was subject to violently sexist abuse (including calls to 'ditch the witch') in the press and parliament. What Lawler pins down, however, is a world where men regard women with a strange mixture of bravado and diffidence. In one scene we see Barney, with stunning insensitivity, suggest to Pearl that she bring her daughter along to partner his new friend, Michael Dowd, for a day at the races. Barney puts it, however, with characteristic bluntness: 'So we just can't land him with anythin', 'n I was thinkin' – how'd you like to bring that girlie of yours along – what's her name?' When Dowd, however, is left alone with the girl next door, who will eventually accompany him to the track, he is almost as nervous as Young Marlow in *She Stoops to Conquer*.

Lawler paints a vivid picture of a world where middle-aged men brag and mature women fantasise and where both are brought up against harsh reality: in that sense, his play is both deeply Australian and in tune with the battle between truth and illusion that haunts modern drama. If there is one character in the play who can see daylight, it is Olive's septuagenarian mum, Emily, who, at the climax, gives Roo a piece of her mind:

> You and Barney are two of a pair. Only the time he spent chasin' wimmen, you spent in being top dog! Both of you champions! Well, that's all very fine and a lot of fun while it lasts but last is one thing it just don't do. There's a time for sowing and a time for reaping – and reapin' is what you're doing now.

Emily is the ratty *raisonneur* in a play that shows not only that, spiritually, old habits die hard but that, sexually, old hards tend to die habits. What Roo and Barney, inseparable as Beckettian tramps, wake up to is the realisation that the party is over and that together they face an empty road. While Australia may have gone on to produce more poetic or militant drama, it has produced no play so unbearably poignant.

80

The Visit

FRIEDRICH DÜRRENMATT
(1921–90)

I've always been fascinated by the work of the Swiss-German writer Friedrich Dürrenmatt. In novels such as *The Inspector Barlach Mysteries* (1951) he uses the police procedural as a basis for philosophical enquiry. And in plays like *The Visit* (1956) and *The Physicists* (1962) he creates macabre fables open to multiple interpretations. *The Visit*, especially, is an obliging work of art. I've seen it given totally antithetical stagings by Peter Brook for H. M. Tennent and Annabel Arden and Simon McBurney for Complicité. I've witnessed a German operatic version presented to the well-heeled patrons of Glyndebourne. It's also been filmed, with Ingrid Bergman and Anthony Quinn, and twice turned into a musical. For all that, no one can ever quite agree on what it is actually about.

I found a helpful clue in an interview Dürrenmatt gave to Martin Esslin in *Plays and Players* just before the London opening of *The Physicists* in 1962. Esslin revealed that he had been criticised for not including Dürrenmatt in his book on *The Theatre of the Absurd*. 'No,' said Dürrenmatt, 'I don't think I am on the same lines as Beckett and Ionesco. I would call my own theatre a "theatre of paradox" because it is precisely the paradoxical results of strict logic that interest me. Ionesco and Beckett attack language and logic as a means of thought and communication. I am concerned with logical thought in its strictest application, so strict that it sets up its own internal contradictions.' It is just those contradictions that you find explored in *The Visit*.

The outline of the plot is, I suspect, well known: as in Gogol's *The Government Inspector*, the arrival of a visitor reveals the depths of corruption in a poor provincial community. In this case, the visitor is Claire Zachanassian, a fabulously wealthy plutocrat who returns to the Middle-European town of Gullen, where she was born. The citizens are praying that she will pour some of her superfluous wealth into the town's ailing economy. What she offers them is a billion marks provided they agree to murder a local shopkeeper, Anton Schill, who, as a young man, seduced, impregnated and then jilted her. The citizens are initially horrified. But Schill notices that all his customers are ordering expensive items on credit. The police chief, the pastor and a local teacher protest their integrity while succumbing to the credit-based spending-spree. Even Schill's wife buys a fur coat and his son a car. Eventually, in strict accordance with democracy, a civic vote is taken, Schill's fate is sealed and, in a chilling climax, the citizens process with Claire to the station accompanied by Schill's coffin.

At the most basic level, you can see this is as a stark fable about good and evil. But Dürrenmatt complicates the issue by suggesting that it is not a confrontation of moral absolutes. Schill, as a young man, denied being the father of Claire's child and, when the case came to court, bribed two of the townsfolk to swear they had slept with her. For her part, Claire was driven from the town as a seventeen-year-old, pelted with stones and forced into a life of prostitution. As she says, in her own defence, 'The world made me into a whore: now I make the world into a brothel.'

If the play is much more than a Manichaean tale of moral

opposites, it can plausibly be interpreted as a political parable, one, as Michael Paterson has pointed out, in which Dürrenmatt reflects on Switzerland's ambiguous relationship with Nazi Germany and on the wealth it acquired through the war. But while the play is palpably about corruption, I see it as proof of Dürrenmatt's point that his plays are really concerned with the paradoxes of strict logic: what he shows, with great skill, is how words like 'democracy' and 'justice' are riddled with contradictions. The citizens of Gullen don't arbitrarily murder Schill, they are driven to it by economic necessity and act in accordance with democratic principles. Equally, Dürrenmatt shows that 'justice' is no mere abstract idea: it is something that operates in a strict financial context. Lest this seem remote from today's world, I would draw attention to Nick Davies's gripping account of the 2013–14 trial in which Rebekah Brooks and Andy Coulson were accused, in their capacity as newspaper editors, of supervising the illegal hacking of private phones. Correct judicial procedures were undoubtedly followed, but Davies pointed out how Rupert Murdoch, as the ultimate employer of Brooks and Coulson, poured millions into their defence while 'the Crown Prosecution Service had only one full-time solicitor attached to the trial and one administrative assistant'. Justice, in short, can never be divorced from money.

But one should not underestimate the theatrical cunning and visual skill with which Dürrenmatt explores his ideas. One of the abiding images is of Claire waiting patiently on her hotel balcony while the townsfolk come to terms with the necessary murder. And although the play is full of Gothic touches such as the accompaniment of Claire by a live panther and a pair of blind castrati, it gains from being staged with a resonant simplicity. That was the beauty of Brook's production, which had a strange, eventful history: it went on a British regional tour in 1958, was shunned by

London managers and only arrived in the West End in 1960 after it had been acclaimed in New York. Long before Brook became the apostle of the empty space, he showed his matchless ability to choreograph human movement on a virtually bare stage: I recall the line of stubborn backs blocking Schill's exit as he sought to escape the town and the sinister glow of lighted cigarettes in the dark as the citizens encircled him for the kill. Alfred Lunt and Lynn Fontanne, Brook's chief actors, were famous at the time for their adornment of lavishly quilted comedies; I remember the excitement of a befurred lady in Stratford-on-Avon looking at a playbill for *The Visit* and ecstatically crying, 'O, darling, the Lunts.' Like everyone else, she was in for a rude shock. Alfred Lunt, with his sagging shoulders and defeated air, was a memorably doomed Schill, and Lynn Fontanne as Claire radiated a devastatingly icy elegance. Brook showed us a believable community propelled towards murder. For all its brilliance, Complicité's 1988 production, with its citizens collectively juddering to convey the passage of an express-train through the station, gave us the impression we were watching a troupe of accomplished mime artists. But Dürrenmatt's play reminds us that great drama can take many forms. In this case, we have a resonantly powerful *Mittel Europa* moral fable, one full of unnerving paradoxes about the fallibility of democracy and the contamination of justice by wealth.

81

All That Fall

SAMUEL BECKETT

(1906–89)

The scene is a café outside the Young Vic, where two critics have just seen a fine production of Beckett's *Happy Days* starring Juliet Stevenson. The two critics, whom we have met before, are Helena and Michael. She is bright, smart and fantastically well-read. He is an ageing, slightly portly figure with dandruff on his collar and bags under his eyes. They relish their random encounters. When they last met, it was to debate the virtues, and occasional vices, of Bernard Shaw. And this evening Beckett is naturally at the forefront of their minds. Helena, pensively stirring her cappuccino, opens the conversation.

Helena: Is it true what I've heard?

Michael: Which is?

H: That you're writing a book on the *101 Greatest Plays*?

M: Perfectly true.

H: I assume Beckett will feature a lot. I guess the difficulty is in choosing which plays to include. You must be torn between *Waiting for Godot*, *Endgame* and *Happy Days*.

M: I'm afraid that you, like a lot of other people, are in for a shock. I've chosen none of those.

H: What! How could you possibly leave them out? What was it Tom Stoppard said about *Godot*? 'It redefined the minima of theatrical validity.' Drama was never the same after Beckett showed how much you could achieve by abandoning linear narrative and focusing on mankind's search for meaning. *Endgame* is also a great poem about life's terminal stages. And, for Christ's sake, we've just seen a wonderful production of *Happy Days*, which says everything about our capacity for endurance.

M: I don't disagree with a word you've said. Beckett did more than anyone since Brecht to change the nature of theatre. I've also lived long enough to see *Godot* transformed from a piece of supposedly avant-garde obscurity into a popular boulevard hit. I recall how *Endgame*, when played by Michael Gambon and Lee Evans, seemed like a distilled *King Lear* – another play, incidentally, I've omitted. And I've seen generations of Winnies, from Peggy Ashcroft to Juliet Stevenson, stoically suffering under a blazing sun.

H: So what's your problem?

M: Maybe it lies within me. While I admire Beckett's integrity as a man and an artist, I'm not temperamentally drawn to his vision of life as an irremediable hell and I don't find his theatrical metaphors necessarily grow more resonant with time. I applaud his musicality, his strict sense of form, his ability to break the theatrical mould. But, much as I love the early work, I don't yearn to see it endlessly revived. Something strange also happens after *Happy Days* in that Beckett uses the stage like a painter or sculptor to create irreducible, unchanging images. The essence of great drama is that it is susceptible to endless reinterpretation, but Beckett's images are too prescriptive to allow that. When Fiona Shaw sought to release May in *Footfalls* from her spatial captivity, it undermined the play and actually led to the Beckett estate banning the production. Even when Peter Brook had the chairbound heroine of *Rockaby* sit motionless – instead of rocking back and forth – it worked against the grain of the text.

H: You're simply citing two productions that didn't work. But that doesn't obscure the fact that Beckett has created a set of images that are part of the lexicon of modern theatre. And if you see Lisa Dwan's terrific performance of *Not I*, *Footfalls* and *Rockaby*, you realise there is scope for interpretative latitude within a disciplined form.

M: Good point. But I have to say that there is one early Beckett play I've always treasured since I heard it receive its première on the BBC Third Programme in 1957.

H: Isn't it cheating a bit to include a radio drama in your top 101 plays?

M: I don't think so, since the play has been staged several times, not least in that beautiful Trevor Nunn production a few years back when Eileen Atkins gave a mesmerising performance as Mrs Rooney.

H: I'm with you on that. But why, given your general hesitancy on Beckett, are you so passionate about *All That Fall*?

M: Partly because of its vivid particularity. As you know, all that really happens is that Maddy Rooney travels along a country road to a railway station to meet her blind husband off a train. But, as Jim Knowlson points out in his brilliant biography, Beckett is writing about people and a world he knew intimately when growing up in Foxrock near Dublin: the carter, the bill-broker, the racecourse-clerk, the station-master are all drawn from memory rather than being exemplary archetypes.

H: OK. But all that proves is something we've all known about for a long time: your own rather dated penchant for observant realism.

M: Maybe so. But I find in the play all the great Beckett themes given flesh and colour. The testy interdependence of Maddy and her husband is to me as moving as that of Vladimir and Estragon in *Godot*.

And while the play is full of images of death and decay, they have none of the determinist bleakness of *Endgame*. When the bill-broker says 'divine day for the meeting', referring to the Leopardstown races, there is a sense of bright hope in the air, one, I admit, that is later offset by Maddy's moans, the omnipresent sense of misfortune and the image of rotting leaves in a summer ditch. But I don't feel, as I do in *Endgame*, that the dice are loaded against humanity from the start: even Mr Rooney's determination to know what's going to happen in Theodor Fontane's novel *Effi Briest* suggests a hunger for life that counterpoints the pervasive dissolution.

H: I'm not denying it's a beautiful work but doesn't it seem slight and pale in comparison with the polyphony of *Godot*?

M: Not for me, it doesn't. Even in *Godot*, I don't find Beckett's tenacious Protestant memory works as powerfully as it does here. Whenever I think of Beckett, I'm reminded of a remark by the Spanish film-maker Luis Buñuel: 'Still an atheist, thank God.' This, to me, is Beckett's sublime contradiction: his denial of a divine purpose and his inability to eradicate his Protestant past. The Rooneys may mock the idea that 'The Lord upholdeth all that fall and raiseth up all that be bowed down', but the phrase still haunts their consciousness. And there are references to Scriptural discrepancies, Christ's resurrection and entry into Jerusalem on a donkey. However much he may reject religion, Beckett remains permeated by its language and ethos.

H: I see your point, even if I still think you're perverse in preferring this play to *Godot*. But you've dodged the big question, which is the curious ending in which Beckett leaves us in suspense as to whether Mr Rooney may have been responsible, in the course of his train journey, for the death of a child.

M: I'm sure the mystery is intentional. But the ending only underscores the obsession with children that courses through the play. Maddy is still plagued by the death of her daughter, and Mr Rooney speaks of his desire to 'nip some young doom in the bud'. If you look through Beckett's plays, they are haunted by images of childlessness and infertility as if he is working out some private anxiety or sorrow. But that is mere impertinent speculation. I doubt I have won you over to my case. I can only say that *All That Fall*, in its localised richness, has a humanity that leaves me more moved than by any other Beckett play. But it's getting late. Let's go.

H: We can't.

M: Why not?

H: We're still waiting for the bill.

82

The Entertainer

JOHN OSBORNE

(1929–94)

I know, I know. *Look Back in Anger* is the play that caused ructions, changed lives, helped reshape the British theatre. But *The Entertainer* both is a better play and offers a more resonant metaphor. Laurence Olivier, the first ever Archie Rice, wrote a heartfelt letter to John Osborne the day the play opened at the Royal Court on 10 April 1957. 'Thank you,' it read, 'for the thrilling and lovely play which will no doubt be in the same Reps Drawer as *The Cherry Orchard* and *The School for Scandal* before the century is out.' Olivier may have been guilty of exaggeration, but, having seen any number of revivals, I can say that Osborne's play both encapsulates the rancorous mood of the 1950s and triumphantly stands the test of time.

What is astonishing, as Osborne reveals in his memoir *Almost a Gentleman*, is that the original production was nearly forestalled. Even with Olivier's name attached, the council of the English Stage Company initially turned the play down. It was only at a second, crisis meeting that a casting vote by Lord Harewood changed the council's original decision. Osborne also records, with wry humour, how he and the play's director, Tony Richardson, were summoned to a casting meeting with the Oliviers, where it was suggested that the beautiful Vivien Leigh might play Archie's ageraddled wife by wearing a rubber mask. Happily, the idea was quickly scotched.

If *The Entertainer* is Osborne's finest play, it is for one basic reason: it uses the British music hall, then in terminal decline, as a symbol for the nation at large. In the mid-1950s bulldozers started to blitz many of the old Victorian and Edwardian variety theatres. Others were hastily converted. A handful survived. Meanwhile, in October 1956, British and French troops, in violation of international law, invaded Colonel Nasser's Egypt over its nationalisation of the Suez Canal. Osborne's inspired idea was to forge a link between these two events. Nor was it an arbitrary one: many of Britain's old theatres, which boasted names like the Chiswick Empire, the Glasgow Empire, the Liverpool Empire, were a testament to an age of imperialist expansion. The kind of tatty touring shows that filled the decaying halls often sought to combine prurience and patriotism: one of Archie's front-cloth numbers includes a gauzy vision of a nude Britannia holding a bulldog and trident. But Osborne's most far-sighted notion was to see that the public protests against the Suez invasion, especially a famous one in Trafalgar Square, were a form of street theatre and that the flakily temperamental prime minister of the time, Anthony Eden, had a touch of the fading matinee idol. One of the least noticed lines in *The Entertainer* comes when Archie says to his father, Billy: 'Are you one of those who don't like the Prime Minister? I think I've grown rather fond of him. I think it was after he went to the West Indies to ask Noël Coward to write a play for him.' The truth is that Eden, after his resignation in January 1957, did indeed go to Coward's Jamaican home to convalesce, a situation that prompted Coward in his *Diaries* to describe Eden as 'a tragic figure who had been cast in a star part well above his capacities.'

Osborne not only pins down the inherent theatricality of the time, he also structures his play as if it were a music-hall show. Illuminated numbers on the sides of the proscenium arch punctuate each scene as if they were items in a music-hall bill. And Osborne, with little-noticed brilliance, relates Archie's front-cloth songs and patter to his private life and the mid-1950s zeitgeist. Archie's first song, 'Why Should I Care?', epitomises the heartless detachment that later turns out to be a key to his character. His second number, 'We're All Out for Good Old Number One', expresses the prevailing political ethos and picks up a phrase used by the new prime minister, Harold Macmillan, about the dangers of a 'drab equality'; Archie puts the credo of selfish individualism into practice by being ready to ditch his wife and exploit his father to save himself from ruin. Archie's third song, 'Thank God I'm Normal' also creepily links male potency and the imperialist urge in a way that anticipates Caryl Churchill's *Cloud Nine*.

Osborne uses the music-hall format to explore the essence of England. He also shows how Archie's rat-a-tat patter bleeds into his ramshackle home life. Yet, for all the performative element of the domestic scenes, they posses the kind of emotional intensity that one associates more with the work of O'Neill or Tennessee Williams than conventional British drama. Osborne once said he wanted to give audiences 'lessons in feeling', which he certainly does here, and it's fascinating that a writer so often accused of misogyny does this best through the beautifully written character of Archie's wife Phoebe. She is not only precisely observed – the sad wife of a womanising second-rater used to following in Archie's wake and terrified of 'being laid out by some stranger in some rotten stinking little hole in Gateshead or West Hartlepool' – she also has the prickliness and deference that Osborne sees as class characteristics. One of the play's best moments is Phoebe's disproportionate rage at Archie's dad for nibbling at the cake she'd bought for her son Mick, supposedly returning from Suez. Phoebe also bridles ferociously at Archie's daughter Jean, when she mocks the patronising gentlemanliness of her wealthy uncle Bill. What Osborne pins down exactly is Phoebe's mixture of deprivation and rattiness.

But that is typical of a play shot through with Osborne's characteristic ambivalence: you feel he sides intellectually with Jean in her anti-Suez anger and sympathises emotionally with Archie's Edwardian dad Billy, who embodies a vanished grace and style. That ambivalence reaches its fulfilment in Archie himself, who, while being a sinking shit, also displays an heroic valour in appearing twice-nightly before audiences who despise him as much as he despises them. It is one of the greatest roles written for any actor in the twentieth century and also susceptible to varying interpretations. No one can quite match Olivier, who, exactly as in the Stratford Macbeth he'd played two years earlier, showed outward bravura and soul-wrenching despair giving way to spiritual emptiness. But every actor brings something different to the role: Max Wall had his own charismatic lugubriousness, Peter Bowles a seedy, pseudo-poshness, David Threlfall a wild eccentricity and Robert Lindsay – the best since Olivier – the self-loathing of a man aware of his moral shabbiness.

Osborne's play was a product of the 1950s, but it both expresses its time and transcends it in its portrait of a country going through its own identity crisis and of a battered comic who is dying, in every sense, before our very eyes.

83

The Fire Raisers

MAX FRISCH

(1911–91)

You cannot, as I hope I've shown, confine drama to a single purpose. It can enlighten, educate and entertain. It can be epic or minimalist. It can rejoice in language or parcel out words parsimoniously. But one of its most basic functions is to provide a metaphor that expands with time and takes on multiple meanings. The Swiss-German writer Max Frisch achieved just that in *The Fire Raisers*. Frisch's idea first took dramatic shape as a radio play in 1953 (and there is a thesis to be written on the influence of radio on modern drama). The stage version was premiered in Zurich in 1958, reached London's Royal Court in 1961 in a Lindsay Anderson production and was briskly revived – in a new translation by Alistair Beaton under the title of *The Arsonists* – at the Court in 2007. Some plays fade with time. Frisch's satiric fable – 'a morality without a moral' he called it – seemed more pertinent than ever.

Frisch's story has a beautiful clarity. Gottlieb Biedermann, an archetypal bourgeois, as his name implies, is a manufacturer of hair tonic in a town plagued by arson attacks. In his professional life, Biedermann behaves with a brutal heartlessness: he rejects a former employee who's claiming a share of the profits from an invention and ultimately provokes the man's suicide. But when a homeless wrestler, Schmitz, turns up at his door, Biedermann gives him food and shelter. To the astonishment of Biedermann and his wife, Babette, Schmitz is soon joined by an ex-waiter, Eisenring. Biedermann suspects the two men are arsonists, and when they stack drums of petrol in his attic and openly fix fuses and detonators in front of him his fears are confirmed. But Biedermann seeks to appease the intruders, even inviting them to a slap-up dinner of goose and red cabbage. Whatever may happen to the rest of the town, he believes that he is safe from attack. All this is observed by a parodic Greek chorus of firemen, who, from the outset, point out that nothing can be put down to fate. As they say in the Beaton version: 'If humans start thinking like that Then they will not deserve Their place on this earth This generous earth That is fruitful and gracious to man.'

The first thing to strike one is Frisch's skill in resurrecting a potent dramatic myth: the danger of showing hospitality to one's destroyers. Sophocles' Oedipus, investigating the source of Theban plague, opens his doors to messengers of doom. Ibsen's Hjalmar Ekdal in *The Wild Duck* welcomes into the family home the fatally idealistic Gregers Werle. Significantly in both cases, as with Babette in *The Fire Raisers*, it is the protagonist's wife who has the foresight to detect the looming disaster.

But, while invoking ancient myth, Frisch's play was prompted by post-war history: specifically, the case of President Beneš of Czechoslovakia. In 1946 Beneš and his foreign minister, Jan Masaryk, had welcomed Czech communists, who had a popular following, into their ruling coalition. Two years later the communists, realising they could never gain power by democratic means, resorted to force. Armed militiamen appeared on the streets, non-communist politicians were arrested, Masaryk was thrown to his death from his ministry window. As the pliant Beneš stood by, Klement Gottwald, the communist boss, said,

'It was like cutting butter with a sharp knife.' But while you can see how this would have sparked Frisch's imagination, you can apply the play's central situation to other historical events, most obviously to the German people's democratic endorsement of Hitler in 1933, scarcely believing that he meant what he said when he spoke of war and global conquest.

The greatness of Frisch's play, however, resides in its openness to interpretation. When the play was seen at the Royal Court in December 1961 – a few months after the Labour Party had decisively rejected CND's calls for unilateral disarmament – it seemed urgently topical. Edna O'Brien, reviewing the Court's production in *Encore*, wrote: 'It is a play about NOW: about the predicament of being alive and helpless in a nuclear age; about the rotting effects of power; about women attending to wreaths (as women will) when the house is falling in; about the need to be loved even by those whom we regard as our inferiors.'

Nearly half a century later, when Frisch's play returned to the Court, it had taken on a different colouration. It still remained a play about a man welcoming agents of destruction into his home, but the situation had taken on countless new meanings. To some, it was a play about our willingness to allow corporate greed and individual selfishness to destroy the planetary eco-system. To others, it was about the surrender of precious liberties, in a post-9/11 world, in the name of the War on Terror. To right-wing nationalists, it might even be seen as a parable about the perils of unchecked immigration.

But as I watched Ramin Gray's sharp-witted 2007 revival, it struck me that Frisch's play, while kaleidoscopically shifting, is also about a timeless subject: bourgeois guilt. Biedermann, as Frisch once insisted, is not stupid. He has, however, the uneasy conscience of the affluent. He also divorces private and public morality: he shows a nervous charity to the arsonists but treats his ex-employee Knechtling with total callousness. It's exactly the division Brecht explored in plays such as *The Good Person of Sezuan* and *Mr Puntila and his Man Matti*. The turning point comes when Biedermann, having threatened to call the police to the arsonists, is confronted by an officer of the law with news of Knechtling's suicide. At the very moment when he could reverse the situation, Biedermann mendaciously reports that the suspect oil-drums are full of hair rejuvenator.

Frisch pursues the idea of guilt right through to the climax. Having invited the resident fire-raisers to dinner, Biedermann hastily hides the candlesticks, finger-bowls and damask linen his wife and maid have provided only to be obliged to reinstate them at the emphatic insistence of his guests. It is both funny and chilling and of a piece with a play that is as much about class as it is about impending catastrophe. Martin Esslin corrals the play into his Theatre of the Absurd on the grounds that it is about the dead world of routine and empty bonhomie. But Frisch's play is much more political than that. It suggests the bourgeoisie turns a blind eye to encroaching evil because of its own internal anxiety. By implication, it also argues that whole nations embrace the seeds of their own destruction through a mix of myopia, inertia and fear. For a play without a moral, it manages to communicate a surprising number of messages. But Frisch's supreme achievement is to have created a fable that, like Dürrenmatt's *The Visit*, has its roots in post-war Europe but that acquires new meaning whenever and wherever it is produced.

84

A Raisin in the Sun

LORRAINE HANSBERRY

(1930–65)

Lorraine Hansberry, who died tragically young, is too often defined by her pioneering achievements. When *A Raisin in the Sun* was produced at New York's Ethel Barrymore Theatre in 1959, Hansberry became not only the first black woman to have a play on Broadway but also the youngest American ever. These are significant landmarks: what they tend to obscure is the fact that Hansberry had also created a magnificent work of art. As Bonnie Greer wrote when the play was revived at London's Young Vic in 2001, 'Come to *A Raisin in the Sun* as you would to any classic. It speaks to us today as it did almost half a century ago.' If one test of a classic is its mythic afterlife, Hansberry's play achieved just that when it inspired Bruce Norris to write *Clybourne Park* in 2010, a play that starts where Hansberry's ends in that it shows the consternation when a white middle-class couple propose to sell their home in the Chicago suburbs to a black family.

I recently asked a class of bright University of Pennsylvania students to pin down the essential factors that make American drama American. Their answers were revealing: 'the degradation of the nuclear family', the collision between fact and fantasy, a fixation with identity and a bias towards domestic realism. And *A Raisin in the Sun* meets all those criteria: what gives it its astonishing freshness and vigour is that it sees them through the distinctive prism of a young black woman's experience.

Family is at the heart of Hansberry's play. At first, she seems to be focusing on the rancorous divisions amongst the Youngers who inhabit a cramped apartment on Chicago's Southside. But where the work of O'Neill, Miller and Williams tends to show the flaws in a practising patriarchy, Hansberry gives us a household in the grip of a big mama, a stoic Christian who views with dismay the fecklessness of her son Walter, chauffeur to a rich white man, and the independent-minded atheism of her daughter Beneatha, whose dream is to be a doctor.

The plot hinges on the $10,000 dollar cheque that Mama is due to get on her late husband's life insurance. It is characteristic of Mama's determination that she puts part of the money down on a deposit for a house in the close-knit white neighbourhood of Clybourne Park. Hansberry not only takes the familiar ingredients of family drama and projects them into a world of racial progress (and this is before the Civil Rights Acts passed under Lyndon Johnson's presidency in the mid-1960s). She also shows how, under the pressure of white bullying, the collapsing family acquires a new cohesion. It is precisely at the moment when Walter has blown the bulk of the insurance money and the Youngers are being bribed to stay out of Clybourne Park that the family comes together. Popular Broadway comedies of the white middle class such as *Life with Father* (1939) made obeisance to the family pieties; Hansberry, writing of the black urban working-class, shows familial closeness to be a by-product of the assertion of racial pride.

As a dramatist, Hansberry is like one of those chefs who create a magical new dish out of existing ingredients. In almost every American play you meet a character steeped in illusion who is confronted by obdurate fact: a Willy Loman in *Death of a Salesman*, a Blanche DuBois in *A Streetcar Named Desire*. But what gives a special pathos to the plight of Walter Younger is that, as a chauffeur, he is a powerless spectator of a world of white affluence. In an odd way he anticipates Martin Luther King's great speech 'I have a dream', except that Walter's dream is less of a world of racial equality than a capitalist fantasy of untold wealth which he plans to achieve by opening a liquor store in partnership with two friends. When one of Walter's chums absconds with the stake money, all looks lost. But one of Hansberry's prime achievements is to show how Walter, in his moment of crisis, sheds his adolescent fantasies to acquire genuine manhood. Ironically it is Walter, the great worshipper of wealth, who finally dismisses the creepy Clybourne Park bagman who comes to try and bribe the Youngers into sticking to their own territory.

It would be easy to mistake *A Raisin in the Sun* for a squarely traditional play but what Hansberry does brilliantly is to rearrange the classical furniture.

Walter's daily tussles with his wife, Ruth, are no standard marital spats but a product of delusional dreams that lead him to declare, 'Here I am a giant – surrounded by ants! Ants who can't even understand what it is the giant is talking about.' And the question of identity that runs through American drama is given extra definition by the predicament of Mama's twenty-year-old daughter Beneatha, the closest thing to an author-figure in the play. Plenty of American heroines, from Emily in Thornton Wilder's *Our Town* to the androgynous Frankie in Carson McCullers's *The Member of the Wedding* have wrestled with their emotional and sexual identities. But Beneatha is torn between her rich assimilationist beau George, who can offer her a parody of the white lifestyle, and her new Nigerian friend Joseph, who teaches her to acknowledge her African heritage. In the end, the contest is easily won by Joseph as Beneatha cuts her hair, performs Yoruba dances and foreshadows the women of the 1960s who embraced Black Power. Once again, Hansberry takes a stock figure and invests her with a new political potency.

You could argue that the play's climactic shift from breast-baring despair to heroic resistance is a shade rushed. But, as so often in world drama, the play's resonance depends on the way it is rooted in closely observed reality. Hansberry paints a precise picture of a world where meals have to be cooked, beds made, bathrooms shared and the whole dingy apartment given a thorough going-over on a Saturday morning. If any predecessor comes to mind, in fact, it is not an American one but O'Casey's *Juno and the Paycock*. Like O'Casey, Hansberry presents us with a strutting, drink-taking fantasist who lives in a state of mutinous disharmony with his hard-working wife and whose dreams are fuelled by the prospect of an inheritance. Admittedly, Hansberry's Walter achieves emotional maturity where O'Casey's Jack Boyle declines into desolate torpor. But that is a measure of the different cultural context in which Hansberry was writing. She has created an American classic about the defiance born of oppression and about a family whose obstinate pride challenges and triumphs over a retrograde white prejudice. The future, you feel, belongs emphatically to the Youngers.

85

Serjeant Musgrave's Dance

JOHN ARDEN
(1930–2012)

The much-touted renaissance of British theatre that began at the
Royal Court in 1956 with *Look Back in Anger* achieved many
notable things. It discovered new voices. It led to a greater fluidity
of form. It invigorated theatrical language. It also frequently
produced a bitter schism between theatrical practitioners and
critical pundits. Of no play was that more true than John Arden's
Serjeant Musgrave's Dance, which opened at the Court in October
1959 to the kind of hostile reviews, with the striking exception
of Philip Hope-Wallace in the *Manchester Guardian*, that British
critics, of whom I am one, reserve for the arrival of a work that
challenges theatrical preconceptions. So angered was the Court
by the response that they published a leaflet, containing ringing
endorsements of Arden's play from a host of luminaries including
Peggy Ashcroft, Michael Redgrave, C. Day-Lewis, Doris Lessing,
Christopher Logue and Arnold Wesker, which was distributed all
over London's coffee bars and universities. Even with such high-
profile advocacy, *Serjeant Musgrave's Dance* played to a paltry 25
per cent at the box-office. But the whirligig of time brings in its
revenges. Arden's play is now an indispensable part of the modern
canon. It was moving to attend a staged reading at the Court, six
months after Arden's death in 2012, for which Peter Gill assembled

a magnificent cast headed by Brendan Coyle as an unforgettable Musgrave.

It is fascinating to trace the multiple influences on the play. Arden himself admitted that, watching a drab dress parade for his play *Live Like Pigs* at the Court in 1958, he felt it would be liberating to see a bright-red military tunic on the modern stage. Arden was also strongly affected by a particular film and play: a 1954 Western, *The Raid*, starring Van Heflin as a fugitive Confederate officer, and John Whiting's *Saint's Day*, dealing with the eruption of military deserters into civilian life, which Arden had seen as a student in Peter Hall's 1952 Cambridge production. But the biggest influence of all was a shocking recent event. British soldiers had been despatched to Cyprus to quell the violence between the island's Greek and Turkish populations and had been forced to resort to brutal tactics: in one notorious episode in 1958 they had killed five innocent people in an anti-terrorist reprisal.

All this stirred Arden's imagination and yielded a play notable for its rich moral complexity and exciting muscular language. It is also a play that takes time to unfold its purpose. We initially see four deserters from a Victorian colonial war turning up in a bleak northern mining town. They pose as recruiters, and the mayor assumes they will help break a strike by inducting agitators into the army. In reality the soldiers are part of a scheme, hatched by the fervently religious 'black Jack Musgrave', to bring home to the townsfolk the merciless nature of war. In a highly theatrical gesture, Musgrave produces the skeleton of a local private, whose furtive killing in a foreign war of occupation prompted a savage military retaliation. By exacting revenge on the inhabitants of the boy's birthplace, Musgrave's plan is 'to work that guilt back to where it began'.

As Arden himself admitted to me, the play initially baffled critics and audiences because they like to have a leading character with whom they can identify. As he said:

You can't latch on to Serjeant Musgrave because he doesn't announce what he's trying to do. And, when he does commit an action, there's something crazily wrong about it. What people would have expected is that Musgrave either be signalled as a dangerous lunatic who had to be stopped or as a hero who had to be defeated but would go down in glory. My story ricochets between those two pillars. But it's become much easier to grasp because audiences now expect this kind of ambivalence.

Arden made that point in 2003, just before Sean Holmes's fine revival for the Oxford Stage Company. But if *Serjeant Musgrave's Dance* has grown in stature, it is not only because audiences no longer crave moral certainty, it is also because the Irish troubles – which in 1972 led to thirteen innocent people being killed in Derry by British soldiers – as well as the 'War on Terror' in Iraq and Afghanistan were all conflicts in which criminal acts were committed by members of the occupying forces. But Arden's point is that, even if professional soldiers perpetuate the cycle of revenge, it has to stop somewhere. As the imprisoned Musgrave is told in the final scene, there is a flaw to his argument that civilians must be made to pay the price for acts of military murder. As his one-time supporter Attercliffe tells him: 'You can't cure the pox by further whoring.'

That last phrase is typical of a play which has the form of a folk-ballad, in the frequency with which characters burst into song, and which, in the richness of its prose, displays a spendthrift vigour. T. S. Eliot argued in 1928 that 'the greatest drama is poetic drama' and that 'prose drama is merely a slight by-product of verse drama'. But Arden is one of many modern dramatists, including Beckett, Osborne and Pinter, who have demonstrated the sinewy vitality of prose. When the missionary-minded Musgrave announces 'our message without God is a bad belch and a hiccup', demotic speech positively sings. When a burly Scottish soldier says of the greengrocer who cuckolded him, 'I saw him four foot ten inch tall and he looked like a rat grinning through a brush,' you get an instantly vivid picture. And when the local barmaid – stunningly played by Maxine Peake in the 2003 revival – tells Musgrave that 'the north wind in a pair of millstones was your father and your mother' the harshness of the protagonist's character is brilliantly evoked. In defiance of Eliot, this is prose achieving the effect of poetry. It's also a reminder that, while a dramatist like Rattigan could generate powerful emotion through verbal restraint, a defining quality of the post-1956 generation of British dramatists was its delight in language.

But Arden's play also possesses a vital quality of great drama in that it simultaneously looks back and forwards. Reaching beyond *Saint's Day*, it bears the imprint of Farquhar's *The Recruiting Officer*, which shows the impact of a group of soldiers on a corrupt local populace. But Arden's play also anticipates an extraordinary speech, written by Dennis Cannan for Peter Brook's 1968 anti-Vietnam War polemic *US*, about what would happen if the horrors of war were visited on a politely manicured English lawn. Looking even further ahead, Sarah Kane's *Blasted* in 1992 showed an event akin to the Bosnian civil war erupting in a Leeds hotel-room. While tangibly absorbing the influences of the past, *Serjeant Musgrave's Dance* was a seminal work. It is also true that its argument about the destructiveness of cyclical violence has grown more distressingly relevant with every year that passes.

86

Chips with Everything

ARNOLD WESKER

(1932–)

In 1955 the conservative columnist Henry Fairlie wrote a hugely influential column in *The Spectator*, defining what he termed the 'Establishment'. Fairlie didn't just mean those in authority.

> Anyone who has at any point been close to the exercise
> of power will know what I mean when I say that the
> 'Establishment' can be seen at work in the activities of not
> only the Prime Minister, the Archbishop of Canterbury
> and the Earl Marshal but of such lesser mortals as the
> chairman of the Arts Council, the Director-General of the
> BBC and even the editor of the *Times Literary Supplement*.

In later life Fairlie began to regret the way the term had been hijacked by the left to justify all kinds of conspiracy theory. Writing in the *New Yorker* in 1968, Fairlie admitted one reason for the term's tenacity was that 'many of the Western democracies have experienced various forms of radical or left-wing government and have found, at the end of the day, that the ways in which a society is governed or managed remain much the same as before'.

I never see Arnold Wesker's *Chips with Everything*, simultaneously premièred at the Royal Court, the Glasgow Citizens and Sheffield

Playhouse in 1962, without thinking of Fairlie's essay, for what Wesker shows, with great skill, is the existence in Britain of a social network that assumes people of a certain class are bound together by indissoluble ties. The play's action is propelled by the attempt of Pip Thompson, one of a group of raw RAF conscripts doing their initial eight weeks' square-bashing, to break those ties. Pip is a general's son who initially defies the officer class by refusing a commission. Instead he sides with his working-class hut-mates and tries to instil in them a mutinous nonconformity. There is a famous scene at a NAAFI party where the officers expect the men to sing a few pop songs and tell dirty jokes; instead Pip encourages a young Scot to recite a Burns poem and an Englishman to chant the folk ballad 'The Cutty Wren'. By the end, Pip's resistance has been broken, and he has joined the military Establishment, but not before Wesker has shown that there is an untapped potential among his former colleagues now transformed into immaculately drilled automata.

I make Wesker's play sound didactic whereas its virtue lies in its rich ambivalence. For a start, Pip himself is anything but a knight in shining armour. He is a self-confessed snob in his dislike of working-class values ('You breed babies and you eat chips with everything') and distrusts the reverence of intellectuals for manual labour. Even less forgivably, he stimulates the thirst for knowledge of a young admirer, Chas, but obstinately refuses to satisfy it (as Chas says, 'You lead and then you run away'). And there is some truth to the observation made by the pilot officer who finally breaks Pip that he enjoys being 'Messiah to the masses'. You feel Wesker admires Pip's rebellious spirit while acknowledging that he lacks the backbone or stamina to stand out against the insidious blandishments of the Establishment.

Wesker's ambivalence extends to his portrait of RAF life. He captures, deftly and economically, the individuality of each of the conscripts: the surly Scot, the autodidact filled with technojargon and, most tragically, the gauche and clumsy Smiley, whose immovable facial grin is treated as a permanent sign of insubordination. The drill instructor, Corporal Hill, is also a memorable creation. Once described as 'a prole who has gone over to the enemy', he occupies a strange no man's land: a bellicose martinet on the square but, off duty, a sad solitary exuding a semi-paternal solicitude. Wesker's own mixed feelings, however, become fully apparent at the play's climax, the Passout Parade, when the men march with glittering precision, the RAF colours are hoisted on the flagpole and the National Anthem resounds through the theatre. Intellectually, one deplores both the military code's capacity to rob the men of their individuality and the organised pointlessness of National Service. At the same time, I never see that scene without a lump coming into my throat: even Wesker once confessed that seeing an uncoordinated rabble turned into an efficient unit, as he did during his own time in the RAF, was a 'mesmerising experience'.

Wesker's play also dismantles the preposterous barrier we erect between 'text-based' and 'physical' theatre. Every great play (and most good ones) from *Hamlet* to *Waiting for Godot* works through a seamless fusion of word and image, and Wesker's is no exception. His text is supple and highly sophisticated, drawing a clear distinction between the jagged, exuberant diction of the conscripts and the leaner, more artificial style of authority. As the PT instructor says, 'I want your body awake and ringing. I want you so light on your feet that the smoke from a cigarette could blow you away, and yet so strong that you could stand firm before hurricanes. I hate thin men and detest fat ones. I want you like Greek gods.' Yet, exactly as in *The Kitchen*, Wesker provides us with scenes of beautifully choreographed action: the mini-uprising in the NAAFI, a silent raid on a coke store and the climactic parade. Wesker's play manages to be, at one and the same time, a subversive critique and an enthralling spectacle.

But just how subversive is it? Harold Hobson in 1962 described it as 'the first anti-Establishment play of which the Establishment has cause to be afraid'. Alan Brien, in contrast, felt Wesker 'underrates the resilience of the ordinary man while he overrates the rigidity of class barriers and the cunning of the Establishment'. Yet, although much has changed since Wesker wrote the play, I feel that his central argument still holds good: that in Britain there is a ruling class that protects the interests of its members and that instinctively absorbs apostates and rebels. I began by quoting a conservative columnist, Henry Fairlie. I would end by citing a left-wing guru, Herbert Marcuse, whose ideas expressed in *One Dimensional Man* (1964) Wesker intriguingly anticipates. It was Marcuse who claimed that capitalism anaesthetises the oppressed by manipulating the means of communication, a notion central to Wesker's *Roots*. Marcuse also argued that a ruling elite, in sanctioning protest, effectively nullifies it, an idea perfectly exemplified in *Chips with Everything*. You have only to note the words of the pilot officer to the rebellious Pip: 'We listen to you, we let other people listen to you but we show no offence . . . We listen but we do not hear, we befriend but do not touch you, we applaud but we do not act.' Nowhere in modern drama is there a more vivid realisation of Marcuse's concept of 'repressive tolerance'.

87

The Homecoming

HAROLD PINTER

(1930–2008)

Our old friends, Michael and Helena, are having one of their periodic encounters. Having argued the toss on Wilde, Shaw and Beckett, they are this time meeting after seeing a revival of *Old Times*, starring Kristin Scott Thomas, Lia Williams and Rufus Sewell at – where else? – the Harold Pinter Theatre. Michael, looking every bit of his seventy-five years, is in pensive mood. So too is his young friend, Helena. They stare lengthily over the pot of coffee that sits between them before Helena breaks the silence.

Helena: So is that your favourite Pinter play?

(*Pause.*)

Michael: I find whichever one I've seen most recently is the one that lodges in my imagination.

H: You're dodging my question. I know you once wrote a book on Pinter so you must have an all-time favourite.

(*Pause.*)

M: You're putting me in a difficult position. I've always loved *The Birthday Party* because Pinter uses the format of the rep thriller to create an atmosphere of menace. But equally I admire *No Man's Land* for its distilled poetry and Eliotesque desolation. And there's no better demonstration of the insecurity of the state oppressor than in *One for the Road* . . .

H: Cut the bullshit. I'm asking you to name an absolute favourite.

M: Since you insist, *The Homecoming*. This is the play for me where all the best elements in Pinter combine: the demotic speech, the sexual tension, the ability to invest each phrase and gesture with significance. I've seen the play in countless versions, from Peter Hall's original production at the Aldwych in 1965 to a recent revival by Luc Bondy at the Odéon in Paris, and each time it acquires new meaning. In particular Ruth, who abandons her sterile life in America to settle with her Hackney in-laws, strikes me as perpetually fascinating.

H: I guessed you'd say that. But I find something creepily offensive about Ruth. If she's really, at the end, agreeing to become the family's surrogate mother and a Soho sex-worker, that's disgusting. And if she's simply using her sexual magnetism as a weapon of control, that argues a very dated idea of how women behave. Pinter's a fabulous writer, but his view of women now looks anachronistic to my generation.

M: I've heard that argument before and I totally refute it. For a start, look at the men in the play: all loners and losers, for all their verbal ebullience. Max, the supposed head of the family, is a bellicose blusterer. The pimping Lenny is entirely routed by Ruth in their first encounter. Joey is a dim-witted boxer with a crudely opportunist approach to women. As for Teddy, Ruth's husband, he seems to regard her as little more than a useful campus trophy. Of course, the play is about a misogynist, male household that sees women as either mothers or whores. But it would be madness to assume that Pinter endorses that attitude. You also have to see *The Homecoming* in the context of his whole oeuvre, where women, more often than not, are active agents rather than passive victims. Emma in *Betrayal* is clearly made of stronger stuff than her husband or lover. And we've just seen *Old Times*, where Kate not only retains her sense of self but fights off the competing claims of Deeley and Anna.

H: I hear what you're saying. But you're overlooking one simple fact: at the end of *The Homecoming*, Ruth is either a putative *putain* or a manipulative minx.

M: That's sheer prudery. What we see is a startling territorial takeover. At the start, Ruth eyes up Max's chair. By the end, having made a deliberate choice, she occupies the seat of power. Joey, still sexually unsatisfied, is kneeling at her feet. Max is reduced to a whimpering wreck. And although Lenny stands behind the chair, Pinter was unusually adamant about the fact that he doesn't exercise control. No Pinter play is ever finally resolved, and we can argue forever about what might happen next. But the more often I see the play, the more it seems to me about a woman who exercises control over a group of hilariously inadequate men whose big-cock talk is belied by the reality of their daily lives.

H: You would say that, wouldn't you? I still think there's an element of male wish-fulfilment lurking within the play. And what I sometimes hunger for is that beautiful Beckettian minimalism you find in later Pinter plays like *Landscape* or the political fury of *One for the Road* or *Mountain Language*. This is Pinter still working within the old-fashioned realistic format.

M: I'd agree with you this is a pivotal moment for Pinter: the last play he writes that draws on the naturalistic tradition. But, like all great dramatists from Chekhov on, Pinter gives it his own peculiar spin. Just look at that night-time battle between Lenny and Ruth I mentioned earlier. Lenny seeks to intimidate Ruth with two exceptionally violent arias. Ruth rattles him first through her provocative silence and then by using a glass of water as a form of sexual challenge. That shows Pinter's ability to achieve, through a simple domestic object, the same kind of big effect that the actors of his youth, such as Donald Wolfit, accomplished through the sweep of a cloak.

H: OK. But you're an old issue-dodging codger. You still haven't addressed my point about the coarseness of this play compared to the sparseness and clarity of later Pinter.

M: That's only because I totally disagree with your point of view. Pinter always finds a diction that is appropriate to the setting and character. Here he's writing about a group of men who have mostly lost the art of conversing with women. He also makes a clear distinction between Max, who is an old East End roaring-boy on the verge of senility ('Even though it made me sick just to look at her rotten stinking face,' he says of his late wife, 'she wasn't such a bad bitch'), and his asexual brother Sam, who adopts the polite servility of a professional chauffeur. And Ruth herself has her own distinct tone: ironically mocking at first, legally precise later. But I could go on forever about this amazing play.

H: And I'm sure you will. I'm a great admirer of Pinter. I just prefer him in more lapidary mode or with political fire in his belly.

M: That is your privilege. But Pinter's work is large and various enough to satisfy all tastes. What is crucial is that it goes on being discovered, as it will, by new generations. But it's getting late and I've neglected my duties . . . Can I take your cup and give you a drop more coffee?

H: If you take that cup, I'll take you.

M: Touché.

(*They stare at each other in silence.*)

88

Black Comedy

PETER SHAFFER

(1926–)

The Homecoming opened at the Aldwych in June 1965. A month later Peter Shaffer's *Black Comedy* made its debut at Chichester. Given that John Osborne's *A Patriot for Me* appeared at the Royal Court in September, it was something of a golden summer.

I have a particularly strong memory of the Shaffer play. A friend of mine was among the peasant crowd in Strindberg's *Miss Julie*, which was part of a double bill with *Black Comedy* in the National Theatre's Chichester season. I was invited down to a Sunday-night public dress rehearsal and remember my friend greeting me somewhat gloomily. He had no great hopes of the Strindberg, and the omens for *Black Comedy* weren't good, with the actors having to cope with frantic rewrites up to the last moment. *Miss Julie*, with Maggie Smith and Albert Finney, was indeed a bit stolid, and I settled down for the Shaffer expecting a disaster. Since the opening dialogue between Brindsley, an impoverished sculptor, and his debby girlfriend Carol was conducted in total darkness, there was a palpable sense of bewilderment. Then, five minutes in, there came a moment when a Sousa march wound down on the turntable and, as Brindsley cried, 'Oh blast! We've blown a fuse,' the stage was flooded with brilliant light. I've never heard anything quite like the spontaneous explosion of laughter that greeted that line. The joy of it was that, as the show's first audience, we were taken totally by surprise.

Everyone now knows that Shaffer based his idea on a scene from the Chinese Classical Theatre, where two men fight in assumed darkness on a fully lit stage. But Shaffer's skill lies in taking a ten-minute display of technical virtuosity and turning it into a fully fledged farce, one of the funniest ever written. Shaffer is famous for plays such as *The Royal Hunt of the Sun* (1964), *Equus* (1973) and *Amadeus* (1979) in which the twin protagonists, invariably male, embody the Apollonian and Dionysiac sides of human nature: a rational hero, in Shaffer, is always racked by envy for an opposite who seems to have access to some divine instinct. What is perfectly plausible in the case of Salieri and Mozart in *Amadeus* seems more tendentious with the psychiatrist Dysart and his patient Alan in *Equus*: given that the latter's capacity for worship leads him to the blinding of horses, I find myself on the side of humanist conformity. But Shaffer's great strength has always been his capacity to create pieces of total theatre in which, as with Wesker, text, mime, movement and music work in conjunctive harmony.

While *Black Comedy* seems outwardly different from the rest of Shaffer's oeuvre, it too depends on a quintessentially theatrical idea: a dark-into-light device that in any other medium would be totally meaningless. Shaffer also obeys a basic rule of farce by showing a hero driven to a state of insane desperation. In this case, Brindsley is out to impress both a multi-millionaire art-dealer and his militaristic future father-in-law. To that end, he has 'borrowed' some classy furniture from his fastidious neighbour Harold. But Brindsley himself predicts it's all going to be 'an A-one, copper-bottomed, twenty-four-carat disaster', and so indeed it proves. First, the lights fuse. Then Harold unexpectedly comes home, and his furniture has to be surreptitiously returned.

To make matters worse, Brindsley's sexy ex Clea arrives and needs to be strenuously placated. A Germanic electrician who comes to mend the fuse is mistaken for the stone-deaf art-dealer. And even that gag is topped by the advent of the actual multi-millionaire.

Panic, mistaken identity, the intransigence of physical objects: these are the stock ingredients of farce. But here Shaffer puts them to brilliant use as we see Brindsley, in apparent darkness, seeking to restore Harold's furniture to its rightful owner. At its height, the play takes on the form of a mad ballet, with Brindsley acting as a demented removal man. He stealthily takes a chair on which the peppery colonel has been sitting and with great effort, involving the entanglement of his feet in an overnight bag, replaces it with his own rickety rocking-chair. Returning from a trip to the drinks-table, the colonel plonks himself squarely on what he thinks to be an upright chair and rocks backwards, ending up arse over tip.

This may not sound unduly sophisticated, but it confirms there is always something faintly sadistic about farce: we enjoy seeing a rigid, ramrod-back dignity literally upended. While it is dangerous to over-intellectualise farce, it strikes me that the genre, at its best, is invariably about something. Michael Frayn's *Noises Off* (1982) was to show that theatre is a perfect metaphor for life in that order is perpetually on the brink of dissolving into chaos. And while it would be absurd to see a message in Shaffer's play, what it vividly demonstrates is that darkness reveals hidden truths. It is only through the lack of light that Brindsley realises he belongs to the Bohemian Clea rather than the Sloaney Carol. Even more fascinating is the discovery that the bisexual Brindsley has been more closely intimate with Harold than with his supposed fiancée: when everyone plays a tactile guessing game, Harold instantly identifies Brindsley's hand in a way Carol signally fails to do.

The stock argument against farce is that it depends on stereotypes, but even those have their basis in life and can be refreshed in performance. I'd concede that Shaffer's teetotal spinster Miss Furnival, who discovers a taste for drink in the dark, is not wildly original. But the martinet colonel, reducing every crisis to a simple formula, is accurately observed. And Harold, Brindsley's preciously possessive neighbour, is a perfectly recognisable figure. As played by Albert Finney in John Dexter's original production, he suggested camp constantly on the verge of being struck. Finney's physical muscularity and Lancastrian accent also lent an extra élan to his riposte to Carol's claim that Brindsley would soon be world famous and that she'd feel like a Mrs Michelangelo. In a tone of salty Salfordian derision, Finney brought the house down with his retort that 'There wasn't a Mrs Michelangelo, actually.'

One of the distinctive features of modern drama is its ability to compress the human dilemma into ninety minutes or less. What Beckett did for tragedy, Shaffer here does for farce. He strips away the lengthy expositions of late-nineteenth century writers like Feydeau or Labiche to give us one continuous act that shows a cornered hero reduced to sweaty desperation through executing a demanding physical task and, in the process, discovering who he is. By an ingenious reversal of theatrical expectation, Shaffer also memorably fulfils an idea poetically expressed by Milton: he triumphantly succeeds in making darkness visible.

89

Absurd Person Singular

ALAN AYCKBOURN
(1939–)

If *Black Comedy* is less highly rated than some of Shaffer's more ostensibly serious plays, that is a sign of the snobbery still attaching to comedy and farce, a formal condescension that has long been applied to the work of Alan Ayckbourn. The sheer quantity of his output – seventy-five plays and still counting – is regarded with suspicion as is his global popularity. The fact that Ayckbourn has no declared agenda, shies away from the word 'political' and has experimented with varieties of comic form means that in Britain he is consistently underrated. Yet I would argue that, in his prodigal inventiveness and observation of human foibles, he is worthy to be placed alongside Molière (it was a German critic who dubbed Ayckbourn 'the Molière of the middle classes') and Goldoni. The range of themes he has tackled is also vast: bereavement (*Absent Friends*), moral evil (*Way Upstream*), madness (*Woman in Mind*), corruption (*A Small Family Business*), media worship of criminality (*Man of the Moment*). He has achieved all this while writing plays that, in the first instance, have to satisfy a fun-seeking, but deeply demanding, audience in his adopted home of Scarborough.

Absurd Person Singular, premièred in Scarborough in 1972 before moving to London a year later, remains one his most perfect plays and arguably the first in which he allies technical brilliance to a socially resonant theme. Structurally, the play offers a sardonic parody of Dickens: the three acts cover Christmas Past, Christmas Present and Christmas Future. Ayckbourn has also recorded how he regards it as his first 'offstage action play'. By setting the play in three different kitchens, he allows us to imagine unseen characters: a couple of insufferably hearty party guests and a murderously menacing dog. In solving the technical challenge of confining the action to three kitchens, Ayckbourn also releases his real subject: the shift in the zeitgeist that sees a wife-bullying property developer rise to the top of the heap while a toffish bank manager and a middle-class architect suffer a correspondingly severe decline.

Without claiming to write a state-of-the-nation play, Ayckbourn reveals his unerring social awareness. It is worth recalling the Britain out of which *Absurd Person Singular* emerged in 1972. On one level, the country was in the throes of a crisis: in January the NUM called a national strike which provoked the government into declaring a state of emergency, shutting down twelve power stations and imposing total black-outs for nine hours a day. It was also the year in which a provincial architect, John Poulson, was charged with bribery and corruption, for which he was later imprisoned. Yet some people did very well out of the crisis: Gross National Product and the FTSE share index both shot up, and house prices rose by three-quarters between mid-1971 and mid-1973. As Andy Beckett records in *When the Lights Went Out*, it was an artificial boom 'too reliant on speculation and one-off government initiatives to last long'. But while this is not the subject of Ayckbourn's play, it forms a vital background. You can see why Ronald Bryden, reviewing the West End transfer in 1973, declared, with excessive optimism, 'it may make many of its audiences think twice before voting again for the free-market economy, individual enterprise and the competitive principle'.

Ayckbourn may not have changed voting intentions but he did foresee the rise of the bustling entrepreneur who came to be venerated in the Thatcherite 1980s. In this sense, the key figure is Sidney Hopcroft, a domestic despot who treats his wife Jane as a social appendage. In the first act he crawls to the local bank manager, Ronald Brewster-Wright, for a loan but by the end he has become a mini-tycoon putting up jerry-built properties ('Half his tenants are asking to be rehoused and they haven't even moved in yet'). Sidney's rise is neatly symbolised by the games he makes people play. In the first act, on home territory, he envisages a modest Pass the Parcel. In the second act, set in the kitchen of a philandering and lazily incompetent architect, Sidney wants to 'get everyone jumping about'. In the final act, Sidney and the newly confident Jane invade the Brewster-Wrights' territory and force the kitchen's cowering occupants to, quite literally, dance to their particular tune. With deft economy, Ayckbourn charts the decline of the patronising, but inefficient, professional classes and the ascent of the go-getting provincial profiteer.

Other writers had detected a similar phenomenon, not least David Turner in a now largely forgotten Jonsonian comedy, *Semi-Detached*, that in 1962 brought Leonard Rossiter to national attention. But Ayckbourn's special gift lay in harnessing his social theme to sexual politics: in particular, the havoc wrought by male oppression, exploitation or casual disregard of women. Everyone remembers the play for its famous middle act in which Eva, driven to despair by her 'sexual flying Dutchman' of a husband, vainly tries to kill herself by leaping off a ledge, running at a kitchen knife, putting her head in the oven, swallowing pills and paint-stripper and hanging herself from the light flex; each time, in a masterpiece of unnerving hilarity, her gesture is hopelessly misinterpreted by her guests. But Eva is not the play's only victim. Even if the manically tidy Jane Hopcroft eventually succumbs to Sidney's power-seeking, she remains the victim of an overweening bully. Perhaps the most poignant case of all is that of Marion Brewster-Wright, who declines into a permanent, bed-bound alcoholic stupor under the uncomprehending gaze of her husband. I still recall Michael Aldridge, in Eric Thompson's 1973 production, looking like a distraught bloodhound as he confessed to his abysmal failure to understand women: 'I mean, damn it all, one minute you're having a perfectly good time and the next you suddenly see them there like – some old sports jacket or something – literally beginning to come apart at the seams.'

It takes a great dramatist to cover so much ground in one play: cataclysmic shifts in the social pecking-order, the buccaneering irresponsibility of the free-market system, the unthinking, or even calculating, cruelty of men towards women and our reflex obeisance to festive rituals such as Christmas. Ayckbourn achieves all this without ever bursting the formal bounds of comedy. Even if, in his own lifetime, he is still largely seen as a popular entertainer – with all the patronage that implies – I am convinced that the whirligig of time will bring in its revenges and that his plays will be revived, along with Harold Pinter's, by generations yet unborn.

90

Bingo

EDWARD BOND

(1934–)

It's a brave dramatist who puts Shakespeare on stage. Shaw, always wrestling with the ghost of his predecessor, did it a couple of times: in *The Dark Lady of the Sonnets* and a puppet-play, *Shakes versus Shav*, in which the Elizabethan becomes the dark side of the Dubliner. Clemence Dane in 1921 wrote a forgotten verse-drama, *Will Shakespeare*. More successfully, Lee Hall's *Shakespeare in Love*, based on a screenplay by Tom Stoppard and Marc Norman, shows the hero as a struggling playwright coping with writer's block and his passion for an ultimately unattainable aristo. But it is Edward Bond's *Bingo* (1973) that not only contains the most plausible dramatic portrait of Shakespeare but also makes him a powerfully moving symbol of the politically impotent artist.

Bond himself occupies a strange position in British theatre: admired for early plays such as *Saved* (1965) and *The Sea* (1973), championed by loyal directors such as Jonathan Kent and Sean Holmes, but honoured more on the continent, especially in France, than at home. His own desire to exercise a measure of artistic control over his work may not help his cause, but he remains an unbudgeable presence and he has given us a number of stony masterpieces, of which *Bingo* (subtitled 'Scenes of Money and Death') seems to me the finest.

What clearly fired Bond's imagination was a palpable contradiction in Shakespeare: the fact that the man who in *King Lear* offered such a scathing portrait of suffering and violence could, in his own life, exhibit the cold calculation of a bourgeois property-owner.

The facts are all there, and Bond has not substantially embroidered them. In 1614 three wealthy landowners came up with a scheme to enclose common land, from some of which Shakespeare drew substantial rents, near Stratford. Stratford Corporation vigorously opposed the enclosure scheme. Popular protests erupted, a court battle ensued, but Shakespeare stayed out of the fight. He had already reached an agreement with the enclosers that, if his tithes were compromised, he would have 'reasonable satisfaction . . . in yearly rent or a sum of money'. According to Stephen Greenblatt in *Will in the World*, 'It is not a terrible story . . . It is merely and disagreeably ordinary.'

But to Bond, it is a terrible story. What it asks is how the dramatist who wrote in *King Lear* of 'poor naked wretches' and argued for equal distribution of wealth could, in his final years in Stratford, fail to support the dispossessed and behave so harshly to his wife and daughter. Bond's play is not, however, a Marxist indictment of Shakespeare; nor do I see it, as some critics have claimed, as an assertion of Bond's moral superiority over his predecessor. 'I wrote *Bingo*,' Bond has said, 'because I think the contradictions in Shakespeare's life are similar to the contradictions in us.' What, to me, makes the play so moving is Shakespeare's incapacity for meaningful action in a society filled with barbarism. For much of the first half, the dramatist is a largely passive figure, contemplatively sitting in his New Place garden. Only at the end do his grief and self-questioning drive him inexorably to suicide.

Dramatically, it is Shakespeare's silence that it so powerful. He listens to the technicalities of William Combe's argument in support of enclosures and the offer of a personal guarantee against loss. He also looks on as his aged gardener is caught having sex with a young female vagrant. But Shakespeare says and does little. Asked if he will sign Combe's legal papers, he remarks he'll 'wait and see'. And although he says of the vagrant 'she must be looked after', he fails to prevent his daughter Judith handing her over to Combe's magistracy, which will ultimately lead to her hanging. Only in the third scene, set in the hills above Stratford, where the vagrant's corpse is displayed on a gibbet, does Shakespeare give voice to his pain in Bond's powerful prose. He is haunted by the horrors he has seen in London. He talks graphically of 'Women with shopping bags stepping over puddles of blood'. With equal vividness he recalls: 'When I go to my theatre I walk under sixteen severed heads on a gate. You hear bears in the pit while my characters talk.' This is not only historically evocative, it also strikes me as Bond's own self-indictment. He may not see heads on poles on his way to the Royal Court or the National Theatre, but he is still a member of a society that perpetuates gross inequality and sanctions illegal acts of military aggression.

Admittedly Bond implies there are alternatives to Shakespeare's detachment. In the second act Shakespeare gets hopelessly drunk with an impoverished Ben Jonson, who envies his rival's serenity and who talks of his own four spells in prison and lucky escape from hanging. The scene is very funny (I always recall Arthur Lowe's Jonson petulantly asking a bewildered Shakespeare in the original Royal Court production, 'What *was The Winter's Tale* about?') but even Jonson's anti-social anger is expended on a literary quarrel rather than the injustices of his world. And Bond's play moves towards a tremendous climax in which the myth of Shakespeare's serenity is exploded as he discards his wife and daughter and becomes an agonised symbol of the artist who records human suffering without being able to change it: 'Every writer,' says Bond's Shakespeare, 'writes in other men's blood.' As Shakespeare edges towards self-slaughter in a deserted bedroom, one question resounds like a tocsin through the play's final moments, 'Was anything done?'

You could make an intellectual case against Bond by invoking the historical record: you could argue that to write *King Lear*, paint *Guernica* or compose *The War Requiem* is to rearrange human consciousness and thereby counter barbarism. But what matters is the emotional impact of a play that stirs our consciences and offers one of the few plausible portraits of creative genius in the dramatic canon. Harold Hobson got it right when, reviewing Jane Howell's original production at the Northcott, Exeter in 1973, he wrote that it is possible to believe Bond's Shakespeare wrote the plays because he never mentions them: 'He simply takes them for granted, and because he does so, we take them for granted too.' Over the years I've seen Bond's Shakespeare memorably incarnated by Bob Peck and John Gielgud, but it was Patrick Stewart's performance, in a production seen first at Chichester and then in the West End in 2012, that confirmed my belief in the play's greatness. Craving financial security yet telling his daughter that 'money always turns to hate', displaying a brusque exterior to a rich landowner yet seeming at ease with his mad gardener, Stewart caught all the contradictions in Bond's Shakespeare. This was an unforgettable portrait of the artist as an old man, unreconciled to his kin or to his tragic ineffectualness in mitigating the world's cruelty.

91

Death and the King's Horseman

WOLE SOYINKA

(1934–)

Like the bulk of British critics, I know relatively little of drama on the African continent. Over the years I've seen a number of visiting Shakespearean productions, including a famous Zulu *Macbeth*. The plays of Athol Fugard have also done a valuable job in raising consciousness about apartheid: Fugard's brilliant collaboration with John Kani and Winston Ntshona on *Sizwe Bansi Is Dead* and *The Island* produced a genuinely vibrant political theatre. But if any one African play from among the few that have penetrated our shocking Western indifference has the authentic feel of a masterpiece, it is Wole Soyinka's *Death and the King's Horseman*. He wrote it in 1975, and it has since had two major British productions: at Manchester's Royal Exchange in 1990 and at the National Theatre, in a stunning Rufus Norris revival, in 2009. Like Chinua Achebe's landmark Nigerian novel *Things Fall Apart*, Soyinka's play is both culturally specific and rich in philosophical resonance.

Soyinka's own extraordinary life straddles many worlds. After studying in Ibadan in Western Nigeria, Soyinka got a scholarship to the University of Leeds and became part of the turbulently creative world of the Royal Court under George Devine in the late 1950s. Returning to Nigeria in 1960, he founded his own company, turned out a number of satirical, humorous plays and in 1967 was imprisoned for twenty-seven months for supposedly conspiring with Biafran rebels during the civil war. In the years since Soyinka has suffered repeated political exile, written plays, novels, memoirs and essays, spent long periods teaching on American campuses and, in 1986, won a Nobel Prize for Literature, the first writer of African descent to do so. But what is striking about Soyinka's drama is its ability to integrate dance, music and action and to use the mythology of his own people – the Yoruba – to explore universal ideas. Soyinka is a Nigerian writer who speaks to us all.

That is certainly true of *Death and the King's Horseman*. The play is based on historic events which took place in the ancient Yoruba city of Oyo in 1946. Soyinka, however, both shifts the action back in time to the Second World War and uses it to explore the transition between the living, the dead and the unborn. The situation is this. At the start of the play Elesin, the eponymous horseman, is about to commit ritual suicide to accompany his late master to the spirit world. But the supremely vital Elesin sees a beautiful young woman in the marketplace and takes her as his bride before his imminent death. Elesin's death, however, is forestalled by Pilkings, the British District Officer, anxious to avoid civic unrest during a visit by the Prince of Wales. To make matters worse, Elesin's eldest son, Olunde, studying at medical school in London, unexpectedly returns at the very moment of his father's arrest. Confronting his father, Olunde angrily accuses him of reneging on his duty to the gods. In a shattering climax, Olunde takes on his father's sacrificial role, thereby finally giving Elesin the courage to take his own life.

Soyinka is adamant in his introduction to the play that it cannot be labelled with the facile tag of 'a clash of cultures'. That, he argues, presupposes a potential equality at all times between two different value systems. Admittedly, seeing the play in 2009 after the Western invasion of Iraq and Afghanistan, it was difficult not to think about the perils of 'humane intervention'. Pilkings believes, above all, that he is acting in everyone's best interests when he uses force to prevent what he calls a 'barbaric' act of suicide. But Soyinka is concerned with something far more complex than colonial incomprehension of indigenous practices. He is really writing about the tension between the overwhelming life-force and ritualised custom, about the power of the spirit world and about the perils of isolation and exile. Like all the best works in world drama, Soyinka's play is richly ambivalent.

Formally, it is extremely adventurous. It starts as folk-drama with song, dance and percussive drumming preparing the way first for Elesin's anticipated suicide and then for his marriage ceremony. It moves into social satire with the portrait of Pilkings and his wife: at one point, they both insensitively don Yoruba masquerade costumes to attend a fancy-dress ball. There is low comedy in the way the village women taunt a local sergeant for his sexual inadequacy. Finally, the play moves into the mode of Greek tragedy as the imprisoned Elesin is confronted by his son's coffin to the accompaniment of a funeral dirge.

But what is most striking is Soyinka's complex, shifting attitude to Yoruba mythology. He accepts the validity of ceremony, ritual and faith in the spirit world. At the same time he makes Elesin a figure of such surging vitality, and sexual potency, that he initially shrinks from death. Crucially, it is not the action of Pilkings but Elesin's own hunger for life that stalls his suicide and that leads him to believe 'there might be the hand of the gods in a stranger's intervention'. Elesin becomes a tragic figure, straight out of Euripides, uneasily caught between two worlds. And his son Olunde adds another dimension to the play, by embodying the pathos of the alienated outsider. Olunde inhabits a strange no man's land: a student in the West, a critic of colonial attitudes yet also a man bound to abide by ancestral custom and tradition. Steeped in secular materialism or a diluted Christianity, many Western spectators may find Soyinka's vision hard to grasp. There is also something disturbing about the assumption that Elesin's bride is simply a means of ensuring the continuity of life. What is moving, however, is to find a play that invests death with moral significance and that, philosophically, regards it as more than 'the great and mighty nothingness' that Ionesco posits in his play about mortality, *Exit the King*.

Soyinka's play is also defined by its sheer theatrical vitality. In Norris's National Theatre production this was enhanced by presenting it with an all-black cast who 'whited up' to play the colonialists: the sight of Lucian Msamati and Jenny Jules as upper-class imperialists was as revealing as seeing a group of Yoruba women mimicking the British habit of primly crossing and uncrossing their legs. But the real virtue of Norris's Brechtian alienation device was that it took us away from a simplistic cultural collision and allowed us to focus on the issues Soyinka was addressing: above all, the idea that the living, the dead and those still to come exist not in separate compartments but in a state of mysteriously numinous co-existence.

92

The Real Thing

TOM STOPPARD

(1937–)

I've been fortunate, as a critic, in being able to chart the career of Tom Stoppard. I first came across his work in 1966, when I was asked to review for the Third Programme two radio plays – *If You're Glad I'll Be Frank* and *The Dissolution of Dominic Boot* – by the then scarcely known Stoppard. Nearly half a century later, in 2015, I found myself wrestling with *The Hard Problem* at the National, a work I found richly invigorating in its portrait of the battle between scientific materialism and selfless virtue. In the interim I've recorded Stoppard's capacity, in works such as *Jumpers, Travesties* and *Arcadia*, to expand the boundaries of theatre, to bring unlikely opposites into flamboyant juxtaposition and to delight in the punning possibilities of language. But of all his plays *The Real Thing* (1982) strikes me as his most durable in its ability to combine emotional depth with structural intricacy.

Stoppard's play turned out to be the third in a sequence in which British middle-aged, male dramatists grappled with questions of adultery. Pinter's *Betrayal* (1978) examined the politics of infidelity and brilliantly reversed conventional chronology. Peter Nichols's *Passion Play* (1981) ingeniously created alter egos for its central characters. But, deeply as I admire both plays, Stoppard's resonates even more strongly in that it branches out from adultery to explore a philosophical question: namely, the nature of 'the real thing' in love, art and politics. It is also a dazzling theatrical construct that presents us with a series of interlocking Chinese boxes.

Reviewing the play in 1982, I was roundly rebuked by Richard Curtis for revealing the calculated artifice of the opening, play-within-a-play scene. But I have no regrets since this is crucial to Stoppard's point. In the first scene we see 'Max' reacting with verbal insouciance to the discovery that his wife 'Charlotte' has forgotten to take her passport on a supposed trip to Switzerland. It transpires that this is one of a series of alleged adulteries which 'Charlotte' has disguised by bringing home appropriate presents such as Rembrandt place-mats after a purported trip to Amsterdam. As Max suavely observes, 'It's those little touches that lift adultery out of the moral arena and make it a matter of style.' But Stoppard goes on to show that in real life people rarely react with such Wildean sophistication to personal crises.

We quickly discover that the opening scene is the work of an acclaimed dramatist, Henry, who is married to Charlotte and who is having a passionate affair with Max's wife Annie. But when Max confronts Annie with the tangible evidence of the affair – through an Othello-like, blood-spotted handkerchief – he reacts with none of the dexterous calm of the stage 'Max': 'You're filthy. You filthy cow. You rotten filthy . . .' he cries before flinging himself on Annie in a violent embrace. Stoppard underlines his point by showing how Henry, admired as a dramatist for his verbal mastery, is similarly bereft when he discovers that Annie, with whom he has now lived for two years, is having a fling with a fellow actor. Left alone, while Annie goes off to meet her lover, Henry puts on a Procul Harum record and utters an anguished cry of 'Oh, please, please, please, please, *don't*.' But Stoppard's play is not simply about the difficulty of dignified cuckoldry. It is about a middle-aged dramatist's sentimental education in discovering that 'the real thing' in love is not an idealised, exclusive passion but a frank acknowledgement by each partner of the other's flawed individuality.

Stoppard is a brilliant writer, but occasionally his meticulous research sits on top of the dramatic action. Here, however, he writes from the heart without sacrificing one iota of his mental agility. He extends his exploration of 'the real thing' to art by having Annie urge Henry to spruce up a ham-fisted play written by Brodie, a soldier who has committed an act of arson at the Cenotaph as a protest against Cruise missiles. Henry famously attacks Brodie's clunky dialogue by comparing good writing to the manual dexterity by which a cricket bat can send a ball speeding to the boundary. It's one of Stoppard's most moving and anthologised speeches. But while Stoppard's play is a passionate plea for the sacredness of words ('If you get the right ones in the right order, you can nudge the world a little or make a poem which children will speak for you when you're dead'), it also raises the question of whether Brodie's original play has a clumsy authenticity which Henry's skilled rewrite can never quite match.

Stoppard is on more controversial ground when he has Henry declare, 'Public postures have the configuration of private derangement,' a resonant line which I quoted in my paean to *Venice Preserv'd*. Henry's point would seem to be confirmed when, later in the play, we learn that Brodie's act of arson was dictated more by a desire to sexually impress Annie than by his innate radicalism. Many have challenged the validity of Henry's proposition and asked whether all anti-nuclear and anti-apartheid protests, or Stoppard's own challenge to the abuse of human rights in his native Czechoslovakia and elsewhere, are the product of private derangement. My own view is that we should not automatically assume Henry's views are Stoppard's. The play has undoubted aspects of autobiography – Henry's musical tastes are very much Stoppard's own – but it is also discreetly critical of a hero who hides behind a mask of verbal wit and emotional detachment and who has to learn about the self-abasement of passion.

What is beyond challenge is the play's emotional power and meta-theatrical skill. Henry, having confessed that he doesn't know how to write love, takes Annie through a scene from Strindberg's *Miss Julie*, one that shows how passion can be expressed through sub-text and that prefigures Annie's later involvement with the working-class Brodie. The dangerous mutual attraction between Annie and her fellow actor Billy – who gets to play Brodie in Henry's rewrite – is also expressed through a scene of forbidden love from Ford's incest-ridden *'Tis Pity She's a Whore*. The whole play is about the teasing and constantly shifting relationship between art and life. It was there in Peter Wood's original London production but was brought out even more strongly in Mike Nichols's 1984 Broadway revival, with Jeremy Irons and Glenn Close: there the opening scene was played in heavily inverted commas in contrast to the emotional reality of what followed. And in Anna Mackmin's 2010 Old Vic production we saw more clearly than ever the rocky path that the two lead characters take on their journey to maturity: Toby Stephens's Henry moved from initial superciliousness, via naked desperation, to a humane understanding while Hattie Morahan's Annie progressed from the reckless excitement of illicit passion to the relative calm of total commitment. If I had to rescue just two Stoppard plays from oblivion, it would be his magnificent TV drama *Professional Foul* and this one. Like all first-rate plays, it appeals simultaneously to head and heart and is, in the words of an American critic, 'the best cricket-bat anyone has written in years'.

93

Top Girls

CARYL CHURCHILL

(1938–)

We can all agree on one thing: Caryl Churchill is the most restlessly experimental dramatist around today.

Every time she puts pen to paper, or finger to laptop, she seems to be breaking the mould and coming up with new theatrical forms. But Churchill's prodigal inventiveness tends to overshadow her skill as a social and political commentator. In *Owners* (1972) she created an exploitative female landlord whose philosophy of life – 'Be clean, be quick, be top, be best' – anticipated the rampant individualism of the following decade. In *Light Shining in Buckinghamshire* (1976) she used verbatim testimony from the debates between Cromwell's army and the Levellers and Ranters as a metaphor for the failure of the revolutionary optimism of the 1960s. And in *Serious Money* (1987) she went on to examine the laddish coarseness of the City of London and the idea that 'sexy-greedy' was part of the zeitgeist. But it was in a play from earlier in that decade, *Top Girls* (1982), that Churchill best explored the role of women today and the idea that feminism will never advance without a total restructuring of society.

The beauty of *Top Girls* is that it is both rich in content and radical in form: Max Stafford-Clark, who directed the original Royal Court production, pointed out to me how unusual the play is in withholding a crucial plot-information until two-thirds of the way through. But arguably the play's most experimental feature is its famous opening scene, in which the modern Marlene, on the eve of taking over the eponymous employment agency, holds a dinner-party for iconic women from myth and history. I confess it took me more than one viewing, or reading, to fully grasp what Churchill was up to: showing that the widely differentiated women on view were both boundary-breaking pioneers and social victims. The adventurous Isabella Bird, the peripatetic Japanese courtesan Lady Nijo, the intellectual Pope Joan all suffered for their defiance of tradition and failed to realise their potential as human beings. Even Brueghel's Dull Gret, leading a crowd of women charging through hell, and Chaucer's archetypally submissive Patient Griselda are part of a pattern in that their roles are defined by men. In their midst sits Marlene, the archetypal 1980s go-getter who, for all her aura of public success, is privately insecure.

Churchill is too sophisticated and elusive a writer to offer anything so simple as a template for modern feminism. What she does in that brilliantly surreal opening scene is to chart the frustration experienced by women down the ages. What she goes on to do, in the rest of the play, is show how women, in seeking to rectify a historical injustice, are in danger of replicating male values. The play appeared three years into Margaret Thatcher's premiership, and part of Churchill's point is that Thatcher's form of abrasive capitalism did not, in itself, signal feminist progress. It's no accident that the puppet-Thatcher in the TV show *Spitting Image* resembled a bullying Mr Punch in a pin-striped suit.

The historic frustration that is the keynote of the first act is rhythmically echoed in the office scenes of the second act, which are sustained by the verbal motif of wanting to 'get away': that applies to the interviewers as much as the interviewees. Marlene may be top-dog, but her two staffers, Win and Nell, simmer with discontent. And the women they interview for potential jobs offer a mix of hopeless dreams and rancorous disappointment: a young woman, Shona, invents a fantasy career based on the model of an expense-account salesman while the forty-six-year-old Louise is the victim both of an ageist culture and personal sacrifice. But the most potent scene is that in which Mrs Kidd, the wife of the man who has been passed over for the top job in the agency, pleads with Marlene to stand down in favour of her husband. It's a brilliant scene – comparable to the one in *Death of a Salesman* where the superannuated Willy Loman is downgraded by his young boss – because it hits one in so many ways. One's intellectual sympathy is entirely with Marlene: why should a woman be expected to give way to a man? But, as Nicholas Wright shrewdly pointed out, there is an 'uneasy undertow' to the scene that makes you see Mrs Kidd's point of view: she has to bear the disappointment of a husband who is the victim not simply of female progress but also of a hard-hearted new entrepreneurial culture that is the essence of the 1980s.

In the third act Churchill both shifts her style and extends her argument. The tone is social realist; the issue is the personal vacancy that lies behind Marlene's success. Marlene confronts her Suffolk-based sister Joyce, who has been left to look after their hospitalised mother and whose own life is one of drudgery and toil. We also realise that the moody, teenage Angie whom Joyce has brought up is the daughter Marlene has abandoned. Many plays have been built around the idea of contrasted female siblings: the worldly opportunist versus the kitchen-bound stay-at-home. But Churchill expands the idea by showing Marlene's acute awareness of what she has lost in sacrificing her daughter and in depicting the unbridgeable gulf between the two sisters. A lesser writer would have hinted at reconciliation. Churchill shows that the personal is political: Marlene trumpets the virtues of Thatcher and Reagan while Joyce obdurately announces, 'I spit when I see a Rolls-Royce, scratch it with my ring.' The real victim, however, is Angie: 'stupid, lazy and frightened' in the words of Joyce and with little hope of whatever potential she possesses ever being realised.

What most shocks one about Churchill's play is its continuing validity. In 1982 it seemed a resonantly topical attack on the prevailing Thatcherite ethos. Seeing it revived by Max Stafford-Clark in 2011, in a co-production between Out of Joint and Chichester, it seemed as pertinent as ever. As played by Suranne Jones and Stella Gonet, the fraught encounter between Marlene and Joyce was edgily moving. But it was the office scenes in the central act that reminded one how little had radically changed. One job applicant is told to conceal her intention to get married. Another, leapfrogged by male rivals, reveals that loyalty goes unrewarded. The glass ceiling may have been mildly splintered since Churchill wrote the play in 1982, but that is not her point. What she is suggesting is that true feminism is impossible without socialism and a restructuring of society. But the great thing about Churchill is that she never hammers us into submission. She expresses her ideas with an inventiveness, vigour and wit that has made her an inspiration to dramatists – men as well as women – the world over.

94

Dancing at Lughnasa

BRIAN FRIEL

(1929–2015)

Some prefer *Faith Healer* (1979), with its brilliantly revealing monologues. Others would plump for *Translations* (1980), which explores the use of language as an instrument of colonial power. But *Dancing at Lughnasa* (1990) has always been Brian Friel's most popular play. In this at least, I am on the side of audiences. It is a play that does everything you could wish for. It is extravagantly theatrical. It moves one to tears through its minute examination of wasted lives. It also makes a strong general point about the primitive, atavistic passions that lurk beneath the surface of ingrained Irish Catholic orthodoxy.

Conventional wisdom links the play to Tennessee Williams's *The Glass Menagerie*. It is true that both are set in 1936 on the cusp of the Second World War. Both are memory-plays relying on a narrator who speaks for the author. And both, as Christopher Murray has pointed out, 'explore the pathos of loved ones incapable of side-stepping, as the artist-narrator himself must (though not without guilt), the snares set by family and community'. But the comparisons end there. Friel's play has a richness of texture and robustness of language that puts me in mind more of Chekhov than Williams. Whenever I see the play, as I did in 1990 at the Lyttelton and again in 2011 at the Old Vic, I am even reminded of Euripides' *The Bacchae*, the grandfather of all dramas that show passion bursting through the pales and forts of reason.

Friel, a Northern Irish Catholic, has never denied his play's autobiographical origins. Its dedication says 'In memory of those five brave Glenties women', and it is no accident that the unseen younger self of the narrator, Michael, is seven years old when the play starts. Yet Friel was not, like Michael, illegitimate. The play also testifies to the vivid unreliability of memory, a recurring theme in all Friel's work. In this he resembles Harold Pinter. Although the sense of the past threads its way through all their plays, they never lapse into the suffocating warmth of nostalgia. Thus in *Dancing at Lughnasa* the narrating Michael recalls that summer in 1936 with great precision but also as 'simultaneously actual and illusory'.

The key metaphor of the play, embedded in the title, is that of dancing: a reminder that, as the Elizabethan poet Sir John Davies wrote, 'dancing is love's proper exercise'. Yet Friel skilfully suggests that it is fraught with different meanings for each of the play's main characters. Take the five sisters. For Kate, the forty-year-old teacher and family breadwinner, dancing carries overtones of forbidden fruit: she is the one who most strenuously objects – echoing Euripides' Pentheus – to the hillside rites celebrating the pagan god Lugh. For Maggie, cook and housekeeper, dancing symbolises the sexual and emotional fulfilment she has been denied: she is still haunted by the memory of a lost love, Brian, and her friend, Bernie, at a village hop ('they were just so beautiful together, so stylish, you couldn't take your eyes off them'). Agnes, a spinster knitter who protects her simple sister Rose, wants to dance but is rarely asked. And when Michael's mother Chris is briefly reunited with her transient lover Gerry how else do they express their passion but through dance? As Michael, in later life, remembers: 'No singing, no melody, no words. Only the swish and whisper of their feet across the grass.'

Friel's supreme skill lies in creating a pervasive metaphor without allowing it to crush the play's spontaneous life. He also extends its possibilities. Dancing is clearly a symbol of the pagan past that lurks beneath Catholic propriety – and not just in Ireland. One of the play's most fascinating characters is Uncle Jack, whose career as a Catholic missionary in Uganda has been abruptly terminated. At first one assumes it may be for undue intimacy with his beloved houseboy, Okawa. Then one realises the truth: Jack has abandoned the Catholic mass for immersion in native Ugandan rituals, such as the Festival of the Sweet Casava, which, like the Irish Festival of Lugh, celebrate nature's bounty: as Jack explains, people paint their faces, drink palm wine 'and then we dance – and dance – and dance'. Everywhere, Friel implies, there are primal impulses that predate organised Christianity and exert a stronger power.

But the play's most famous moment comes when the five sisters surrender to the magnetic voodoo of an Irish tune on the Marconi radio and break into a wild, abandoned dance. Even here, Friel preserves their essential character. Maggie is the first on her feet, emitting a raucous, exuberant, banshee-like cry; Kate, cautious, repressed and puritanical, is the last of the five to join in and even then 'dances alone, totally concentrated, totally private'. But it is one of the defining images of modern theatre. I can still recall the weird exhilaration of Patrick Mason's original production where the five sisters – played by Frances Tomelty, Anita Reeves, Brid Ni Neachtain, Brid Brennan and Catherine Byrne – suddenly released their pent-up passions like Ballybeg Bacchantes.

The paradox of Friel is that he is a master of language who frequently invokes the emotions that lie beyond words. In *Translations* the colonising soldier Captain Yolland falls in love with the hedge-school student Maire, though he can't speak a word of Gaelic nor she of English. And in *Dancing at Lughnasa*

Michael's recollections, pitched between reality and illusion, are sparked by memories of 1930s music and the hushed rhythms and hypnotic movements of people dancing – 'dancing as if language no longer existed because words were no longer necessary'.

But there is no false romanticism in Friel's play. Like Chekhov – whose work he has frequently adapted – Friel is haunted by what-might-have-been and by the sacrificial waste of individual lives. Moreover, the waste is always related to the wider social and political picture: as we know from *The Freedom of the City*, based on the Derry shootings of Bloody Sunday, and *Translations*, Friel's writing has never been divorced from actuality. In *Dancing at Lughnasa* Kate loses her teaching job because of Catholic prejudice against her apostate brother. As freelance knitters, Agnes and Rose are made redundant by machines and forced to go to England, where they become victims of mass unemployment. Chris's fantasising lover, Gerry, goes off to fight in the Spanish Civil War, from which he returns a maimed veteran. In some ways Friel paints a bleak picture of lives that are circumscribed, stunted, unfulfilled both because of individual character and historical circumstance. Yet behind that lies the image of the dance and of a moment, however transitory, when these deprived sisters achieved ecstatic rapture.

95

Racing Demon

DAVID HARE

(1947–)

David Hare is a romantic realist. No dramatist, with the possible exception of the admirable David Edgar, has so assiduously examined British institutional life or the changing temper of the times. But Hare's attentive observation is flecked with romanticism. His plays almost invariably end with a positive image: classic examples are a flood of sunlight in *Plenty*, a life-changing journey in *A Map of the World*, the joy of a good meal in *Skylight*. Hare also sees women as potential agents of change, although he has not always been thanked by feminist critics, who have often accused him of excessive idealisation. Above all, Hare's plays constantly explore the tenacity of virtue in a corrupt, diminished world.

One of Hare's greatest gifts is that he is an excellent reporter. Before writing a trilogy about the church, the law and the Labour Party, Hare burrowed inside all of them and produced a book, *Asking Around* (1993), which combined the rigorous detail of Anthony Sampson's *Anatomy of Britain* with the unvarnished truth-telling of George Orwell. But Hare is also a first-rate dramatist, and in *Racing Demon* (1990) he created a play that combines acute analysis of the Church of England with an intuitive compassion for the victims of its schisms. The play is about a divided institution still – at the time the work was written – agonising over society's increasing secularisation, gay clerics, women bishops. Yet the play, in its vivid portrait of the battle between ineffectual pragmatists and crusading idealists, has the resonance of metaphor. In 1990 Hare told me in an interview that it was blindingly obvious the play was really about the Labour Party. Today it strikes me it could be about any polarised institution, whether it be the BBC, the NHS or even a national daily newspaper.

The play dramatises a quintessential conflict. On the one hand, you have the decent, bumblingly apologetic rector Lionel Espy, leading his ministerial team in a struggling south London parish. On the other hand, you have the forces for change, led by the young, zealous, fiercely evangelical Tony and the beleaguered Bishop of Southwark, who tells Lionel, 'You stand in the centre of the parish like some great, fat wobbly girl's blouse.'

Such conflicts have their origins in real life. In *Asking Around* Hare tells the story of a vicar called Walter who similarly crossed swords with his bishop and who, when he asked what would happen if he took legal advice, was roundly informed, 'I can tell you what will happen. You will never get a job in the Church of England again.' But, whether consciously or not, Hare was also invoking the battles between moderates and evangelicals that run through nineteenth-century English fiction. George Eliot's *Scenes of Clerical Life* – which itself might be an apt title for Hare's play – constantly returns to the subject. In 'The Sad Fortunes of the Reverend Amos Barton' Eliot provides a humane portrait of a modest cleric ('It was not in his nature to be superlative in anything; unless indeed he was superlatively middling, the quintessential extract of mediocrity') who might almost be a forerunner of Lionel Espy. But in 'Janet's Repentance' Eliot gives an equally sympathetic picture of an earnest Evangelical, the Rev.

Edgar Tryan, whose only fault was that 'he made the mistake of identifying Christianity with a too narrow doctrinal system; that he saw God's work too exclusively in antagonism to the world, the flesh and the devil'. Much the same could be said of Hare's Rev. Tony Ferris.

Hare is clearly more sympathetic to Lionel and his team than he is to Tony. A key point of Hare's trilogy, written at the end of a Thatcherite decade, is that it is left to modestly paid clerics, policemen and social workers to repair the damage done by those blessed with ideological certainty. But although it is clear where Hare's emotional sympathies lie, he still asks big, searching questions in *Racing Demon*. What is the nature of faith in the modern world? Is the Church of England becoming a spiritual soup kitchen devoid of fervour and hope? And does enlightened humanism offer any more convincing answer to life's inexplicable cruelties than organised religion?

What is impressive is that Hare addresses these questions not just through dramatic action but through direct prayer, and each prayer is a revelation of character. Lionel addresses God in the perplexed tones of a man puzzled by His 'perpetual absence'. Tony is more irate in his search for fundamentalist rigour ('Christ didn't come to sit on a committee. He didn't come to do social work. He came to preach repentance'). Frances, Tony's ex-lover and the agnostic product of a clerical family, finds it impossible to reconcile the idea of God with the injustice of a cruel universe. Harry, a gay vicar victimised by the press, tries to find it in his heart not to hate his persecutors. Best of all, perhaps, is 'Streaky' Bacon, another member of Lionel's team, who sees God's love manifested in the earthly delights of Gilbert and Sullivan, the pleasure of drink, the love of friends. Perhaps the only character you can't imagine baring his soul to God is the politicised Bishop of Southwark, whose 'brass balls clang as he walks'.

Hare offers no easy answers to the questions he poses. He doesn't even create heroes and villains. Lionel is a good man but culpable in his neglect of his wife and unseen, runaway daughter. Tony is vehement, insensitive, cack-handed at personal relations but does actually get the locals to attend a weekly Bible class. Even the Bishop of Southwark, who like Barberini in Brecht's *Galileo* becomes more dogmatic as he dons his official vestments, is not wholly without merit: as an increasingly isolated conservative in a faction-ridden institution, he says, with some truth, that 'the church has been turned into a ghastly parody of government'. That is very much part of Hare's point: that in almost every field of activity – whether it be religion, politics or the mass media – internal strife and tactical battles have replaced any awareness of the original purpose.

But Hare's accuracy as a commentator often leads people to overlook his theatrical quality. This is a play about big issues invested with real warmth: it is there in Streaky's naive delight in taking drinks at the Savoy, in Lionel's understated attraction to Frances, in the quiet loyalty of Harry's lover to his clerical friend. Hare also writes beautifully for actors. Oliver Ford Davies was a superbly doubt-ridden Lionel in Richard Eyre's original 1990 production, while Malcolm Sinclair, in Daniel Evans's brilliant Sheffield Crucible revival in 2011, reminded us of the hidden gutsiness in a man prepared to fight for the retention of his parish. Hare is a realist in his close observation of institutional in-fighting but an idealist – perhaps even a romantic – in his faith in individual goodness. Nowhere is that tension better expressed than in this luminous play.

96

The Weir

CONOR MCPHERSON

(1971–)

It was one of those nights no one who was there will ever forget: 4 July 1997 and the first performance of Conor McPherson's *The Weir* in the relocated Theatre Upstairs above London's Ambassadors Theatre. The writer himself was not unknown. Many of us had seen *This Lime Tree Bower* at the Bush in 1995: a series of intercut monologues about a small-town heist that took its title from a Coleridge poem which claims that 'no sound is dissonant which tells of life'. It's a phrase you could apply to McPherson himself. He vindicated his early promise with *St Nicholas*, seen at the Bush in 1997, a supernatural solo about a Dublin theatre critic, brilliantly played by Brian Cox, who becomes fixated on an actress, pursues her to London and falls in with a nest of vampires. Clearly McPherson had grasped an essential point: there is something of the night about all us parasitic talent-suckers. But nothing had quite prepared us for *The Weir*, a play that seems to consist of little except people telling ghost stories in a rural bar but which is filled with McPherson's Chekhovian gift for the minute particular and his understanding of the Ireland that lies beyond Dublin's affluent swagger. In the 1990s the Celtic tiger was still rampant, and big money was being made, especially out of the property boom. But McPherson is fascinated by the tenacity of myth in a country that lies at the western edge of Europe and that still has a sparsely populated hinterland.

The soft thing to say about *The Weir* is that it shows McPherson reconciling his capacity for monologue with a flair for dialogue. But that's a minor technical point. What really counts is his narrative power, his gift for language and his ability to excavate the quiet desperation of the unfulfilled. He also has the born dramatist's ability to reveal character through action, something demonstrated in the first seconds of the play. Jack, an old codger, enters in a slightly ill-fitting suit, a hint that tonight is a special occasion. You can tell Jack is a regular by the way he goes behind the bar to get himself a drink. But there is something a touch tetchy in his realisation that the Guinness tap is empty and he'll have to make do with bottled stout. You also get a glimpse of Jack's bachelor fussiness in the way he carefully examines the booze prices, puts his money in the till and takes the precise change. Nothing has yet been said, but McPherson has started to build a character-portrait through an accumulation of detail: a tiny example of the durable power of naturalism.

But the beat of McPherson's play lies in the disruption of routine by the introduction into the bar of a newcomer. The garage-owning Jack, the dim, kindly Jim and the taciturn barman Brendan are all used to each other and habituated to a life of communal solitude. Tonight, however, Finbar, the local boy who made good and runs a hotel in Carrick, is expected to arrive with his latest housebuyer and a refugee from Dublin, Valerie. Instantly, this gives an edge to proceedings. You sense the resentment of the regulars towards Finbar: not just for his money but because, although married, he's the one with a girl on his arm. The men also up their game in the presence of an attractive woman: Jack starts to brag of the way Jim, a studious gambler, once won £220 on the horses at Cheltenham. With infinite subtlety, McPherson establishes a mood of sexual tension and ancestral competitiveness.

We get to know the people individually before we hear the stories they tell. We get to know them even better *through* the stories they tell. McPherson doesn't give us a pot-pourri of M. R. James or Sheridan Le Fanu-style spooky tales. Instead he shows how the frightening fables the men relate, clearly designed to impress Valerie, reveal something of their own essential character. Jack, a lonely old sod haunted by the ghosts of his past, tells a tale about fairy knockings on the door of the house Valerie has just bought. Finbar, the big fella, discloses his inner panic in a tale about a spiritual manifestation. Jim, the cosseted loner living with a ma who's been 'fading fast now, for years' comes up with an eerie tale about a graveyard visitant desperate to be buried next to a young girl: a story that seems to echo Jim's own introverted sexuality. Finally, Valerie caps the men's stories with an account of hearing her own recently dead young daughter's voice on the phone: clearly the source of Valerie's estrangement from her husband and of her flight from Dublin.

This is not simply a Celtic version of that classic British movie *Dead of Night*, in which a group of rural visitors recount their spine-tingling dreams. McPherson is showing how in Ireland the past is eternally present and how the supernatural reflects our own anxieties and fears. But what is impressive is the way a young writer – and McPherson was only twenty-six at the time – shows an intuitive understanding of wasted lives. Left alone with Brendan and Valerie, Jack launches into a heartbreaking remembrance of missed opportunities that might be the source of a William Trevor story. Jack recalls how he let the love of his life escape him, attended her Dublin wedding to a member of the Garda, took refuge in a pub, where he encountered an act of consoling kindness. But the pay-off comes in Jack's description of his current life: 'Down in the garage. Spinning small jobs out all day. Taking hours to fix a puncture. Stops you thinking about what might have been and what you should have done.' But when Jack reveals that not a morning passes without his lost love's name being in the room, you realise that he is the most haunted of all McPherson's characters.

Jim Norton had just the right air of marinated solitude in Ian Rickson's original production. And the play has never looked better than in the room above the Ambassadors, where, as McPherson said, 'the audience were sitting in the bar on all those little higgeldy-piggeldy different kinds of chairs and benches and were right in on top of the action'. Later I saw the same production on Broadway, where the play looked a bit lost as the bar expanded to resemble a saloon in a John Ford Western. My faith was restored, however, when Josie Rourke revived the play at the Donmar in 2013. Brian Cox was a magnificently cantankerous Jack, and the play's quiet comedy emerged strongly. When Dervla Kirwan's Valerie protested that the vast nightcap offered to her by Peter McDonald's Brendan was 'an awful lot', he replied, 'Ah, it's not really,' as if brandy, like beauty, was in the eye of the beholder. McPherson has gone on in excellent later plays such as *Dublin Carol* (2000), *Shining City* (2004) and *Night Alive* (2013) to explore his favoured themes of loneliness, loss and the redemptive power of individual kindness. But nowhere does his capacity for using the unearthly to explore our humanity work better than in this mesmerising study of life in a boozy rural backwater.

97

Copenhagen

MICHAEL FRAYN
(1933–)

Conor McPherson enlarges our human sympathies; Michael Frayn, as a novelist and dramatist, gets us to think differently. This is not to deny the intellectual sinew of McPherson's work or Frayn's emotional resonance. But what is striking about Frayn's plays – from a comedy about classification such as *Alphabetical Order* to a farce about theatre like *Noises Off* – is that it is underpinned by a note of philosophical enquiry. Frayn, the most eloquent of self-analysts, once defined the theme that runs through all his work as 'the way in which we impose our ideas on the world around us'. He went on to explain that the central puzzle of life is that 'the world plainly exists independently of us – and yet it equally plainly exists only through our consciousness of it'. That tension between the objective universe and our subjective perception lies at the heart of his masterpiece, *Copenhagen*, a play first staged at the Cottesloe in 1998 that went on to become an international success and that has had a tenacious afterlife. Since Frayn wrote the play new information has come to light about its subject – the meeting between Niels Bohr and Werner Heisenberg in Copenhagen in 1941 – without substantially altering the play's point about the partiality of memory and the inexplicable mystery of life itself.

One of the first things to say about the play is that it is part of modern theatre's urge to grapple with scientific ideas. As Kirsten Shepherd-Barr points out in *Science on Stage*, the subject has always been with us since *Doctor Faustus* and *The Alchemist*. But one could draw up a long list of recent plays, including Tom Stoppard's *Arcadia* (1993), Timberlake Wertenbaker's *After Darwin* (1998), Complicité's *Mnemonic* (1999) and Tom Morton-Smith's *Oppenheimer* (2015), that wrestle with complex scientific ideas. Audiences have also not flinched from – indeed have shown a positive hunger for – staged lectures on the catastrophic consequences of population explosion and climate change in works such as Stephen Emmott's *Ten Billion* and Chris Rapley and Duncan Macmillan's *2071*. Drama has played a vital role in demolishing the barrier between what C. P. Snow called 'the Two Cultures', not just by engaging with big issues but also by showing that theatre is a place where scientific principles can be manifested as well as discussed.

In the case of *Copenhagen*, Frayn starts with an historical conundrum. What did actually happen in 1941, when the German atomic physicist Werner Heisenberg travelled to Nazi-occupied Denmark to see his former mentor and 'spiritual father', the Danish physicist Niels Bohr? And what was said that caused Bohr to react so angrily and that clouded the friendship between the two men? Part of Frayn's point is that there can be no definitive answer and that the two men's varying accounts testify to the subjectivity of memory and the partiality of perception. But Frayn's skill lies in showing Bohr, his wife Margarethe and Heisenberg offering alternative readings, from beyond the grave, of what actually took place. Many other dramatists have explored the fluctuating mystery of memory: it is a constant theme of Harold Pinter from *The Collection* to *Old Times*. What gives *Copenhagen* special purchase is that private uncertainty has global implications: Heisenberg's visit came at a time when Nazi Germany was apparently on the threshold of developing its own atomic capability. Did Heisenberg come to Denmark seeking absolution, affirmation or technical information?

In order to come up with a possible answer, Frayn's play necessarily contains a good deal of scientific detail. But, as Shepherd-Barr points out, Frayn shrewdly lets 'anecdotes define the ideas before giving them their scientific labels'. Thus the uncertainty principle – which is central to the play – is first introduced by a discussion about skiing in which Heisenberg's rapidity is contrasted with Bohr's deliberation. As Bohr says to his old friend of his prowess on the slopes: 'At the speed you were going you were up against the uncertainty relationship. If you knew where you were when you were down, you didn't know how fast you'd got there. If you knew how fast you were going, you didn't know you were down.' Later on, the two men recall a train journey made by Bohr in the 1920s from Copenhagen to Leiden, where Bohr was greeted by physicists at all the major terminals anxious to know his latest theories about the variable spin of electrons: the attempt of the physicists to pin Bohr down becomes a perfect metaphor for the scientific desire to measure the exact position of a particle in its trajectory.

I can think of no play about science – not even Brecht's *Galileo* – that so successfully makes ideas tangible. Michael Blakemore's stunning original production also lent them theatrical visibility. The three actors – David Burke, Matthew Marsh and Sara Kestelman – circled round Peter Davison's set, consisting of a white disc painted on a black floor, as if embodying the principles the play was discussing. In an article in the *New York Times*, Blakemore even likened the act of putting on a play to a scientific experiment: 'You go into a rehearsal room, which is a sort of atom, and then a lot of these rather busy particles, the actors, do their work, and circle around the nucleus of a good text. And then you sell tickets to a lot of photons, that is an audience, who will shine the light of their attention on what you've been up to.'

Frayn's play is obviously speculative, but it suggests the crucial meeting between Bohr and Heisenberg may have had cosmic consequences. Bohr's anger conceivably derived from Heisenberg's question 'Does one as a physicist have the moral right to work on the practical exploitation of atomic energy?' Assuming this to be a reference to a Nazi bomb, Bohr abruptly curtails a conversation which could have led Heisenberg to see past a vital stumbling-block in the bomb's development. It is equally possible that Heisenberg's question, and his uncharacteristic myopia about the scientific data, was prompted by a secret desire to halt the progress of the Nazis' atomic programme. We can never be sure. But Frayn underlines his argument about the accidental nature of good and evil by pointing out that Heisenberg, while working for the Nazis, delayed their weapons of mass destruction. The virtuous Bohr, on the other hand, went to Los Alamos and contributed his knowledge to the Allies' atomic bomb. This is not, however, a play filled with retrospective irony or knowing authorial omniscience. It is a philosophical enquiry into the limitless possibilities of history. And what, in the end, makes it deeply moving is that it combines a hymn to the beauty of life – everything from family and friends to music and nature – with a frank acknowledgement of 'that final core of uncertainty at the heart of things'.

98

The Goat

EDWARD ALBEE

(1928–)

Edward Albee once told me that, as a young man, he delivered telegrams for Western Union. As a dramatist, however, he has always avoided the transmission of straightforward messages. But I resist the attempt by Martin Esslin to link him with the Absurdists. At his best, Albee reveals a troubled social conscience and strong political awareness. His most famous play, *Who's Afraid of Virginia Woolf?* (1962), isn't just a ferocious marital ding-dong, it is also, as its references to Spengler confirm, about the decline of Western civilisation. For all that play's emotional intensity, I actually prefer *A Delicate Balance* (1967), in which an affluent suburban family is visited by old friends who have had a vision of existential terror. But the Albee play that haunts me is *The Goat* (2002), which is significantly subtitled 'Who is Sylvia? (Notes towards a definition of tragedy)'. It is transgressive, provocative, philosophically challenging and emotionally disturbing: it is, after all, about a man who falls in love, spiritually and physically, with a goat.

Albee is not the first writer to confront bestiality. I remember New York's La Mama visiting London in the late 1960s with Rochelle Owens's *Futz*, a play, about a farmer who treated his pet pig as a wife, that in the hippie spirit of the times seemed to be celebrating love's wilder manifestations. Woody Allen's 1972 film, *Everything You Always Wanted to Know About Sex (But Were Afraid to Ask)* contained a sketch about a New York GP who fell in love with a sheep called Daisy. The tone was wry and sophisticated, as Allen translated the standard properties of adultery comedy to unfamiliar territory: at one point the doctor's suspicious wife detected a persistent lamb-chop smell about her husband. But Albee's play, while shocking and subversive, isn't really about bestiality, it asks whether there are limits to our tolerance and whether we ever examine the values to which we liberally subscribe.

Where Owens endorses the strange byways of sexuality and Allen uses bestiality as a mischievous metaphor, Albee is writing a variant on classical tragedy. The word 'tragedy' itself derives from the Greek *tragoidia*, a literal combination of *tragos* ('goat') and *oide* ('song' or 'ode'). So Albee clearly knows what he is doing in having his hero fixated by a goat. What is also striking is the way his play fulfils the Aristotelian definition of tragedy. Albee's hero, Martin, is of suitably elevated stature: he's at the peak of his fame, has won architecture's equivalent of the Nobel Prize (the 'Pritzker') and been chosen to design a $27 billion city to rise in the wheatfields of the Midwest. Martin indisputably suffers a tragic flaw (*hamartia*) in his unchecked passion for a goat, and the action hinges on a crucial change of fortune (*peripeteia*) from prosperity to adversity: in this case, a letter written by Martin's best friend, Ross, to Martin's wife Stevie, informing her of her husband's secret passion. Whether the play achieves the Aristotelian ideal of catharsis is a matter of personal taste. Seeing the play on Broadway in 2002 and in London in 2004, where it starred a memorably fraught Jonathan Pryce, I both times felt emotionally shattered at the downfall of a good man and loving husband.

Albee has written an *Oedipus Rex* for the affluent society. At the same time, his play is flecked with comedy. You see this in the opening exchanges, where Martin is being interviewed at home by his friend Ross for a TV series called *People Who Matter*. The interview is a disaster, as Martin hides his inner turmoil under a verbal pedantry that reminds me irresistibly of Simon Gray's hero Simon Hench in *Otherwise Engaged*. It is also Albee's way of poking sly fun at the banality of the celebrity interview, as Ross becomes increasingly exasperated by Martin's stonewalling:

> ROSS: For the Pritzker Prize! Where were you when they told you?
> MARTIN: I was at the gym; I'd taken all my clothes off, and Stevie called me there.
> ROSS: Stevie is your wife.
> MARTIN: I know that.
> ROSS: How did it make you feel?
> MARTIN: Stevie being my wife?
> ROSS: No, the prize!

But the semantic precision that cloaks Martin's anxiety reaches its climax when he finally shows Ross a photo of his beloved goat:

> ROSS: This is Sylvia.
> MARTIN: Yes.
> ROSS: This is Sylvia . . . who you're fucking.
> MARTIN: (*winces*) Don't say that. (*It just comes out.*) Whom.

In the theatre, the line always gets a laugh. It is also a symptom of the moral no man's land in which Martin is thrashing around. He himself describes his passion for Sylvia as 'a love of an un-i-mag-in-able kind'. Within the framework of classical tragedy,

Albee is asking us to examine our own consciences and question how we define the parameters of what is sexually acceptable. Stevie, Martin's wife, is revolted by her husband's double life and systematically wrecks their beautifully designed living room before wreaking bloody revenge on Sylvia herself. But both Martin and Stevie cheerfully accept that their teenage son Billy is 'gay as the nineties', which raises the question of at what point same-sex love, vigorously condemned in the Bible, achieved the respectability it enjoys today. If society's attitude to homosexuality can change so radically within living memory, where does that leave other practices we currently condemn? Albee is bold enough to push the point by having Billy kiss Martin with a quasi-incestuous passion, by quoting the story of a parent who found himself sexually excited by his baby and by citing the erotic element in religious paintings such as the martyrdom of Saint Sebastian. When a disgusted Ross asks Martin, 'Is there anything you people don't get off on?' Martin coldly replies, 'Is there anything anyone doesn't get off on, whether we admit it or not?'

Behind the play lies an inherited moral framework that sees Martin's plight as fundamentally tragic. But this also strikes me as one of the boldest plays in the Western canon in that it deals openly with the uncontrollable impulses of sex and asks us to examine our own instinctive assumptions – or, as Albee himself put it, to question 'whether the stuff we have armoured ourselves with against the world is still valid'. It does so without either cynicism or sensationalism and reminds us that Albee, who suffered a long period of neglect by American mainstream theatre, remains one of its most durable products and fiercely probing intellects.

99

The History Boys

ALAN BENNETT

(1934–)

Edward Albee's play is about a man who loves a goat. Alan Bennett's *The History Boys* (2004) is about a teacher who gropes his pupils. Like Albee's play, it is, of course, about many other things as well. Given recent revelations about the abuse of young people by media icons and members of the political hierarchy, you might expect Bennett's play to be stigmatised. In fact in 2013 it was voted 'the nation's favourite play' in a poll of 7,000 people conducted by English Touring Theatre. Having started its life at the National Theatre, it has played in the West End and on Broadway, toured widely and been made into a movie. But just what is it about *The History Boys* that makes it, whatever the peculiarities of its hero, such a massively popular work?

The first thing to say is that it belies the notion that Bennett is a cosy writer who snugly endorses established values. From the start, he's always struck me as complex figure: a dramatist who constantly experiments with different forms and whose desire for social change is balanced by a preoccupation with the past. Bennett's peculiar radical nostalgia was evident in his first play, *Forty Years On* (1968). It was both an elegy for a vanishing England and a satire on rooted privilege. Bennett's bifocal complexity was equally apparent in *Enjoy* (1980), which evoked northern, working-class culture while attacking the absurdity of turning it into a museum artefact. Bennett's divided self is also apparent in his capacity to both celebrate and demystify art and literature: he cherishes them deeply while arguing they should never become the property of a self-perpetuating elite. One of my favourite Bennett plays is *A Question of Attribution*, in which a shrewdly perceptive Elizabeth II confronts the Marxist aesthete Anthony Blunt. I suspect Bennett's real sympathy, however, lies with a dogged cop desperate to acquire the basics of art appreciation.

The great thing about Bennett is that he is brilliantly unpindownable. Is he a radical conservative? A romantic socialist? Probably a bit of both. In the introduction to *The History Boys* he says, 'I'm old-fashioned enough to believe that private education should long since have been abolished and that Britain has paid too high a price in social inequality for its public schools.' Yet his play is set in a Leeds school that aspires to fee-paying status and that elects to be judged by the number of bright sixth-formers it can get into Oxford and Cambridge. I understand Bennett's point about our elevation of the ancient universities to iconic status, yet Bennett himself, as he'd be the first to admit, was the beneficiary of an Oxford scholarship and first came to public prominence as part of the Oxbridge quartet that performed *Beyond the Fringe* in Edinburgh in 1960.

Bennett's tantalising equivocation lies at the heart of *The History Boys*. At first glance, the play looks simple enough: a joyous celebration of an eccentric teacher, Hector, who breaks all the rules, makes learning fun and regards exams as 'the enemy of education'. One reason for the play's popularity is that Hector is the kind of teacher everyone wishes they had had – and that some people actually did. My own equivalent of Hector – though not, I hasten to add, a genital groper – was a sixth-form English teacher who'd invite selected boys to his house for Saturday supper, where we would discuss a play, a book, a film in the style of a then popular BBC radio programme, *The Critics*. Hector is a similar life-enhancer: nothing in Bennett's play is more moving than the scene where he gets Posner to read and analyse Hardy's poem 'Drummer Hodge'. The point is that we feel as enlightened, by the end of the scene, as Posner. And we too share Hector's delight in literature's communicative power and the sense that 'it's as if a hand has come out and taken yours'.

But Bennett's play is much more than an updated *Goodbye Mr Chips*, a paean to an inspirational teacher. For all the warmth of the writing and the rich performances of Richard Griffiths and Stephen Moore, the play is not uncritical of Hector. The play obviously contrasts Hector's delight in learning as an end in itself with the calculated tactics of the supply teacher Irwin, a man who encourages the pupils to deploy a flashy originality to impress the Oxbridge examiners. But Mrs Lintott, Hector's loving colleague, accuses Hector of sentimentality in believing that learning poetry by heart will be a hedge against ultimate failure. Hector himself confesses that it's time he left the school because he wants the boys to 'show off' by flourishing handy quotes. There is also the not inconsiderable matter of Hector's copping a feel of the boys' balls as they ride pillion on his motorbike. Hector describes it as a laying-on of hands 'more in benediction than gratification or anything else'. Mrs Lintott instantly cuts through the cant by saying, 'A grope is a grope. It is not the Annunciation.' However, I don't agree – as both Rosie Millard and Johan Hari argued in the *Independent* – that Bennett makes light of sexual abuse. As I see it, Bennett is suggesting that human character doesn't come in neat packages: that a teacher who stimulates boys' imaginations may also be one who seeks to excite them in more dubious ways. The play is not a licence for paedophilia, rather, a recognition of the fact that inspirational mentors may also be morally imperfect.

But that is in keeping with a play rich in ambivalence. It endorses Hector's freewheeling teaching techniques, yet it suggests the boys would get nowhere without the ability of Mrs Lintott – the play's real hero – to meet the factual demands of A-Level. The play is also openly critical of Irwin's presentational showmanship, yet he gets all the boys into Oxbridge. Above all, the play's apparent formlessness is accompanied by a surreptitiously tight structure: scenes are linked by hidden verbal echoes and something as seemingly random as our first sight of Irwin, addressing a group of MPs from his wheelchair, acquires a momentous pay-off when we learn that he was the victim of Hector's notorious unreliability on a motorbike.

Bennett has written many fine plays. But this one, I believe, will outlive them all because it covers so much ground: the hidden eroticism of the teacher–pupil relationship, the pervasive elitism of our educational system, the debasement of a culture in which everything depends on presentation. Yet you can't reduce a Bennett play to the issues it covers. What moves one is the paradoxical mix of the elegiac and the exuberant and Bennett's realisation of the tragic ephemerality of the teaching process and the permanent value of being able to 'pass the parcel'.

Of all Bennett's plays, *The History Boys* is the one most full of glorious contradictions.

100

Jerusalem

JEZ BUTTERWORTH
(1969–)

It's no exaggeration to say that Mark Rylance gave one of the great performances in modern drama as Johnny 'Rooster' Byron in Jez Butterworth's play. But the actor was so mesmeric that it is easy to overlook Butterworth's ambivalence towards his self-mythologising hero. I don't wish to take anything away from Rylance. Off stage, he is a relatively slight figure with a receding hairline and delicate features. On stage, he is a natural shape-shifter who has Alec Guinness's gift for total physical transformation. At Shakespeare's Globe, which he ran for a decade, Rylance was equally persuasive as a robustly militaristic Henry V and a fastidiously mincing Olivia in *Twelfth Night*. In modern drama, he has switched from the shyly amorous, Stan Laurel-like hero of Marc Camoletti's *Boeing Boeing* to the strutting, muscular, whizz-dispensing Wiltshire Falstaff in Butterworth's strangely beautiful and disturbing study of a changing England.

Falstaff immediately came to mind when I first saw *Jerusalem* at the Royal Court in 2009, and in that comparison lies the clue to the play's cunning. As I've suggested before, Falstaff is a multi-dimensional character: a natural spellbinder but also a figure of casual cruelty who displays total indifference to his ragged recruits and who wilfully ignores the regal dismissal that is staring him in the face. Butterworth invests Johnny Byron with something of that same definition-defying diversity. Like Falstaff, Johnny is a born fabulist and, although his natural terrain is the Wiltshire woods rather than a London tavern, he keeps his sylvan court totally enraptured. His charm for his young acolytes lies not just in his ability to dispense drink and drugs but also in his capacity to tell magical tales. Sometimes his stories are of the tallest, as in his account of meeting a giant on the A14 outside Upavon ('About half a mile from the Little Chef'). At other times he persuades his audience – in this case, his abandoned wife – that he has been kidnapped by four Nigerian traffic wardens in Marlbororough. Johnny, in resisting the right of the local council to remove him from his chosen turf, also invokes the folkloristic heroes of old England. As he says in his final speech, 'Rise up! Rise up, Cormoran. Woden. Jack-of-Green. Jack-in-Irons. Thunderbell, Buri, Blunderbore, Gog and Magog, Galligantus, Vili and Ve, Yggdrasil, Brutus of Albion.' It's a stirring list, but it's significant that today we hardly recognise any of the names in this litany of the 'ghosts who walk these green plains still'.

It is easy to be seduced by Johnny and overlook what Butterworth's complex fable is really telling us.

For a start, Butterworth's portrait of this romantic Romany is decidedly equivocal. Johnny finds it easier to play the role of pie-eyed piper to the village youths than to talk to his own six-year-old son, has been banned from all the local pubs, depends on a monthly subsidy (because of his rare blood-group) from the state he strenuously despises and, as one of his followers points out, is not exactly the neighbour that residents of a new housing estate would have chosen. Like Falstaff, Johnny is both a natural enchanter and a symbol of the Vanity depicted in the medieval morality plays whose eventual dismissal is inevitable. Johnny also seems to shrink in solitude: I always recall the moment when, left alone, Rylance hunted for his carefully hidden granny specs to read the small print in the expulsion order.

The art of Butterworth's play depends, as with so many of the key works in world drama, on its double vision. It appeals to our nostalgia for a vanished England and the loss of local identity. One of the funniest episodes is an attack on the BBC's regional *Points West* for extending its territory into Wales ('Local is Bedwyn. Local is Devizes,' as one of Johnny's followers points out). But while Butterworth laments what is lost, he also exposes the absurdity of artificially preserving tradition. You see that in the character simply called Professor, a village teacher who gets high as several kites and who wanders through the St George's Day action woozily talking of abandoning oneself to 'the rhythms of the earth'. But how does one do that, Butterworth implicitly asks, in an age of global culture, new technology and corporate domination? Even the local Flintock Fair is 'sponsored by John Deere Tractors and Arkell Ale', and when the publican, Wesley, reveals that he has been designated to be the Barley Sword Bearer, it transpires that the morris dancers are an ad hoc troupe created by a Swindon-based brewery. Forced by Johnny to demonstrate his skills in exchange for drugs, Wesley announces that his dance connotes the sun god's mastery over the infinite chaos of the galaxy. In a devastating put-down, Johnny declares, 'I'm no expert but to me it says "I have completely lost my self-respect."'

Butterworth does many remarkable things in this play. He asks whether the kind of ancient rituals memorialised by J. G. Frazer in *The Golden Bough* have any real meaning in our modern, mechanised age. He exposes the hypocrisy of a society that condemns Johnny as a misleader of youth while forgetting their own indiscretions and failing to provide recreational facilities for hyperactive teenagers. And in Johnny himself he creates a larger-than-life character who combines the attraction of the social outcast with the pathos of the gregarious loner. If the play has any obvious precedent – apart from Shakespeare's *Henry IV* – it is in John Arden's 1958 drama, *Live Like Pigs*, which set an anarchic group of sturdy beggars next to a respectable, petty-bourgeois family and left audiences to decide for themselves where the balance of sympathy lay.

Butterworth remains a strange, unclassifiable talent. In *Mojo* he wrote a compelling study of gangland violence in the Soho of the 1950s. In *Parlour Song* he explored the desolation of life in exactly the kind of new housing estates being erected in *Jerusalem*. But it would be a mistake to see Butterworth as a romantic sentimentalist or reactionary ally of the Countryside Alliance, lamenting the erosion of old customs. His skill in *Jerusalem* lies in creating one of the iconic heroes in modern drama, one whom other actors will relish playing once the recollection of Rylance has begun to fade. Butterworth is also posing the fundamental question of what it means to be English today. We live in a world where 'Jerusalem', in Parry's version of Blake's poem, has been appropriated as a surrogate national anthem and symbol of knee-jerk patriotism belted out with camp fervour at the Last Night of the Proms. Echoing Blake's original poem, Butterworth asks how ancestral memories can be reconciled with rapid, technological change. He has no easy answer but he poses the question with the vitality, vigor and ambivalence that are the unmistakeable hallmarks of first-rate drama.

101

King Charles III

MIKE BARTLETT

(1980–)

So how to bring my top 101 to a conclusion? I have chosen Mike Bartlett's *King Charles III* not because I think it is a timeless masterpiece but because I believe it raises, with stylish wit and verbal élan, serious questions about the future of Britain and the nature of good governance. Shaw once said that *A Doll's House* would be forgotten when *A Midsummer Night's Dream* was still being performed but that it would have done 'more work in the world'. In fact, Ibsen's play has achieved classic status, but Shaw's idea that drama can be judged by its capacity to shape and mould opinion strikes me as perfectly valid.

Shaw provides a good starting point for any discussion of Mike Bartlett's play. In 1929 Shaw wrote *The Apple Cart*, which looked forward to Britain at the end of the twentieth century. It was a world in which giant corporations were bigger than national governments, Britain survived largely as a clearing-house for international capital, and American cultural colonialism dominated the globe. No one can accuse the old boy of lacking foresight. Shaw also envisioned a king, Magnus, who refused to be reduced to the role of constitutional puppet by mediocre politicians. That is roughly the starting-point for Bartlett's play, where Charles III, even before he has been crowned, refuses to give royal assent to a bill proposing stricter regulation of the press. The big difference between *The Apple Cart* and *King Charles III* is that Bartlett is peering only a few years ahead and is dealing with living royals rather than fictive inventions. His play also has the supreme merit of basing its vision of the near future on present realities. As Prince of Wales, Charles has made known his strong views on organic farming, environmental preservation and traditional architecture. It is also a fact, as Tim Stanley pointed out in an article in the *New Republic*, that since 2005 ministers from six departments have felt compelled to seek his approval for a dozen bills on subjects ranging from gambling to children's rights. The immediate question posed by Bartlett's play is whether Charles, on succeeding his mother, will be able to accept the limits of a constitutional monarchy and adopt a largely ceremonial role. Bartlett's emphatic answer is that he will not.

Many things, however, make Bartlett's play far more than a piece of speculative theatrical journalism. One is the character of Charles himself. Initially, he cuts a somewhat diffident figure uneasy, as Tim Pigott-Smith showed in his superb performance, in his own skin and acutely aware of his predicament: 'My life,' he declares in the pastiche pentameters adopted by Bartlett, 'has been a ling'ring for the throne.' Even Charles's opposition to Labour's press regulation bill is cautiously expressed. It is only when the Machiavellian Conservative leader urges him to exercise his power of veto that he digs in his heels. Realising that to sign a bill that he sees as anti-democratic would be a form of self-betrayal, Charles claims, 'Without my voice, and spirit, I am dust.' What follows is an inexorable downward spiral in which Charles becomes a genuinely tragic figure. Driven to ever more drastic expedients to preserve his moral integrity, he brings the nation to the brink of civil war and ends up isolated, unloved and deposed.

Bartlett's decision to tell the story in iambic pentameters is not merely a clever technical device, it reinforces the Shakespearean resonances that give the play depth and substance. The idea of kingship as a burden, producing an insomniac loneliness, is one that reverberates through all Shakespeare's History plays. Sometimes the echoes are even more specific.

When the deposed Charles places the hollow crown on William's head, he replicates the embittered irony of Richard II as he cries:

God save King William, unking'd Charles says,
And send him many years of sunshine days!

Prince Harry's public rejection of his girlfriend, Jess, in the interests of familial loyalty and 'the firm' is also a direct nod to another Hal's dismissal of his boon companion. Less noticed was the way Diana's ghost, like a mix of Hamlet's father and the weird sisters in *Macbeth*, urges on both Charles and William to acts of recklessness as if still seeking revenge for her own maltreatment. Far from being a decorative add-on or a game of Spot the Bard, the Shakespearean allusions are crucial to an understanding of a play about the dilemmas and contradictions posed by constitutional monarchy in the modern age.

That seems to me at the heart of Bartlett's richly intriguing play. Rationally, it suggests the monarchy is an anachronistic survivor in a democratic age that has disowned the hereditary principle. But Bartlett also implies there is an emotional case for monarchy as a source of stability and continuity. Shaw once said that monarchy was a bulwark against dictatorship; Bartlett suggests that, for all its imperfections, the institution can act as a counter to overweening politicians. One of the play's pivotal scenes, written in prose, shows Harry encountering a kebab seller who laments the withering of the British state through cuts to the NHS, the armed forces and the Post Office and who asks, 'When does Britain get so cut down that it's not Britain any more?' For the kebab seller, the queen was the force holding a fissiparous society together. Without explicitly endorsing it, Bartlett hints that the future may lie with Kate's vision of a modernised monarchy in which power is regally shared between husband and wife and the principle of female succession fully endorsed. As Susannah Clapp perceptively observed, Bartlett's play starts as a provocation and develops into something rich and unsettling.

Bartlett's play, directed with exemplary self-restraint by Rupert Goold first at the Almeida and then in the West End, was devoured by the public because it was vividly written and dealt with issues that matter. What kind of Britain do we want? Do we need a formal constitution? And how do we proceed if a modern monarch exceeds what Walter Bagehot saw as his or her basic constitutional prerogative: namely 'the right to warn'? The passage of time – and Charles's eventual accession – may make Bartlett's play look dated. But if I end my book with it, it is because it feels exactly the right play for this particular moment in history. I also fall back on what I'd call the William Archer defence articulated in his book *The Old Drama and the New* nearly a century ago, which is that, in paying due tribute to the past, we seriously undervalue modern drama. Archer warned us against jeering at living lions while worshipping dead dogs, and I would endorse his argument that great plays are still within our compass and that the art of the drama is alive and well. Today it faces different pressures from those outlined by Archer in 1925: the solo-authored play now has to contend with democratically devised work, the rising power of the director, an anti-verbal culture, not to mention the multiple choices and escalating distractions afforded by a hi-tech society. Yet, happily, people persist in writing plays and audiences still crave the excitement of encountering a strongly subjective, vivaciously expressed vision of the world. Only a defeatist would argue that the bright day is done and that we are for the dark.

Acknowledgements

In the course of writing this book, I have dipped into, plundered and quoted from a large number of critical works, biographies and even novels. I should like to record my profound debt to the following:

James Agate, *Brief Chronicles* (Jonathan Cape)
William Archer, *The Old Drama and the New* (Heinemann)
—— *Play-Making* (Heinemann)
Anne Barton, *Ben Jonson Dramatist* (Cambridge University Press)
Jacques Barzun, *From Dawn to Decadence* (HarperCollins)
Andy Beckett, *When the Lights Went Out* (Faber & Faber)
Eric Bentley, *The Modern Theatre* (Robert Hale)
—— *The Life of the Drama* (Methuen)
Christopher Bigsby, *A Critical Introduction to Twentieth-Century American Drama* (Cambridge University Press)
Michael Blakemore, *Stage Blood* (Faber & Faber)
Harold Bloom, *How to Read and Why* (Fourth Estate)
Elisabeth Bond-Pable, Introduction to *Spring Awakening* (Methuen)
C. M. Bowra, *Landmarks in Greek Literature* (Weidenfeld and Nicolson)

Erik Braun, *Meyerhold* (Methuen)

Peter Brook, *The Empty Space* (Penguin)

Simon Callow, *Orson Welles: The Road to Xanadu* (Jonathan Cape)

Thomas Carlyle, *The French Revolution* (Folio Society)

David Castillejo, *Spanish Classical Drama* (Oberon)

Harold Clurman, *The Collected Works of Harold Clurman*
   (Applause Books)

Peter Conrad, *Cassell's History of English Literature* (Cassell)

Michael Cordner, Introduction to *A Mad World My Masters*
   (RSC programme)

Noël Coward, *The Noël Coward Diaries* (Weidenfeld and
   Nicolson)

Bonamy Dobrée, *Restoration Comedy 1660–1720* (Clarendon
   Press)

——— *Restoration Tragedy 1660–1720* (Clarendon Press)

Evgeny Dobrenko and Marina Balina, *Cambridge Companion to
   Twentieth-Century Russian Literature* (Cambridge University
   Press)

Michael Dobson, Introduction to *Twelfth Night* (Penguin
   Shakespeare)

Margaret Drabble, *The Garrick Year* (Penguin)

T. S. Eliot, *Selected Essays* (Faber and Faber)

Richard Ellmann, *James Joyce* (Oxford University Press)

——— *Oscar Wilde* (Hamish Hamilton)

William Empson, *Seven Types of Ambiguity* (Methuen)

Arthur and Barbara Gelb, *O'Neill* (Harper Brothers, New York)

Pat Gill, *Cambridge Companion to Restoration Theatre*
   (Cambridge University Press)

David Gunby, *The Works of John Webster* (Cambridge University
   Press)

Edith Hall and Fiona Macintosh, *Greek Tragedy and the British
   Theatre* (Oxford University Press)

Peter Hall, *Diaries* (Oberon Books)

Nicholas de Jongh, *Politics, Prudery and Perversions* (Methuen)

Dennis Kennedy, Introduction to *Plays by Harley Granville Barker* (Cambridge University Press)

Frank Kermode, *Shakespeare's Language* (Allen Lane)

John Kerrigan, Introduction to *Love's Labour's Lost* (Penguin Shakespeare)

Declan Kibberd, *Irish Classics* (Granta Books)

Bernard Knox, Introduction to *The Theban Plays* (Penguin Classics)

Alexander Leggatt, *English Drama: Shakespeare to the Restoration* (Longman)

Melveena McKendrick, *Theatre in Spain, 1490–1700* (Cambridge University Press)

Toril Moi, *Henrik Ibsen and the Birth of Modernism* (Oxford University Press)

George Jean Nathan, *Encylopedia of the Theatre* (Farleigh Dickinson University Press)

Benedict Nightingale, *An Introduction to 50 Modern British Plays* (Pan Books)

Fintan O'Toole, *Sheridan: A Traitor's Kiss* (Granta Books)

Michael Paterson, *The Oxford Dictionary of Plays* (Oxford University Press)

Adrian Poole, Introduction to *Henry IV Parts One and Two* (Penguin Shakespeare)

Erich Segal, Introduction to *The Plays of Plautus* (Oxford World's Classics)

Kirsten Shepherd-Barr, *Science on Stage* (Princeton University Press)

Konstantin Stanislavsky, *My Life in Art* (Penguin)

G. M. Trevelyan, *A History of England* (Prentice Hall Press)

Simon Trussler, Introduction to *The Rover* (Methuen)

ACKNOWLEDGEMENTS

Martin Turnell, *The Classical Moment* (Hamish Hamilton)
Kenneth Tynan, *Curtains* (Longman)
Stephen Unwin, *A Guide to the Plays of Bertolt Brecht* (Methuen)
Philip Vellacott, Introduction to *The Persians* (Penguin Classics)
Stanley Wells, *Shakespeare: A Dramatic Life* (Sinclair Stevenson)
Glynne Wickham, *Shakespeare's Dramatic Heritage* (Routledge)
Nicholas Wright, *99 Plays* (Methuen)

I have quoted from a number of indispensable translations of foreign plays. I should like to pay tribute to the following,

Kaite O'Reilly, *The Persians* (unpublished)
Don Taylor, *Oedipus the King* (Methuen)
Frank McGuinness, *Oedipus the King* (Faber & Faber)
Frank McGuinness, *Helen* (Faber & Faber)
Erich Segal, *The Brothers Menaechmus* (Oxford World's Classics)
Stephen Halliwell, *Assembly Women* (Oxford World's Classics)
Tony Harrison, *The Mysteries* (Faber & Faber)
Adrian Mitchell, *Fuenteovejuna* (Absolute Classics)
Meredith Oakes, *Punishment without Revenge* (Oberon Classics)
Gwynne Edwards, *Life Is a Dream* (Methuen)
Ranjit Bolt, *The Illusion* (Absolute Classics)
Ranjit Bolt, *Tartuffe* (Oberon Books)
Tony Harrison, *The Misanthrope* (Rex Collings)
Eric Korn, *Andromache* (Applause Theatre Books)
John Walters, *The Game of Love and Chance* (Methuen)
Lee Hall, *A Servant to Two Masters* (Methuen)
Mike Alfreds, *La Triologia della Villegiatura* (unpublished)
John Wood, *The Marriage of Figaro* (Penguin Classics)
Robert David Macdonald, *Don Carlos* (Oberon Books)
Peter Oswald, *Mary Stuart* (Oberon Books)
David Constantine, *The Broken Jug* (New Directions Books)

ACKNOWLEDGEMENTS

Neil Bartlett, *The Prince of Homburg* (Oberon Books)

Edward Kemp, *Nathan the Wise* (Nick Hern Books)

John Mackendrick, *Woyzeck* (Methuen)

Lynn and Theodore Hoffman, *An Italian Straw Hat* (Doubleday Anchor Books)

Geoffrey Hill, *Brand* (Heinemann)

Alan Ayckbourn, *The Forest* (Faber & Faber)

Frank McGuinness, *A Doll's House* (Faber & Faber)

Christopher Hampton, *The Wild Duck* (Faber & Faber)

Arthur Hopkins, *The Power of Darkness* (Fredonia Books)

John Osborne, *The Father* (Faber & Faber)

Edward Bond, *Spring Awakening* (Methuen)

Kenneth McLeish, *Sauce for the Goose* (Methuen)

Michael Frayn, *Uncle Vanya* (Methuen)

Andrew Upton, *The Cherry Orchard* (Faber & Faber)

Nick Dear, *Summerfolk* (Faber & Faber)

J. M. Q. Davies, *Professor Bernhardi* (Oxford World's Classics)

Tom Stoppard, *Henry IV* (Faber & Faber)

Christopher Hampton, *Tales from the Vienna Woods* (Faber & Faber)

Peter Tegel, *The Suicide* (Samuel French)

Gwynne Edwards, *The House of Bernarda Alba* (Methuen)

Desmond Vesey and John Willett, *Life of Galileo* (Methuen)

John Willett, *Mr Puntila and His Man Matti* (Methuen)

Martin Crimp, *The Chairs* (Faber & Faber)

Maurice Valency, *The Visit* (Samuel French)

Alistair Beaton, *The Arsonists* (Methuen)

One of the many pleasures of writing this book has been that of burrowing into old play-texts. I should like to thank the staff of the London Library for their constant help, Kaite O'Reilly for sending me a copy of her translation of *The Persians* and Lucinda

Morrison, head of Press at the National Theatre, for dispatching a copy of Mike Alfreds' translation of *La Triologia della Villegiatura* with consummate speed. I'd also like to thank Alastair Macaulay for both fact-checking the text and adding his stimulating suggestions and David Watson for his scrupulous and detailed copy-editing. Most of all, I should like to thank my editor at Faber, Dinah Wood, for offering shrewd counsel, moral support and constructive criticism in perfect proportion as always. The choice of plays is entirely mine. But, even though I suspect hers would have been slightly different, Dinah never gave me anything less than her full-hearted backing.

Index